CAGE of EDEN

VOLUME 6

Yoshinobu Yamada

Translated and Adapted by Mari Morimoto

Lettered by Bobby Timony

KC
KODANSHA
COMICS

A Kodansha Comics Trade Paperback Original

Cage of Eden volume 6 copyright © 2010 Yoshinobu Yamada

English translation copyright © 2012 Yoshinobu Yamada

Published in the United States by Kodansha Comics, an imprint of Kodansha USA Publishing, LLC, New York.

Publication rights for this English edition arranged through Kodansha Ltd., Tokyo.

First published in Japan in 2010 by Kodansha Ltd., Tokyo, as *Eden no Ori*, volume 6.

ISBN 978-1-61262-050-3

Printed in the United States of America

www.kodanshacomics.com

9 8 7 6 5 4 3 2 1

Translator: Mari Morimoto
Lettering: Bobby Timony

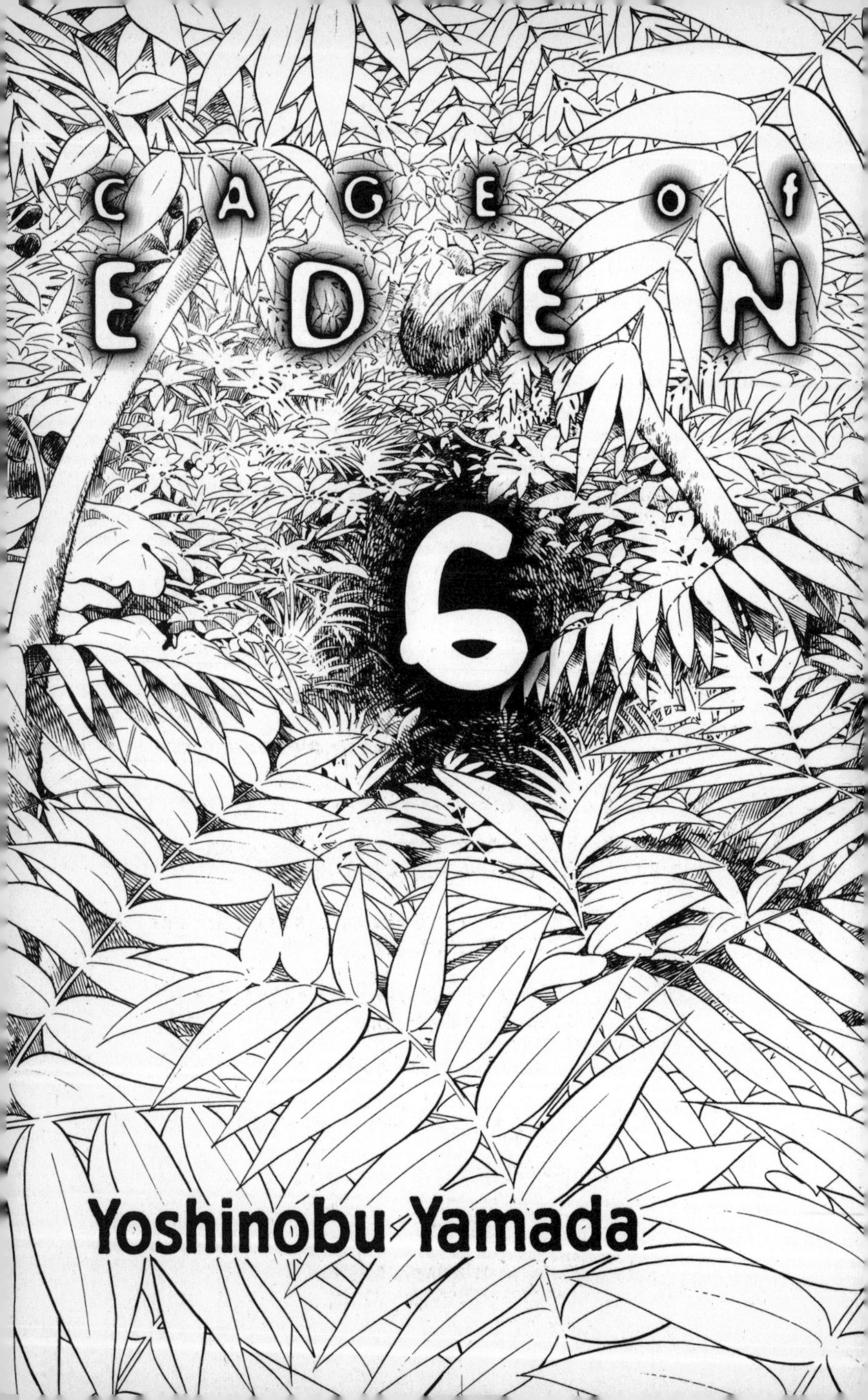
CAGE of
EDEN
6
Yoshinobu Yamada

CAGE of EDEN

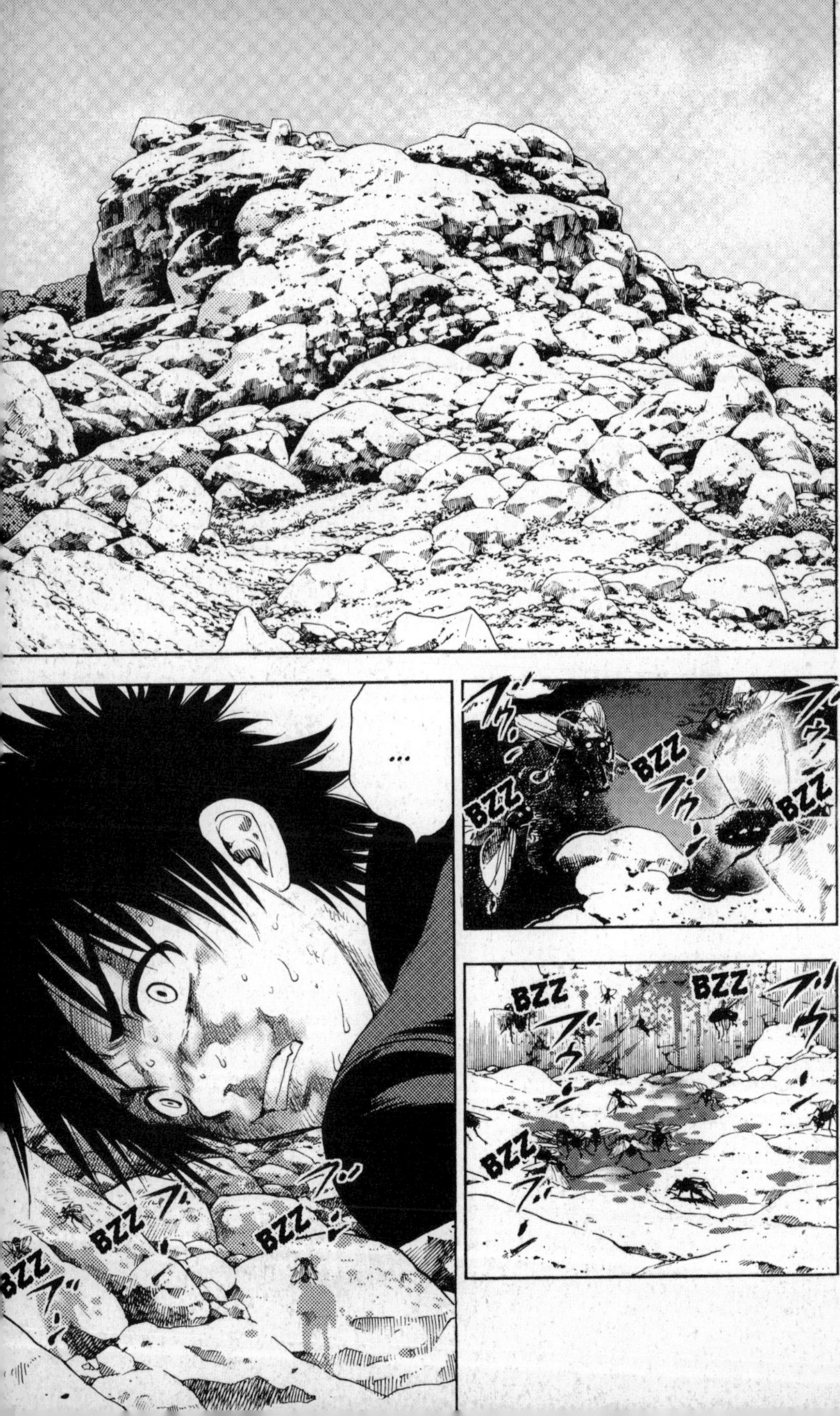
BZZ
BZZ
BZZ
BZZ
BZZ
BZZ
...
BZZ
BZZ
BZZ

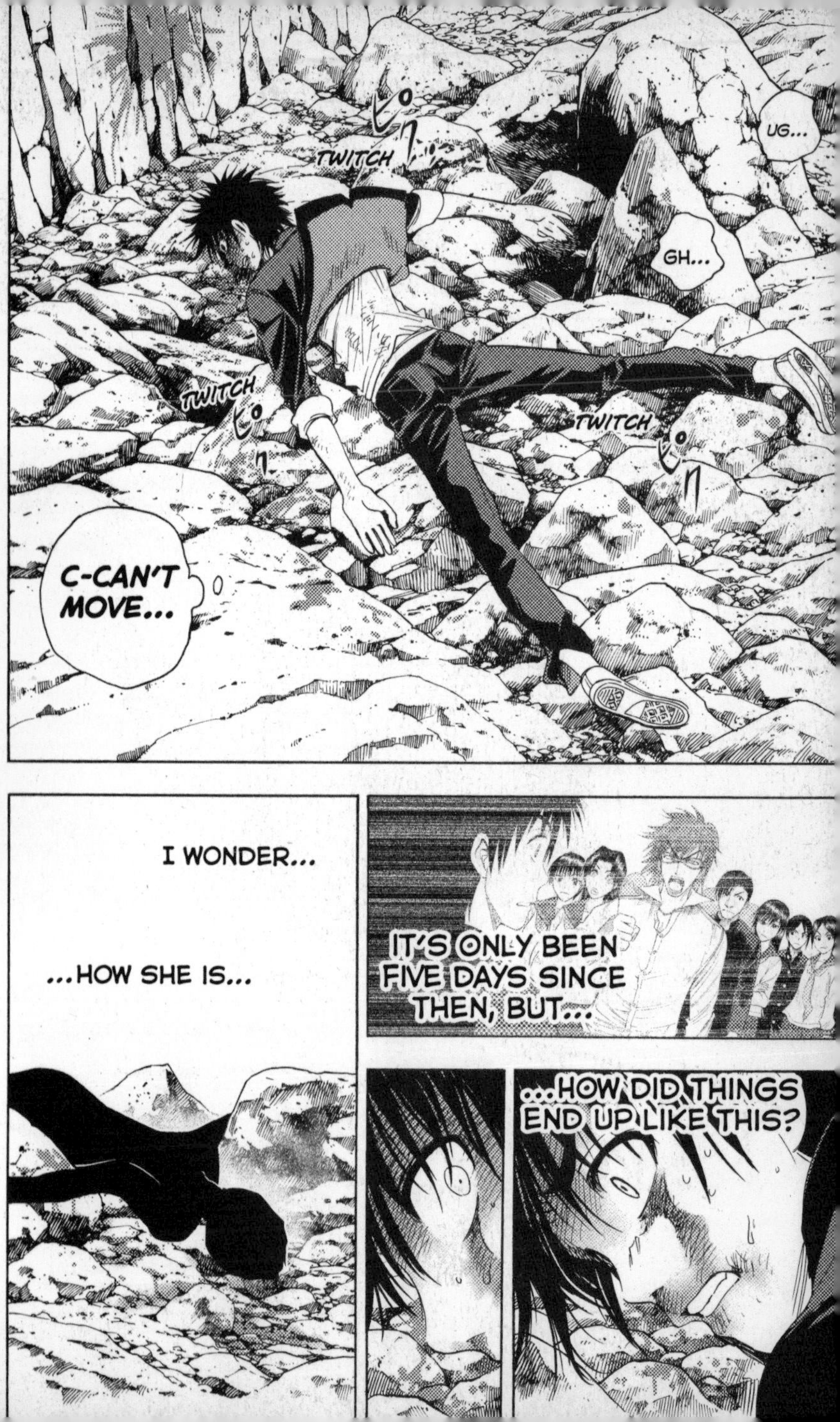
UG...
GH...
TWITCH
TWITCH
TWITCH
C-CAN'T MOVE...
I WONDER...
...HOW SHE IS...
IT'S ONLY BEEN FIVE DAYS SINCE THEN, BUT...
...HOW DID THINGS END UP LIKE THIS?

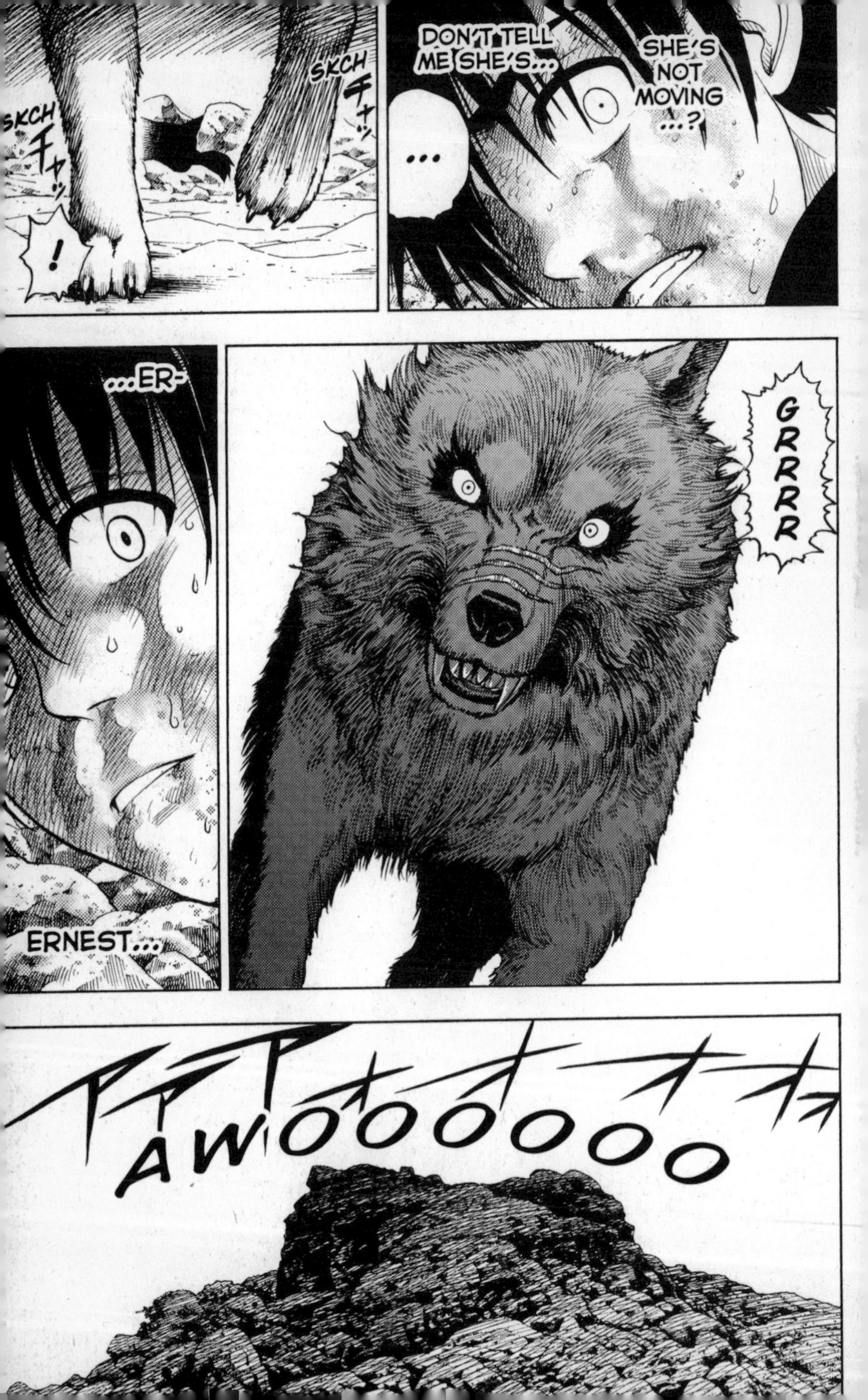
SHE'S NOT MOVING ...?
DON'T TELL ME SHE'S...
...
SKCH
チャッ
SKCH
チャッ
!
GRRRR
...ER-
ERNEST...
AWOOOOOO

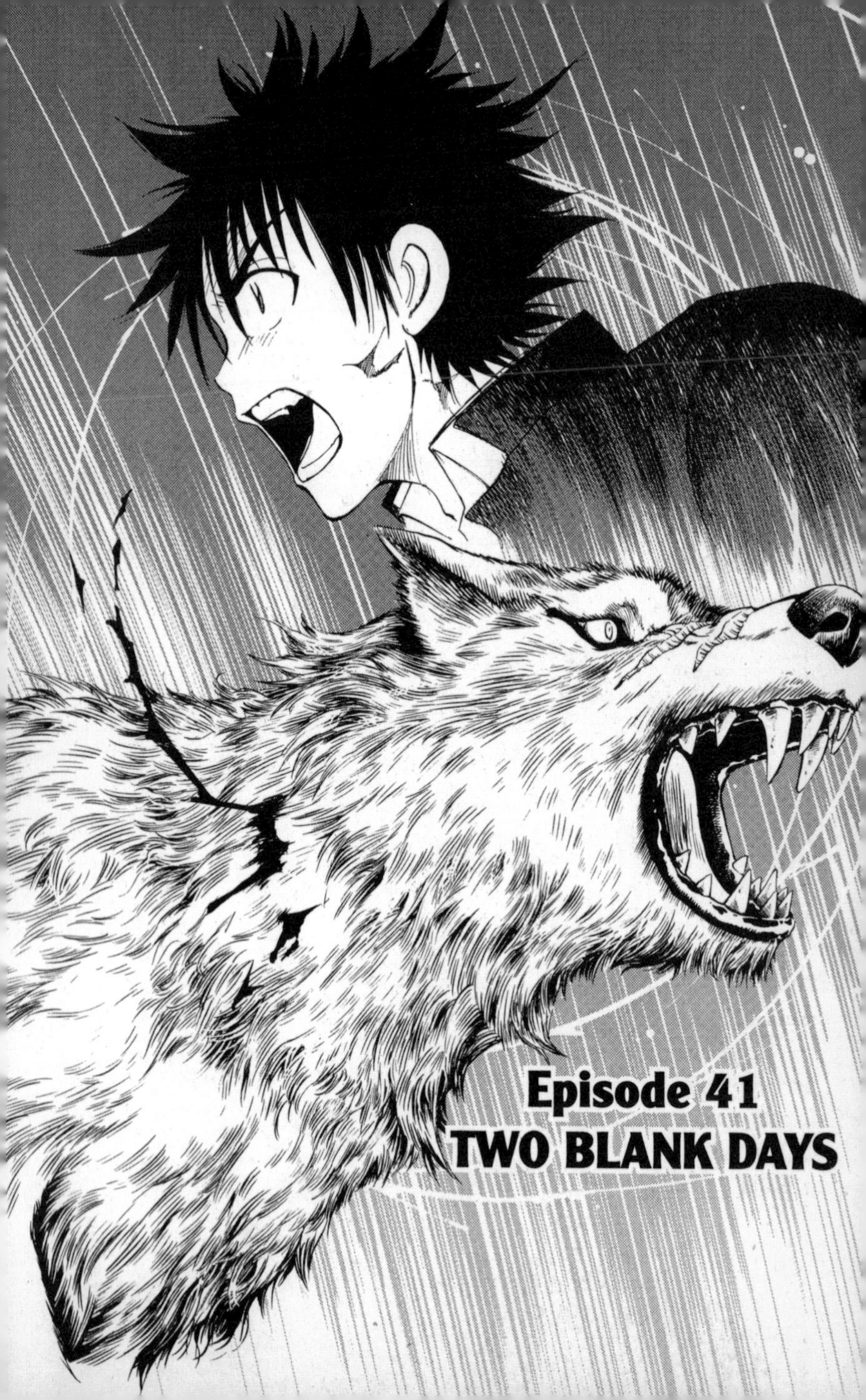
Episode 41
TWO BLANK DAYS

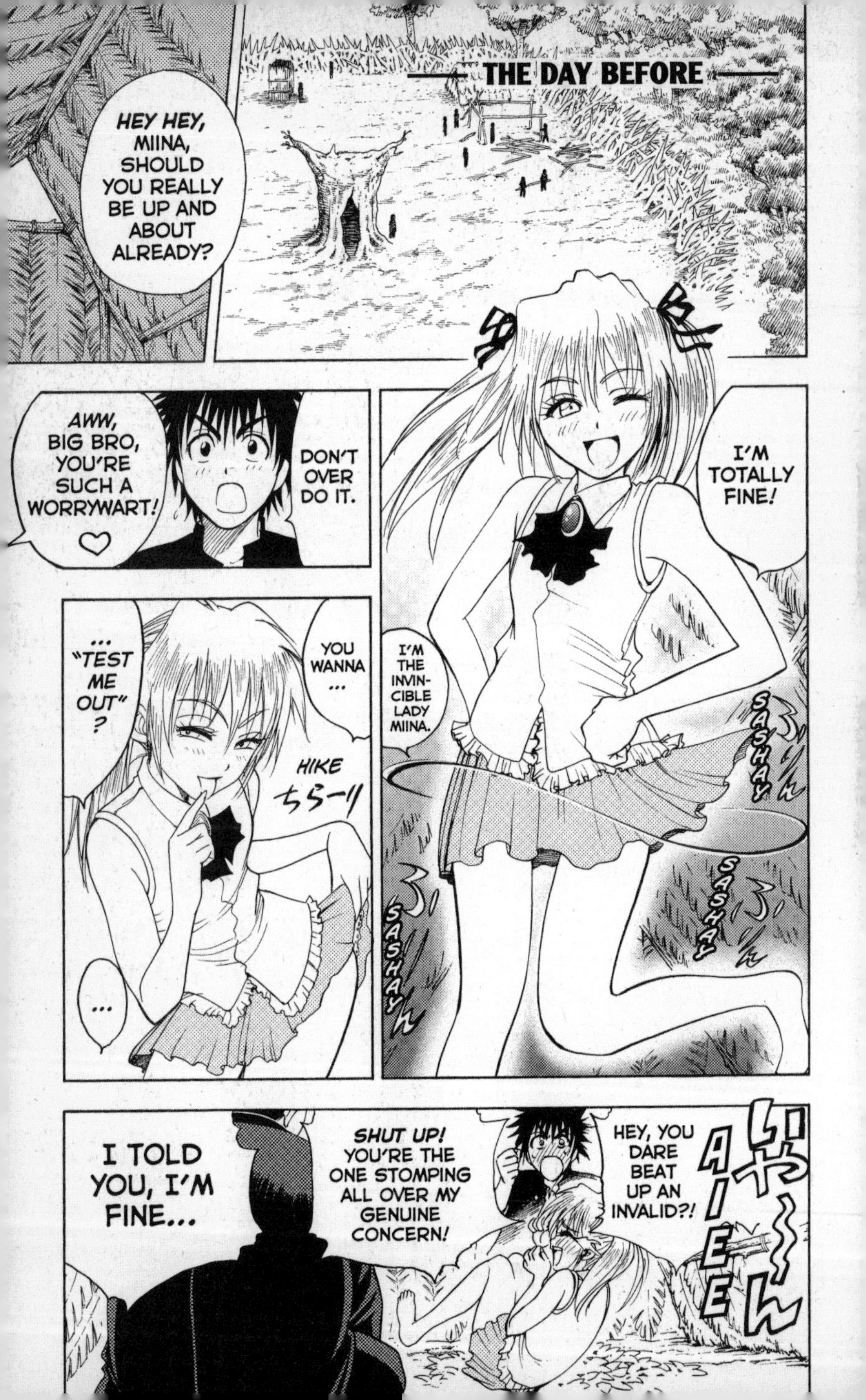
—THE DAY BEFORE—
HEY HEY, MIINA, SHOULD YOU REALLY BE UP AND ABOUT ALREADY?
I'M TOTALLY FINE!
I'M THE INVINCIBLE LADY MIINA.
SASHAY
SASHAY
SASHAY
DON'T OVER DO IT.
AWW, BIG BRO, YOU'RE SUCH A WORRYWART! ♡
YOU WANNA ...
... "TEST ME OUT"?
HIKE
ちらーリ
...
AIEEE
いやーん
HEY, YOU DARE BEAT UP AN INVALID?!
SHUT UP! YOU'RE THE ONE STOMPING ALL OVER MY GENUINE CONCERN!
I TOLD YOU, I'M FINE...

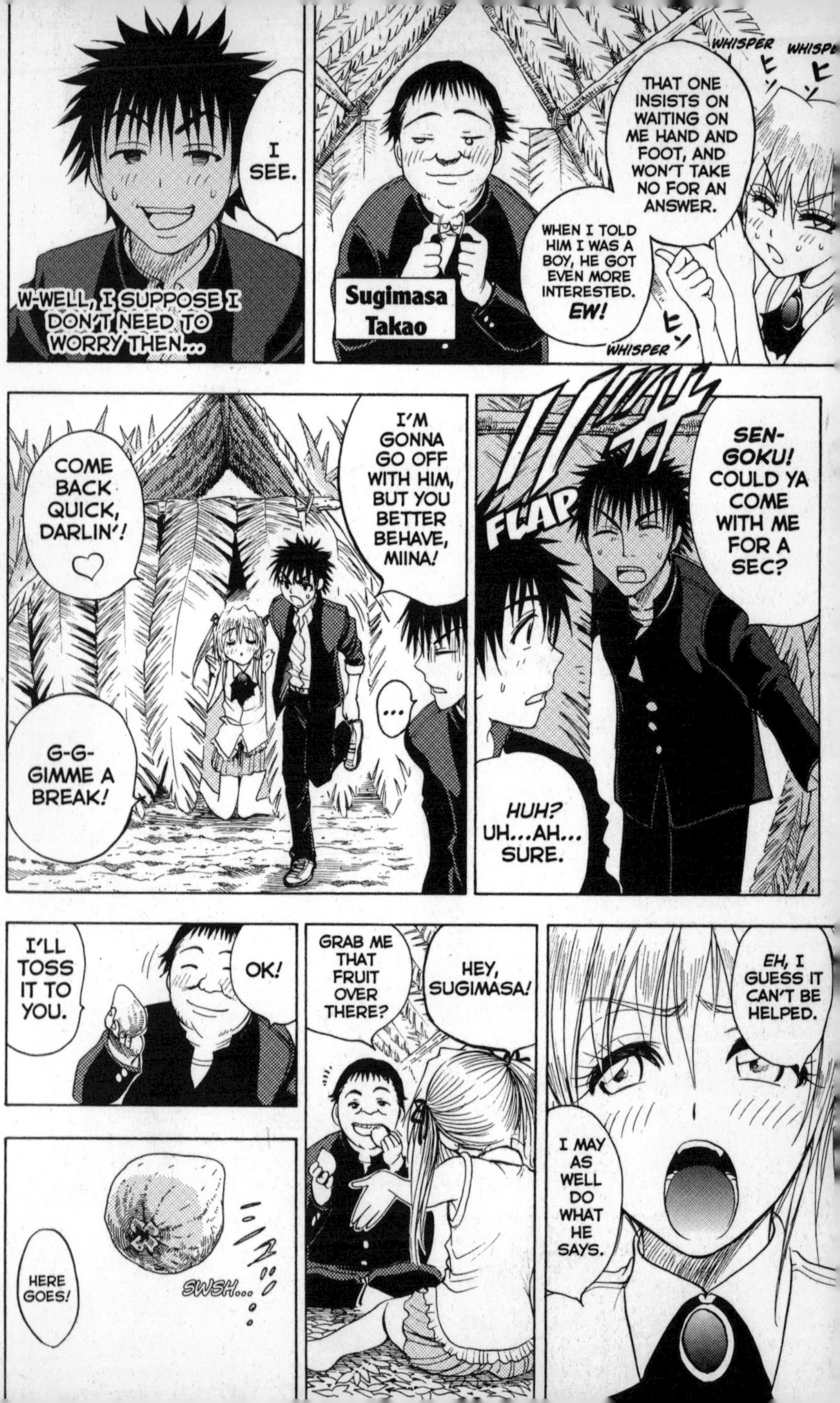
WHISPER
WHISPER
THAT ONE INSISTS ON WAITING ON ME HAND AND FOOT, AND WON'T TAKE NO FOR AN ANSWER.
WHEN I TOLD HIM I WAS A BOY, HE GOT EVEN MORE INTERESTED. EW!
WHISPER
Sugimasa Takao
I SEE.
W-WELL, I SUPPOSE I DON'T NEED TO WORRY THEN...
FLAP
SEN-GOKU! COULD YA COME WITH ME FOR A SEC?
HUH? UH...AH... SURE.
I'M GONNA GO OFF WITH HIM, BUT YOU BETTER BEHAVE, MIINA!
...
COME BACK QUICK, DARLIN'! ♡
G-G-GIMME A BREAK!
EH, I GUESS IT CAN'T BE HELPED.
I MAY AS WELL DO WHAT HE SAYS.
HEY, SUGIMASA!
GRAB ME THAT FRUIT OVER THERE?
OK!
I'LL TOSS IT TO YOU.
HERE GOES!
SWSH...

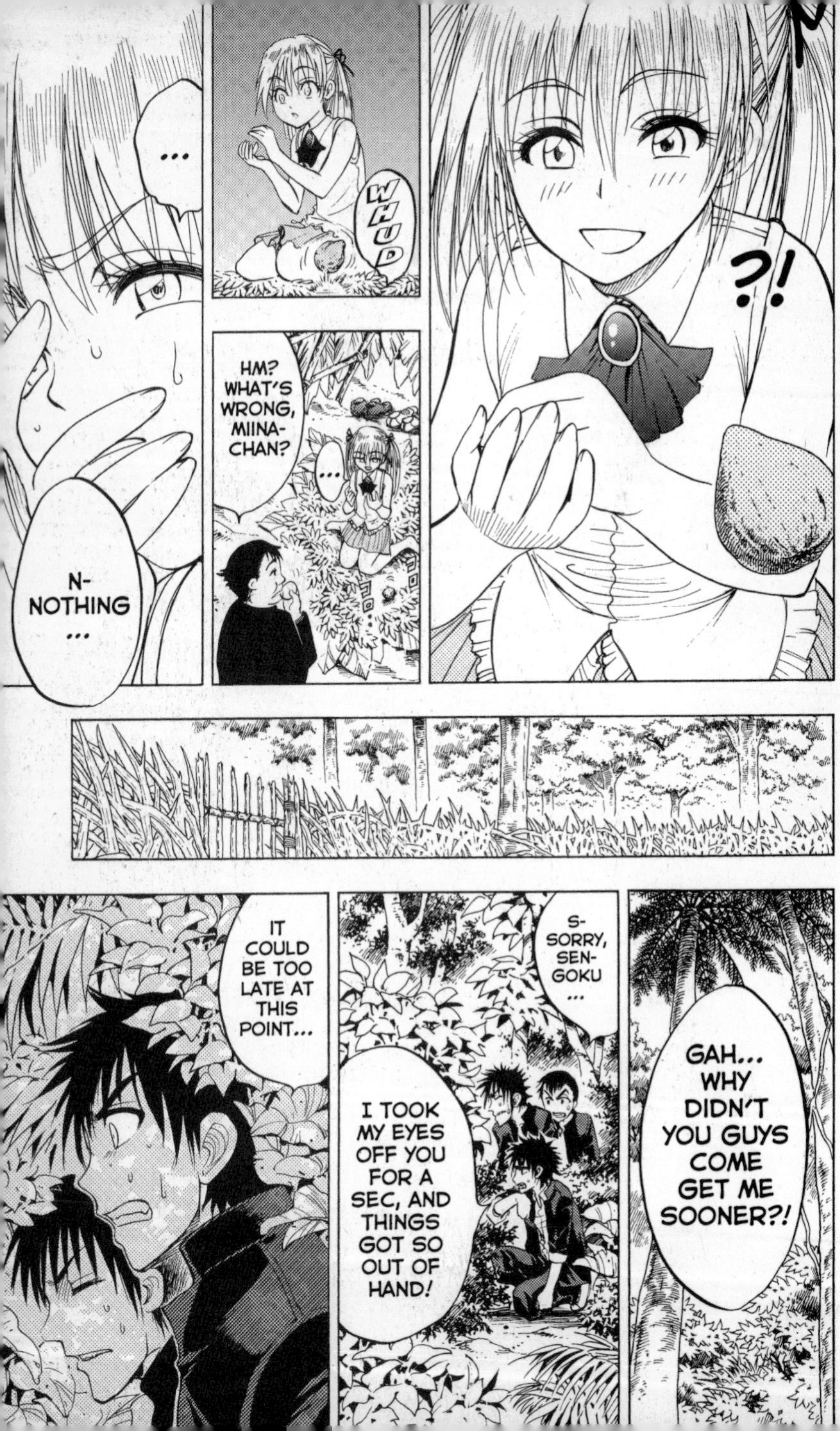
?!
WHUD
HM? WHAT'S WRONG, MIINA-CHAN?
...
...
N-NOTHING...
GAH... WHY DIDN'T YOU GUYS COME GET ME SOONER?!
S-SORRY, SEN-GOKU...
I TOOK MY EYES OFF YOU FOR A SEC, AND THINGS GOT SO OUT OF HAND!
IT COULD BE TOO LATE AT THIS POINT...

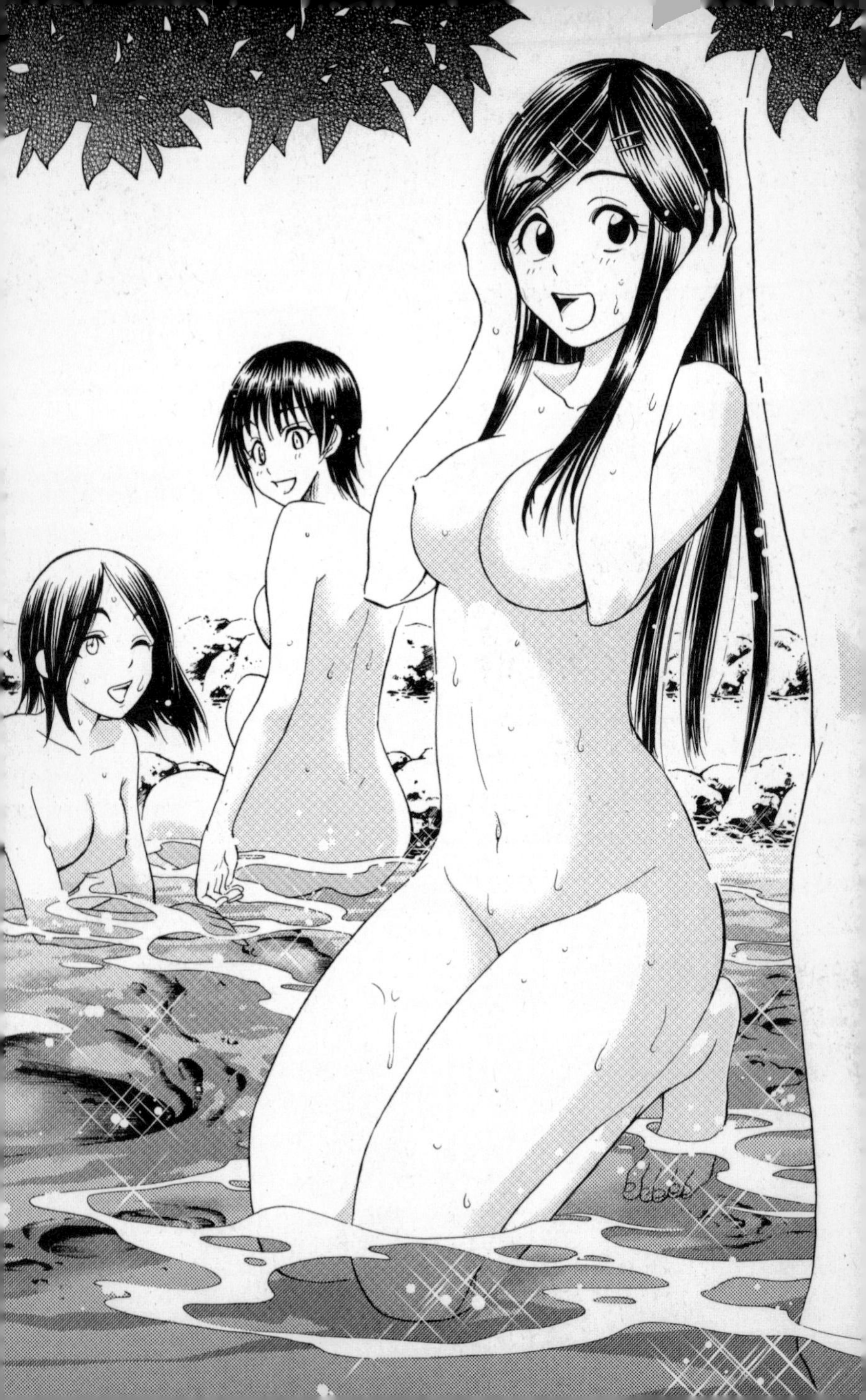

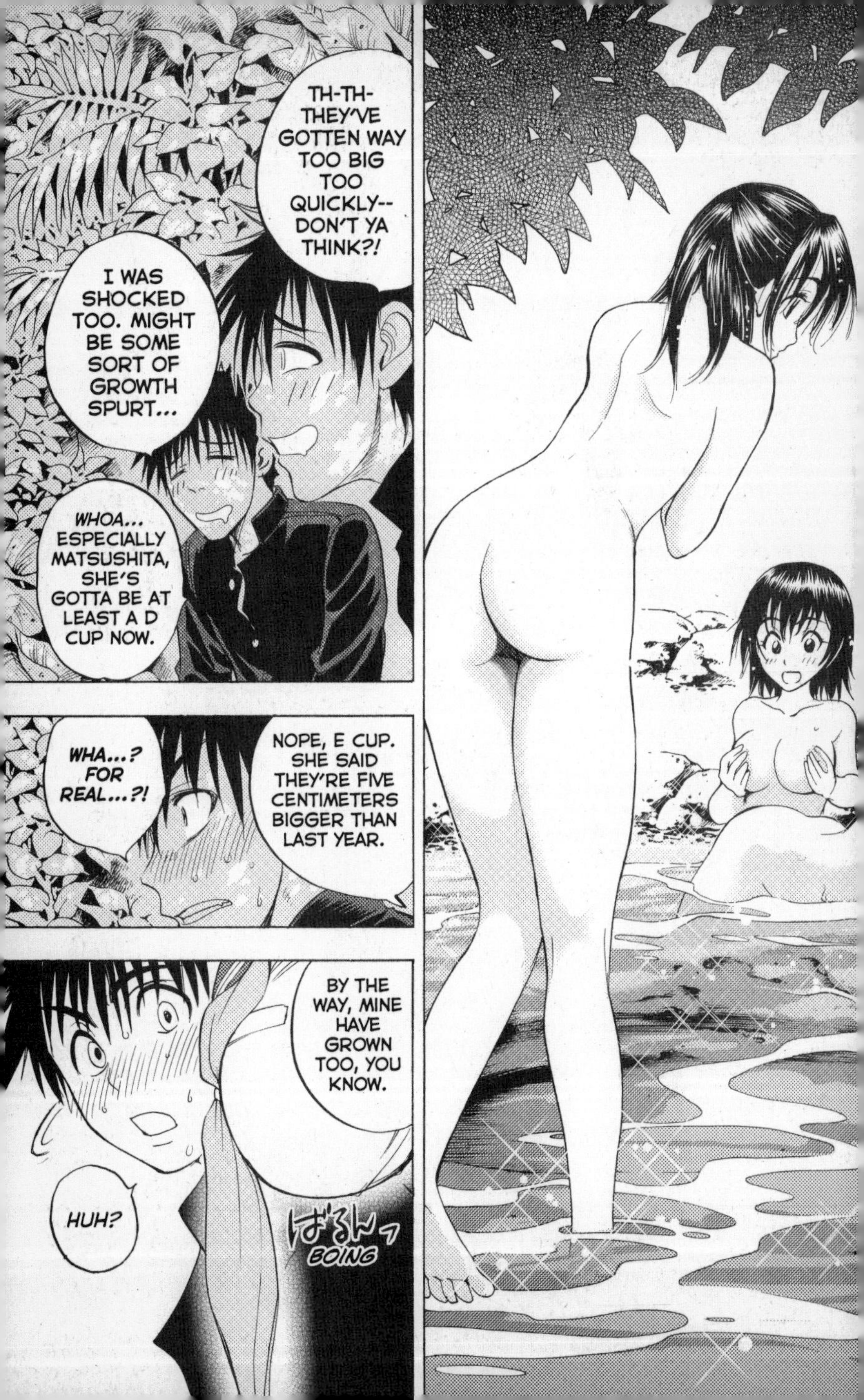
TH-TH-THEY'VE GOTTEN WAY TOO BIG TOO QUICKLY-- DON'T YA THINK?!
I WAS SHOCKED TOO. MIGHT BE SOME SORT OF GROWTH SPURT...
WHOA... ESPECIALLY MATSUSHITA, SHE'S GOTTA BE AT LEAST A D CUP NOW.
NOPE, E CUP. SHE SAID THEY'RE FIVE CENTIMETERS BIGGER THAN LAST YEAR.
WHA...? FOR REAL...?!
BY THE WAY, MINE HAVE GROWN TOO, YOU KNOW.
HUH?
ばるんっ
BOING

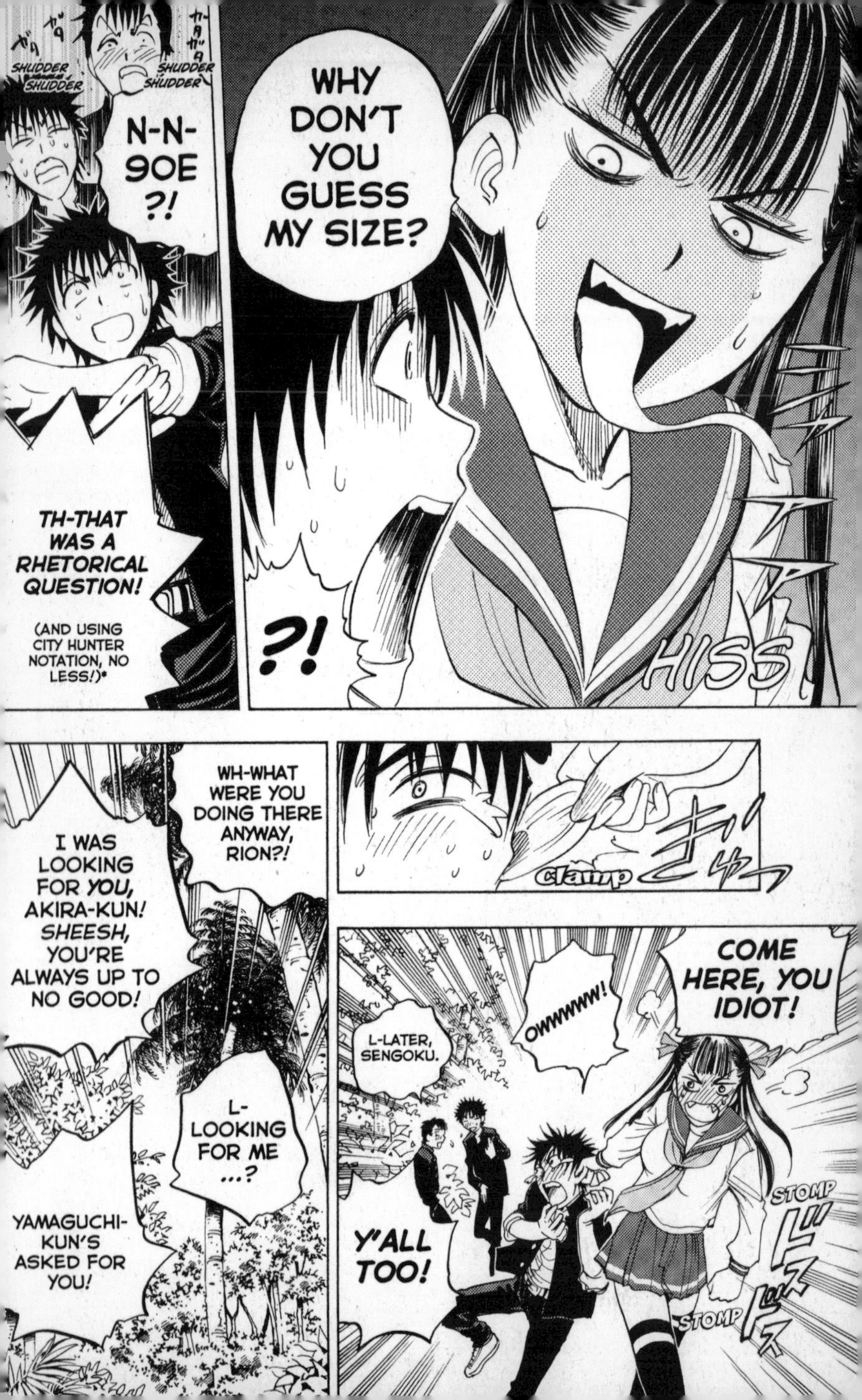
WHY DON'T YOU GUESS MY SIZE?
?!
HISS
SHUDDER SHUDDER
SHUDDER SHUDDER
N-N-90E ?!
TH-THAT WAS A RHETORICAL QUESTION!
(AND USING CITY HUNTER NOTATION, NO LESS!)*
Clamp
COME HERE, YOU IDIOT!
OWWWWW!
L-LATER, SENGOKU.
Y'ALL TOO!
STOMP
STOMP
WH-WHAT WERE YOU DOING THERE ANYWAY, RION?!
I WAS LOOKING FOR YOU, AKIRA-KUN! SHEESH, YOU'RE ALWAYS UP TO NO GOOD!
L-LOOKING FOR ME ...?
YAMAGUCHI-KUN'S ASKED FOR YOU!

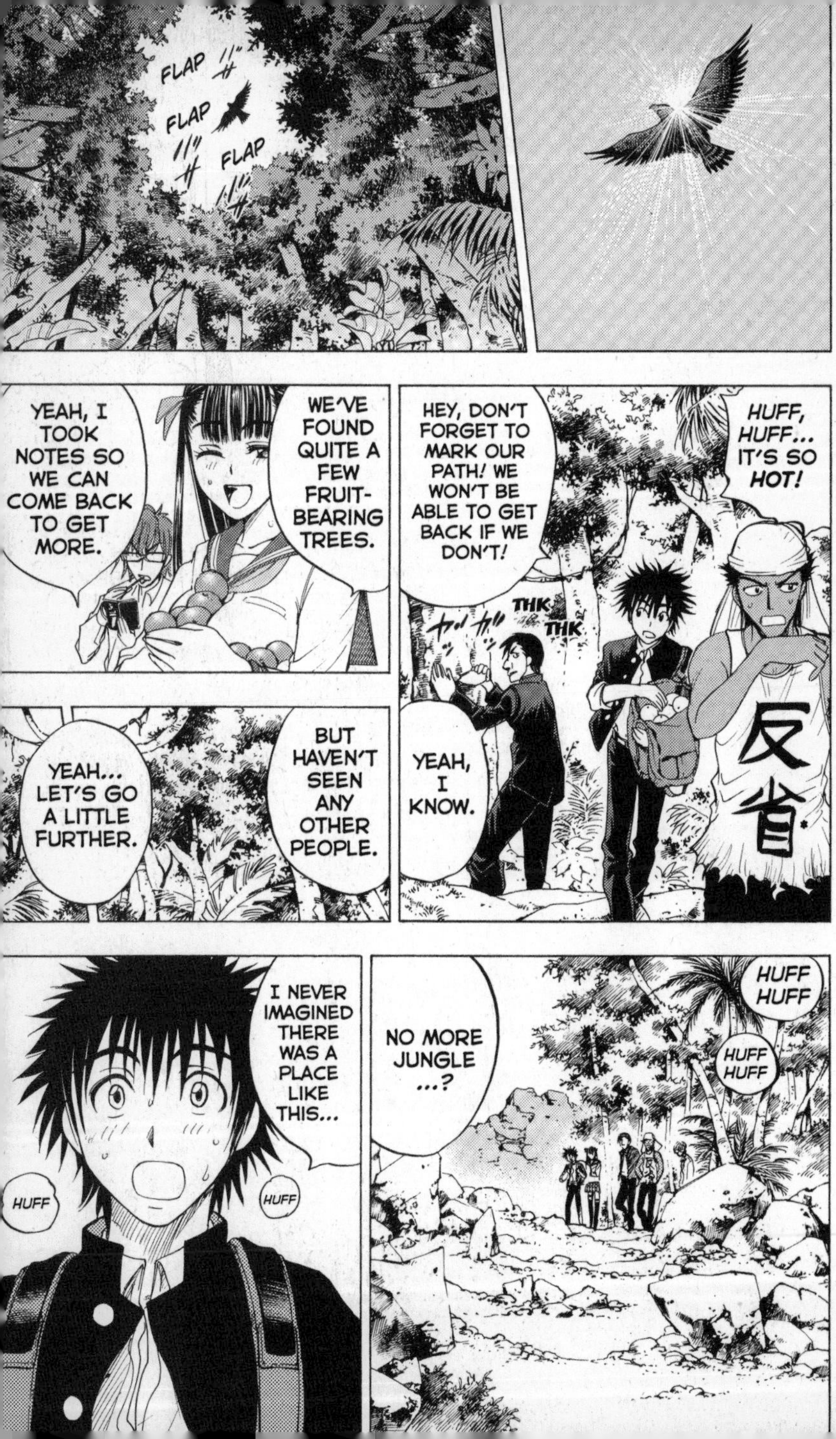
FLAP
FLAP
FLAP
HUFF, HUFF... IT'S SO *HOT!*
HEY, DON'T FORGET TO MARK OUR PATH! WE WON'T BE ABLE TO GET BACK IF WE DON'T!
THK
THK
YEAH, I KNOW.
反省
WE'VE FOUND QUITE A FEW FRUIT-BEARING TREES.
YEAH, I TOOK NOTES SO WE CAN COME BACK TO GET MORE.
BUT HAVEN'T SEEN ANY OTHER PEOPLE.
YEAH... LET'S GO A LITTLE FURTHER.
HUFF HUFF
HUFF HUFF
NO MORE JUNGLE ...?
I NEVER IMAGINED THERE WAS A PLACE LIKE THIS...
HUFF
HUFF

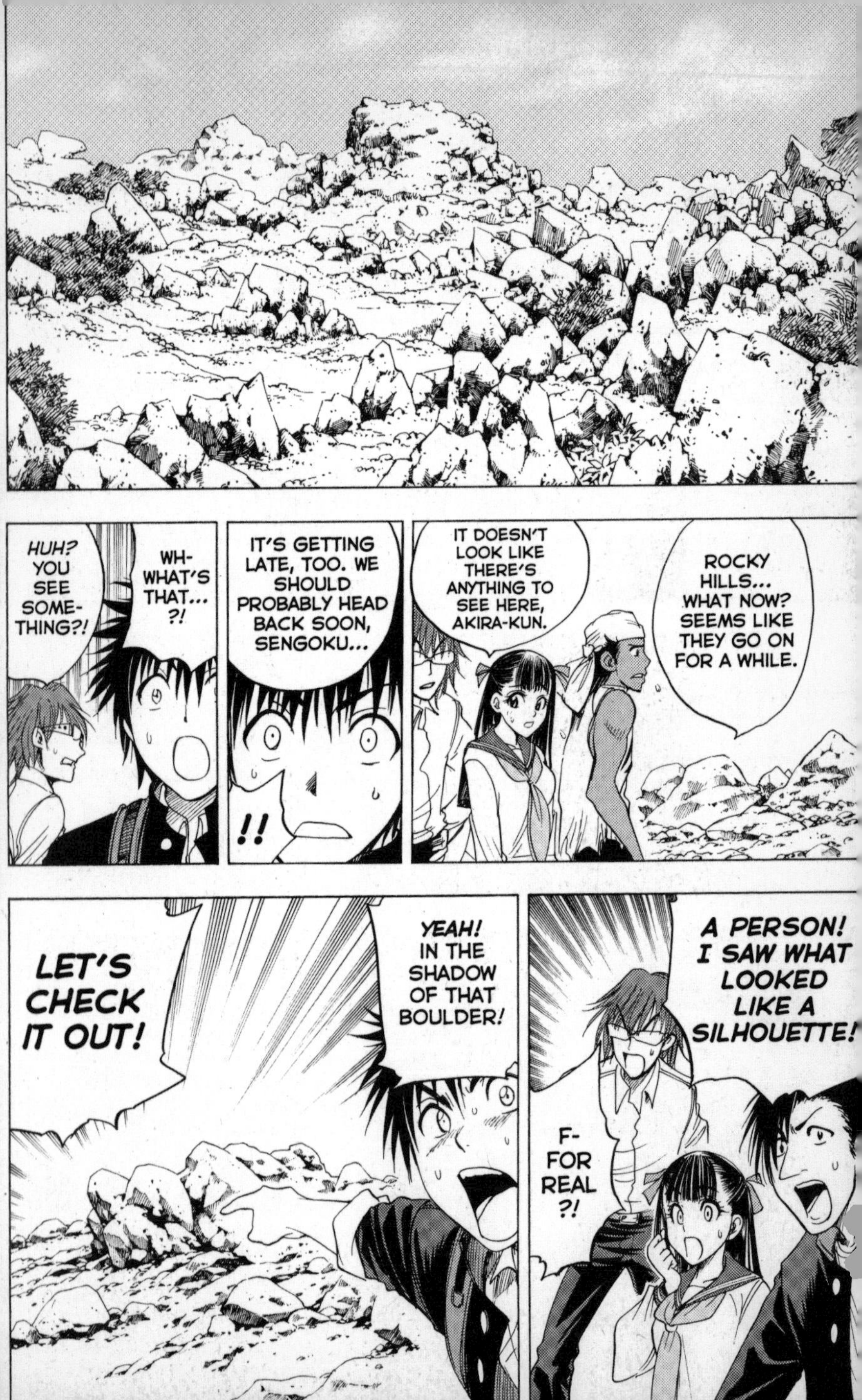
ROCKY HILLS... WHAT NOW? SEEMS LIKE THEY GO ON FOR A WHILE.
IT DOESN'T LOOK LIKE THERE'S ANYTHING TO SEE HERE, AKIRA-KUN.
IT'S GETTING LATE, TOO. WE SHOULD PROBABLY HEAD BACK SOON, SENGOKU...
!!
WH- WHAT'S THAT...?!
HUH? YOU SEE SOME- THING?!
A PERSON! I SAW WHAT LOOKED LIKE A SILHOUETTE!
F- FOR REAL?!
YEAH! IN THE SHADOW OF THAT BOULDER!
LET'S CHECK IT OUT!

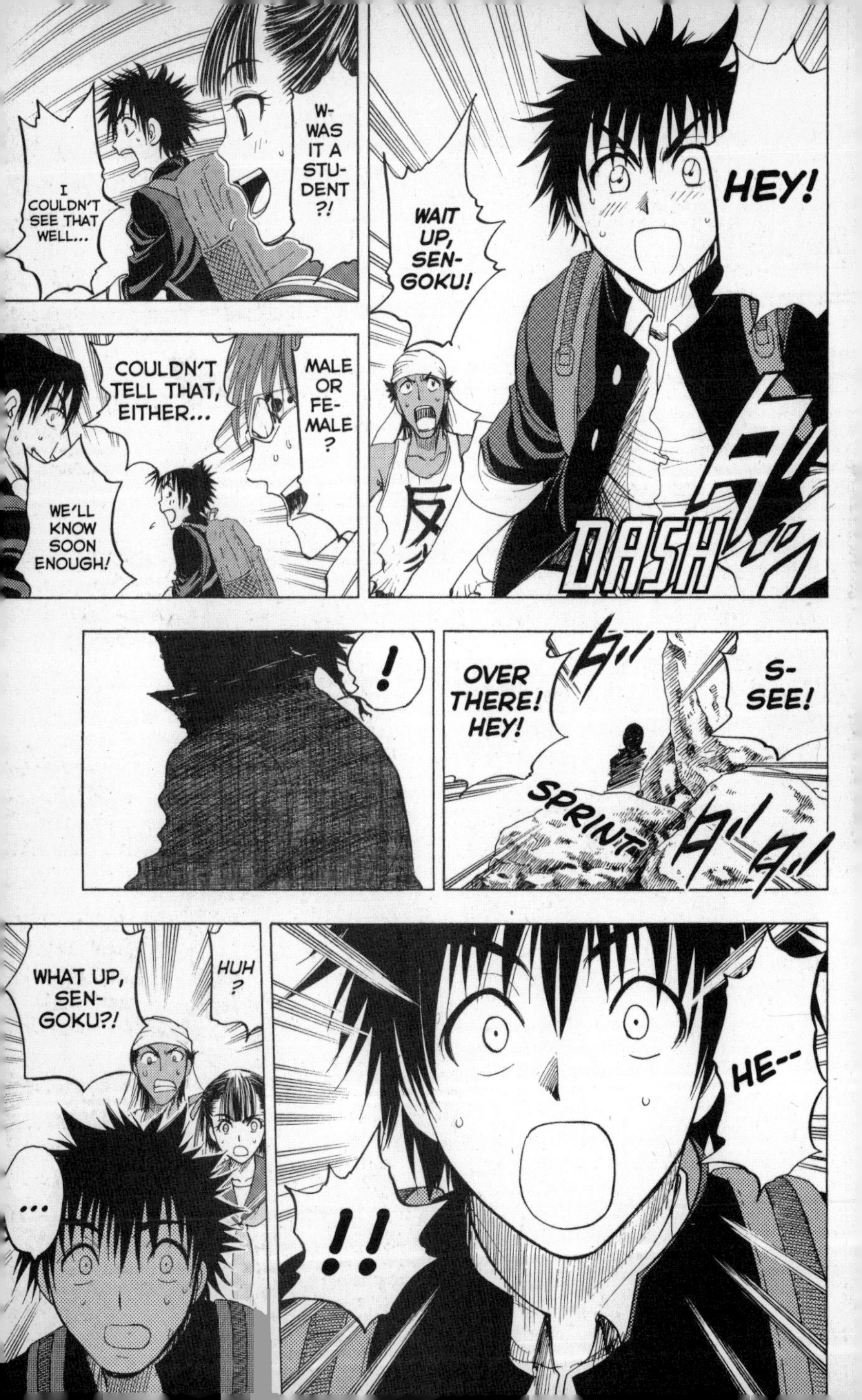

HEY!
WAIT UP, SEN-GOKU!
DASH
W-WAS IT A STU-DENT?!
I COULDN'T SEE THAT WELL...
MALE OR FE-MALE?
COULDN'T TELL THAT, EITHER...
WE'LL KNOW SOON ENOUGH!
S-SEE!
OVER THERE! HEY!
SPRINT
!
HE--
!!
HUH?
WHAT UP, SEN-GOKU?!
...

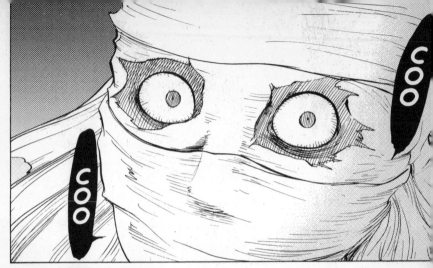

H-H-HIS WHOLE FACE IS COVERED IN GAUZE...?!

AIEEE!

PEOPLE, THERE ARE PEOPLE HERE!

HUH?!

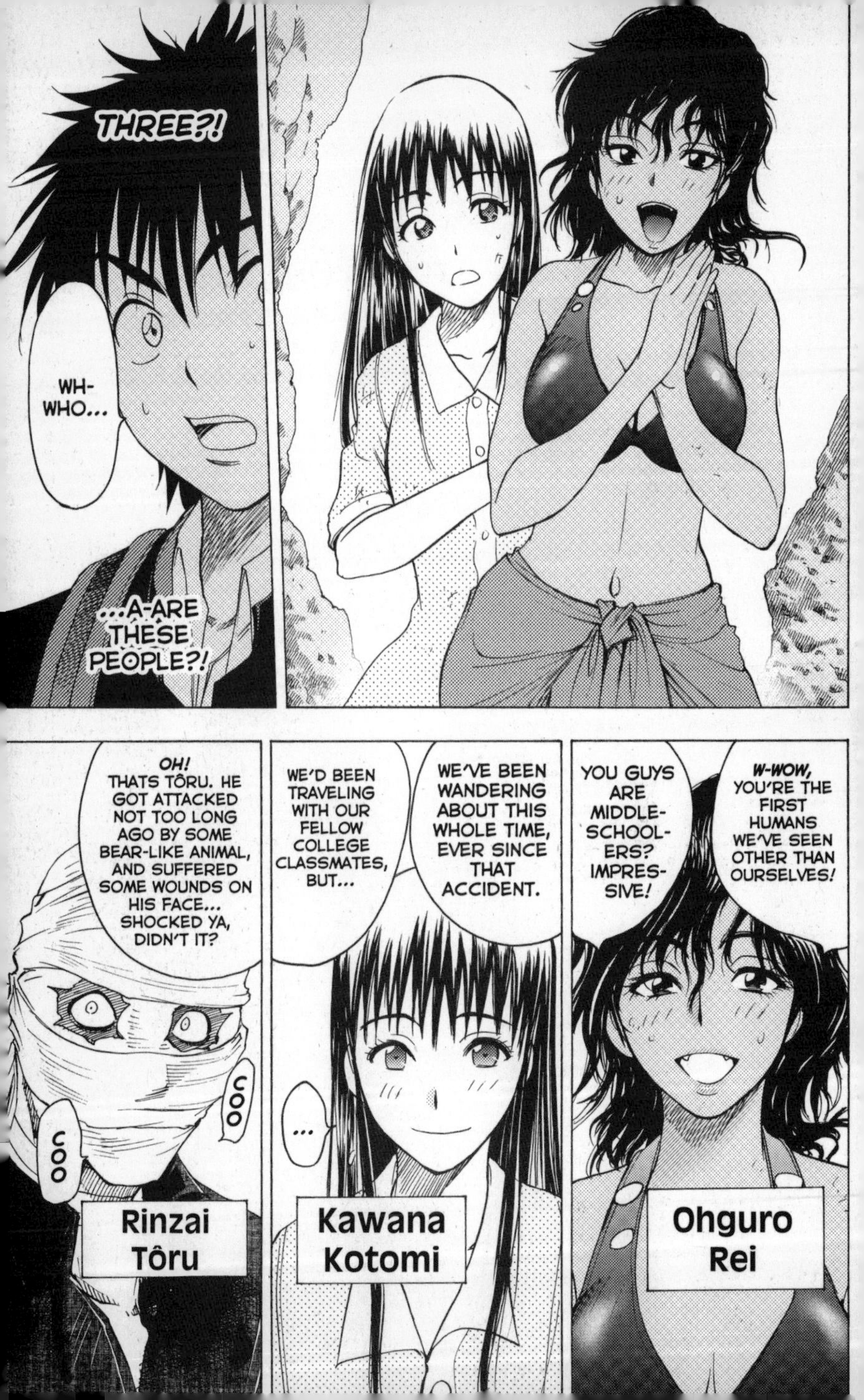
THREE?!
WH-WHO...
...A-ARE THESE PEOPLE?!
W-WOW, YOU'RE THE FIRST HUMANS WE'VE SEEN OTHER THAN OURSELVES!
YOU GUYS ARE MIDDLE-SCHOOLERS? IMPRESSIVE!
Ohguro Rei
WE'VE BEEN WANDERING ABOUT THIS WHOLE TIME, EVER SINCE THAT ACCIDENT.
WE'D BEEN TRAVELING WITH OUR FELLOW COLLEGE CLASSMATES, BUT...
...
Kawana Kotomi
OH! THATS TÔRU. HE GOT ATTACKED NOT TOO LONG AGO BY SOME BEAR-LIKE ANIMAL, AND SUFFERED SOME WOUNDS ON HIS FACE... SHOCKED YA, DIDN'T IT?
COO
COO
Rinzai Tôru

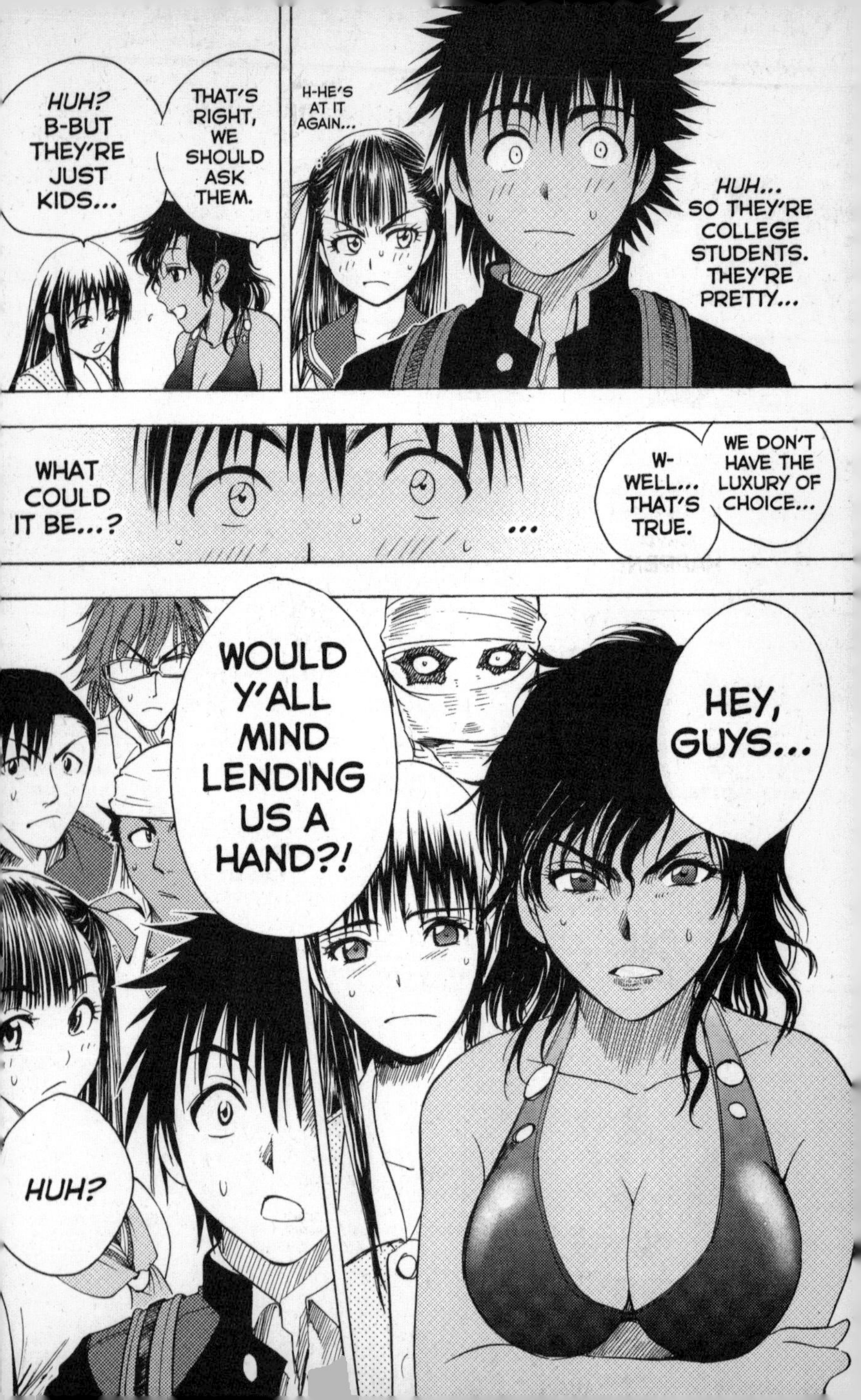
HUH... SO THEY'RE COLLEGE STUDENTS. THEY'RE PRETTY...
H-HE'S AT IT AGAIN...
THAT'S RIGHT, WE SHOULD ASK THEM.
HUH? B-BUT THEY'RE JUST KIDS...
WE DON'T HAVE THE LUXURY OF CHOICE...
W-WELL... THAT'S TRUE.
...
WHAT COULD IT BE...?
HEY, GUYS...
WOULD Y'ALL MIND LENDING US A HAND?!
HUH?

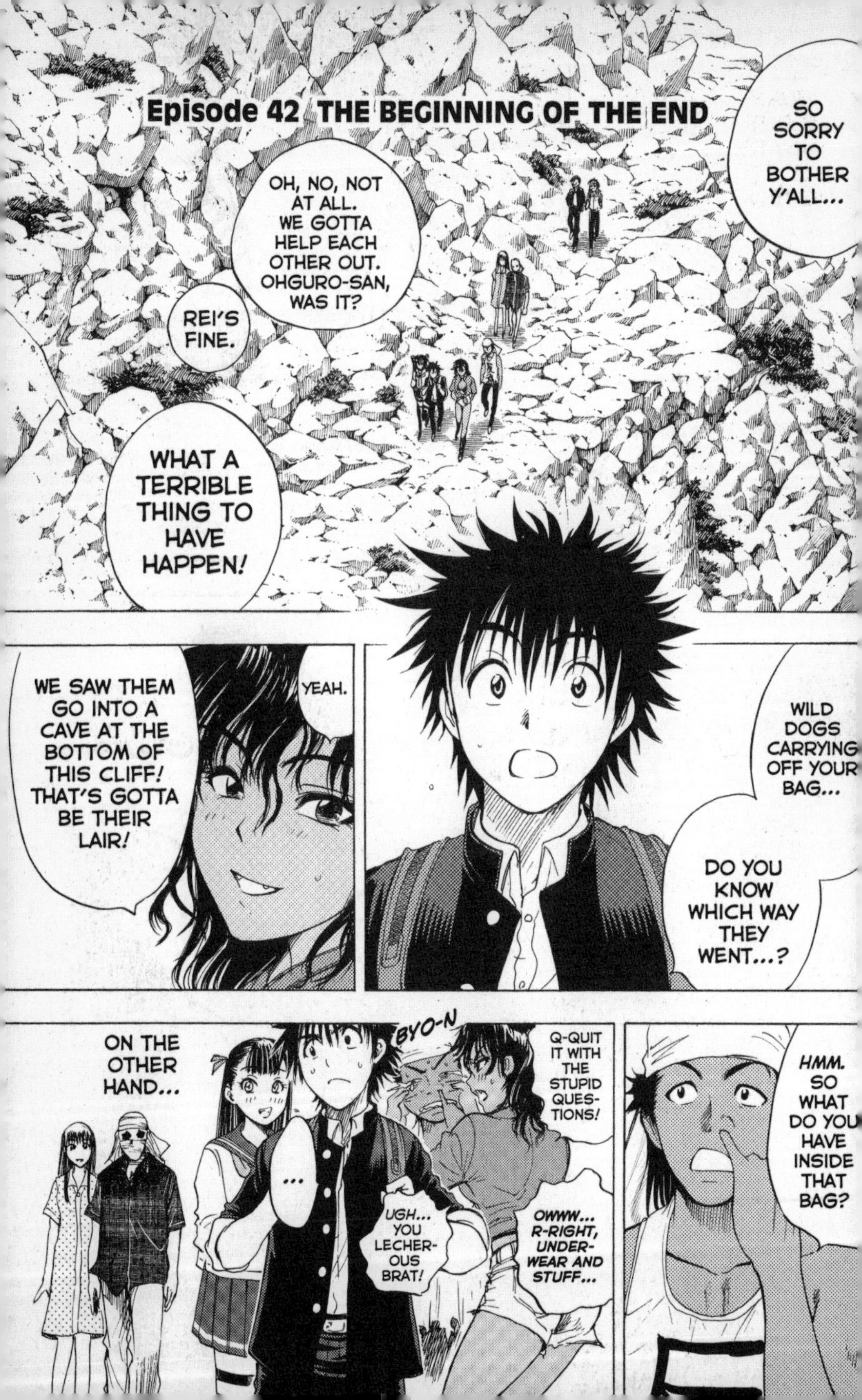
Episode 42 THE BEGINNING OF THE END
SO SORRY TO BOTHER Y'ALL...
OH, NO, NOT AT ALL. WE GOTTA HELP EACH OTHER OUT. OHGURO-SAN, WAS IT?
REI'S FINE.
WHAT A TERRIBLE THING TO HAVE HAPPEN!
WILD DOGS CARRYING OFF YOUR BAG...
DO YOU KNOW WHICH WAY THEY WENT...?
YEAH.
WE SAW THEM GO INTO A CAVE AT THE BOTTOM OF THIS CLIFF! THAT'S GOTTA BE THEIR LAIR!
HMM. SO WHAT DO YOU HAVE INSIDE THAT BAG?
Q-QUIT IT WITH THE STUPID QUES-TIONS!
BYO-N
OWWW... R-RIGHT, UNDER-WEAR AND STUFF...
UGH... YOU LECHER-OUS BRAT!
...
ON THE OTHER HAND...

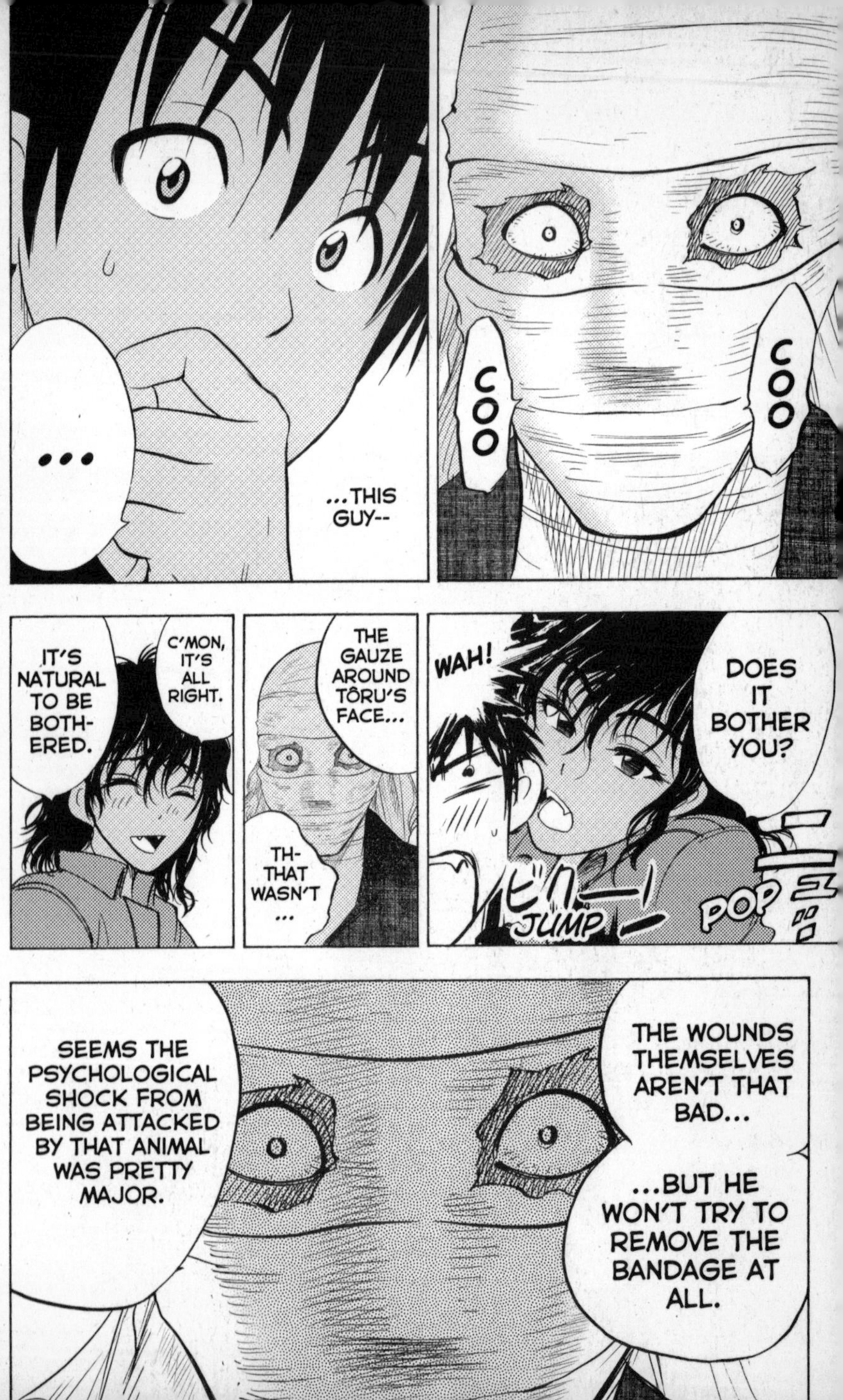
COO
COO
...
...THIS GUY--
DOES IT BOTHER YOU?
WAH!
JUMP
POP
THE GAUZE AROUND TÔRU'S FACE...
TH-THAT WASN'T...
C'MON, IT'S ALL RIGHT.
IT'S NATURAL TO BE BOTH-ERED.
THE WOUNDS THEMSELVES AREN'T THAT BAD...
...BUT HE WON'T TRY TO REMOVE THE BANDAGE AT ALL.
SEEMS THE PSYCHOLOGICAL SHOCK FROM BEING ATTACKED BY THAT ANIMAL WAS PRETTY MAJOR.

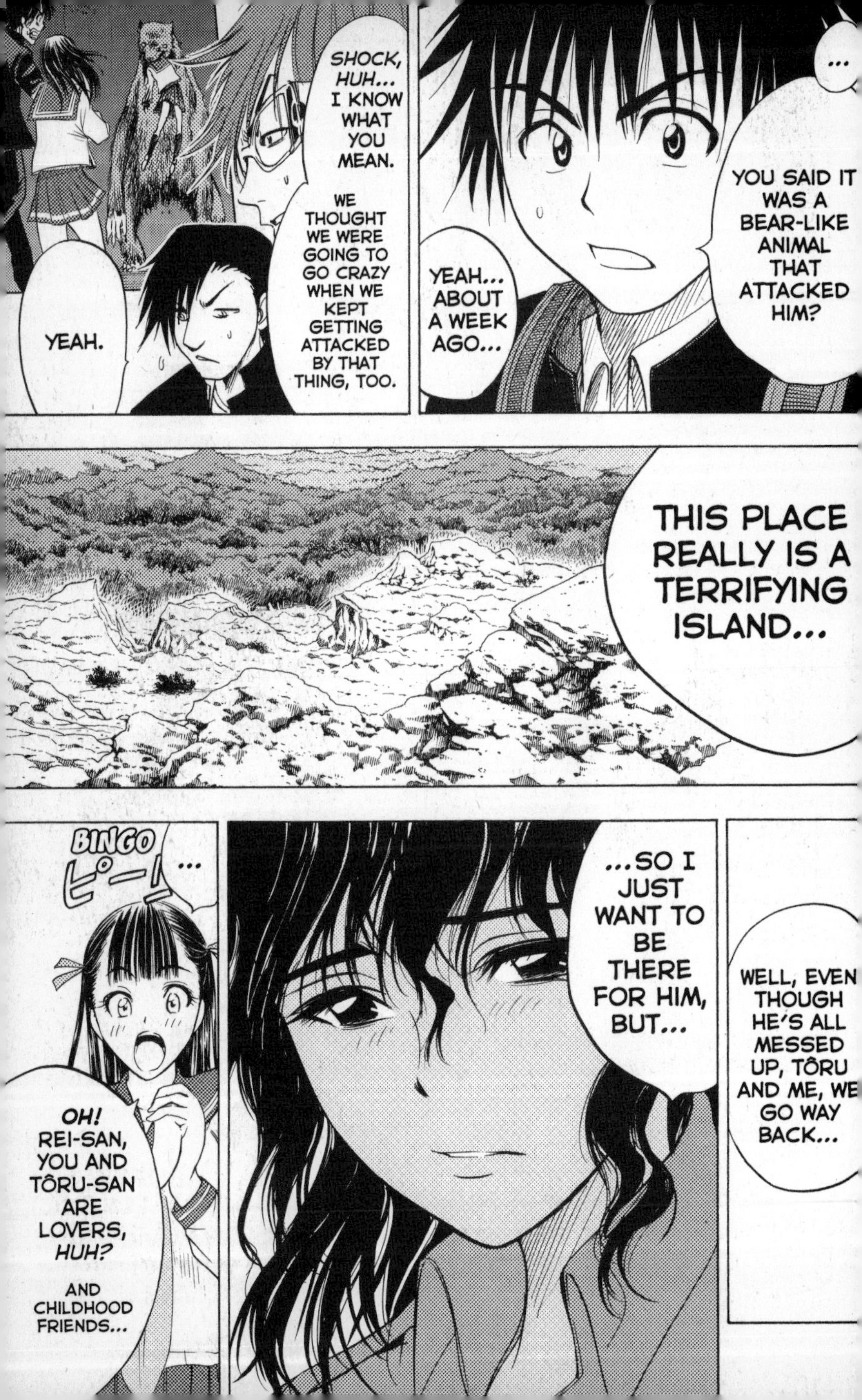
...
YOU SAID IT WAS A BEAR-LIKE ANIMAL THAT ATTACKED HIM?
YEAH... ABOUT A WEEK AGO...
SHOCK, HUH... I KNOW WHAT YOU MEAN.
WE THOUGHT WE WERE GOING TO GO CRAZY WHEN WE KEPT GETTING ATTACKED BY THAT THING, TOO.
YEAH.
THIS PLACE REALLY IS A TERRIFYING ISLAND...
WELL, EVEN THOUGH HE'S ALL MESSED UP, TÔRU AND ME, WE GO WAY BACK...
...SO I JUST WANT TO BE THERE FOR HIM, BUT...
BINGO
ピーー
...
OH! REI-SAN, YOU AND TÔRU-SAN ARE LOVERS, HUH?
AND CHILDHOOD FRIENDS...

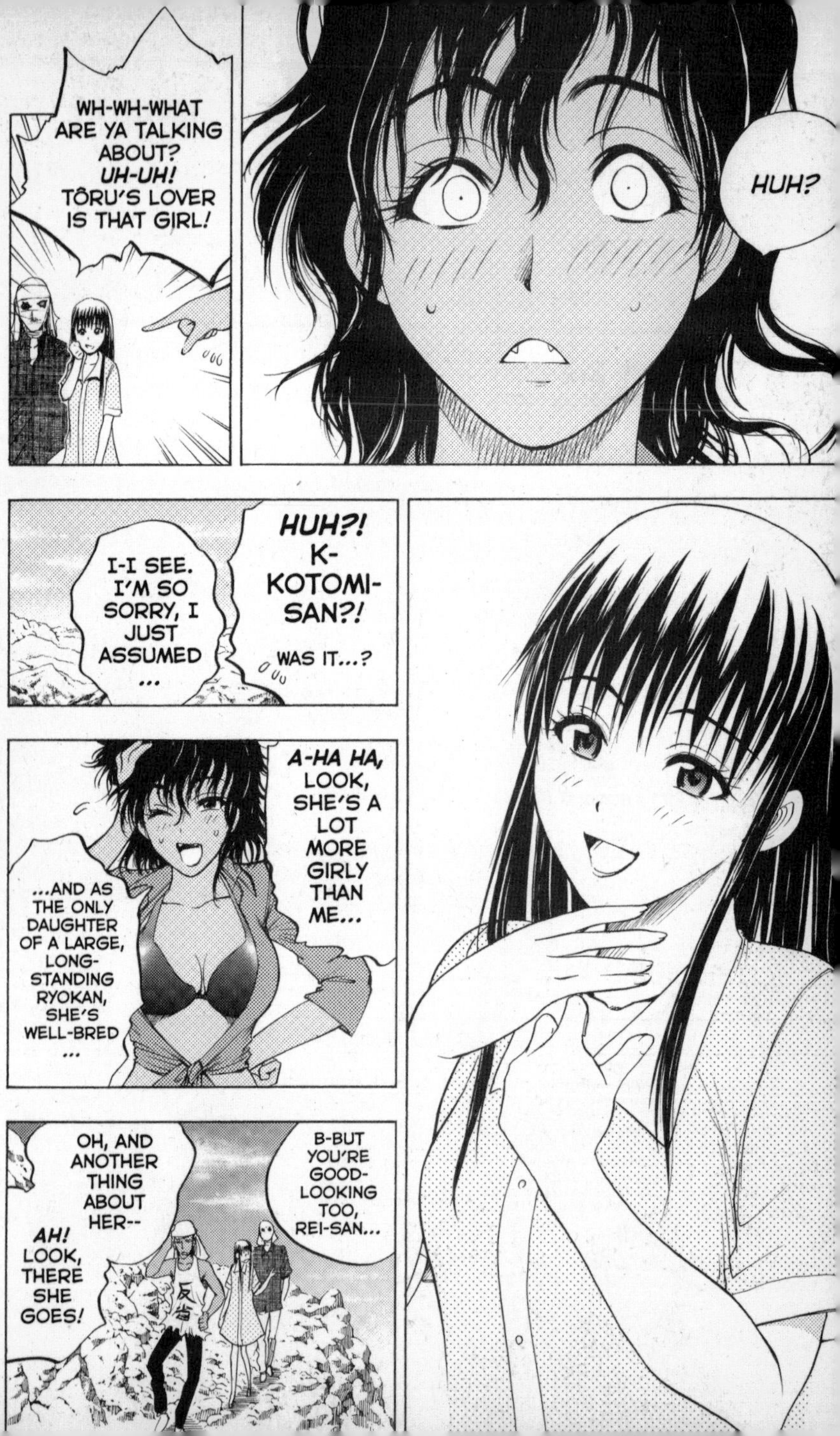
HUH?
WH-WH-WHAT ARE YA TALKING ABOUT? UH-UH! TÔRU'S LOVER IS THAT GIRL!
HUH?! K-KOTOMI-SAN?!
WAS IT...?
I-I SEE. I'M SO SORRY, I JUST ASSUMED ...
A-HA HA, LOOK, SHE'S A LOT MORE GIRLY THAN ME...
...AND AS THE ONLY DAUGHTER OF A LARGE, LONG-STANDING RYOKAN, SHE'S WELL-BRED ...
B-BUT YOU'RE GOOD-LOOKING TOO, REI-SAN...
OH, AND ANOTHER THING ABOUT HER--
AH! LOOK, THERE SHE GOES!

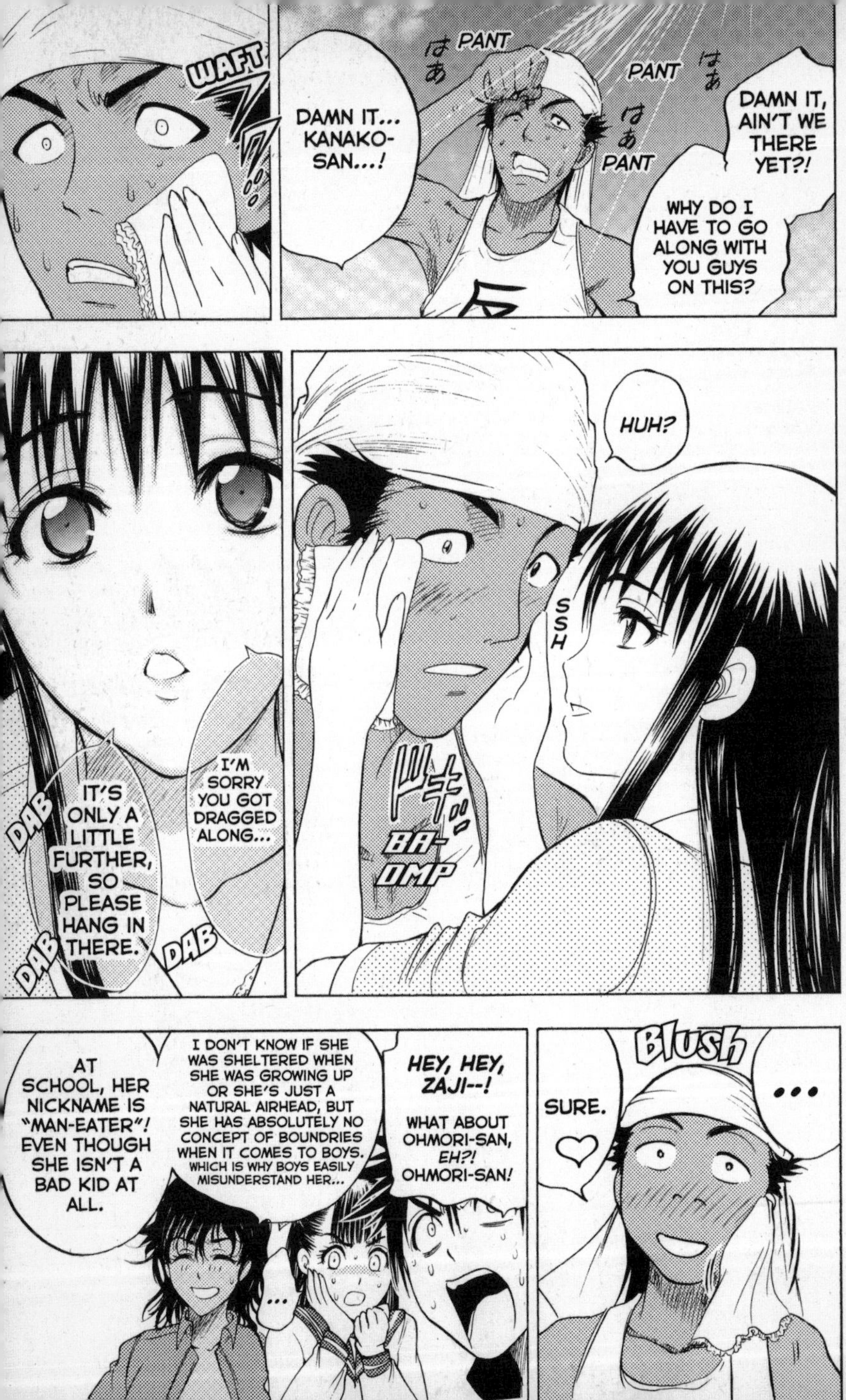
はあ PANT
PANT はあ
はあ PANT
DAMN IT, AIN'T WE THERE YET?!
WHY DO I HAVE TO GO ALONG WITH YOU GUYS ON THIS?
DAMN IT... KANAKO-SAN...!
WAFT
HUH?
SSH
BA-DOMP
I'M SORRY YOU GOT DRAGGED ALONG...
IT'S ONLY A LITTLE FURTHER, SO PLEASE HANG IN THERE.
DAB
DAB
DAB
Blush
...
SURE. ♡
HEY, HEY, ZAJI--!
WHAT ABOUT OHMORI-SAN, EH?! OHMORI-SAN!
I DON'T KNOW IF SHE WAS SHELTERED WHEN SHE WAS GROWING UP OR SHE'S JUST A NATURAL AIRHEAD, BUT SHE HAS ABSOLUTELY NO CONCEPT OF BOUNDRIES WHEN IT COMES TO BOYS. WHICH IS WHY BOYS EASILY MISUNDERSTAND HER...
AT SCHOOL, HER NICKNAME IS "MAN-EATER"! EVEN THOUGH SHE ISN'T A BAD KID AT ALL.
...

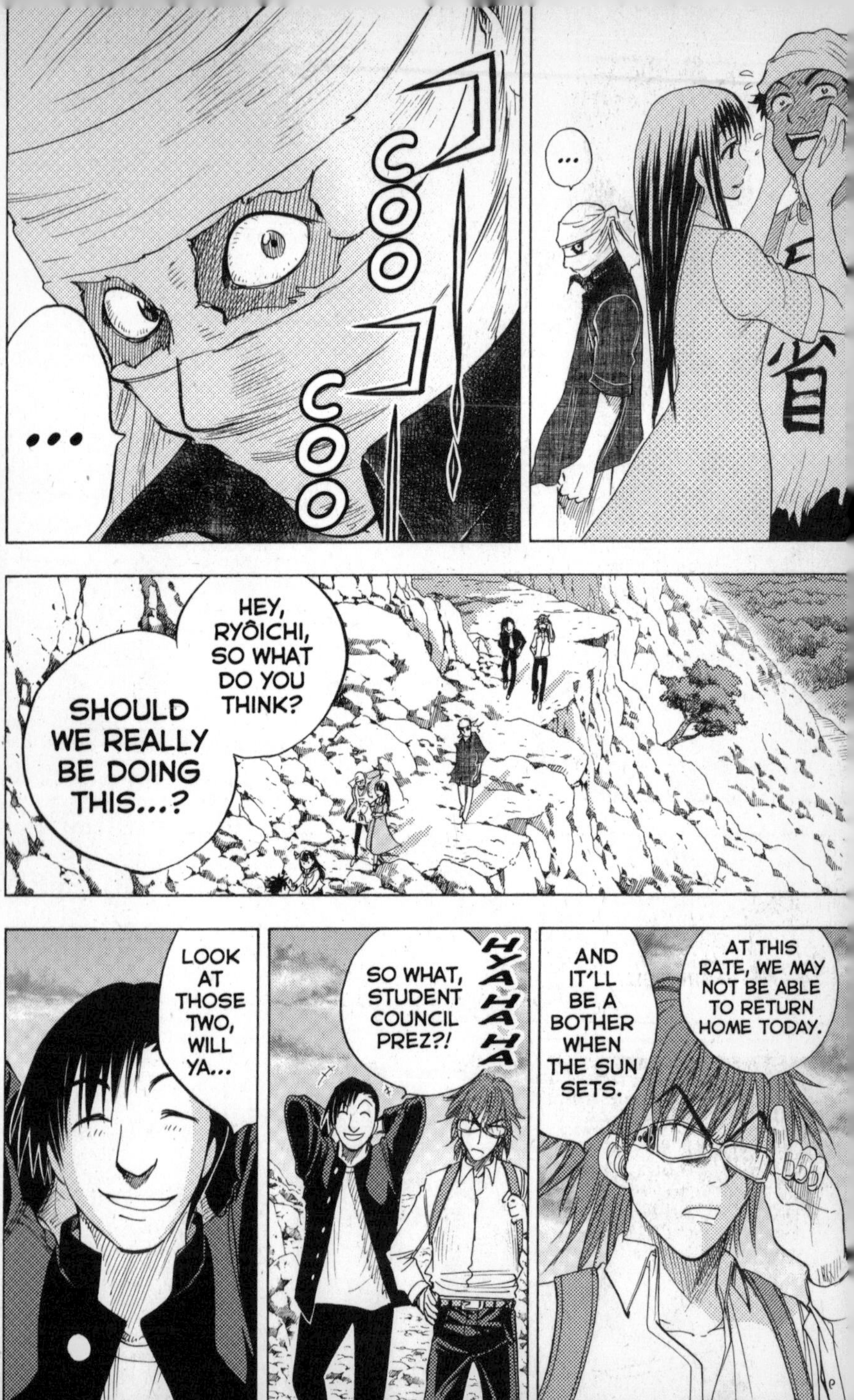
...
...
COO COO
HEY, RYÔICHI, SO WHAT DO YOU THINK?
SHOULD WE REALLY BE DOING THIS...?
AT THIS RATE, WE MAY NOT BE ABLE TO RETURN HOME TODAY.
AND IT'LL BE A BOTHER WHEN THE SUN SETS.
HYAHAHAHA
SO WHAT, STUDENT COUNCIL PREZ?!
LOOK AT THOSE TWO, WILL YA...

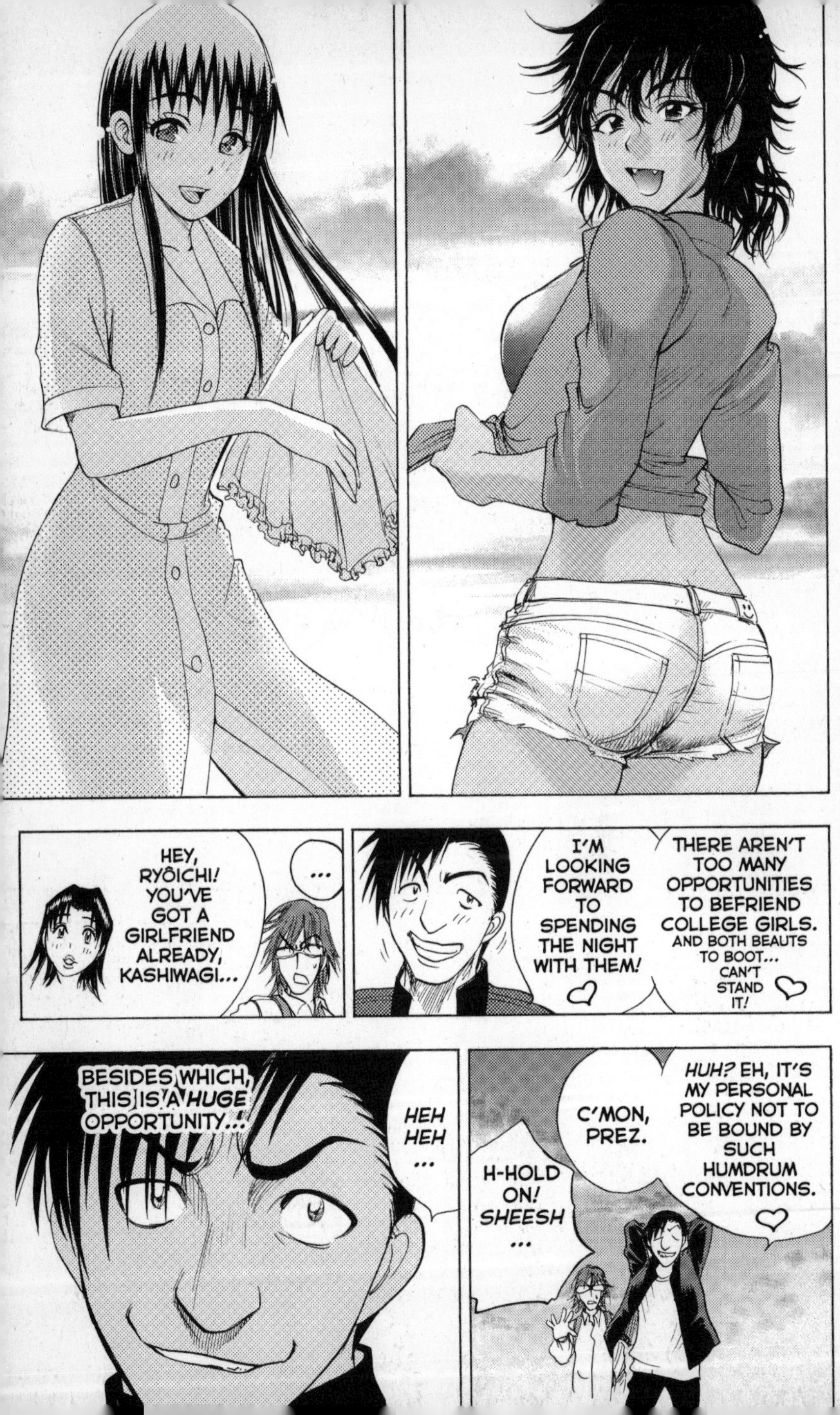
THERE AREN'T TOO MANY OPPORTUNITIES TO BEFRIEND COLLEGE GIRLS.
AND BOTH BEAUTS TO BOOT... CAN'T STAND IT!
I'M LOOKING FORWARD TO SPENDING THE NIGHT WITH THEM!
...
HEY, RYÔICHI! YOU'VE GOT A GIRLFRIEND ALREADY, KASHIWAGI...
HUH? EH, IT'S MY PERSONAL POLICY NOT TO BE BOUND BY SUCH HUMDRUM CONVENTIONS.
C'MON, PREZ.
H-HOLD ON! SHEESH...
HEH HEH...
BESIDES WHICH, THIS IS A *HUGE* OPPORTUNITY...

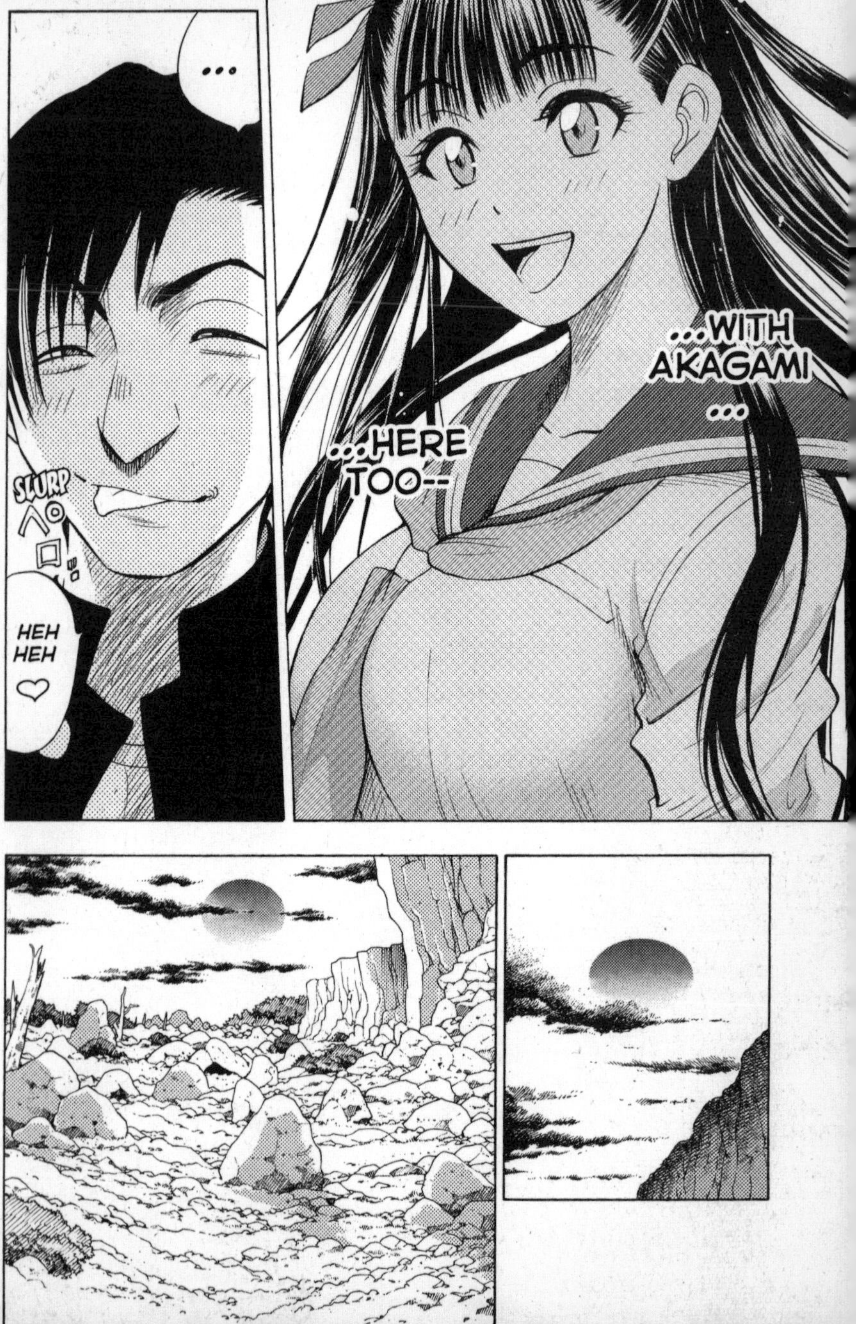
...WITH AKAGAMI ...
...HERE TOO--
...
SLURP
HEH HEH ♡

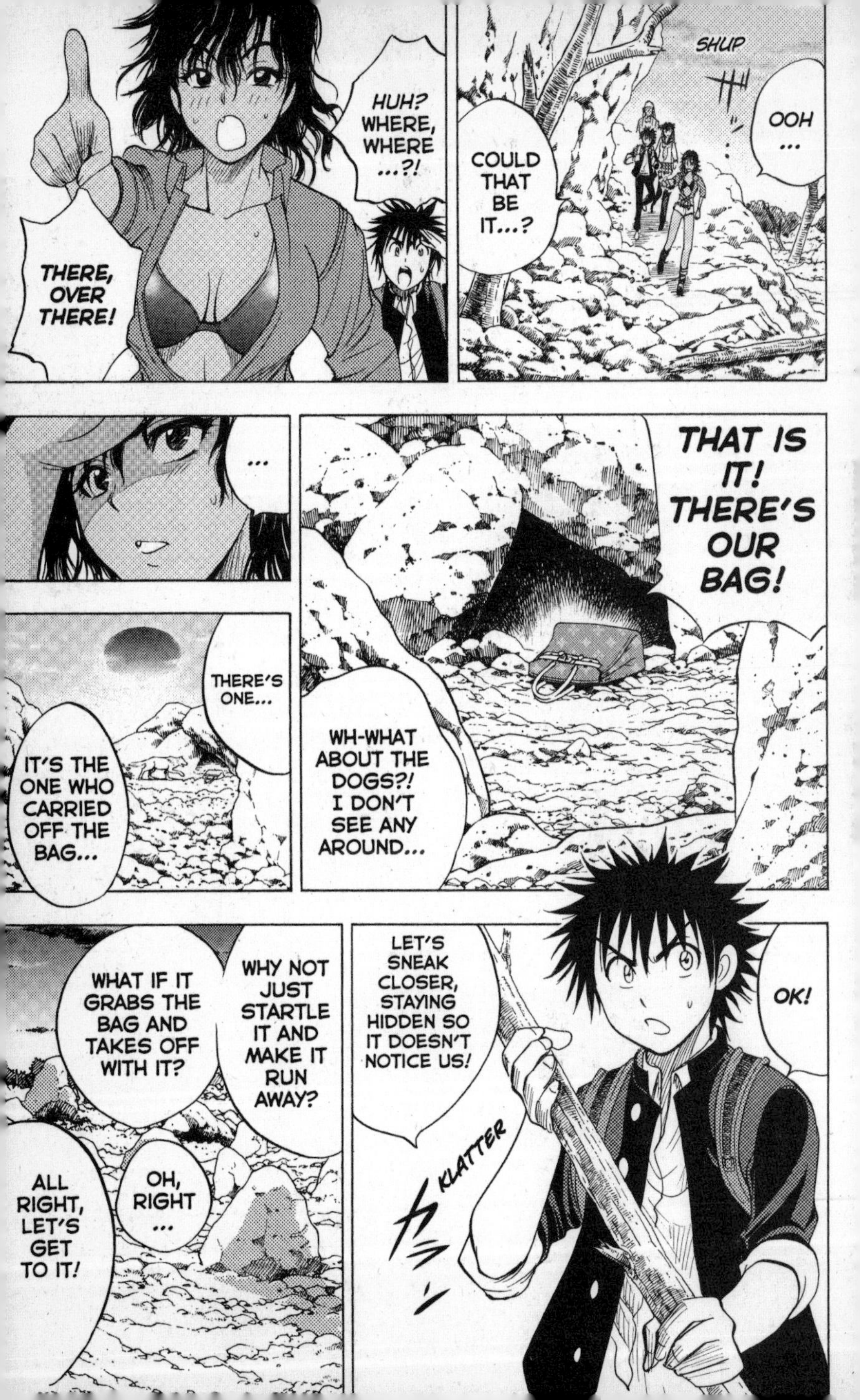
SHUP
OOH ...
COULD THAT BE IT...?
HUH? WHERE, WHERE ...?!
THERE, OVER THERE!
THAT IS IT! THERE'S OUR BAG!
WH-WHAT ABOUT THE DOGS?! I DON'T SEE ANY AROUND...
...
THERE'S ONE...
IT'S THE ONE WHO CARRIED OFF THE BAG...
OK!
LET'S SNEAK CLOSER, STAYING HIDDEN SO IT DOESN'T NOTICE US!
KLATTER
WHY NOT JUST STARTLE IT AND MAKE IT RUN AWAY?
WHAT IF IT GRABS THE BAG AND TAKES OFF WITH IT?
OH, RIGHT ...
ALL RIGHT, LET'S GET TO IT!

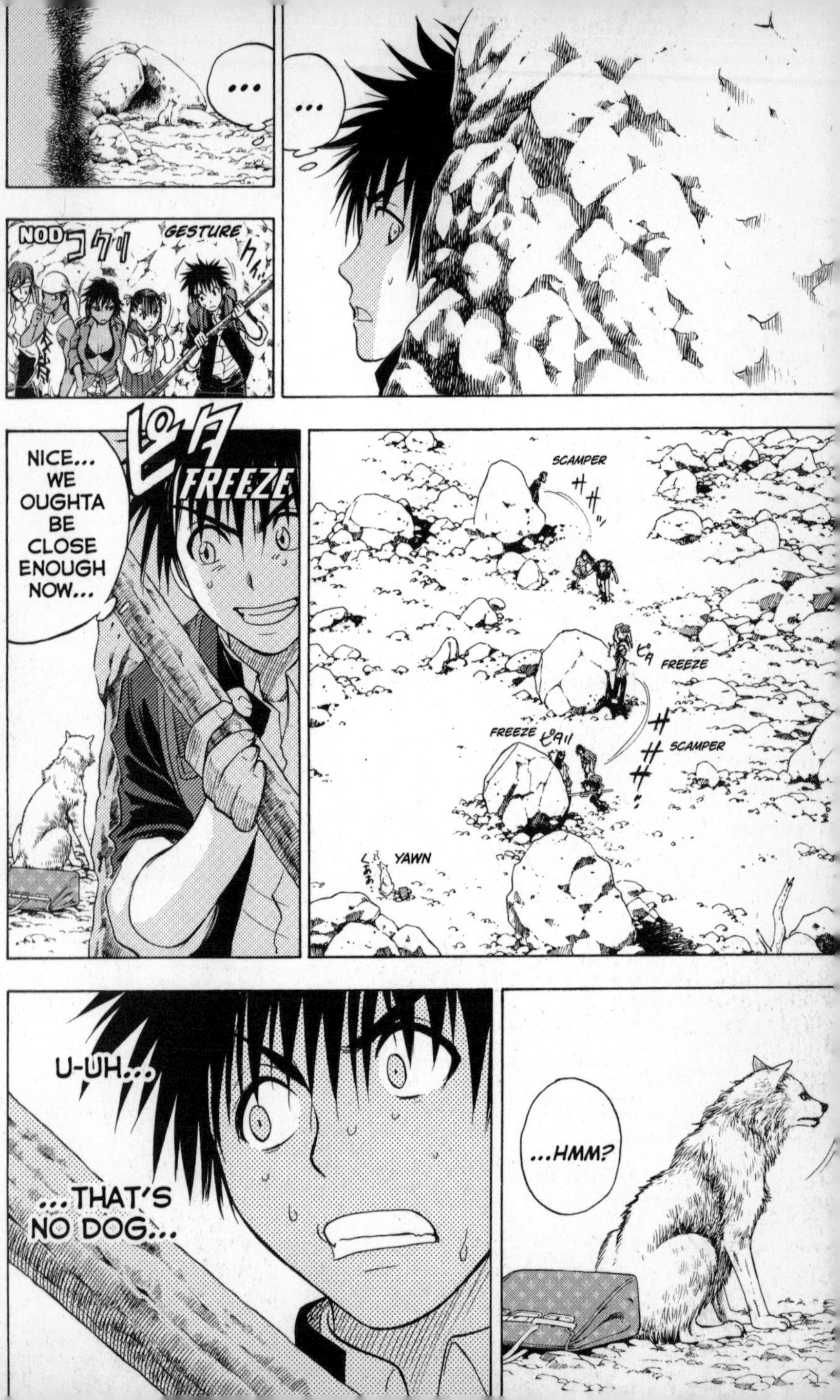
...
...
NOD コクリ
GESTURE
SCAMPER
FREEZE
SCAMPER
FREEZE
YAWN
FREEZE
NICE... WE OUGHTA BE CLOSE ENOUGH NOW...
...HMM?
U-UH...
...THAT'S NO DOG...

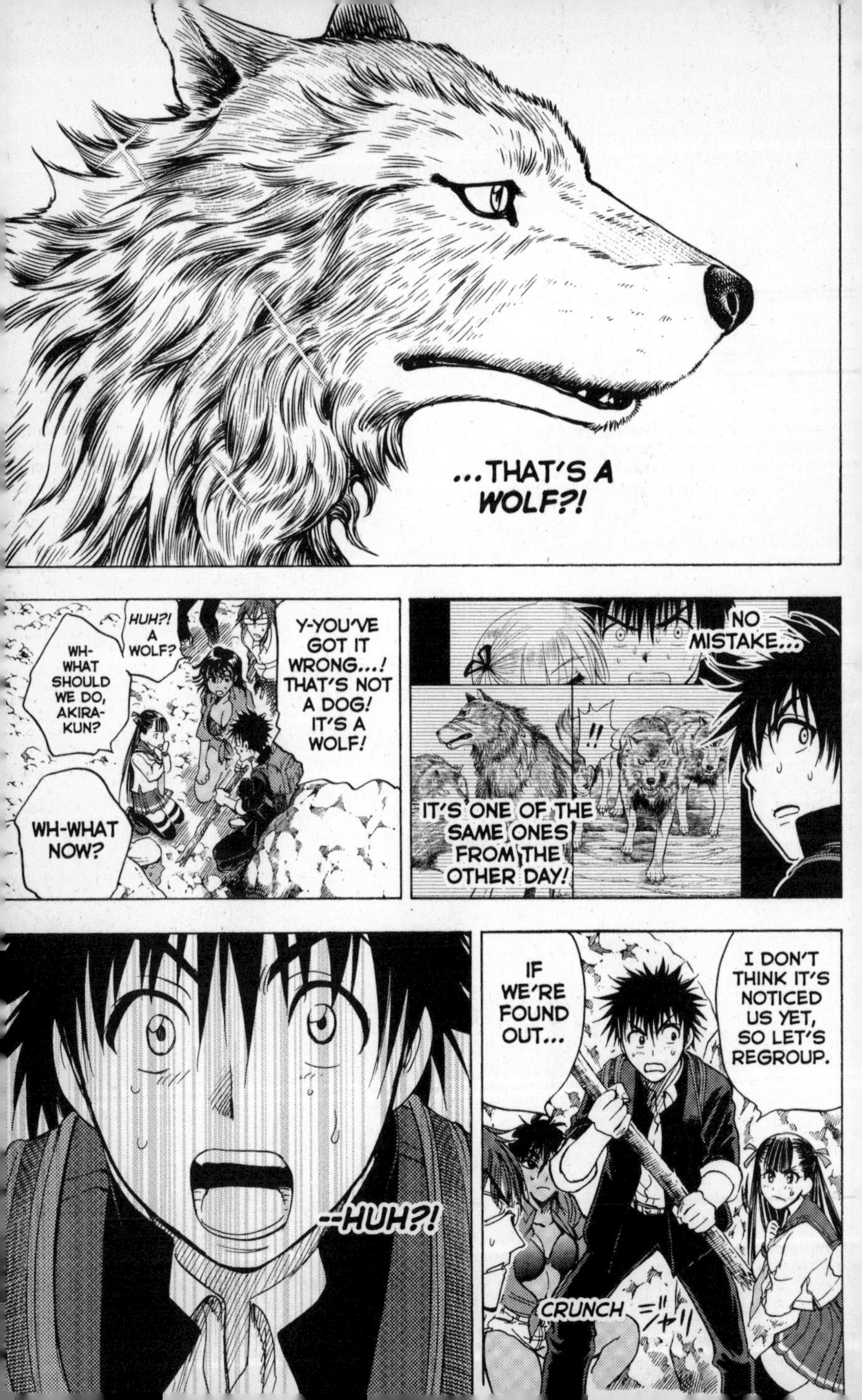
...THAT'S A WOLF?!
NO MISTAKE...
!!
IT'S ONE OF THE SAME ONES FROM THE OTHER DAY!
Y-YOU'VE GOT IT WRONG...! THAT'S NOT A DOG! IT'S A WOLF!
HUH?! A WOLF?
WH-WHAT SHOULD WE DO, AKIRA-KUN?
WH-WHAT NOW?
I DON'T THINK IT'S NOTICED US YET, SO LET'S REGROUP.
IF WE'RE FOUND OUT...
CRUNCH
--HUH?!

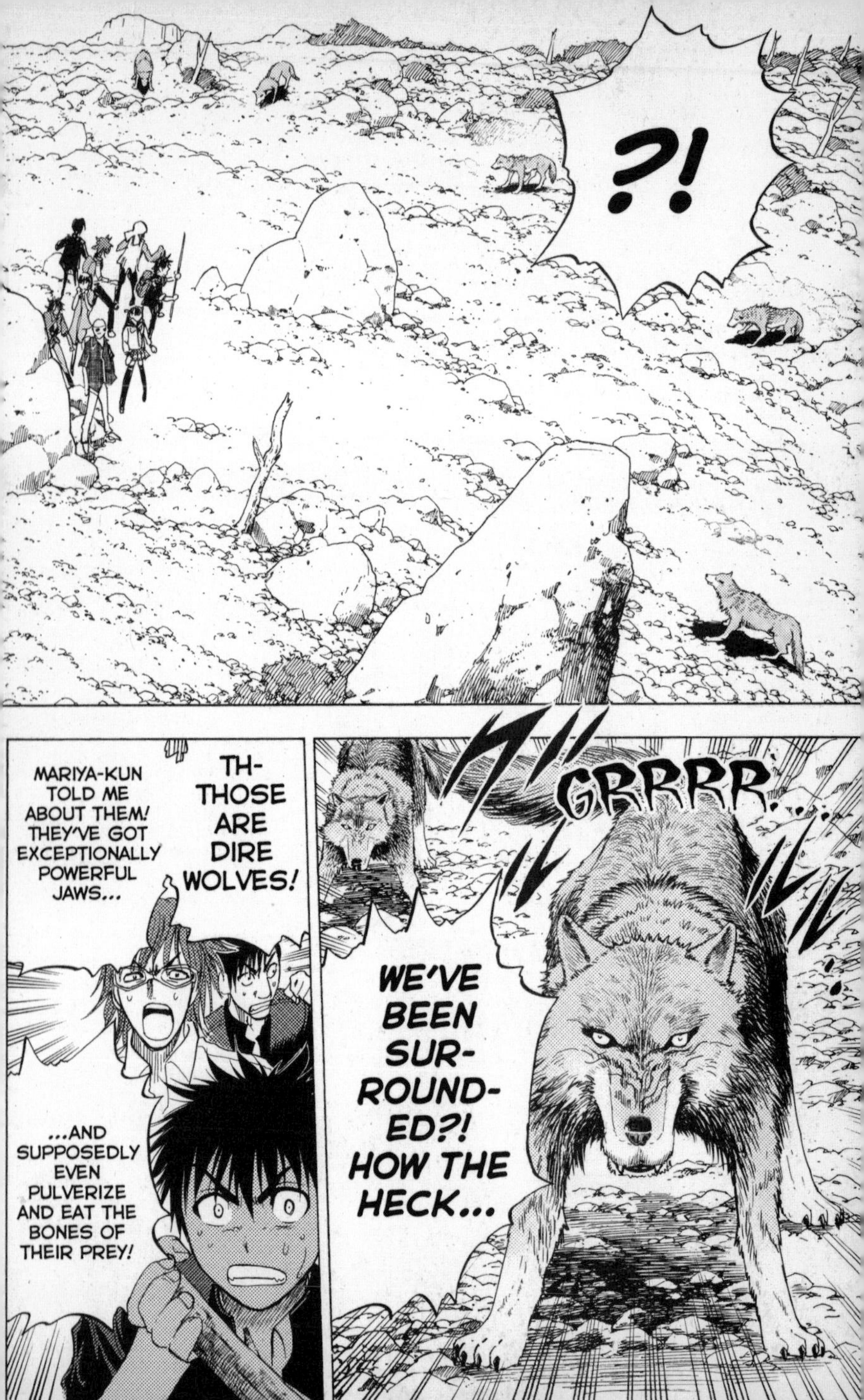
?!
GRRRR...
WE'VE BEEN SUR-ROUND-ED?! HOW THE HECK...
TH-THOSE ARE DIRE WOLVES!
MARIYA-KUN TOLD ME ABOUT THEM! THEY'VE GOT EXCEPTIONALLY POWERFUL JAWS...
...AND SUPPOSEDLY EVEN PULVERIZE AND EAT THE BONES OF THEIR PREY!

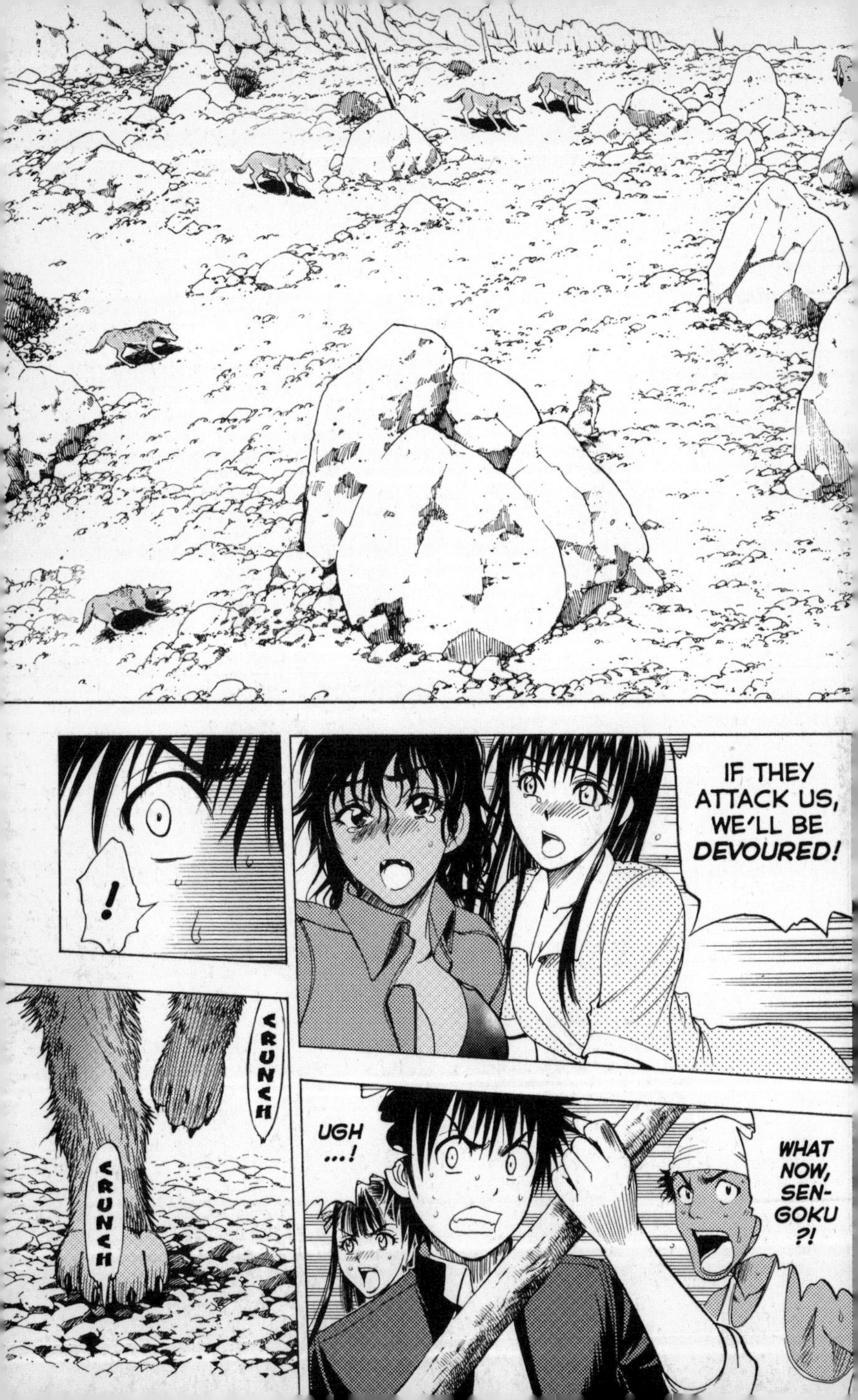
IF THEY ATTACK US, WE'LL BE DEVOURED!
!
WHAT NOW, SEN-GOKU?!
UGH...!
CRUNCH
CRUNCH

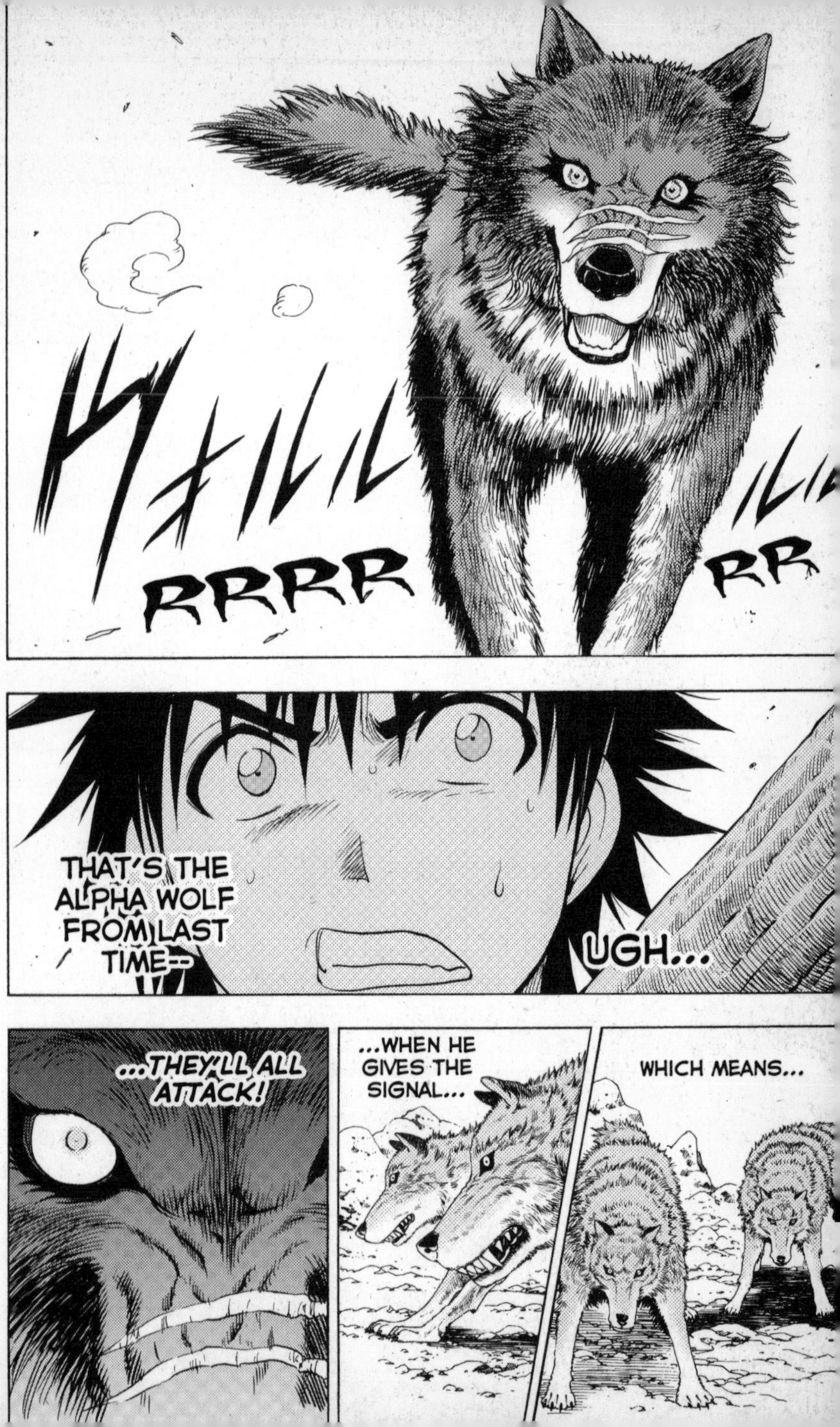
ヴォルルル
RRRRR
ルル
RR
UGH...
THAT'S THE ALPHA WOLF FROM LAST TIME--
WHICH MEANS...
...WHEN HE GIVES THE SIGNAL...
...THEY'LL ALL ATTACK!

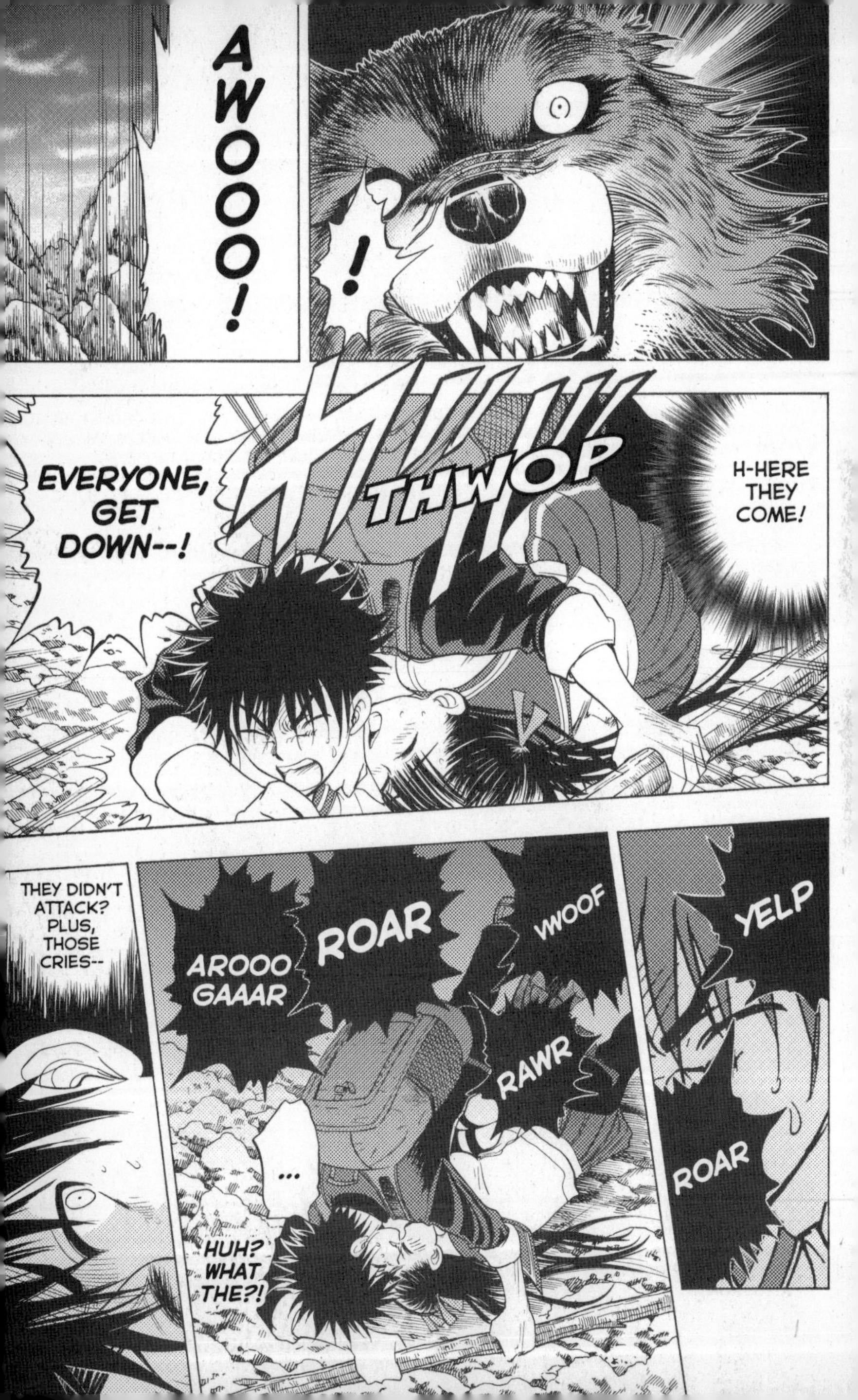
!
AWOOOO!
H-HERE THEY COME!
THWOP
EVERYONE, GET DOWN--!
YELP
ROAR
WOOF
ROAR
AROOO GAAAR
RAWR
...
HUH? WHAT THE?!
THEY DIDN'T ATTACK? PLUS, THOSE CRIES--

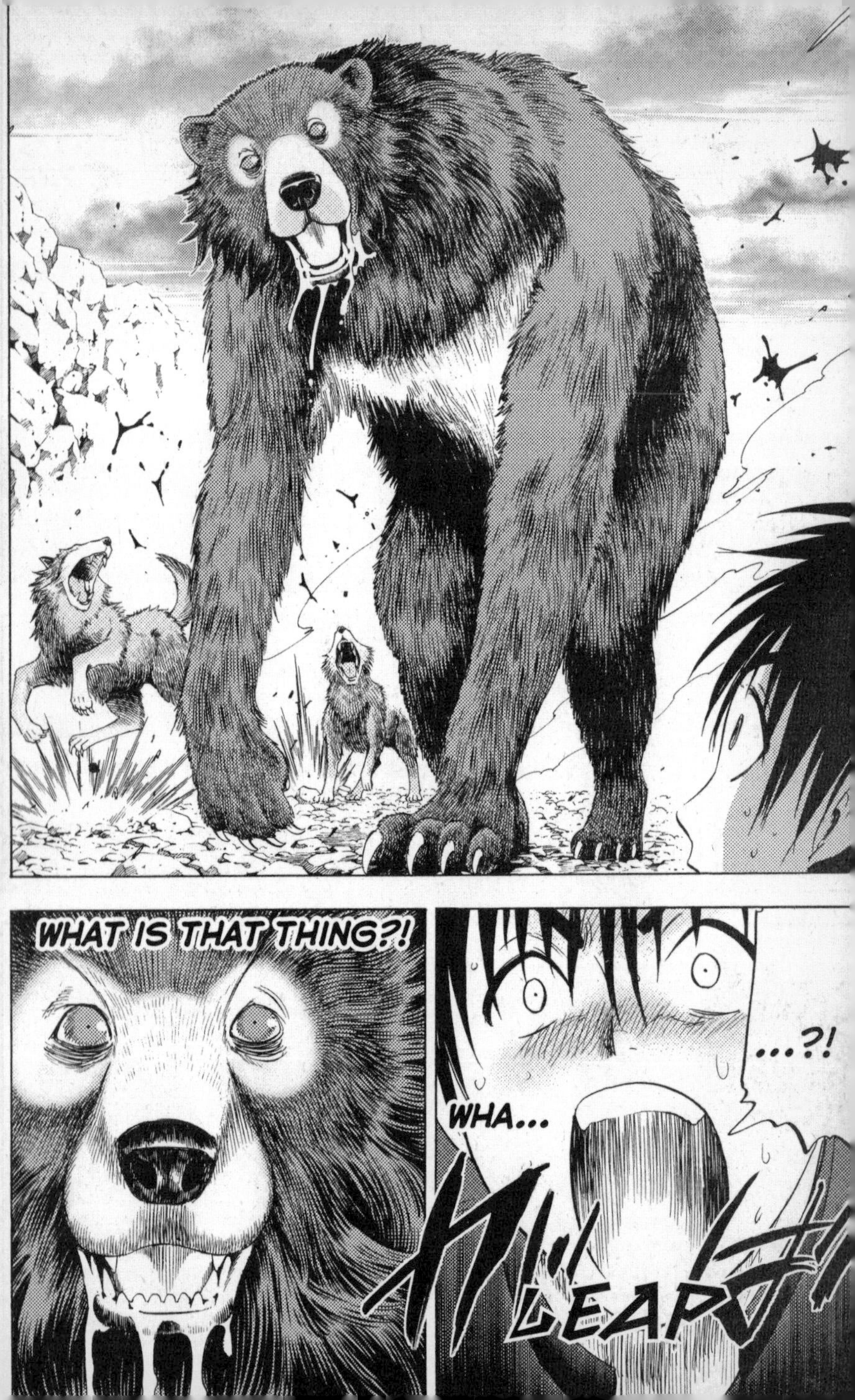
...?!
WHA...
LEAP
WHAT IS THAT THING?!

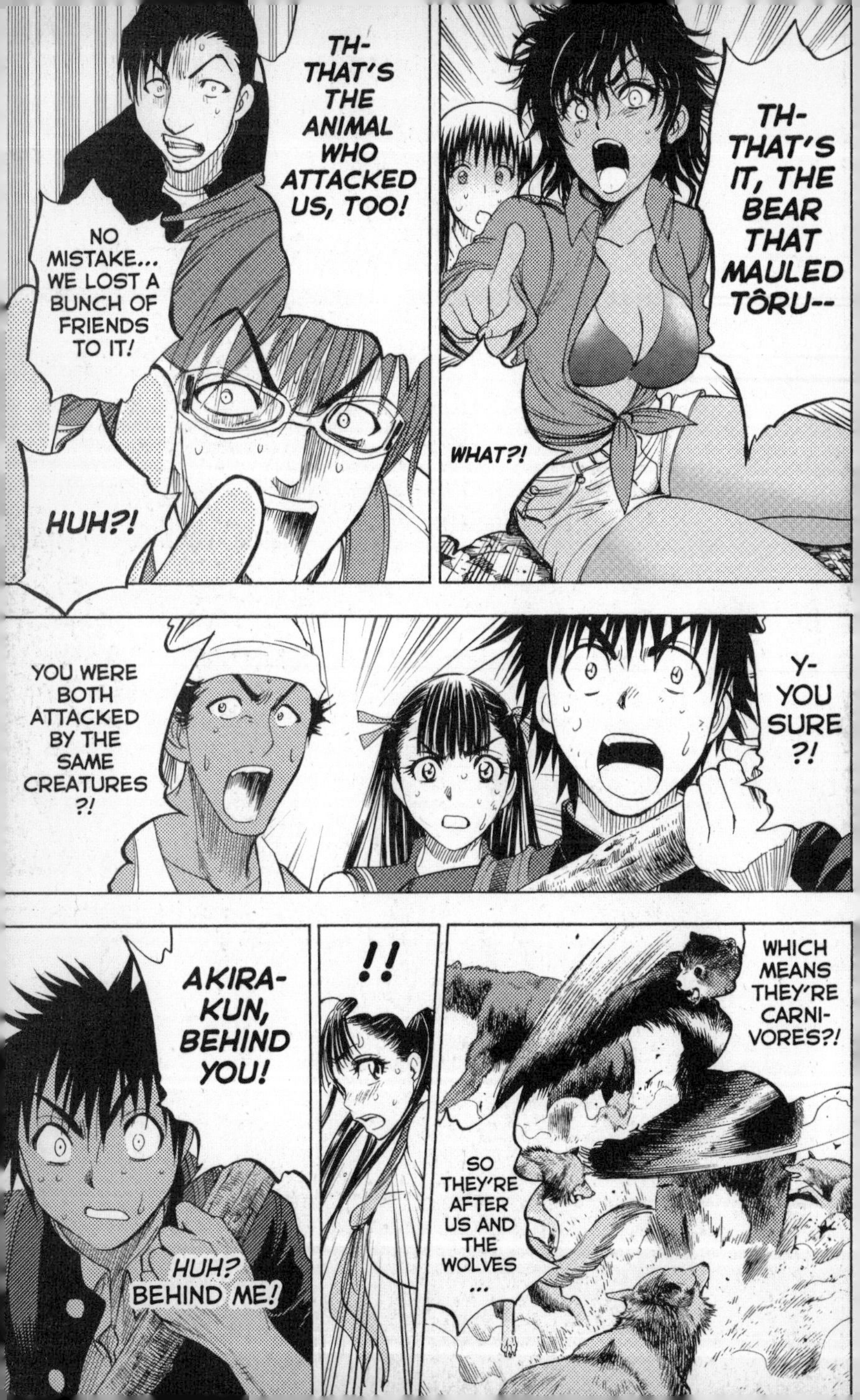
TH-THAT'S IT, THE BEAR THAT MAULED TÔRU--
WHAT?!
TH-THAT'S THE ANIMAL WHO ATTACKED US, TOO!
NO MISTAKE... WE LOST A BUNCH OF FRIENDS TO IT!
HUH?!
Y-YOU SURE?!
YOU WERE BOTH ATTACKED BY THE SAME CREATURES?!
WHICH MEANS THEY'RE CARNIVORES?!
SO THEY'RE AFTER US AND THE WOLVES...
!!
AKIRA-KUN, BEHIND YOU!
HUH? BEHIND ME!

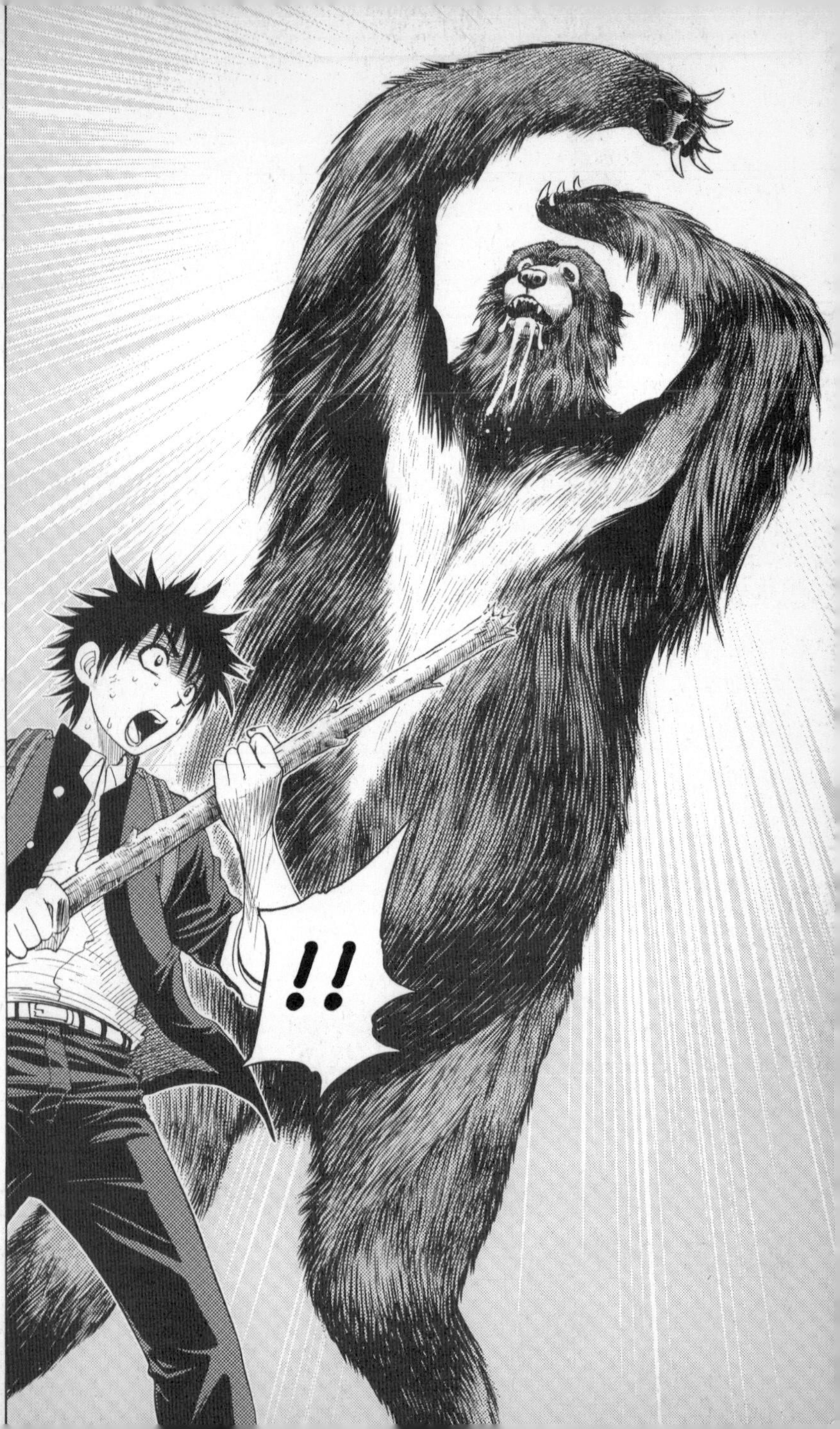
!!

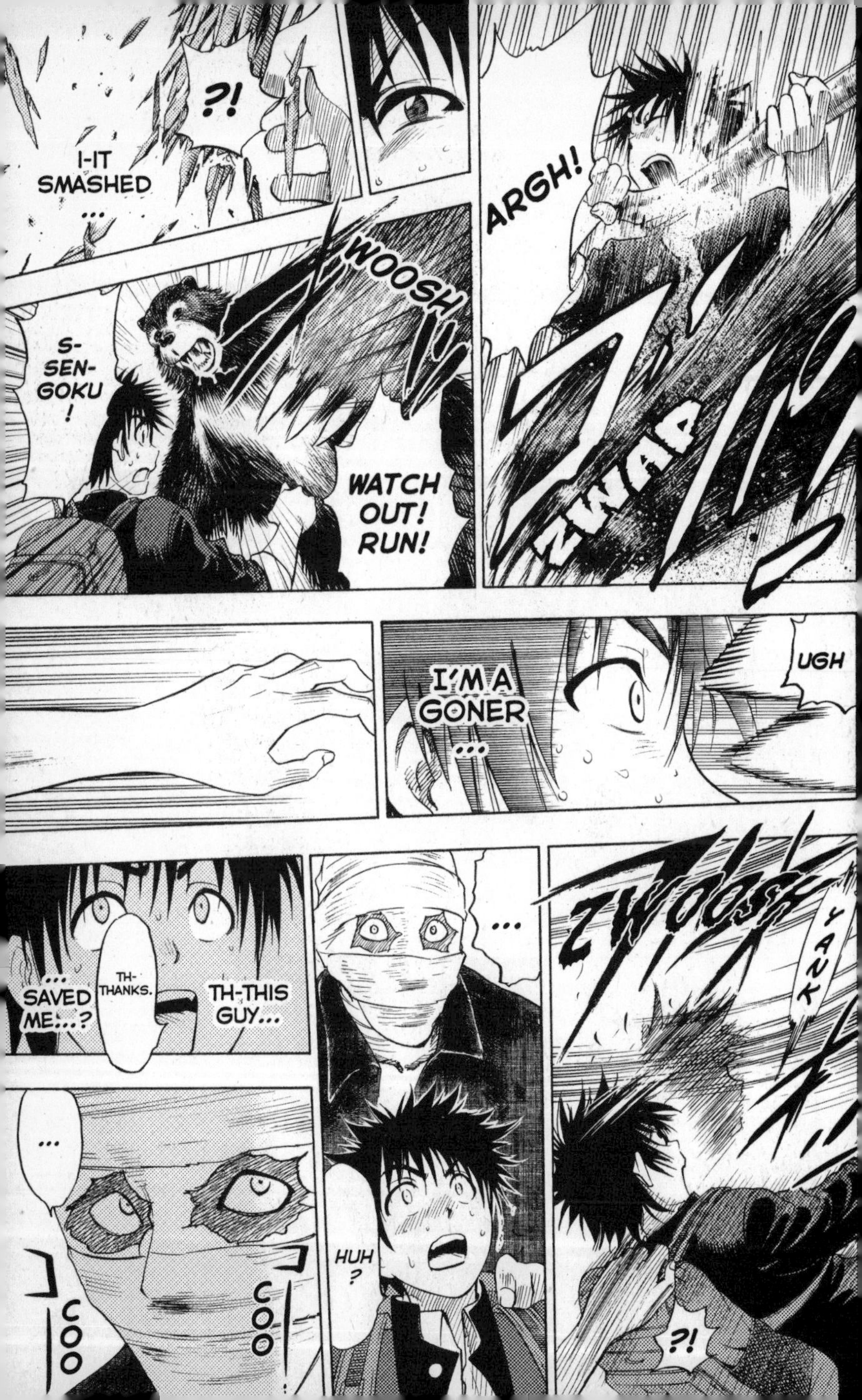
ARGH!
ZWAP
?!
I-IT SMASHED ...
WOOSH
WATCH OUT! RUN!
S-SENGOKU!
UGH
I'M A GONER ...
ZWOOSH
YANK
?!
...
HUH?
TH-THIS GUY...
TH-THANKS.
... SAVED ME...?
...
COO
COO

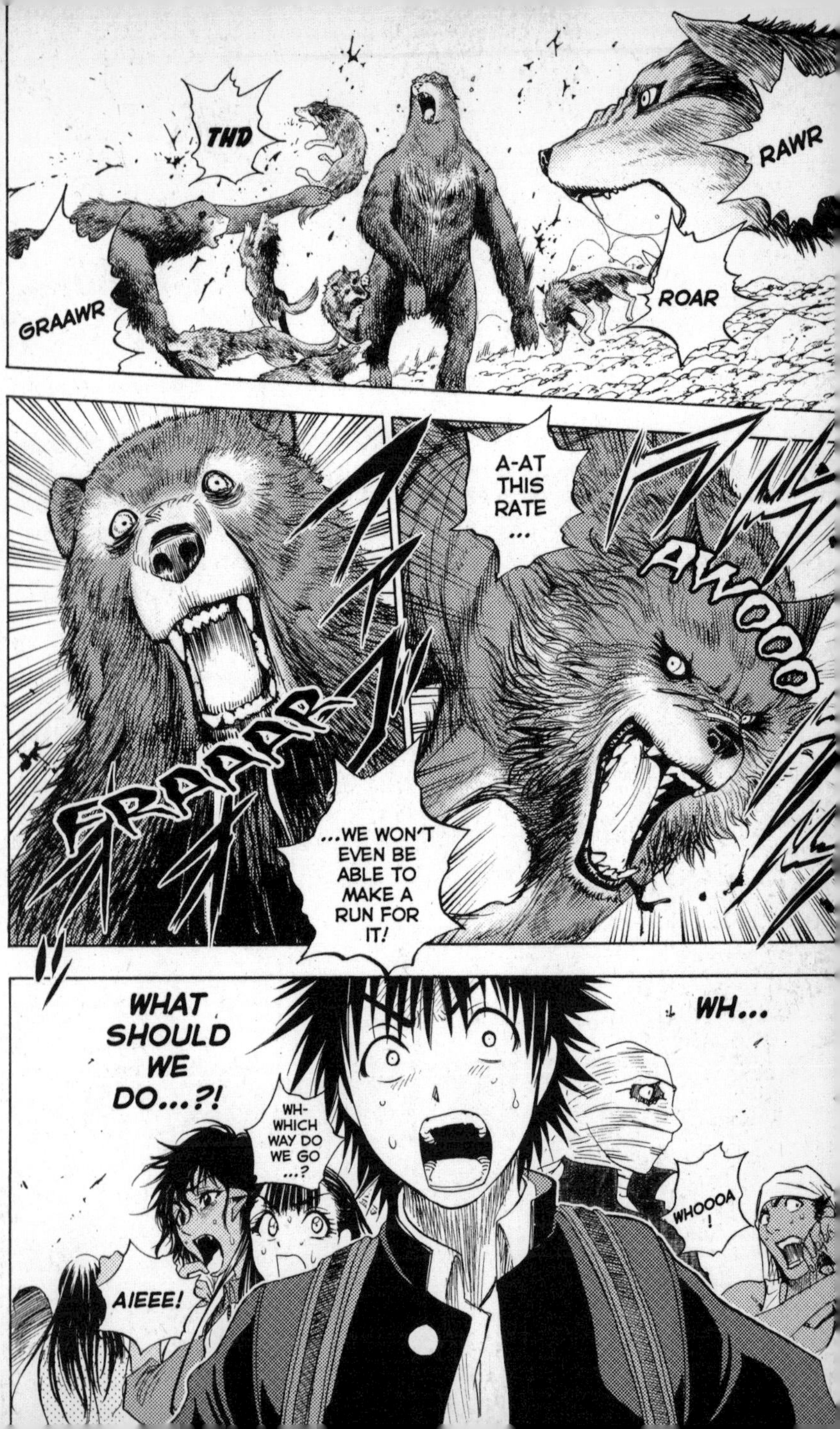
RAWR
ROAR
THD
GRAAWR
A-AT THIS RATE ...
AWOOO
FRAAAR
...WE WON'T EVEN BE ABLE TO MAKE A RUN FOR IT!
WH...
WHOOOA!
WHAT SHOULD WE DO...?!
WH-WHICH WAY DO WE GO ...?
AIEEE!

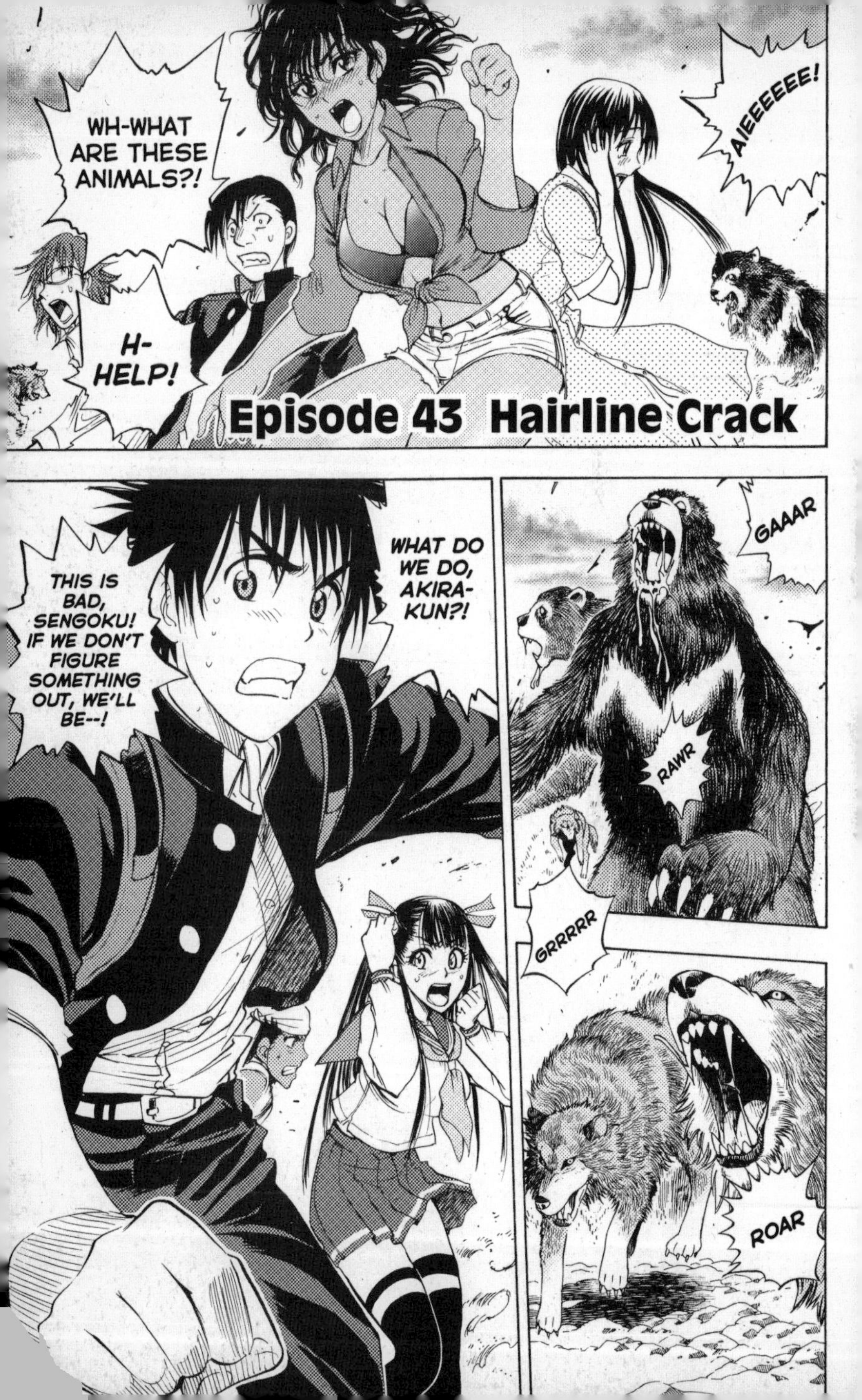
AIEEEEEE!
WH-WHAT ARE THESE ANIMALS?!
H-HELP!
Episode 43 Hairline Crack
GAAAR
RAWR
GRRRRR
ROAR
WHAT DO WE DO, AKIRA-KUN?!
THIS IS BAD, SENGOKU! IF WE DON'T FIGURE SOMETHING OUT, WE'LL BE--!

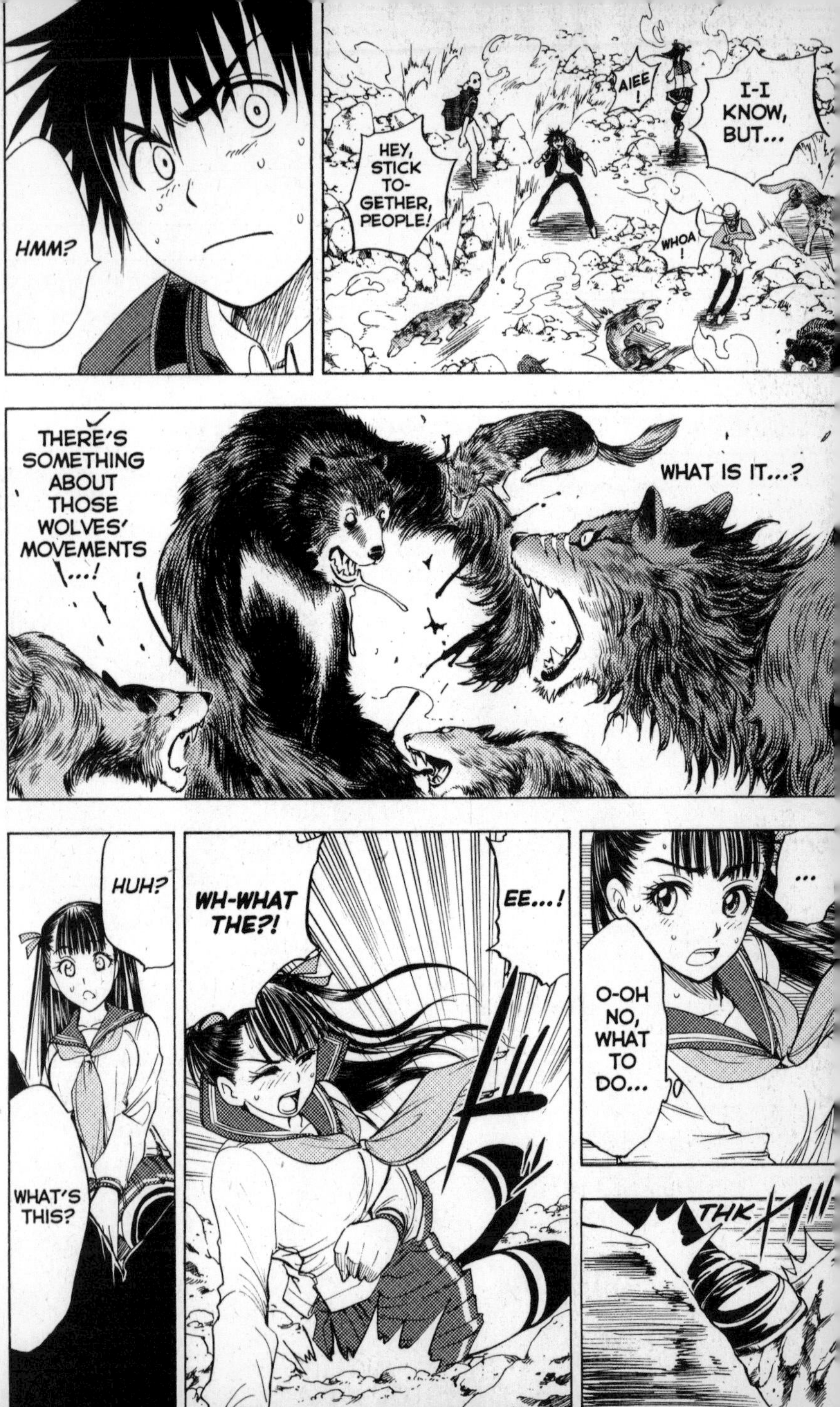
I-I KNOW, BUT...
AIEE!
HEY, STICK TO-GETHER, PEOPLE!
WHOA!
HMM?
WHAT IS IT...?
THERE'S SOMETHING ABOUT THOSE WOLVES' MOVEMENTS...!
...
O-OH NO, WHAT TO DO...
THK
EE...!
WH-WHAT THE?!
HUH?
WHAT'S THIS?

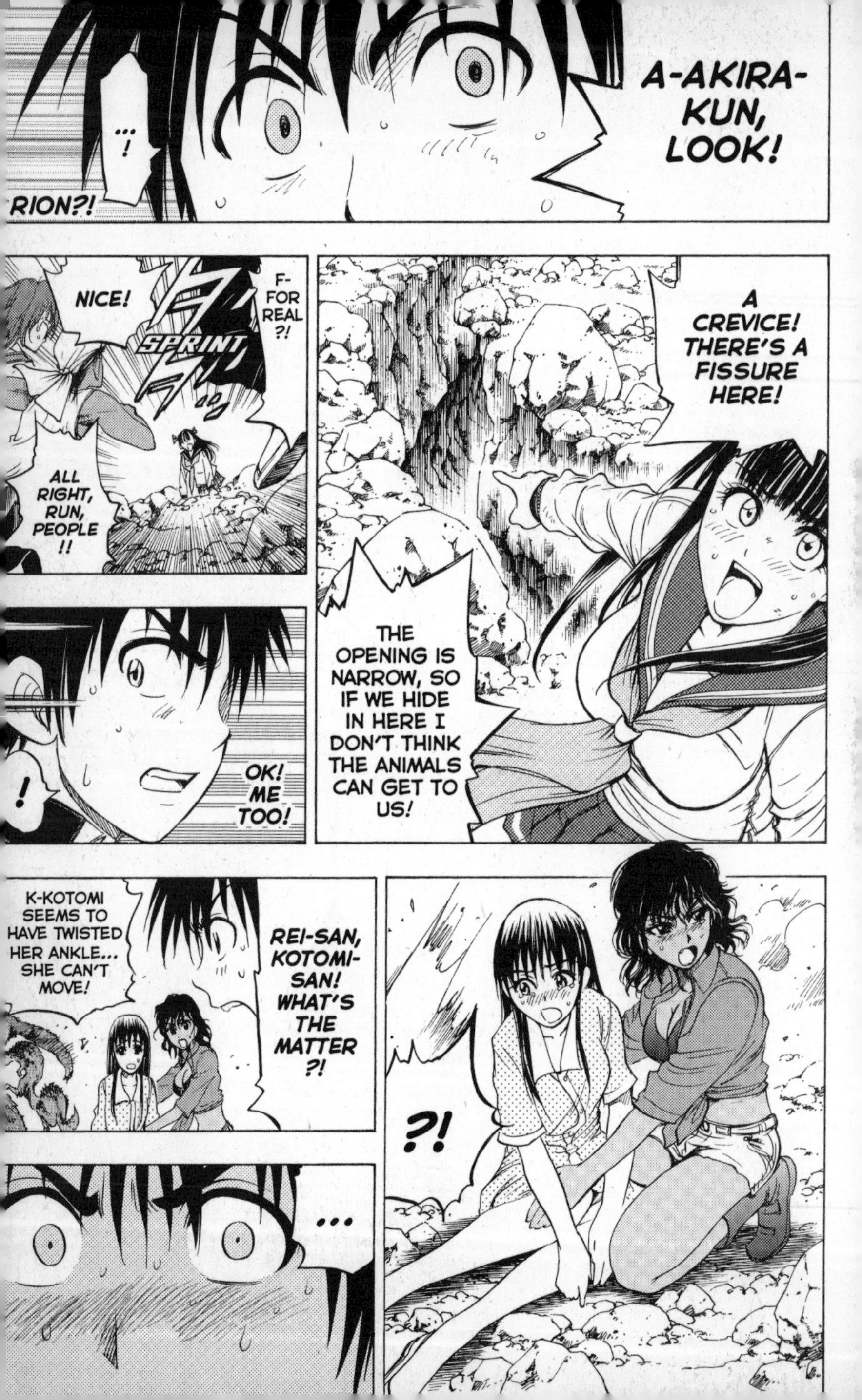
A-AKIRA-KUN, LOOK!
...!
RION?!
A CREVICE! THERE'S A FISSURE HERE!
THE OPENING IS NARROW, SO IF WE HIDE IN HERE I DON'T THINK THE ANIMALS CAN GET TO US!
F- FOR REAL?!
NICE!
SPRINT
ALL RIGHT, RUN, PEOPLE!!
OK! ME TOO!
!
?!
REI-SAN, KOTOMI-SAN! WHAT'S THE MATTER?!
K-KOTOMI SEEMS TO HAVE TWISTED HER ANKLE... SHE CAN'T MOVE!
...

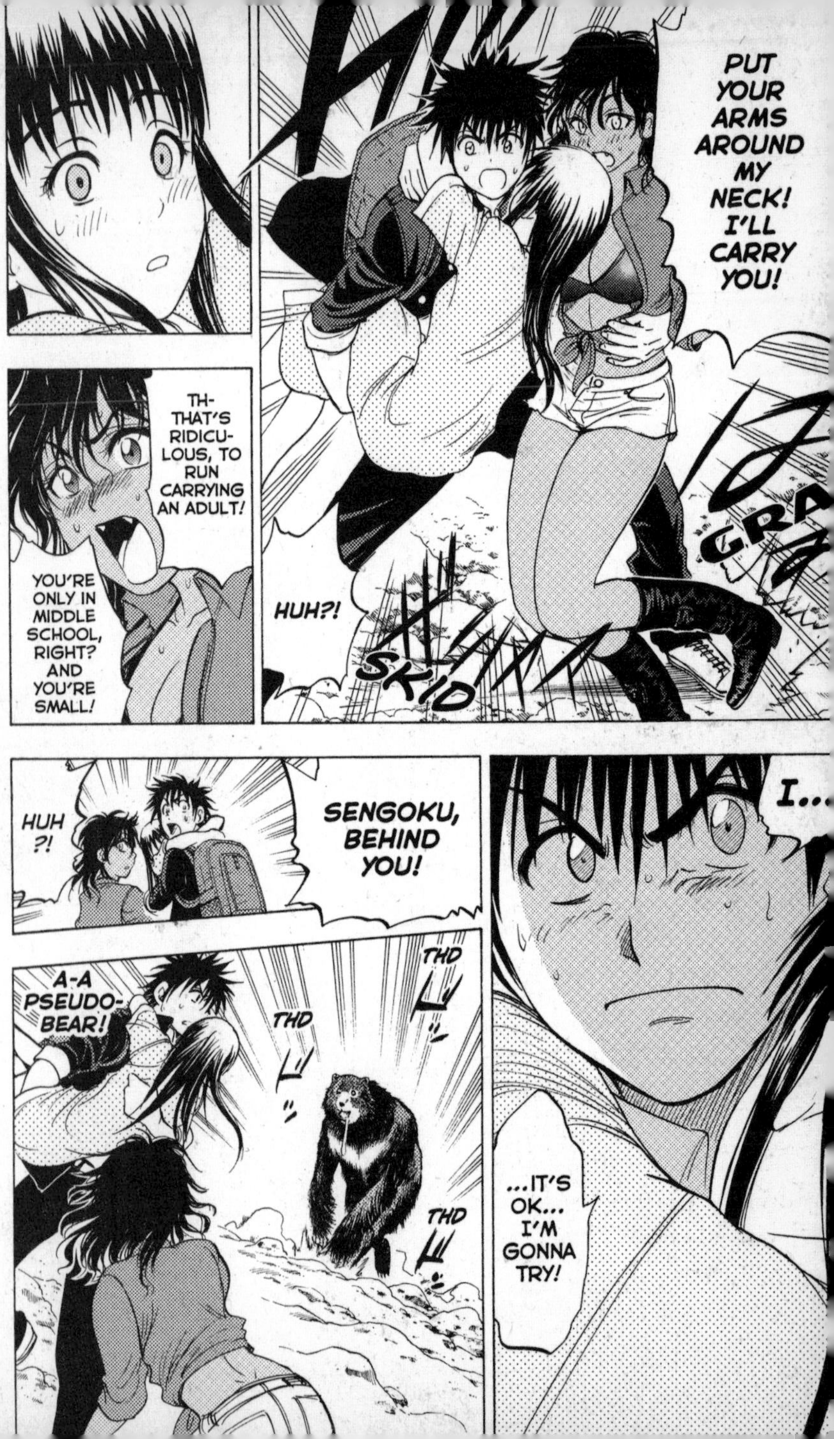
PUT YOUR ARMS AROUND MY NECK! I'LL CARRY YOU!
GRA
SKID
HUH?!
TH-THAT'S RIDICULOUS, TO RUN CARRYING AN ADULT!
YOU'RE ONLY IN MIDDLE SCHOOL, RIGHT? AND YOU'RE SMALL!
I...
...IT'S OK... I'M GONNA TRY!
SENGOKU, BEHIND YOU!
HUH ?!
A-A PSEUDO-BEAR!
THD
THD
THD

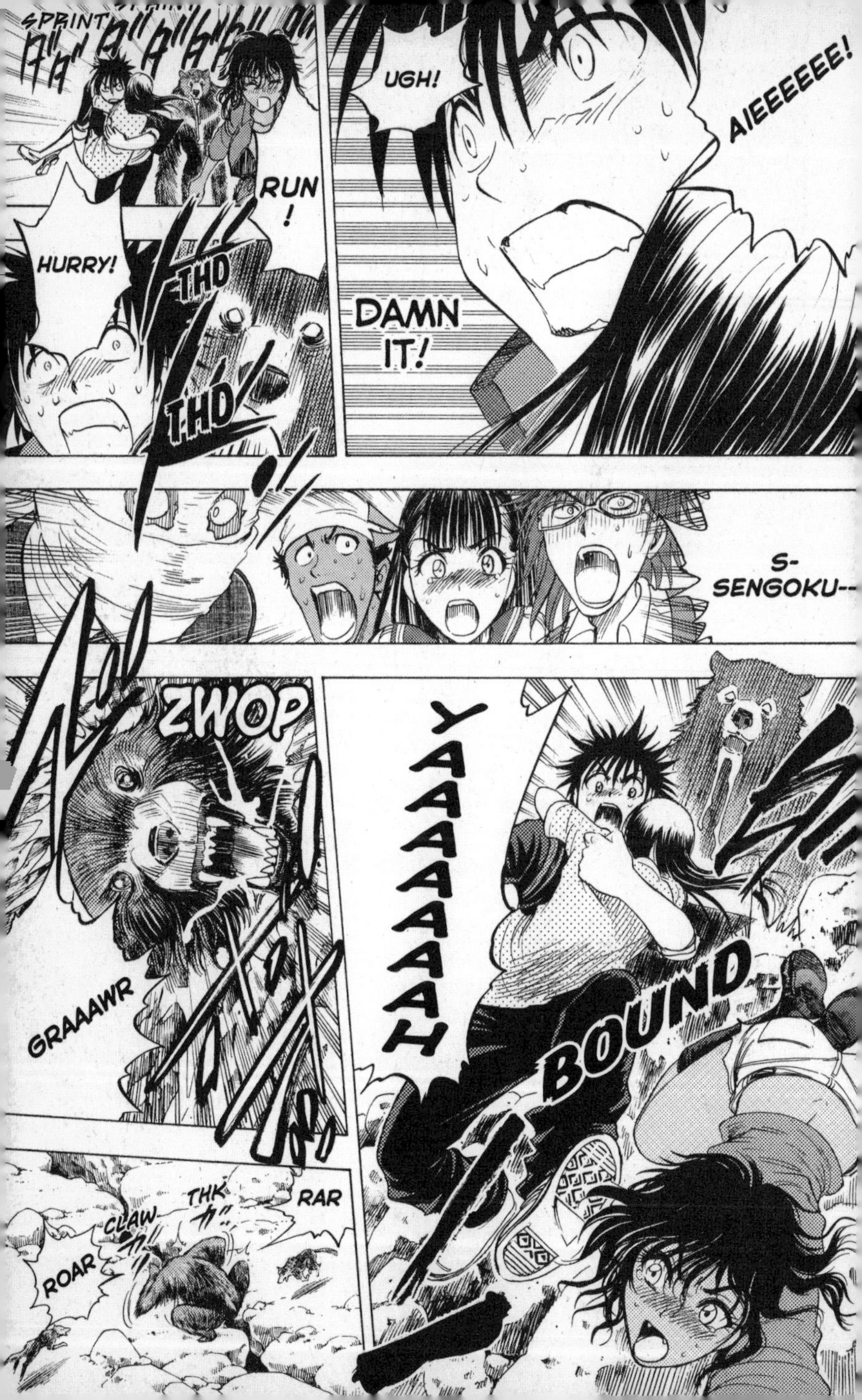
AIEEEEEE!
UGH!
DAMN IT!
SPRINT
RUN!
HURRY!
THD
THD
S-SENGOKU--
YAAAAAAAH
BOUND
ZWOP
GRAAAWR
RAR
THK
CLAW
ROAR

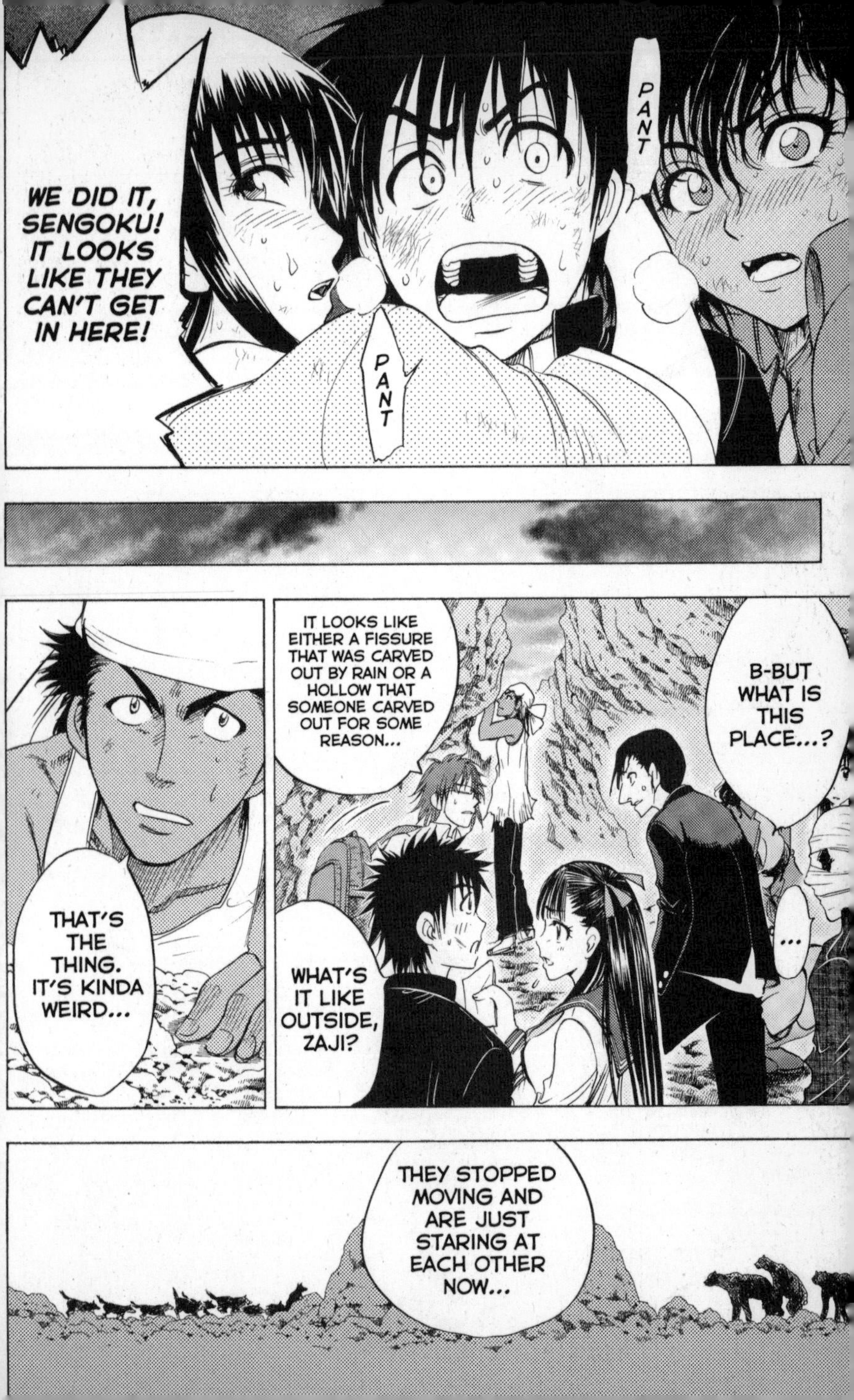
PANT PANT
WE DID IT, SENGOKU! IT LOOKS LIKE THEY CAN'T GET IN HERE!
PANT PANT
B-BUT WHAT IS THIS PLACE...?
IT LOOKS LIKE EITHER A FISSURE THAT WAS CARVED OUT BY RAIN OR A HOLLOW THAT SOMEONE CARVED OUT FOR SOME REASON...
...
WHAT'S IT LIKE OUTSIDE, ZAJI?
THAT'S THE THING. IT'S KINDA WEIRD...
THEY STOPPED MOVING AND ARE JUST STARING AT EACH OTHER NOW...

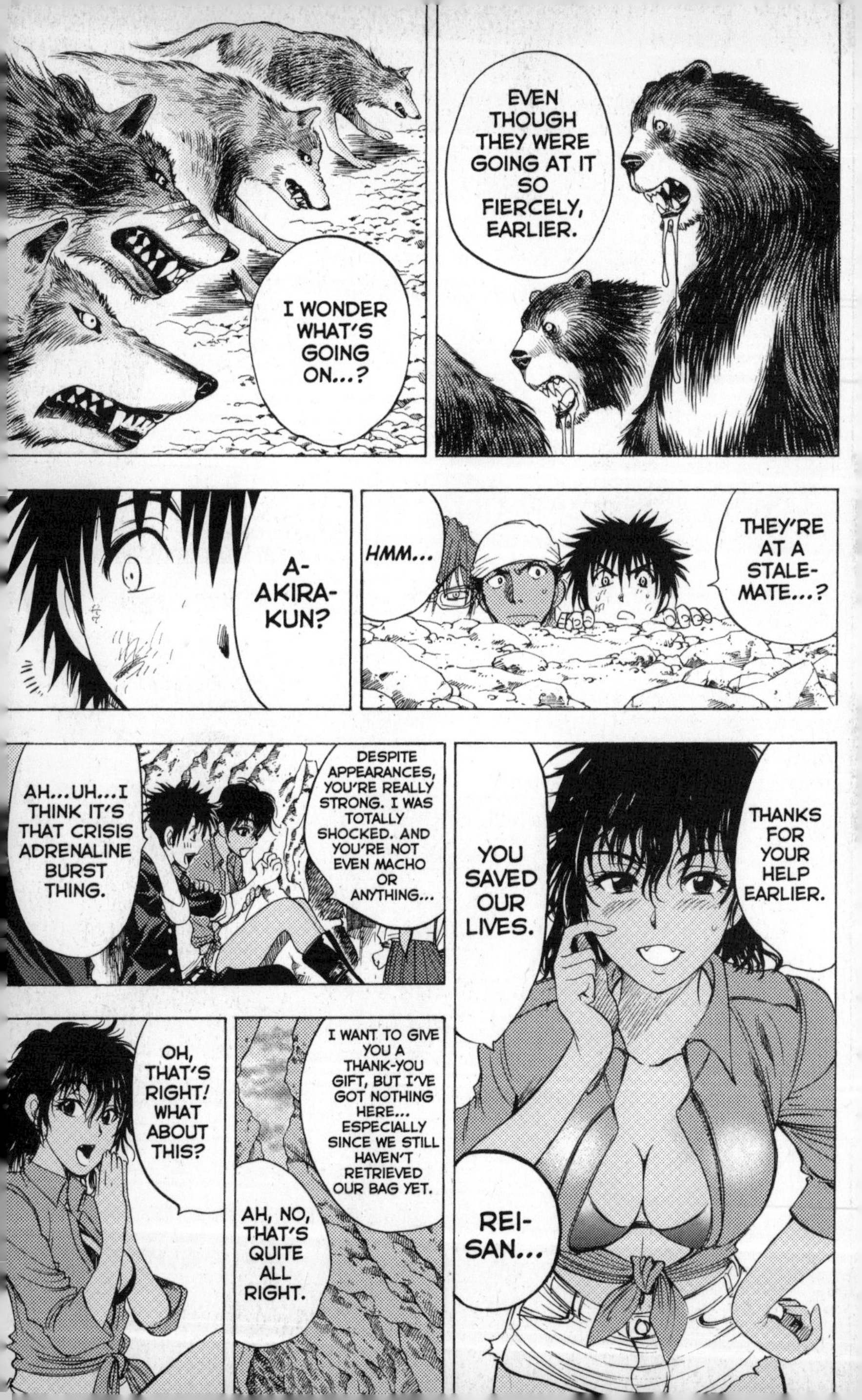
EVEN THOUGH THEY WERE GOING AT IT SO FIERCELY, EARLIER.
I WONDER WHAT'S GOING ON...?
THEY'RE AT A STALEMATE...?
HMM...
A-AKIRA-KUN?
THANKS FOR YOUR HELP EARLIER.
YOU SAVED OUR LIVES.
REI-SAN...
DESPITE APPEARANCES, YOU'RE REALLY STRONG. I WAS TOTALLY SHOCKED. AND YOU'RE NOT EVEN MACHO OR ANYTHING...
AH...UH...I THINK IT'S THAT CRISIS ADRENALINE BURST THING.
I WANT TO GIVE YOU A THANK-YOU GIFT, BUT I'VE GOT NOTHING HERE... ESPECIALLY SINCE WE STILL HAVEN'T RETRIEVED OUR BAG YET.
AH, NO, THAT'S QUITE ALL RIGHT.
OH, THAT'S RIGHT! WHAT ABOUT THIS?

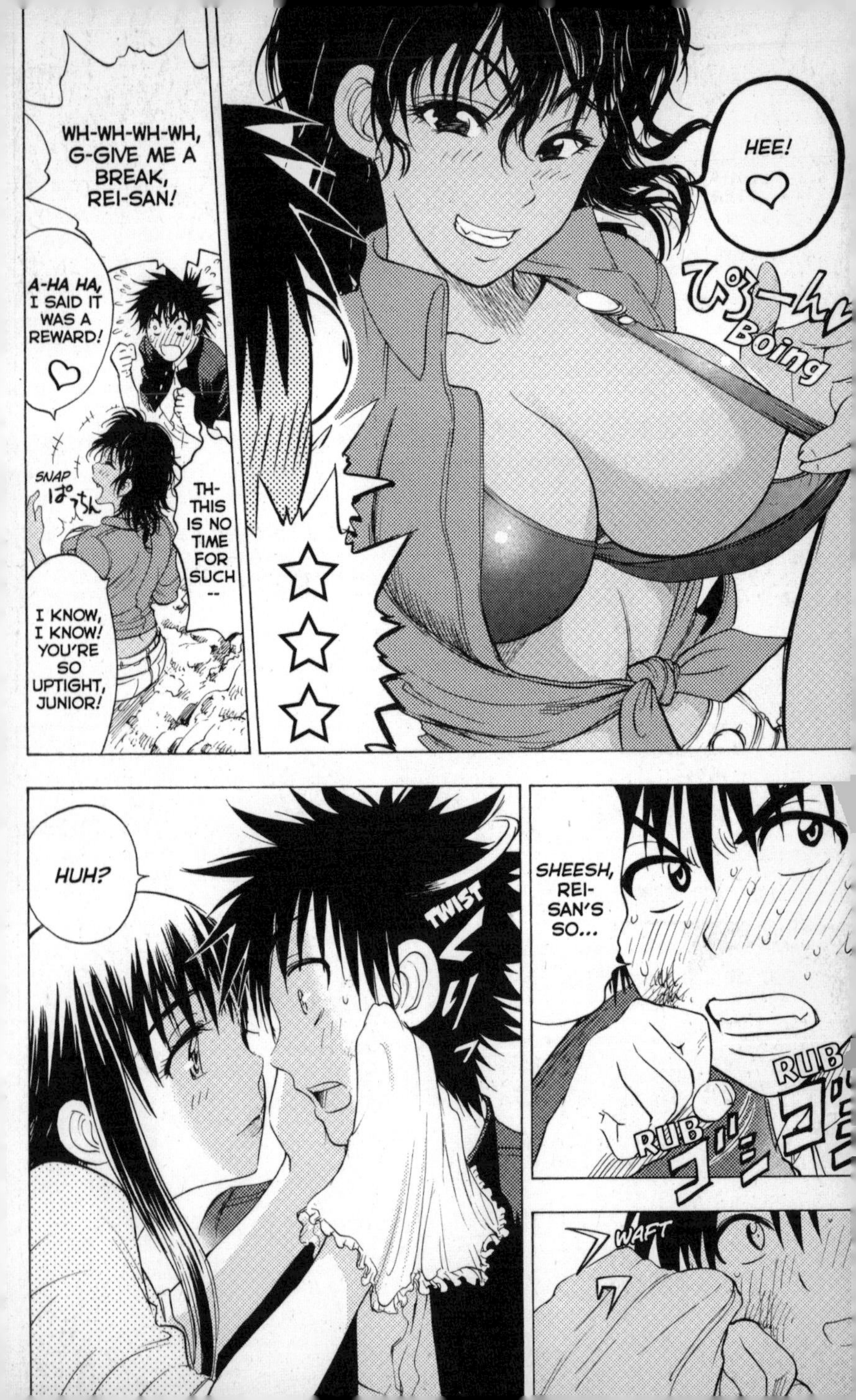
HEE! ♡
ぴろーん
Boing
WH-WH-WH-WH, G-GIVE ME A BREAK, REI-SAN!
A-HA HA, I SAID IT WAS A REWARD! ♡
TH-THIS IS NO TIME FOR SUCH --
SNAP
ぱっちん
I KNOW, I KNOW! YOU'RE SO UPTIGHT, JUNIOR!
SHEESH, REI-SAN'S SO...
RUB
RUB
WAFT
TWIST
HUH?

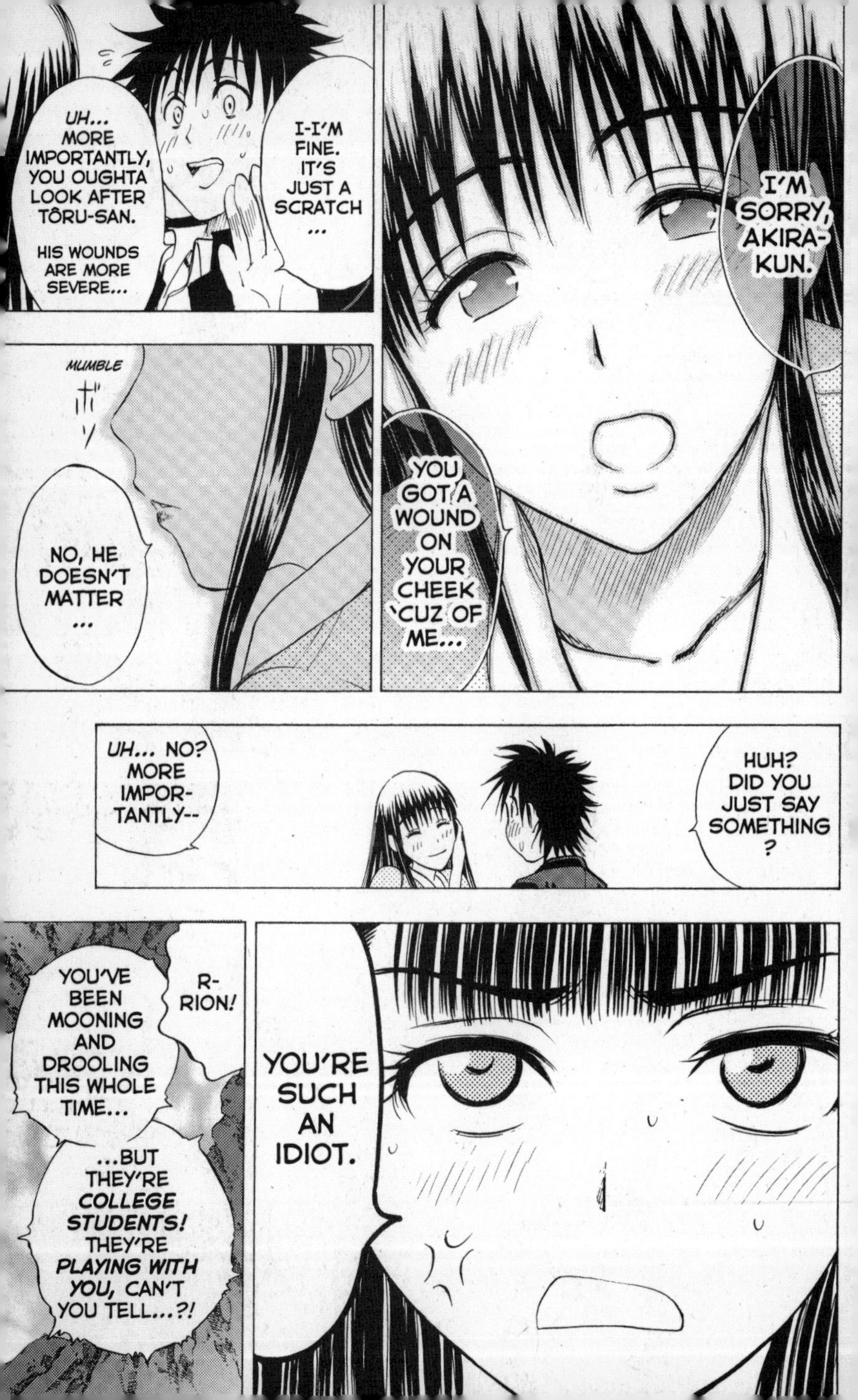
I'M SORRY, AKIRA-KUN.
YOU GOT A WOUND ON YOUR CHEEK 'CUZ OF ME...
I-I'M FINE. IT'S JUST A SCRATCH...
UH... MORE IMPORTANTLY, YOU OUGHTA LOOK AFTER TÔRU-SAN.
HIS WOUNDS ARE MORE SEVERE...
MUMBLE
ボソ
NO, HE DOESN'T MATTER...
HUH? DID YOU JUST SAY SOMETHING?
UH... NO? MORE IMPORTANTLY--
YOU'RE SUCH AN IDIOT.
R-RION!
YOU'VE BEEN MOONING AND DROOLING THIS WHOLE TIME...
...BUT THEY'RE *COLLEGE STUDENTS!* THEY'RE *PLAYING WITH YOU,* CAN'T YOU TELL...?!

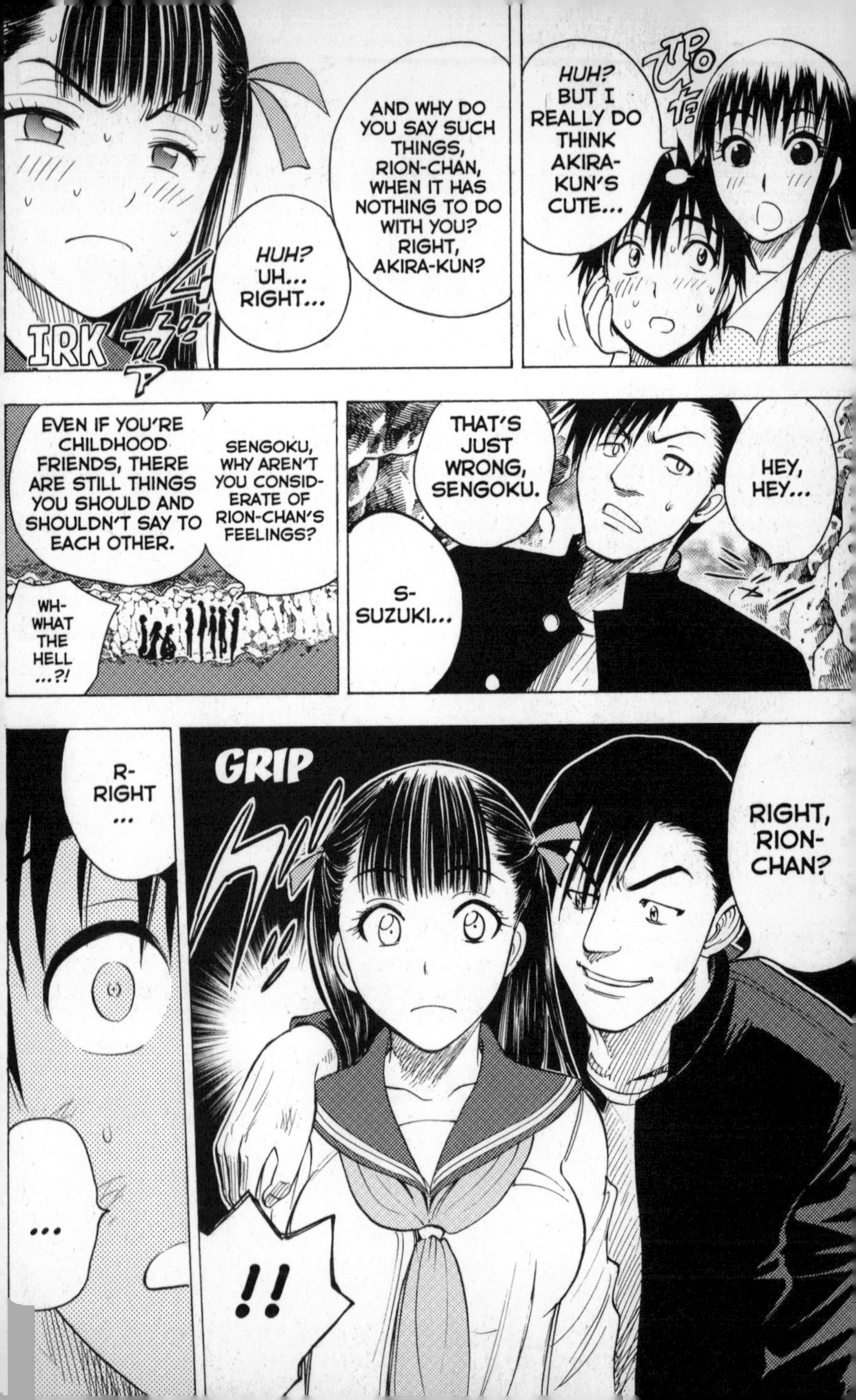
HUH? BUT I REALLY DO THINK AKIRA-KUN'S CUTE...
AND WHY DO YOU SAY SUCH THINGS, RION-CHAN, WHEN IT HAS NOTHING TO DO WITH YOU? RIGHT, AKIRA-KUN?
HUH? UH... RIGHT...
IRK
HEY, HEY...
THAT'S JUST WRONG, SENGOKU.
S-SUZUKI...
SENGOKU, WHY AREN'T YOU CONSIDERATE OF RION-CHAN'S FEELINGS?
EVEN IF YOU'RE CHILDHOOD FRIENDS, THERE ARE STILL THINGS YOU SHOULD AND SHOULDN'T SAY TO EACH OTHER.
WH-WHAT THE HELL...?!
RIGHT, RION-CHAN?
GRIP
!!
R-RIGHT...
...

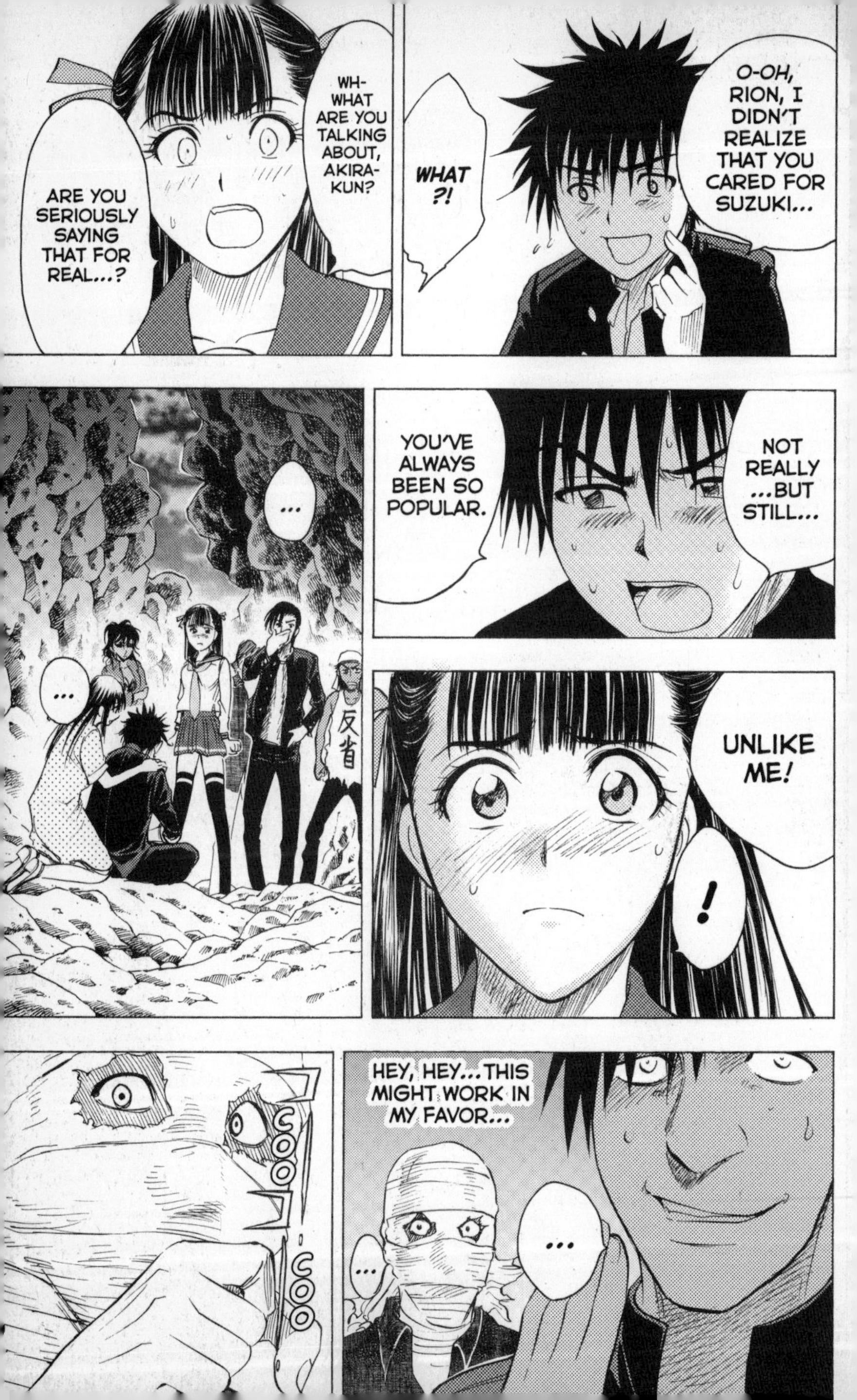
O-OH, RION, I DIDN'T REALIZE THAT YOU CARED FOR SUZUKI...
WHAT ?!
WH-WHAT ARE YOU TALKING ABOUT, AKIRA-KUN?
ARE YOU SERIOUSLY SAYING THAT FOR REAL...?
NOT REALLY ...BUT STILL...
YOU'VE ALWAYS BEEN SO POPULAR.
UNLIKE ME!
!
...
...
反省
HEY, HEY... THIS MIGHT WORK IN MY FAVOR...
...
...
COO
COO

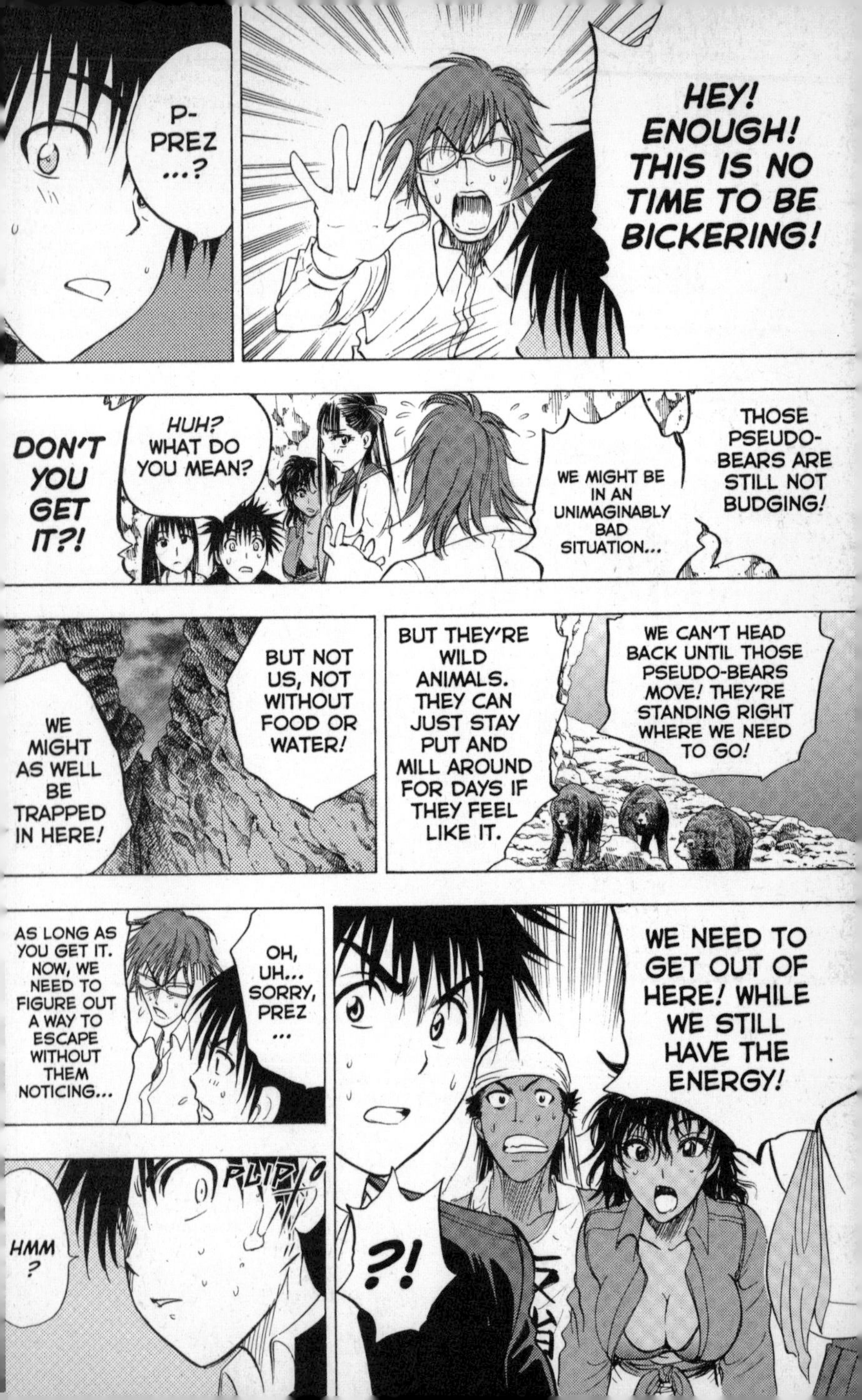
HEY! ENOUGH! THIS IS NO TIME TO BE BICKERING!
P-PREZ ...?
THOSE PSEUDO-BEARS ARE STILL NOT BUDGING!
WE MIGHT BE IN AN UNIMAGINABLY BAD SITUATION...
HUH? WHAT DO YOU MEAN?
DON'T YOU GET IT?!
WE CAN'T HEAD BACK UNTIL THOSE PSEUDO-BEARS MOVE! THEY'RE STANDING RIGHT WHERE WE NEED TO GO!
BUT THEY'RE WILD ANIMALS. THEY CAN JUST STAY PUT AND MILL AROUND FOR DAYS IF THEY FEEL LIKE IT.
BUT NOT US, NOT WITHOUT FOOD OR WATER!
WE MIGHT AS WELL BE TRAPPED IN HERE!
WE NEED TO GET OUT OF HERE! WHILE WE STILL HAVE THE ENERGY!
?!
OH, UH... SORRY, PREZ ...
AS LONG AS YOU GET IT. NOW, WE NEED TO FIGURE OUT A WAY TO ESCAPE WITHOUT THEM NOTICING...
PLIP
HMM ?

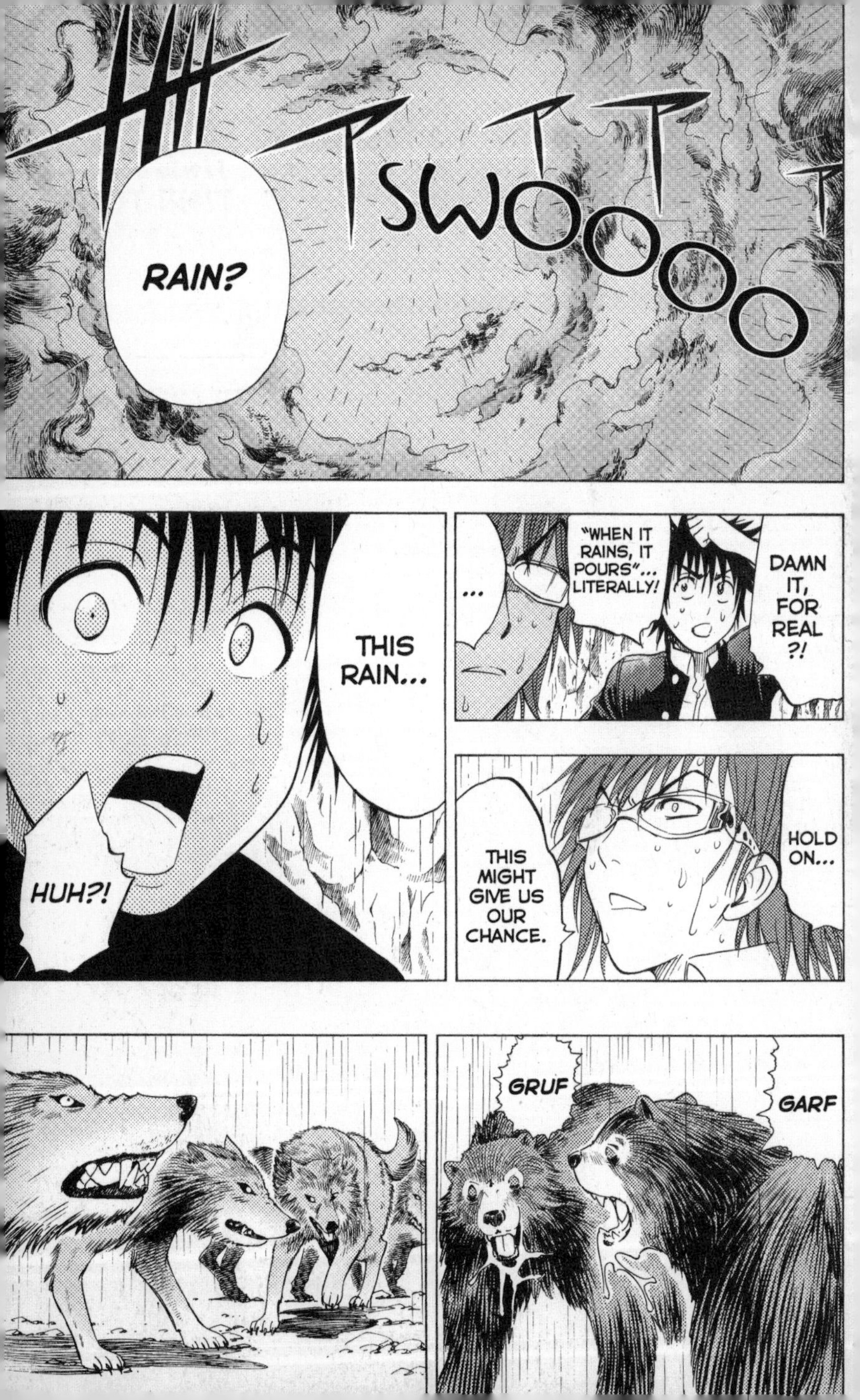
SWOOOOO
RAIN?
DAMN IT, FOR REAL?!
"WHEN IT RAINS, IT POURS"... LITERALLY!
...
HOLD ON...
THIS MIGHT GIVE US OUR CHANCE.
THIS RAIN...
HUH?!
GARF
GRUF

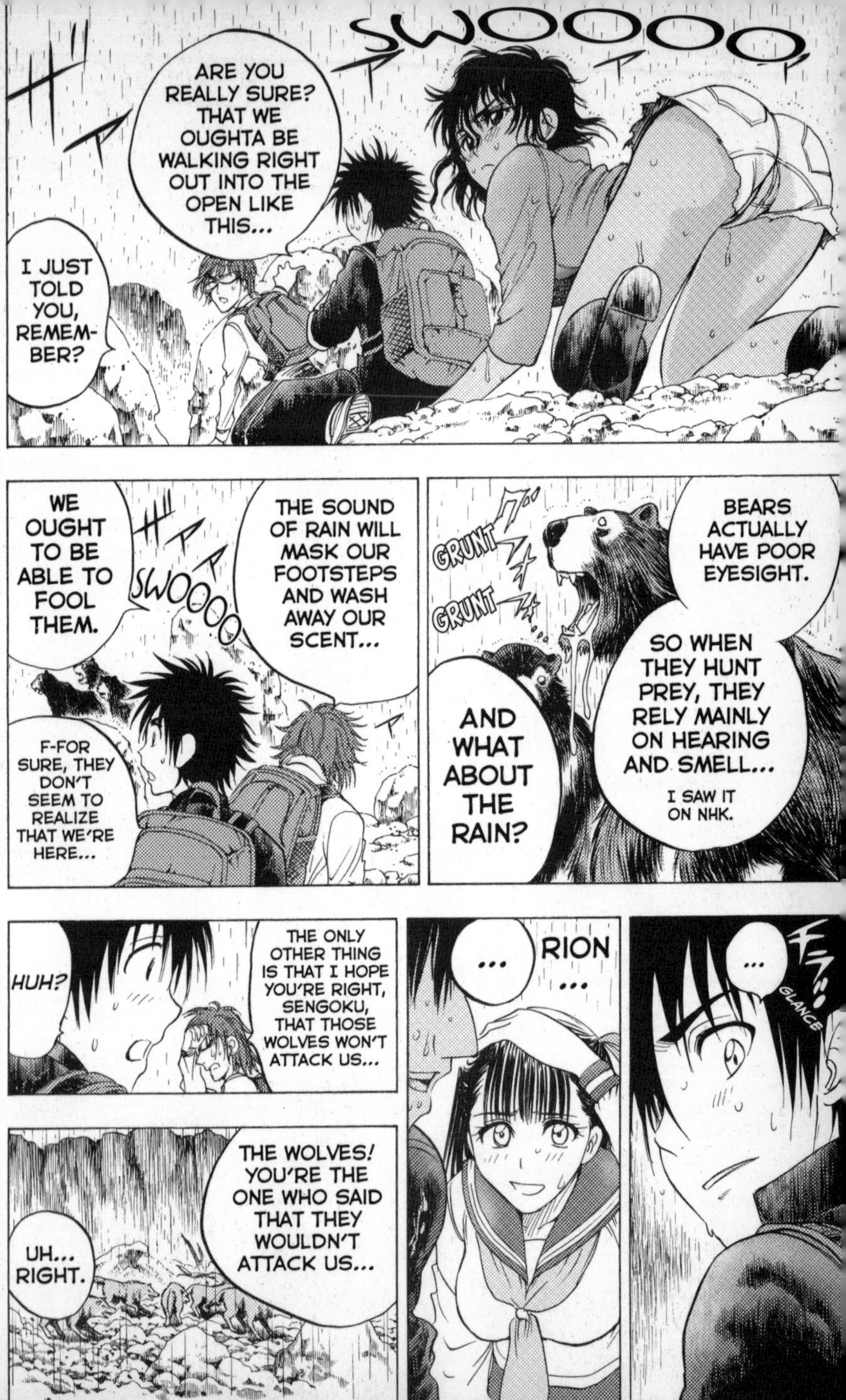
SWOOOO
ARE YOU REALLY SURE? THAT WE OUGHTA BE WALKING RIGHT OUT INTO THE OPEN LIKE THIS...
I JUST TOLD YOU, REMEM-BER?
BEARS ACTUALLY HAVE POOR EYESIGHT.
SO WHEN THEY HUNT PREY, THEY RELY MAINLY ON HEARING AND SMELL...
I SAW IT ON NHK.
GRUNT
GRUNT
AND WHAT ABOUT THE RAIN?
THE SOUND OF RAIN WILL MASK OUR FOOTSTEPS AND WASH AWAY OUR SCENT...
WE OUGHT TO BE ABLE TO FOOL THEM.
SWOOOO
F-FOR SURE, THEY DON'T SEEM TO REALIZE THAT WE'RE HERE...
...
GLANCE
RION ...
...
THE ONLY OTHER THING IS THAT I HOPE YOU'RE RIGHT, SENGOKU, THAT THOSE WOLVES WON'T ATTACK US...
HUH?
THE WOLVES! YOU'RE THE ONE WHO SAID THAT THEY WOULDN'T ATTACK US...
UH... RIGHT.

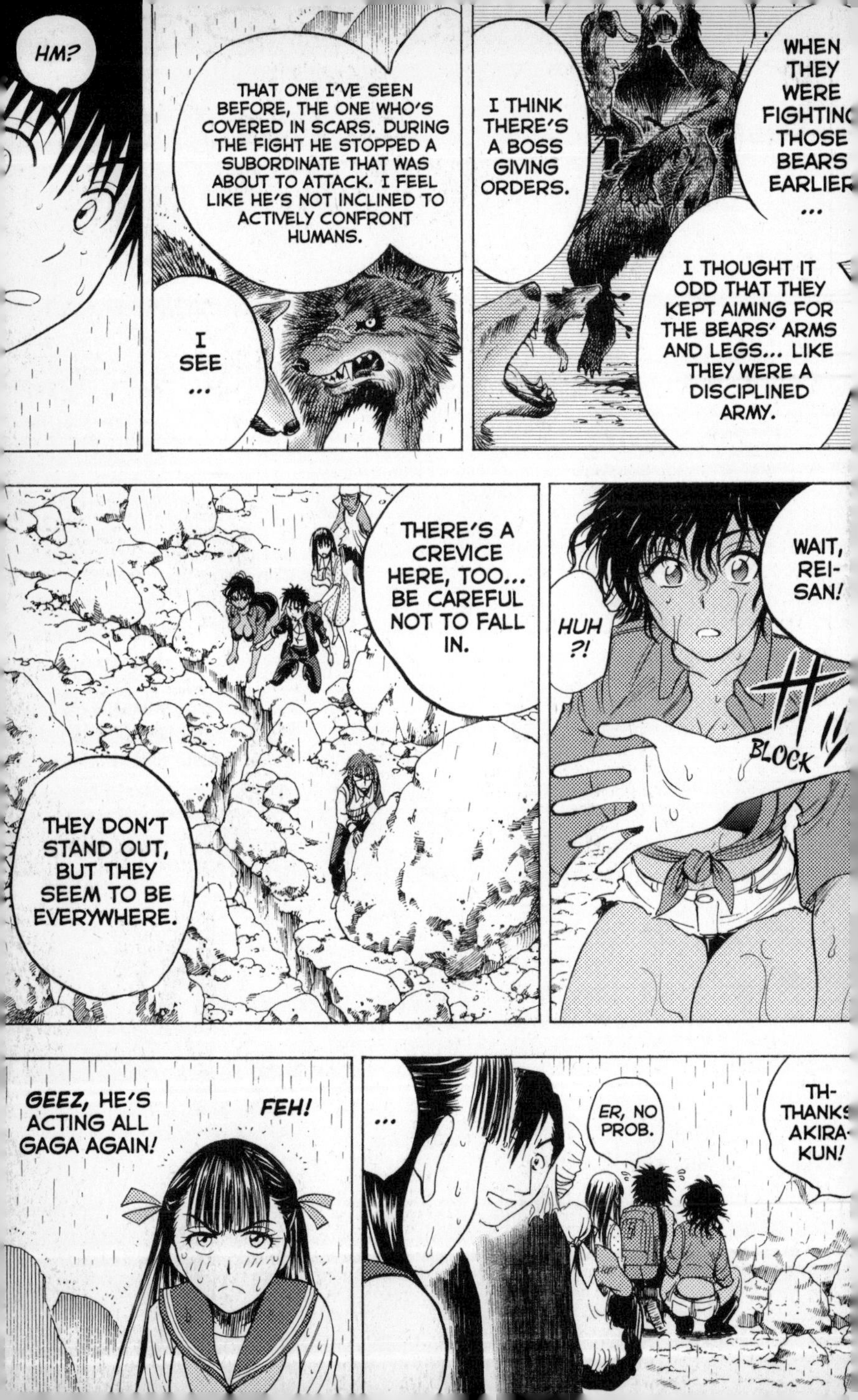

WHEN THEY WERE FIGHTING THOSE BEARS EARLIER...
I THOUGHT IT ODD THAT THEY KEPT AIMING FOR THE BEARS' ARMS AND LEGS... LIKE THEY WERE A DISCIPLINED ARMY.
I THINK THERE'S A BOSS GIVING ORDERS.
THAT ONE I'VE SEEN BEFORE, THE ONE WHO'S COVERED IN SCARS. DURING THE FIGHT HE STOPPED A SUBORDINATE THAT WAS ABOUT TO ATTACK. I FEEL LIKE HE'S NOT INCLINED TO ACTIVELY CONFRONT HUMANS.
I SEE...
HM?
WAIT, REI-SAN!
HUH?!
BLOCK
THERE'S A CREVICE HERE, TOO... BE CAREFUL NOT TO FALL IN.
THEY DON'T STAND OUT, BUT THEY SEEM TO BE EVERYWHERE.
TH-THANKS AKIRA-KUN!
ER, NO PROB.
...
FEH!
GEEZ, HE'S ACTING ALL GAGA AGAIN!

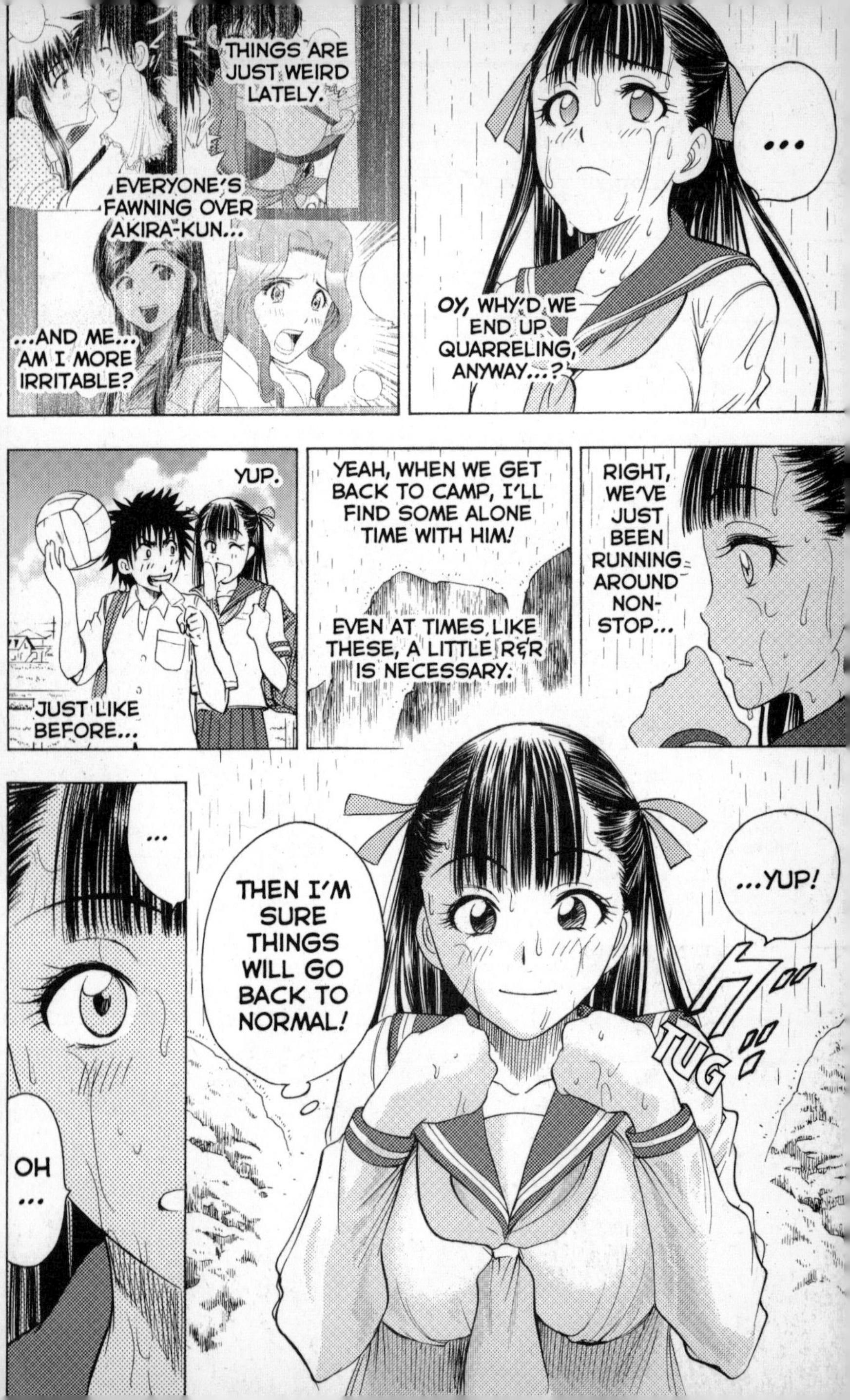
...
OY, WHY'D WE END UP QUARRELING, ANYWAY...?
THINGS ARE JUST WEIRD LATELY.
EVERYONE'S FAWNING OVER AKIRA-KUN...
...AND ME... AM I MORE IRRITABLE?
RIGHT, WE'VE JUST BEEN RUNNING AROUND NON-STOP...
YEAH, WHEN WE GET BACK TO CAMP, I'LL FIND SOME ALONE TIME WITH HIM!
EVEN AT TIMES LIKE THESE, A LITTLE R&R IS NECESSARY.
YUP.
JUST LIKE BEFORE...
...YUP!
TUG
THEN I'M SURE THINGS WILL GO BACK TO NORMAL!
...
OH ...

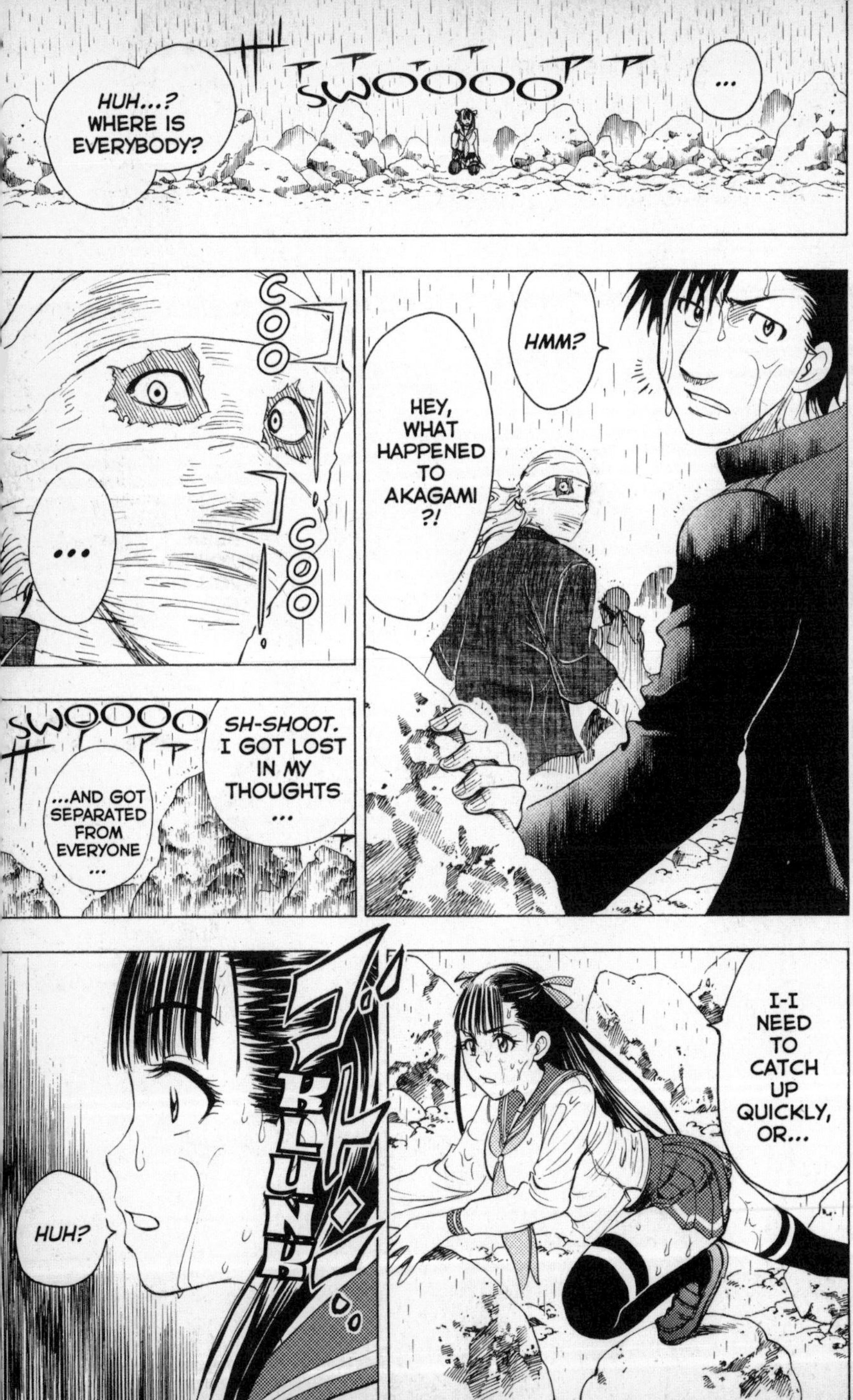
...
SWOOOO
HUH...? WHERE IS EVERYBODY?
HMM?
HEY, WHAT HAPPENED TO AKAGAMI ?!
COO COO
...
SH-SHOOT. I GOT LOST IN MY THOUGHTS ...
SWOOOO
...AND GOT SEPARATED FROM EVERYONE ...
I-I NEED TO CATCH UP QUICKLY, OR...
KLUNK
HUH?

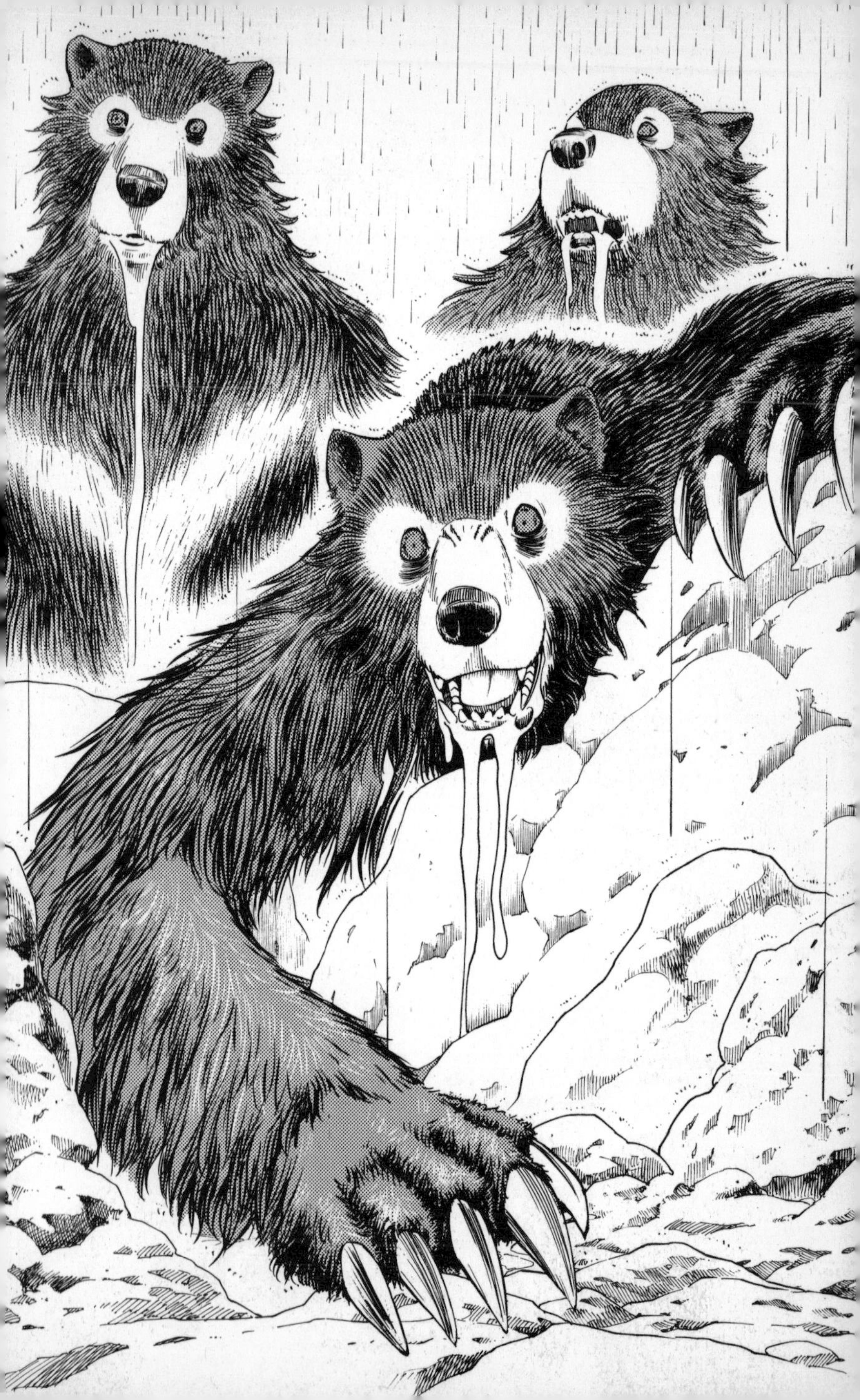

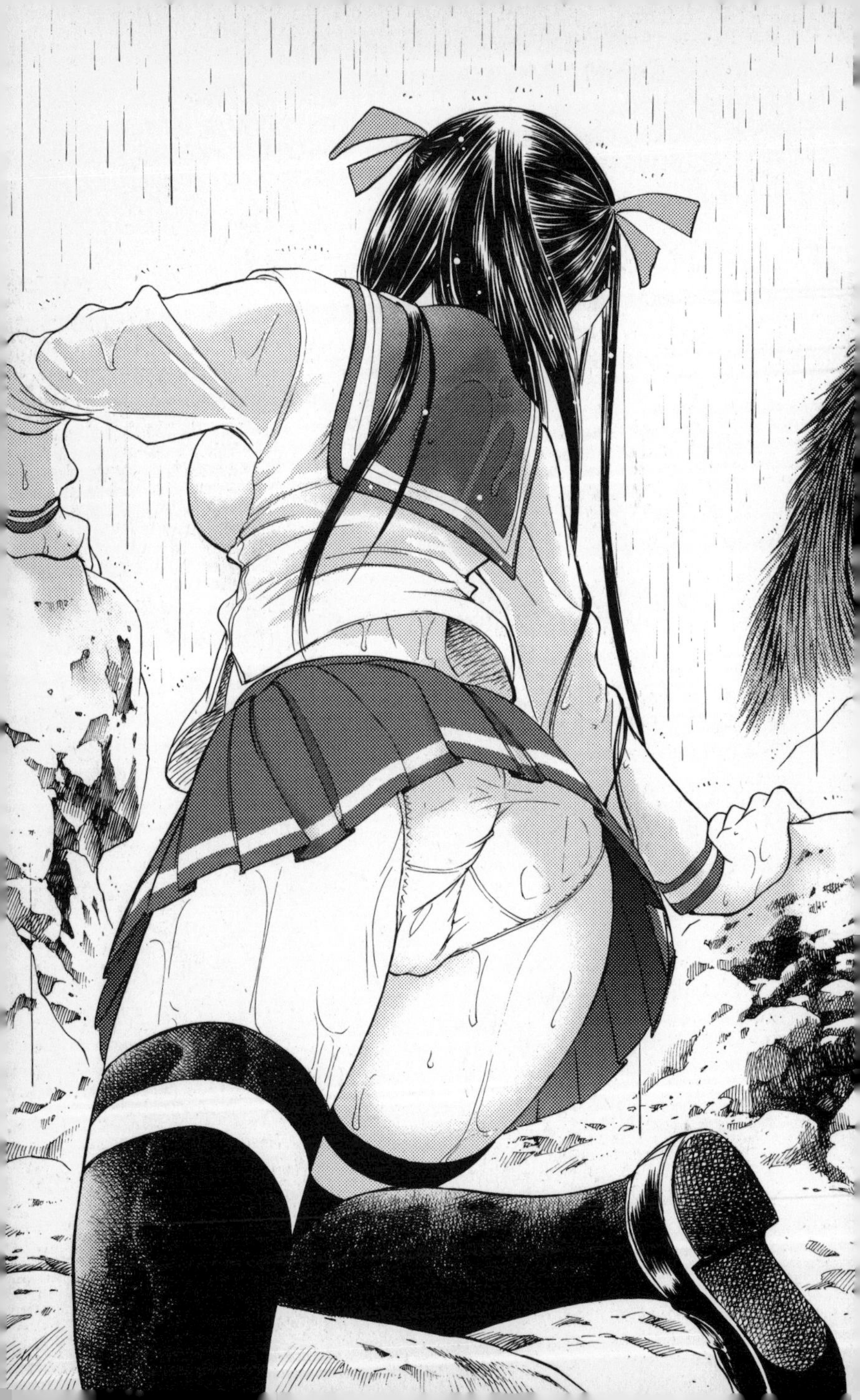

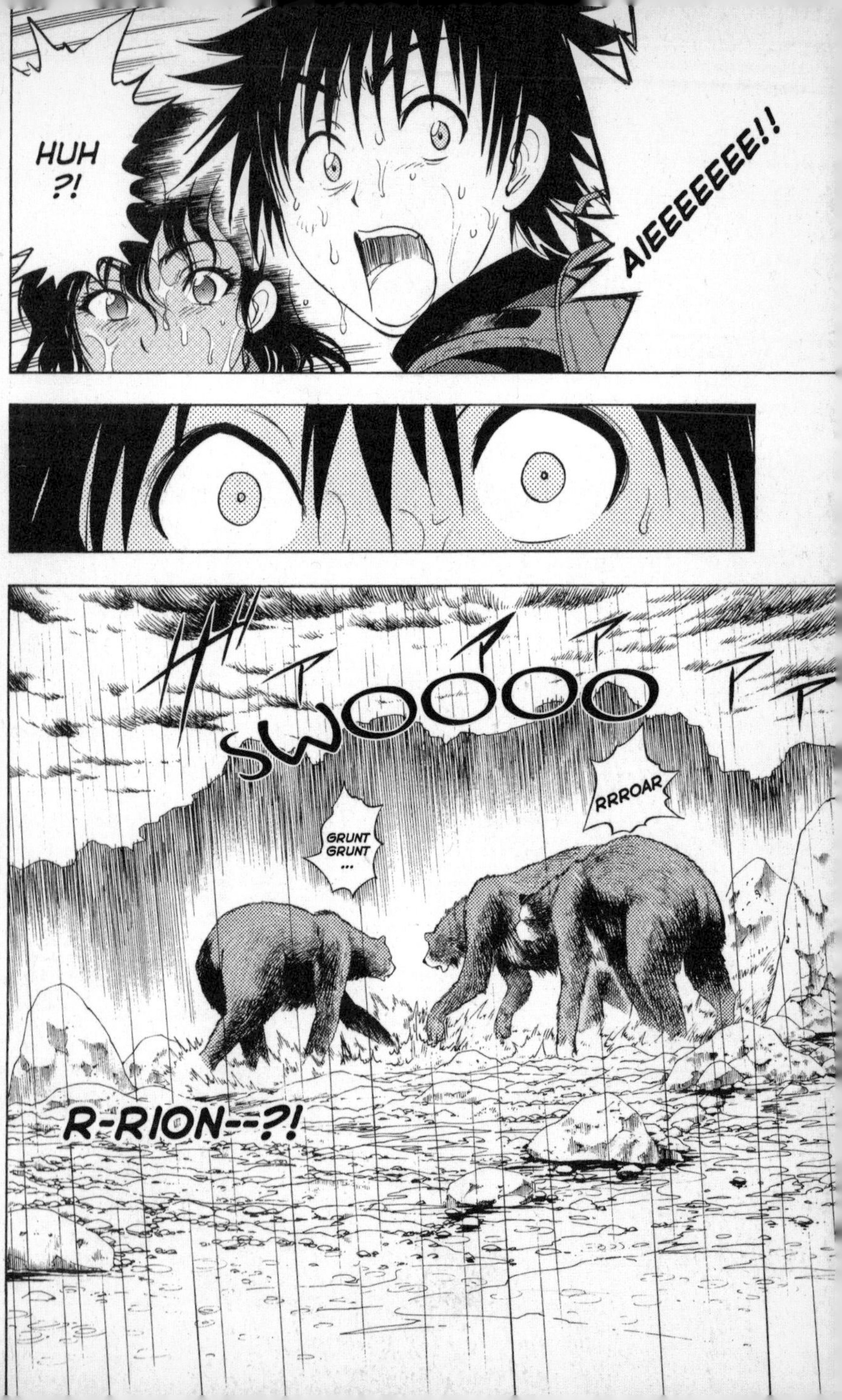
AIEEEEEEE!!
HUH ?!
SWOOOO
RRROAR
GRUNT GRUNT ...
R-RION--?!

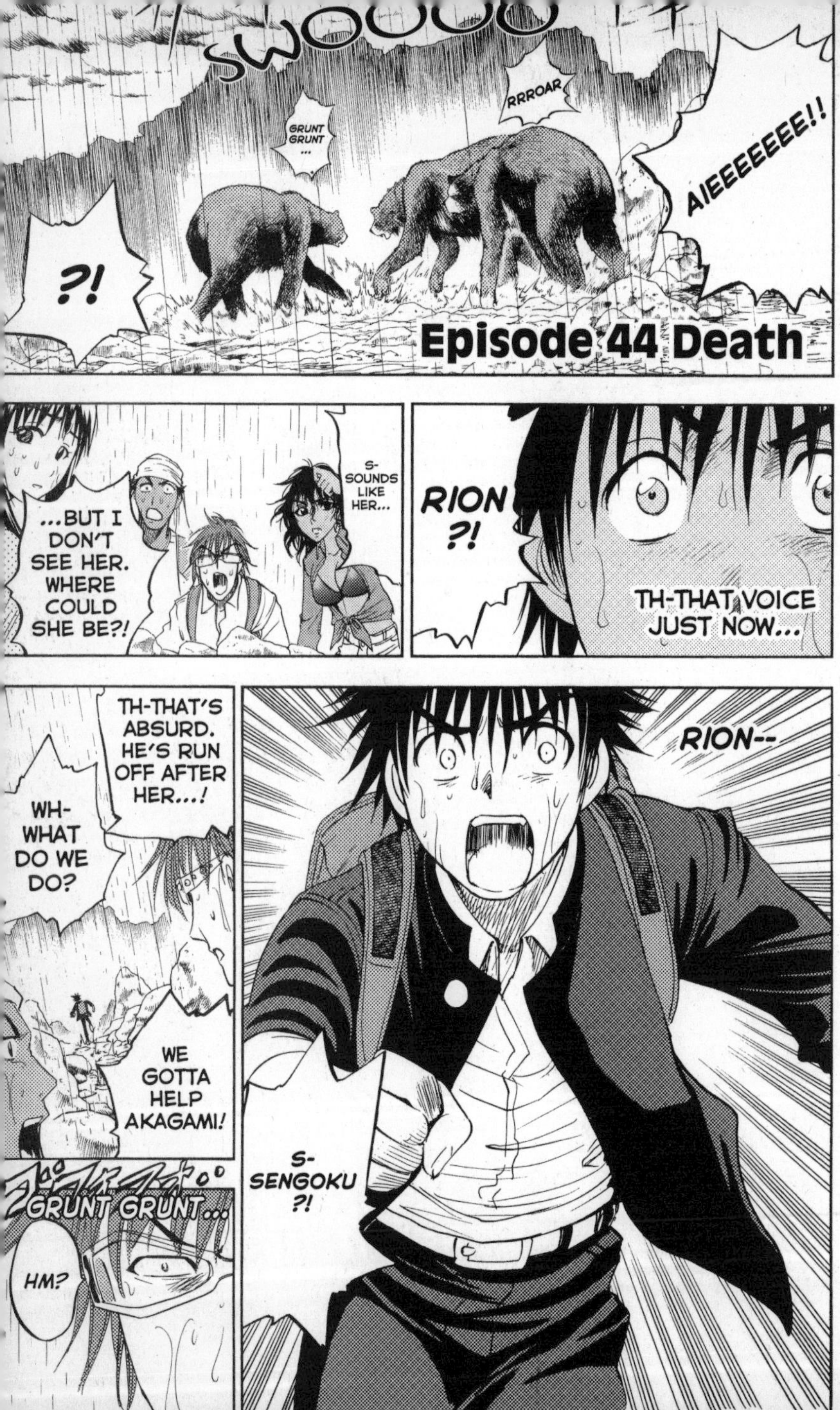
AIEEEEEEE!!
RRROAR
SWOOOO
GRUNT GRUNT ...
?!
Episode 44 Death
TH-THAT VOICE JUST NOW...
RION ?!
S-SOUNDS LIKE HER...
...BUT I DON'T SEE HER. WHERE COULD SHE BE?!
RION--
S-SENGOKU ?!
TH-THAT'S ABSURD. HE'S RUN OFF AFTER HER...!
WH-WHAT DO WE DO?
WE GOTTA HELP AKAGAMI!
GRUNT GRUNT...
HM?

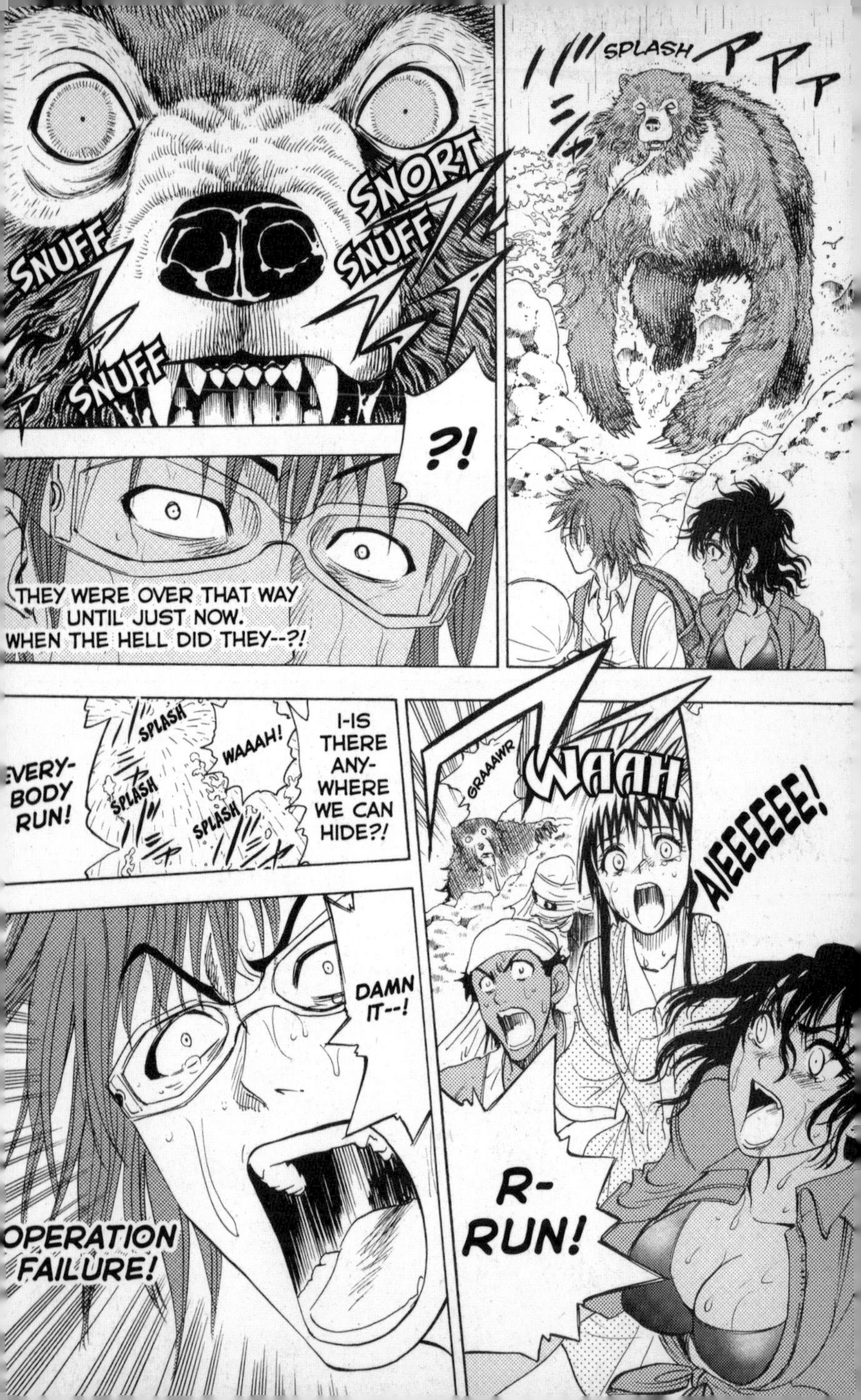
SPLASH
SNORT
SNUFF
SNUFF
SNUFF
?!
THEY WERE OVER THAT WAY UNTIL JUST NOW. WHEN THE HELL DID THEY--?!
GRAAAWR
WAAH
AIEEEEEE!
R-RUN!
I-IS THERE ANYWHERE WE CAN HIDE?!
WAAAH!
SPLASH
SPLASH
SPLASH
EVERYBODY RUN!
DAMN IT--!
OPERATION FAILURE!

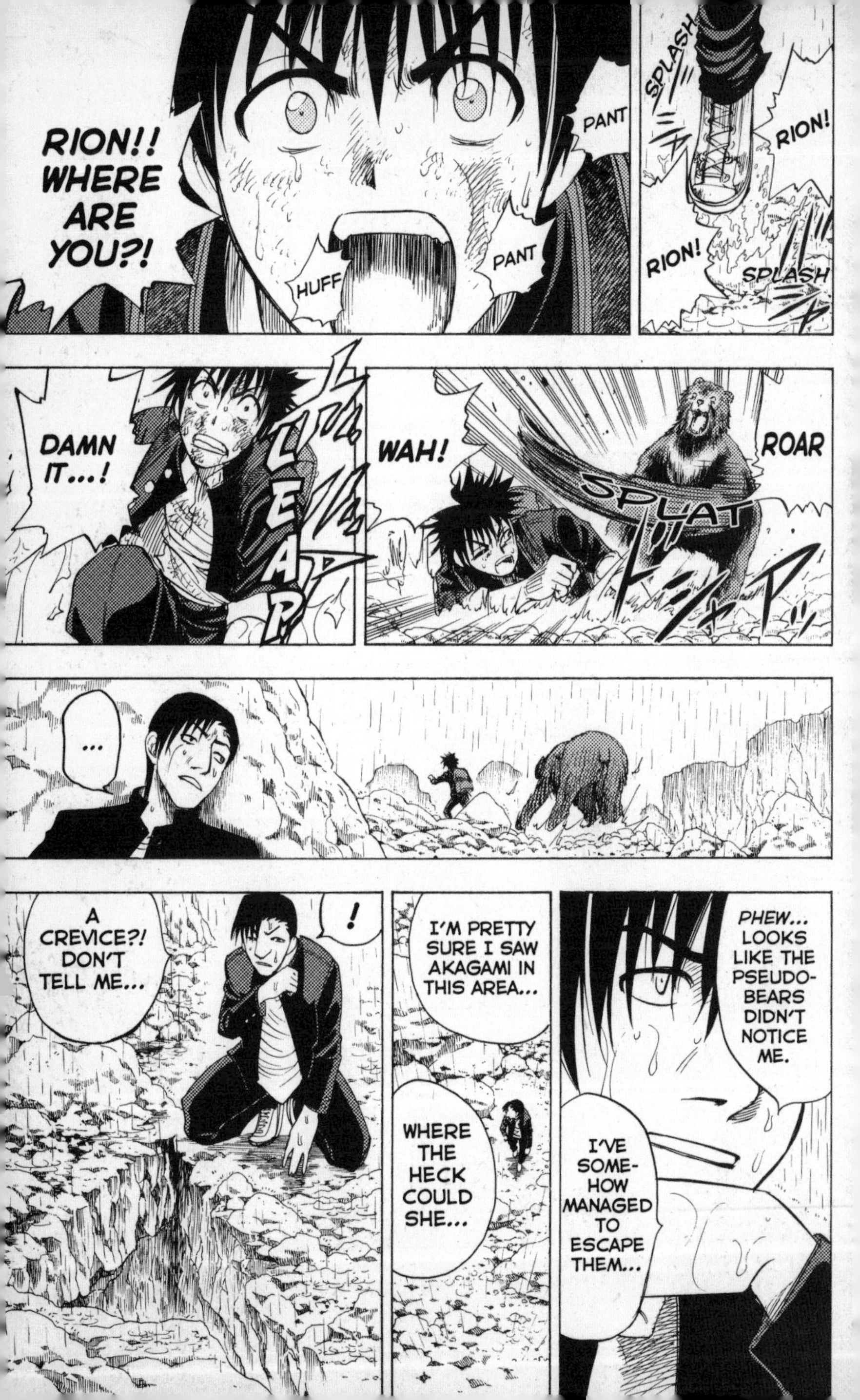
SPLASH
RION!
RION!
SPLASH
PANT
RION!! WHERE ARE YOU?!
PANT
HUFF
ROAR
SPLAT
WAH!
LEAP
DAMN IT...!
...
PHEW... LOOKS LIKE THE PSEUDO-BEARS DIDN'T NOTICE ME.
I'VE SOME-HOW MANAGED TO ESCAPE THEM...
I'M PRETTY SURE I SAW AKAGAMI IN THIS AREA...
WHERE THE HECK COULD SHE...
!
A CREVICE?! DON'T TELL ME...

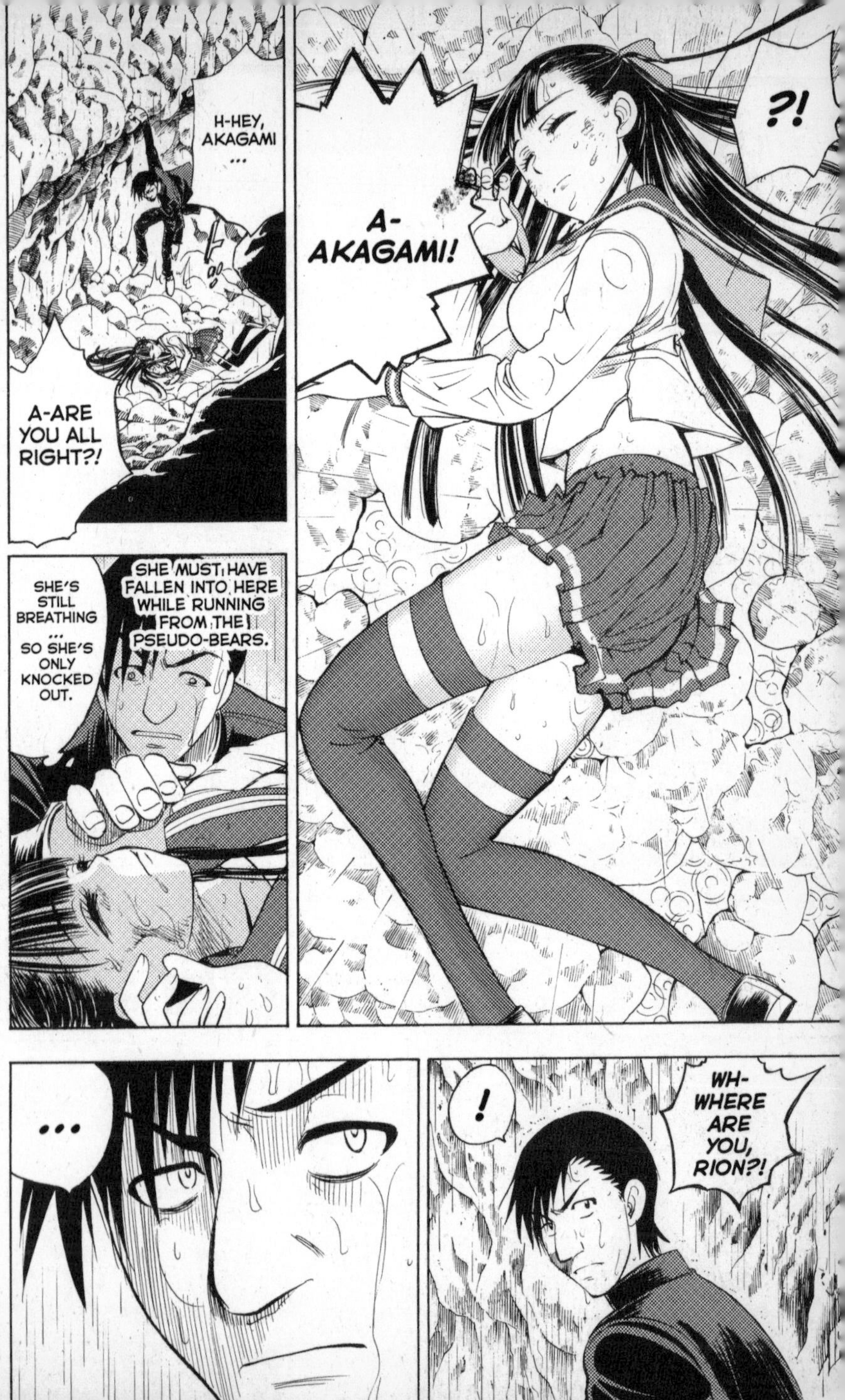
?!
A-AKAGAMI!
H-HEY, AKAGAMI ...
A-ARE YOU ALL RIGHT?!
SHE MUST HAVE FALLEN INTO HERE WHILE RUNNING FROM THE PSEUDO-BEARS.
SHE'S STILL BREATHING ... SO SHE'S ONLY KNOCKED OUT.
WH-WHERE ARE YOU, RION?!
!
...

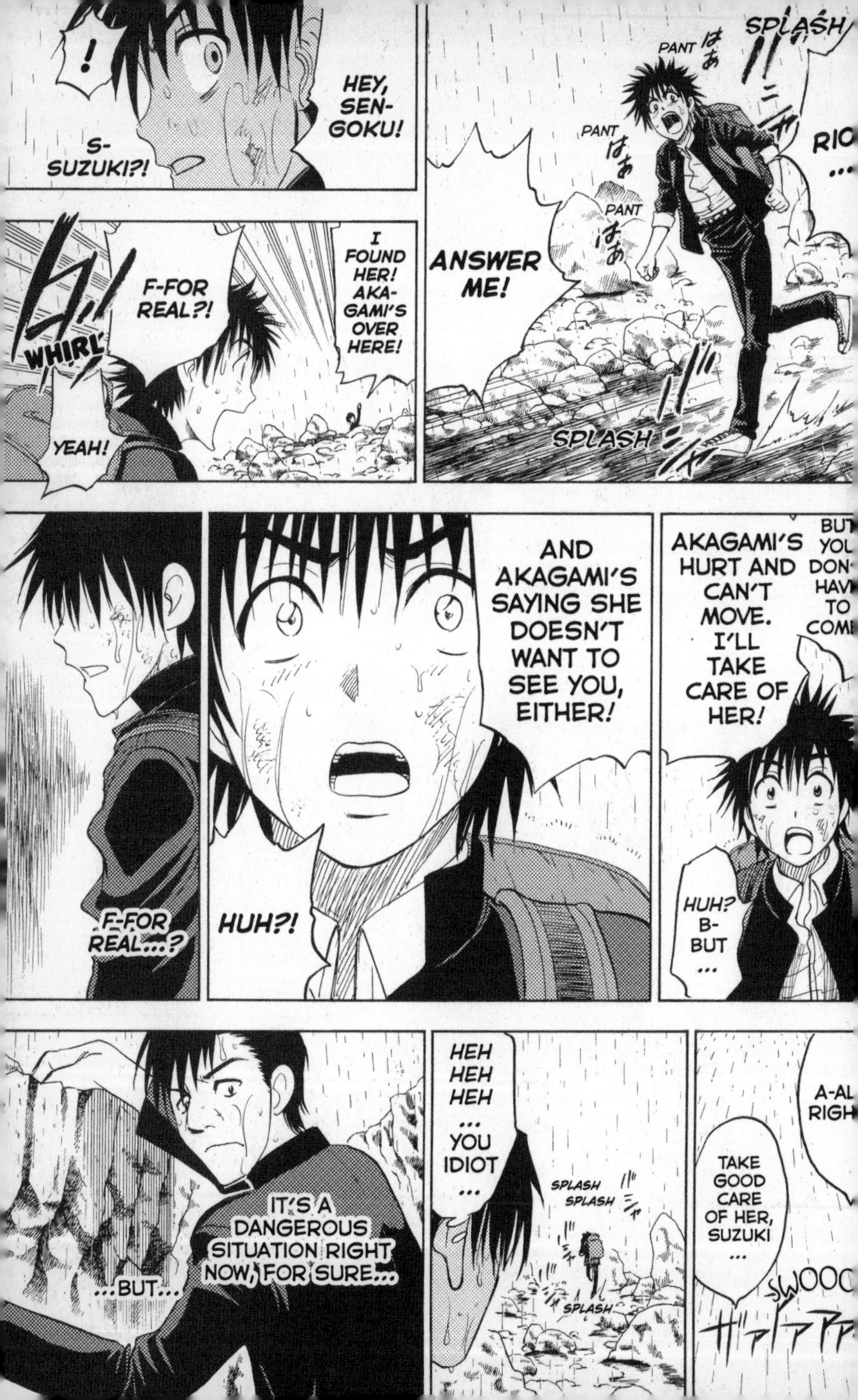
RIO...
SPLASH
PANT はぁ
PANT はぁ
PANT はぁ
ANSWER ME!
SPLASH
HEY, SEN-GOKU!
!
S-SUZUKI?!
I FOUND HER! AKA-GAMI'S OVER HERE!
F-FOR REAL?!
WHIRL
YEAH!
BUT YOU DON- HAV TO COM
AKAGAMI'S HURT AND CAN'T MOVE. I'LL TAKE CARE OF HER!
HUH? B-BUT ...
AND AKAGAMI'S SAYING SHE DOESN'T WANT TO SEE YOU, EITHER!
HUH?!
F-FOR REAL...?
A-AL RIGH
TAKE GOOD CARE OF HER, SUZUKI ...
SWOOO
HEH HEH HEH ... YOU IDIOT ...
SPLASH SPLASH
SPLASH
IT'S A DANGEROUS SITUATION RIGHT NOW, FOR SURE...
...BUT...

...I'M NEVER GONNA HAVE A CHANCE LIKE THIS AGAIN.

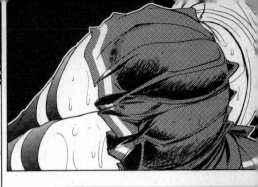

GULP!

I AIN'T LETTING IT SLIP BY!

...

AND AKAGAMI'S SAYING SHE DOESN'T WANT TO SEE YOU, EITHER...

SPLASH

SPLASH

SPLASH

?!

SHOVE

DUCK--!

HEY, SENGOKU! WHAT'RE YOU ZONING OUT, FOR?

HUH ?!

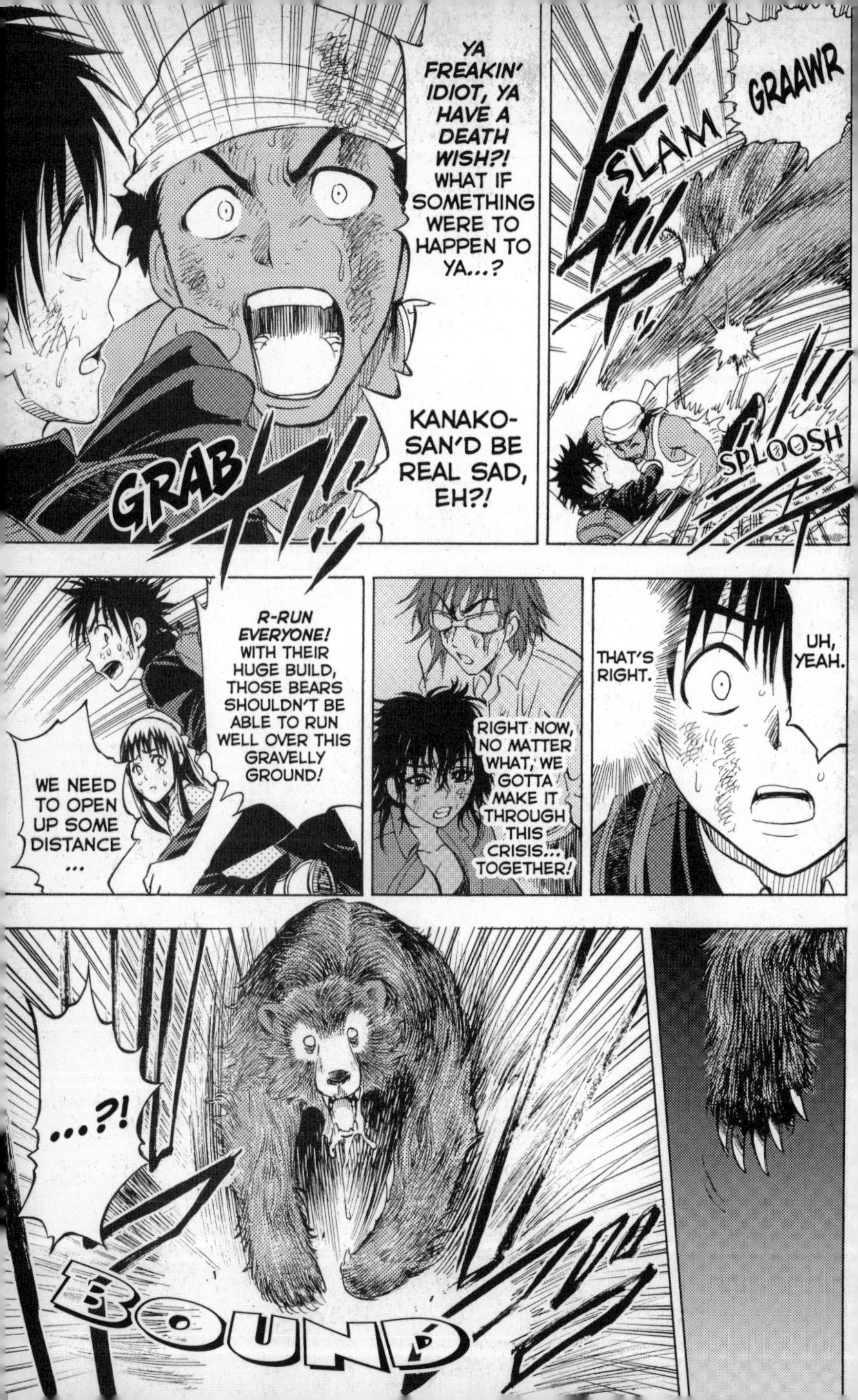
GRAAWR
SLAM
SPLOOSH
YA FREAKIN' IDIOT, YA HAVE A DEATH WISH?! WHAT IF SOMETHING WERE TO HAPPEN TO YA...?
KANAKO-SAN'D BE REAL SAD, EH?!
GRAB
UH, YEAH.
THAT'S RIGHT.
RIGHT NOW, NO MATTER WHAT, WE GOTTA MAKE IT THROUGH THIS CRISIS... TOGETHER!
R-RUN EVERYONE! WITH THEIR HUGE BUILD, THOSE BEARS SHOULDN'T BE ABLE TO RUN WELL OVER THIS GRAVELLY GROUND!
WE NEED TO OPEN UP SOME DISTANCE ...
...?!
BOUND

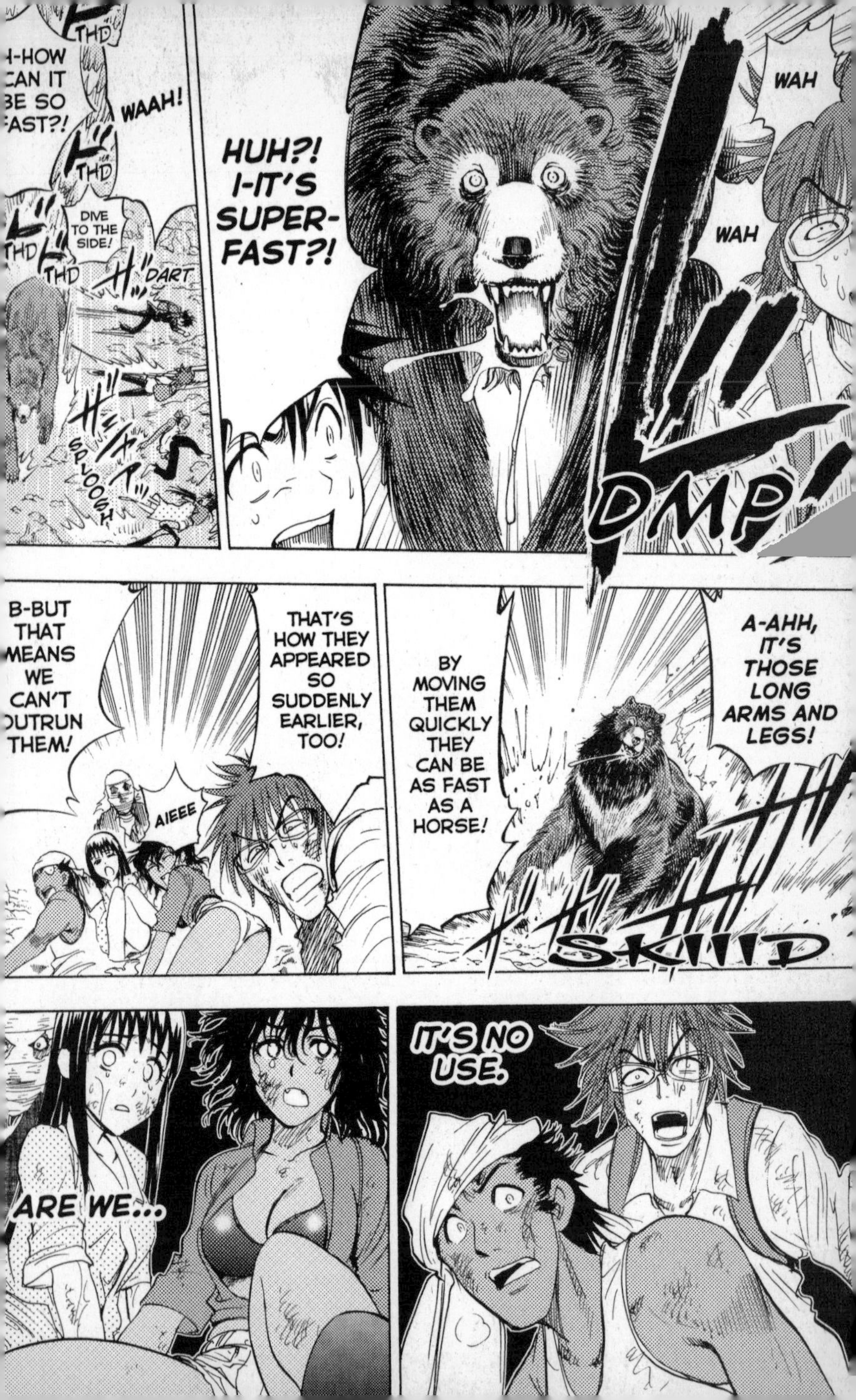
WAH
WAH
DMP!
HUH?! I-IT'S SUPER-FAST?!
THD
WAAH!
H-HOW CAN IT BE SO FAST?!
THD
DIVE TO THE SIDE!
THD
THD
DART
SPLOOSH
A-AHH, IT'S THOSE LONG ARMS AND LEGS!
BY MOVING THEM QUICKLY THEY CAN BE AS FAST AS A HORSE!
SKIIID
THAT'S HOW THEY APPEARED SO SUDDENLY EARLIER, TOO!
B-BUT THAT MEANS WE CAN'T OUTRUN THEM!
AIEEE
IT'S NO USE.
ARE WE...

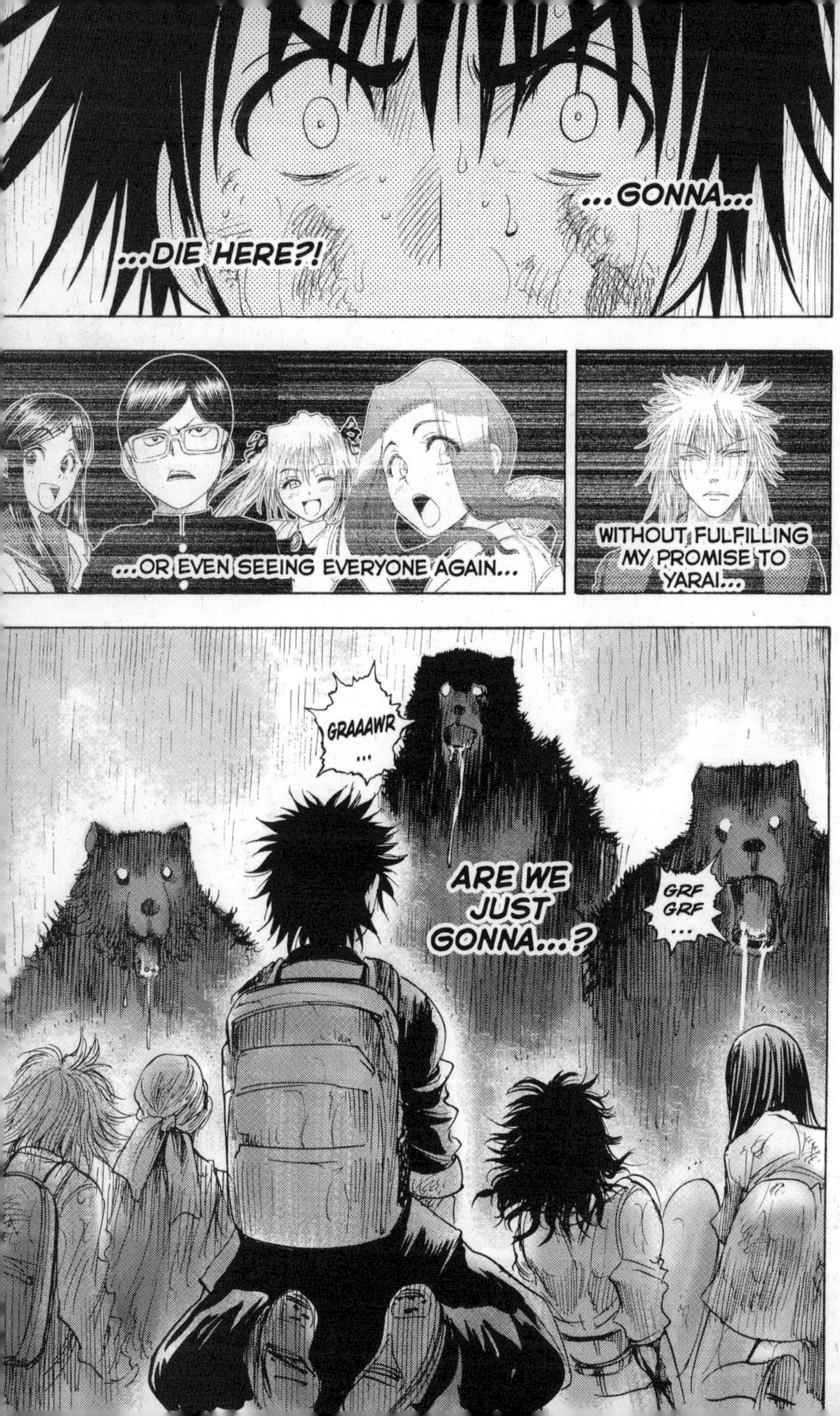
...GONNA...
...DIE HERE?!
WITHOUT FULFILLING MY PROMISE TO YARAI...
...OR EVEN SEEING EVERYONE AGAIN...
GRAAAWR ...
GRF GRF ...
ARE WE JUST GONNA...?

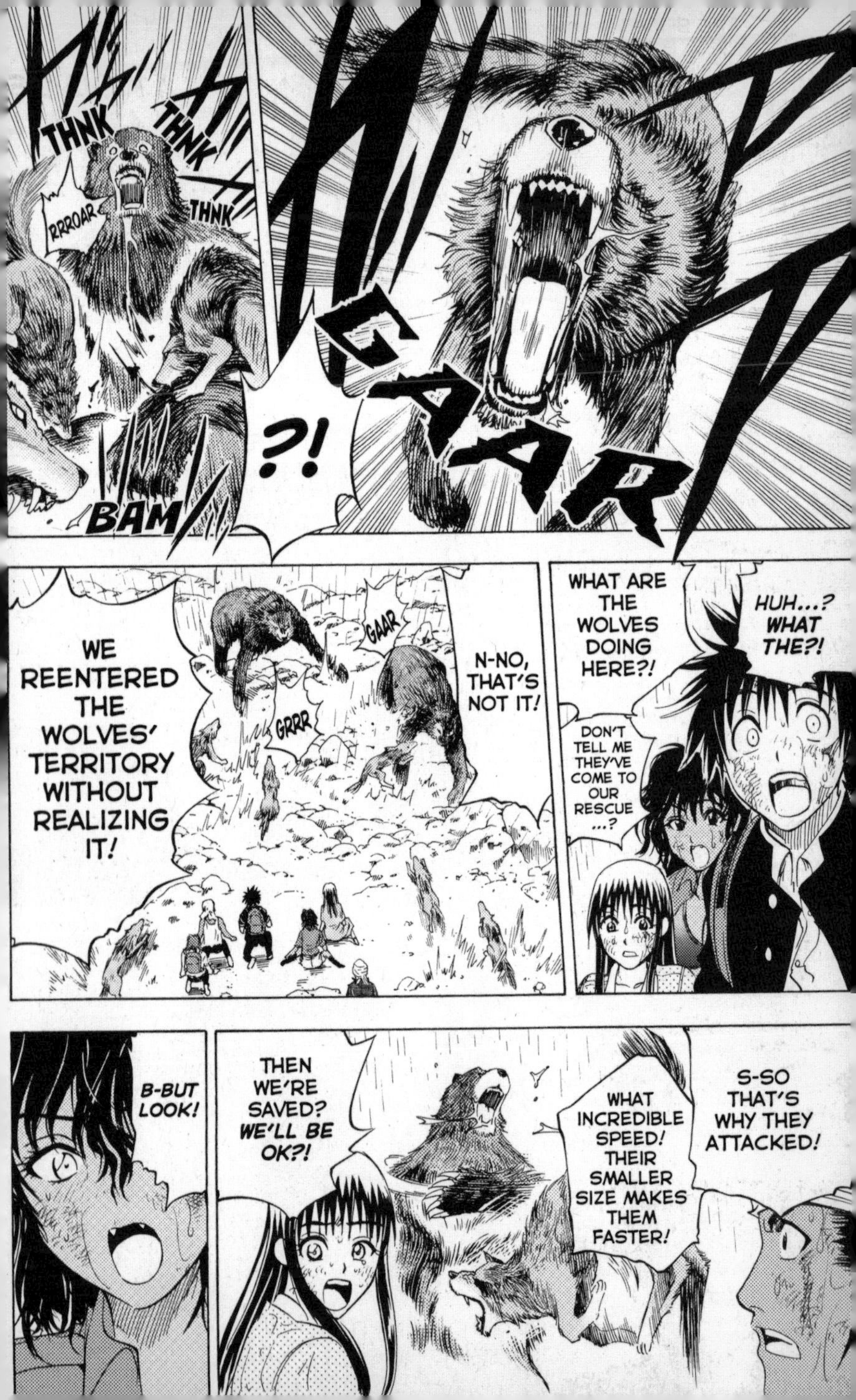
GAAR
?!
THNK
THNK
THNK
RRROAR
BAM
HUH...? WHAT THE?!
WHAT ARE THE WOLVES DOING HERE?!
DON'T TELL ME THEY'VE COME TO OUR RESCUE ...?
N-NO, THAT'S NOT IT!
GAAR
GRRR
WE REENTERED THE WOLVES' TERRITORY WITHOUT REALIZING IT!
S-SO THAT'S WHY THEY ATTACKED!
WHAT INCREDIBLE SPEED! THEIR SMALLER SIZE MAKES THEM FASTER!
THEN WE'RE SAVED? WE'LL BE OK?!
B-BUT LOOK!

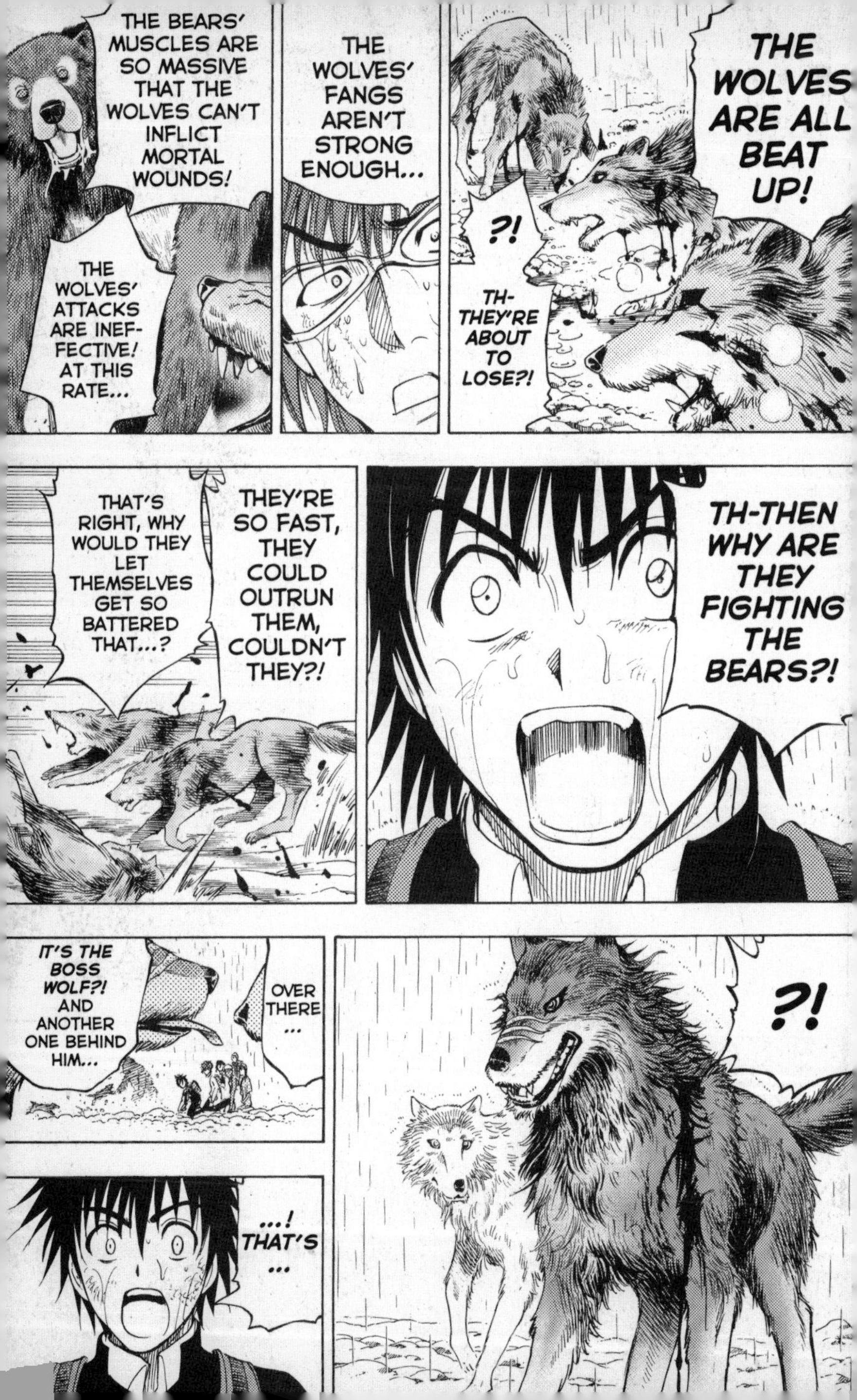
THE WOLVES ARE ALL BEAT UP!
?!
TH- THEY'RE ABOUT TO LOSE?!
THE WOLVES' FANGS AREN'T STRONG ENOUGH...
THE BEARS' MUSCLES ARE SO MASSIVE THAT THE WOLVES CAN'T INFLICT MORTAL WOUNDS!
THE WOLVES' ATTACKS ARE INEF-FECTIVE! AT THIS RATE...
TH-THEN WHY ARE THEY FIGHTING THE BEARS?!
THEY'RE SO FAST, THEY COULD OUTRUN THEM, COULDN'T THEY?!
THAT'S RIGHT, WHY WOULD THEY LET THEMSELVES GET SO BATTERED THAT...?
?!
OVER THERE...
IT'S THE BOSS WOLF?! AND ANOTHER ONE BEHIND HIM...
...! THAT'S...

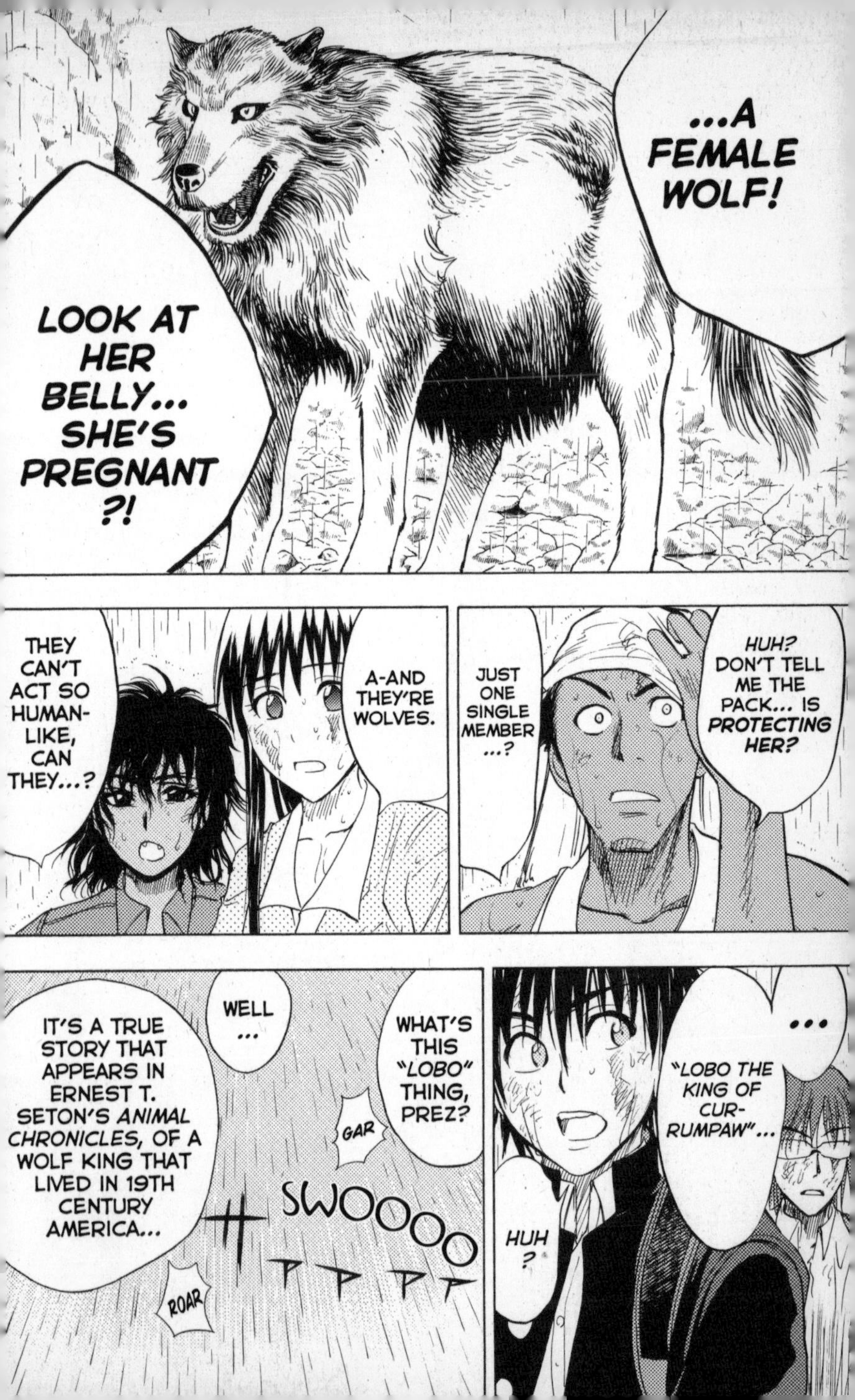
...A FEMALE WOLF!
LOOK AT HER BELLY... SHE'S PREGNANT?!
HUH? DON'T TELL ME THE PACK... IS PROTECTING HER?
JUST ONE SINGLE MEMBER...?
A-AND THEY'RE WOLVES.
THEY CAN'T ACT SO HUMAN-LIKE, CAN THEY...?
...
"LOBO THE KING OF CURRUMPAW"...
HUH?
WHAT'S THIS "LOBO" THING, PREZ?
GAR
WELL...
IT'S A TRUE STORY THAT APPEARS IN ERNEST T. SETON'S ANIMAL CHRONICLES, OF A WOLF KING THAT LIVED IN 19TH CENTURY AMERICA...
SWOOOOOPPPP
ROAR

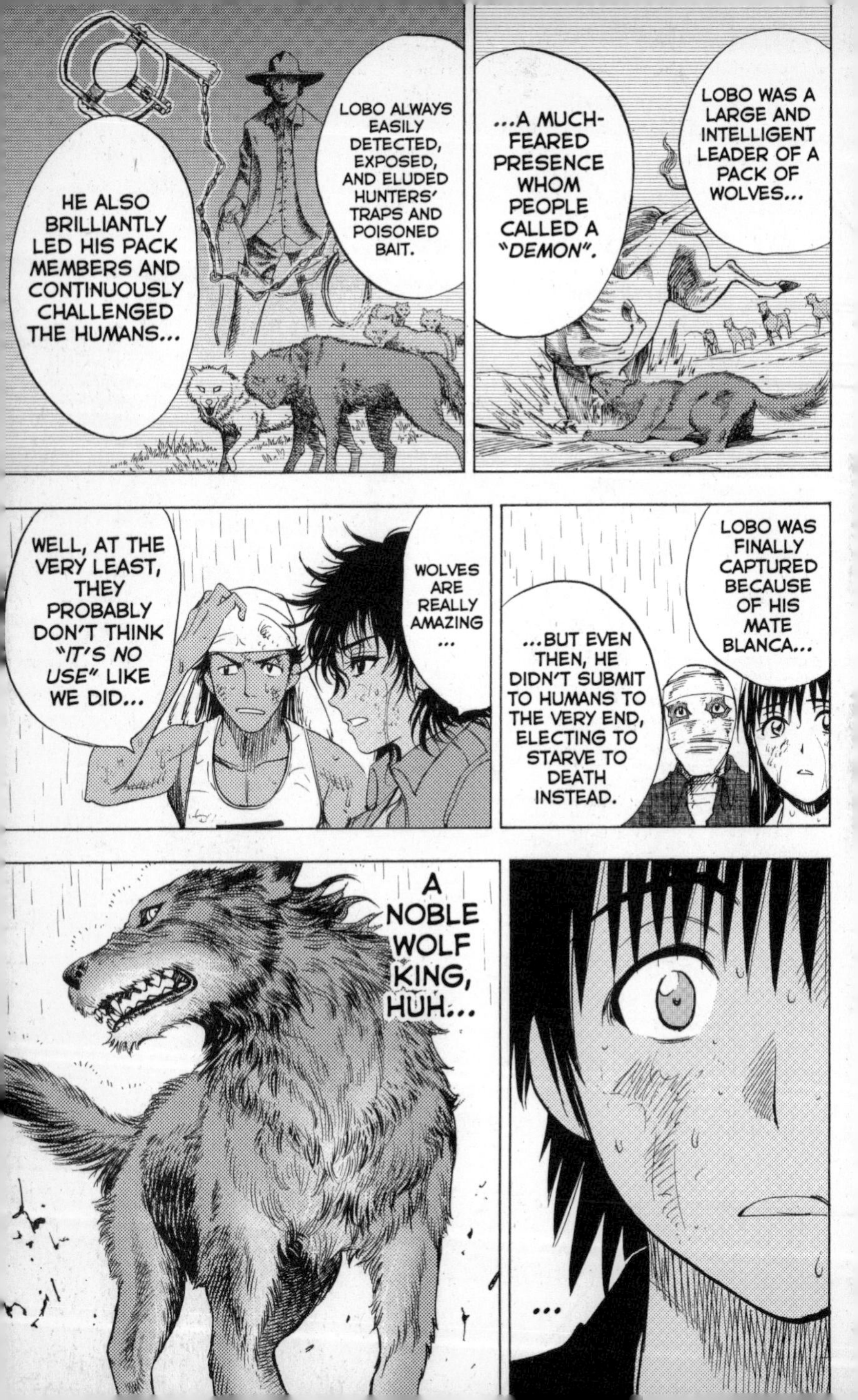
LOBO WAS A LARGE AND INTELLIGENT LEADER OF A PACK OF WOLVES...
...A MUCH-FEARED PRESENCE WHOM PEOPLE CALLED A "*DEMON*".
LOBO ALWAYS EASILY DETECTED, EXPOSED, AND ELUDED HUNTERS' TRAPS AND POISONED BAIT.
HE ALSO BRILLIANTLY LED HIS PACK MEMBERS AND CONTINUOUSLY CHALLENGED THE HUMANS...
LOBO WAS FINALLY CAPTURED BECAUSE OF HIS MATE BLANCA...
...BUT EVEN THEN, HE DIDN'T SUBMIT TO HUMANS TO THE VERY END, ELECTING TO STARVE TO DEATH INSTEAD.
WOLVES ARE REALLY AMAZING...
WELL, AT THE VERY LEAST, THEY PROBABLY DON'T THINK "*IT'S NO USE*" LIKE WE DID...
...
A NOBLE WOLF KING, HUH...

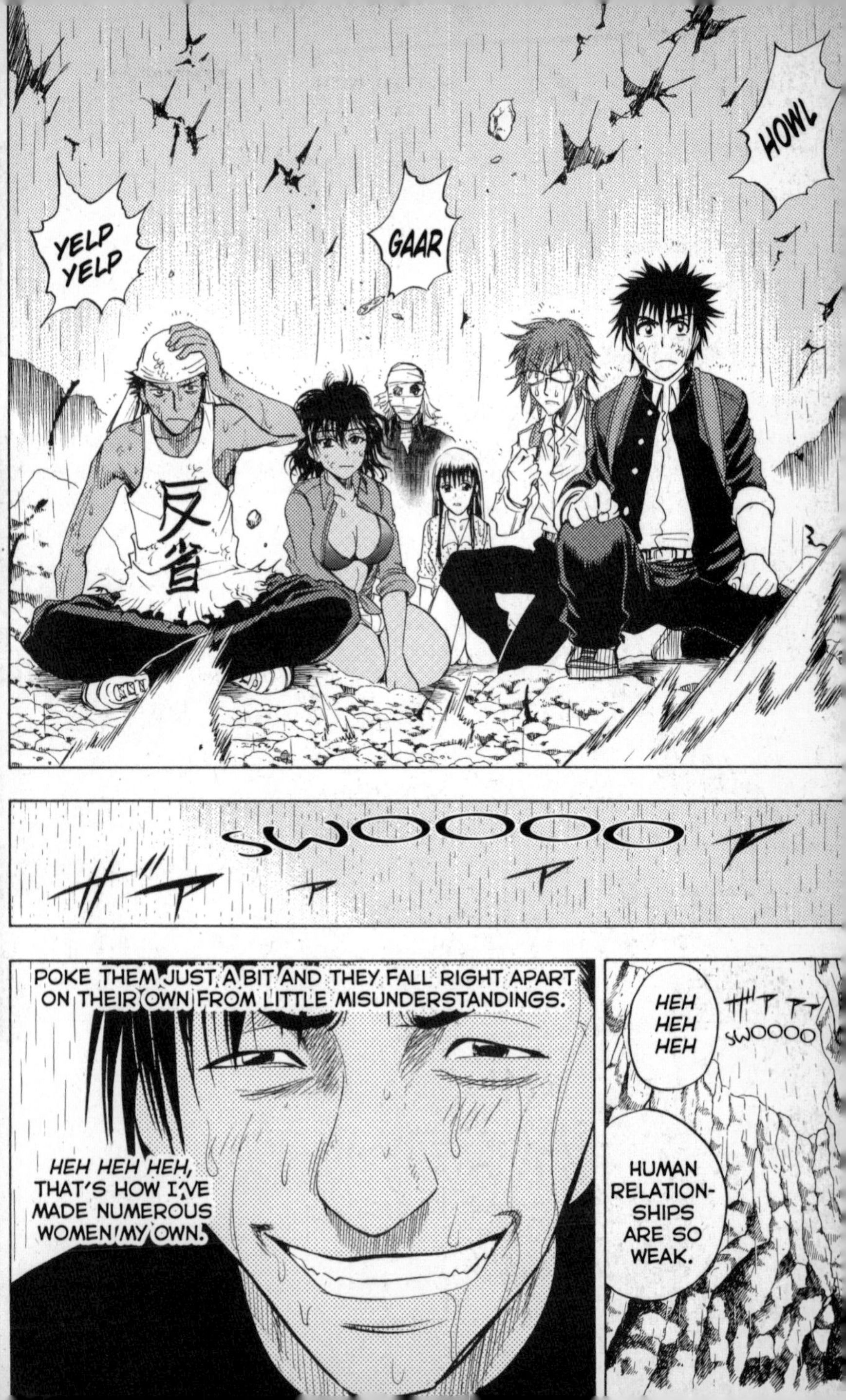
HOWL
GAAR
YELP YELP
SWOOOOO
HEH HEH HEH
SWOOOO
HUMAN RELATION-SHIPS ARE SO WEAK.
POKE THEM JUST A BIT AND THEY FALL RIGHT APART ON THEIR OWN FROM LITTLE MISUNDERSTANDINGS.
HEH HEH HEH, THAT'S HOW I'VE MADE NUMEROUS WOMEN MY OWN.

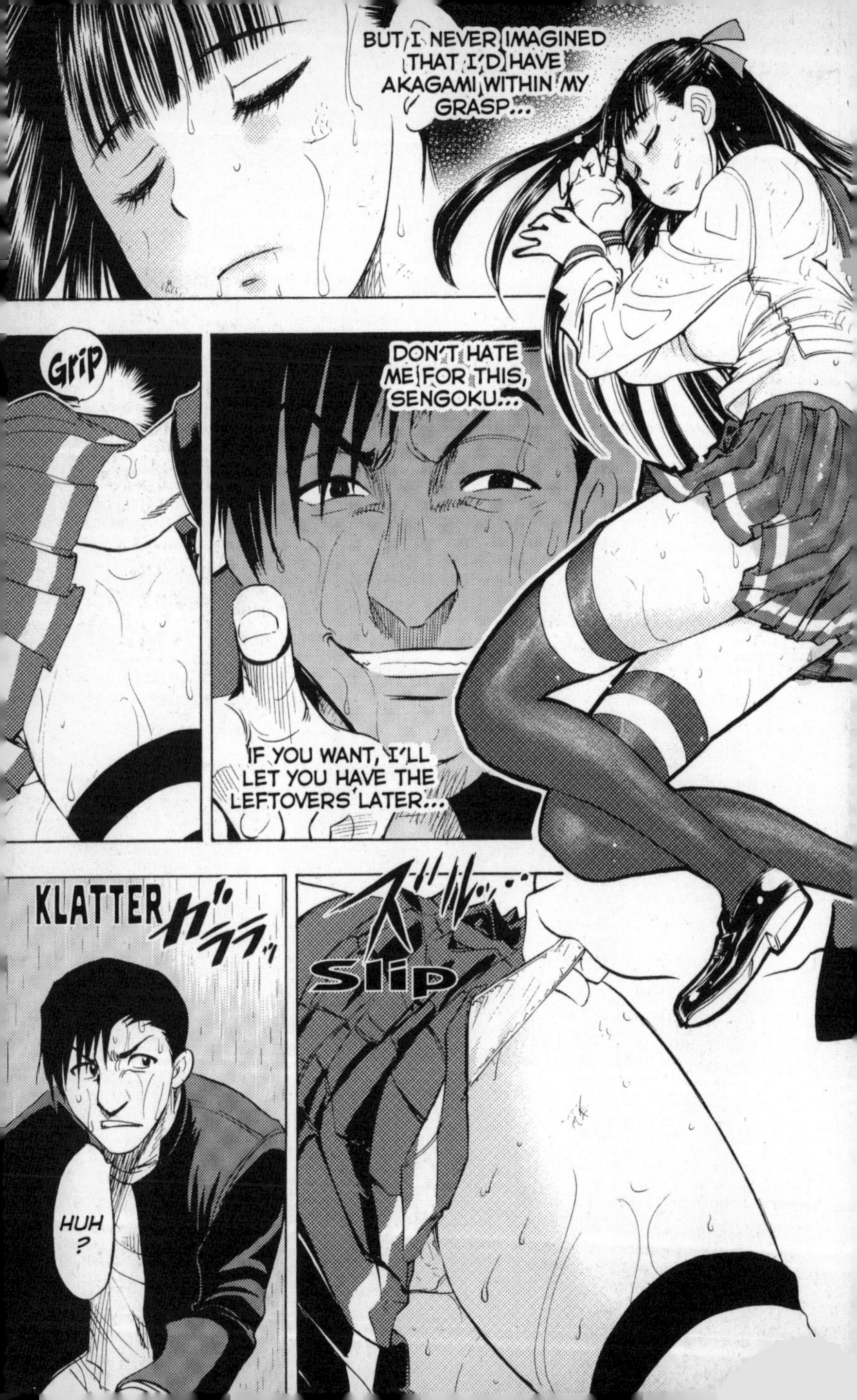
BUT I NEVER IMAGINED THAT I'D HAVE AKAGAMI WITHIN MY GRASP...
DON'T HATE ME FOR THIS, SENGOKU...
IF YOU WANT, I'LL LET YOU HAVE THE LEFTOVERS LATER...
Grip
Slip
KLATTER
ガララッ
HUH ?

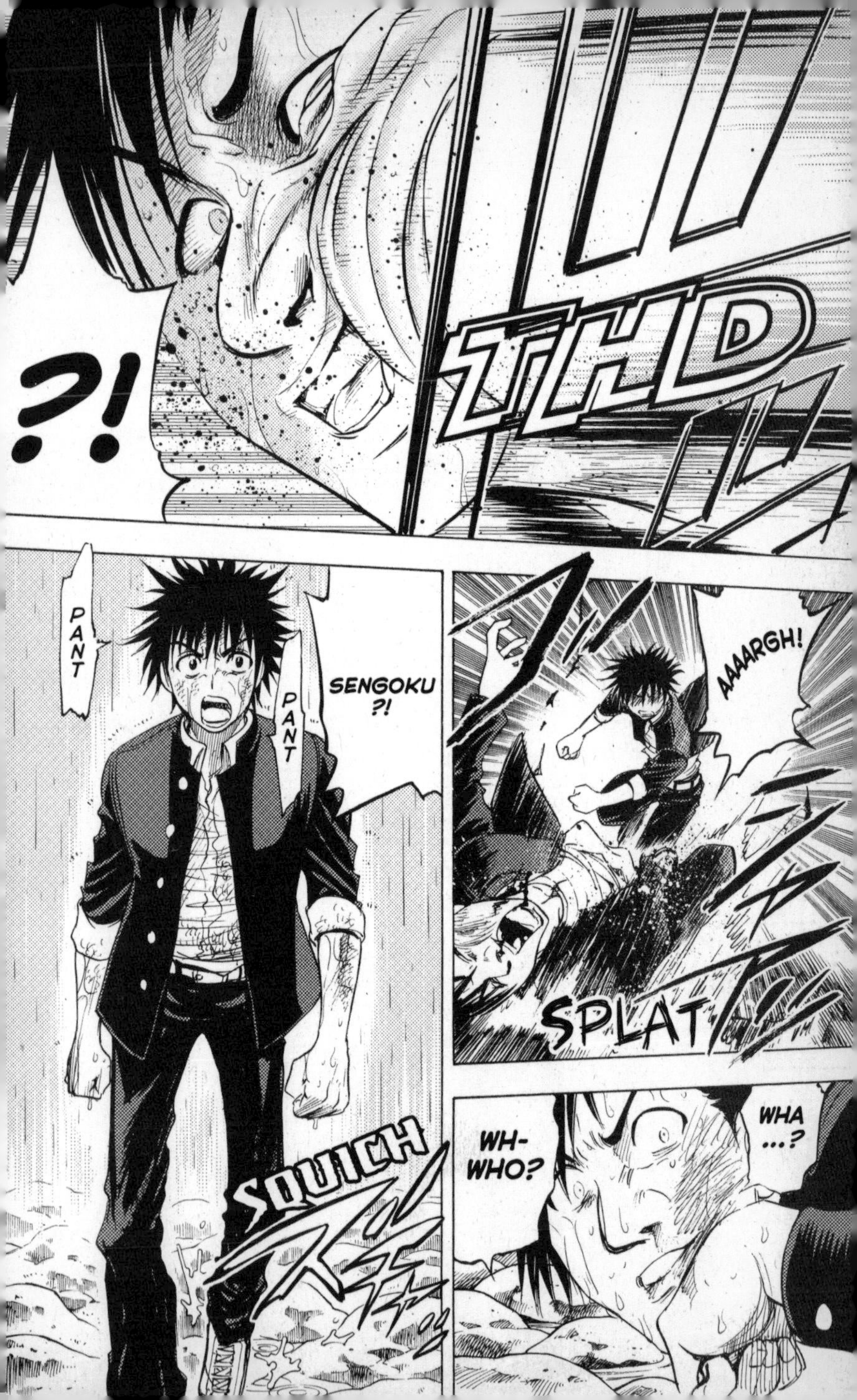
ZTHD
?!
AAAARGH!
SPLAT
WHA ...?
WH- WHO?
SENGOKU ?!
PANT
PANT
SQUICH

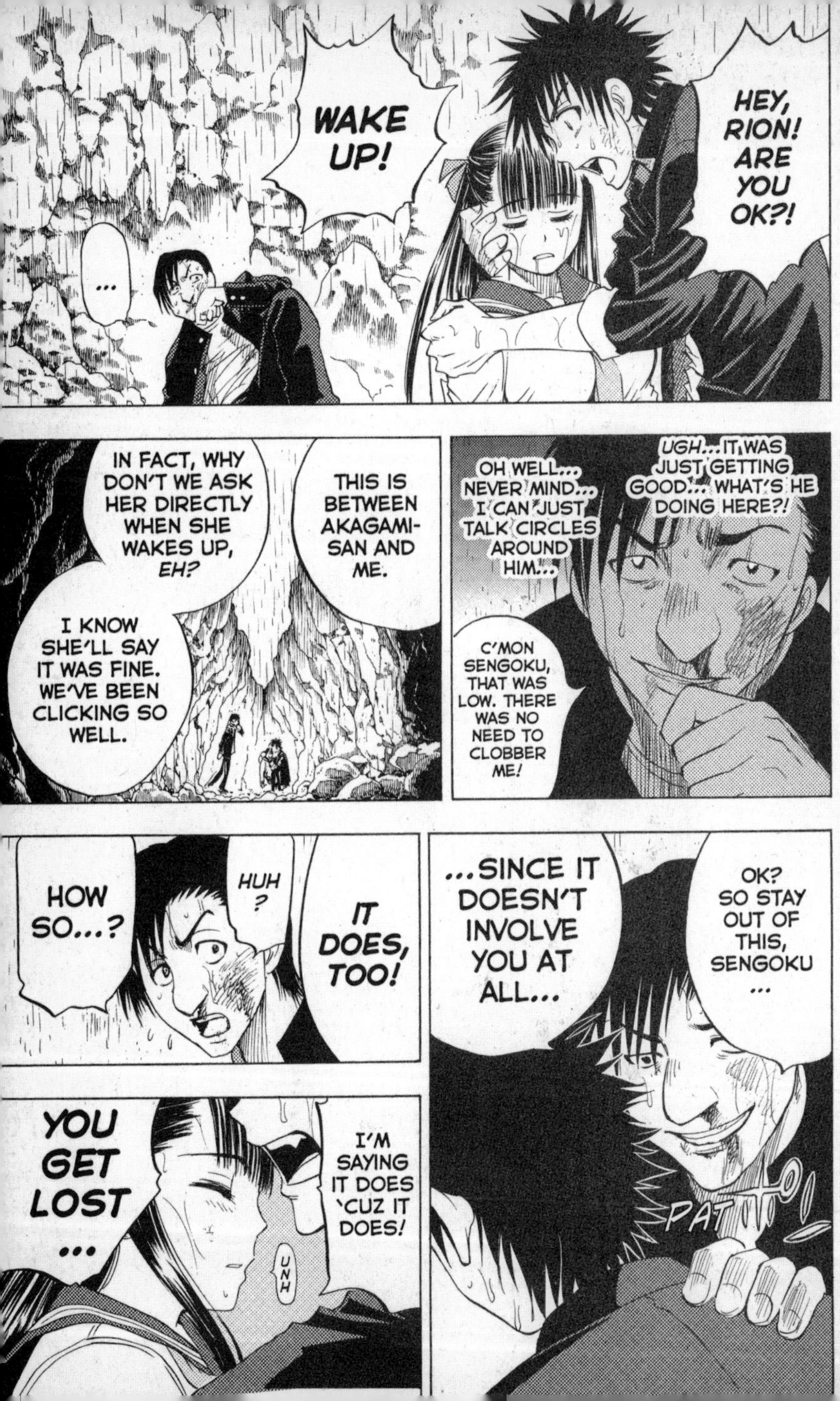
HEY, RION! ARE YOU OK?!
WAKE UP!
...
UGH... IT WAS JUST GETTING GOOD... WHAT'S HE DOING HERE?!
OH WELL... NEVER MIND... I CAN JUST TALK CIRCLES AROUND HIM...
C'MON SENGOKU, THAT WAS LOW. THERE WAS NO NEED TO CLOBBER ME!
THIS IS BETWEEN AKAGAMI-SAN AND ME.
IN FACT, WHY DON'T WE ASK HER DIRECTLY WHEN SHE WAKES UP, EH?
I KNOW SHE'LL SAY IT WAS FINE. WE'VE BEEN CLICKING SO WELL.
OK? SO STAY OUT OF THIS, SENGOKU ...
...SINCE IT DOESN'T INVOLVE YOU AT ALL...
PAT
IT DOES, TOO!
HUH?
HOW SO...?
I'M SAYING IT DOES 'CUZ IT DOES!
UNH
YOU GET LOST ...

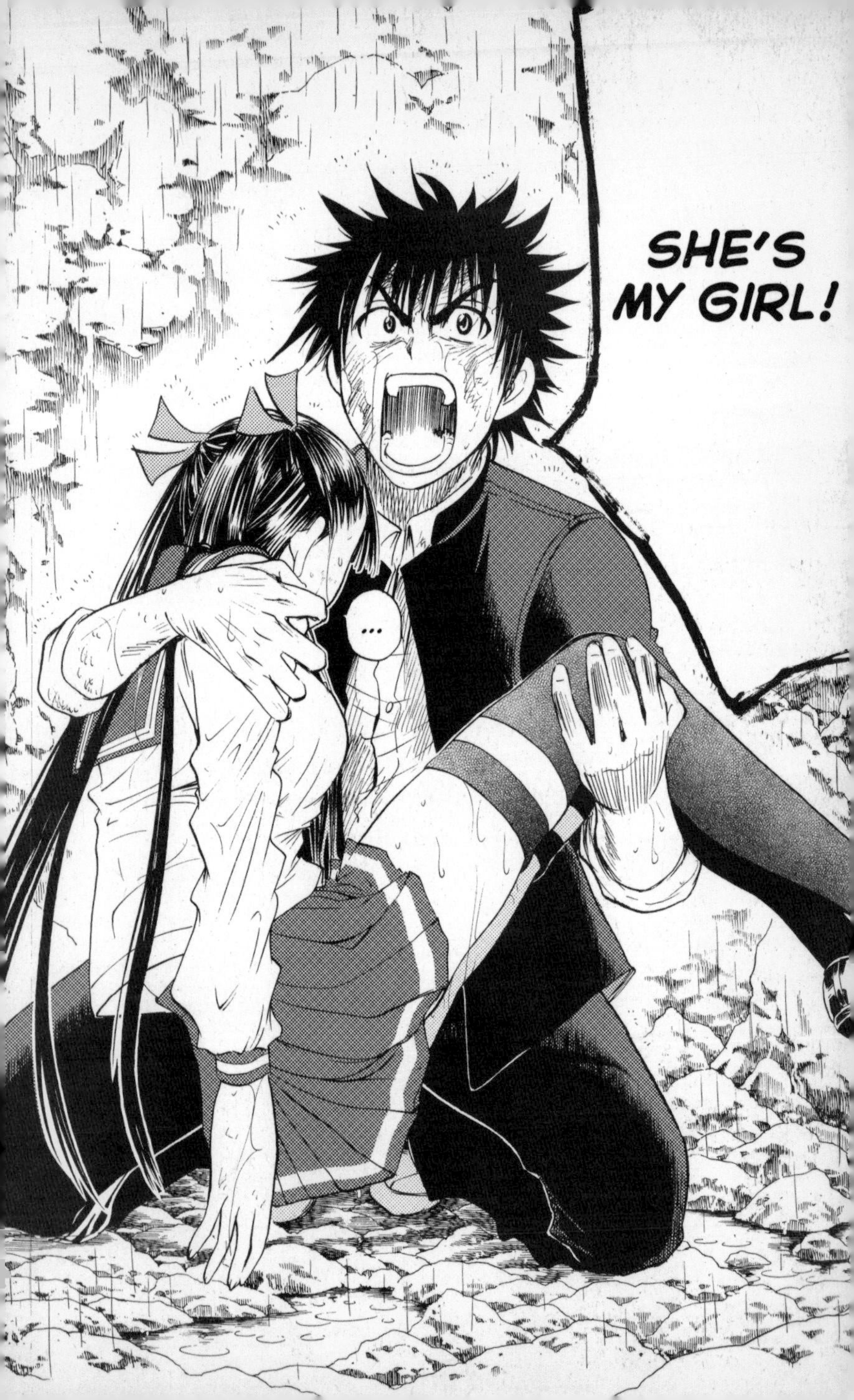
SHE'S MY GIRL!
...

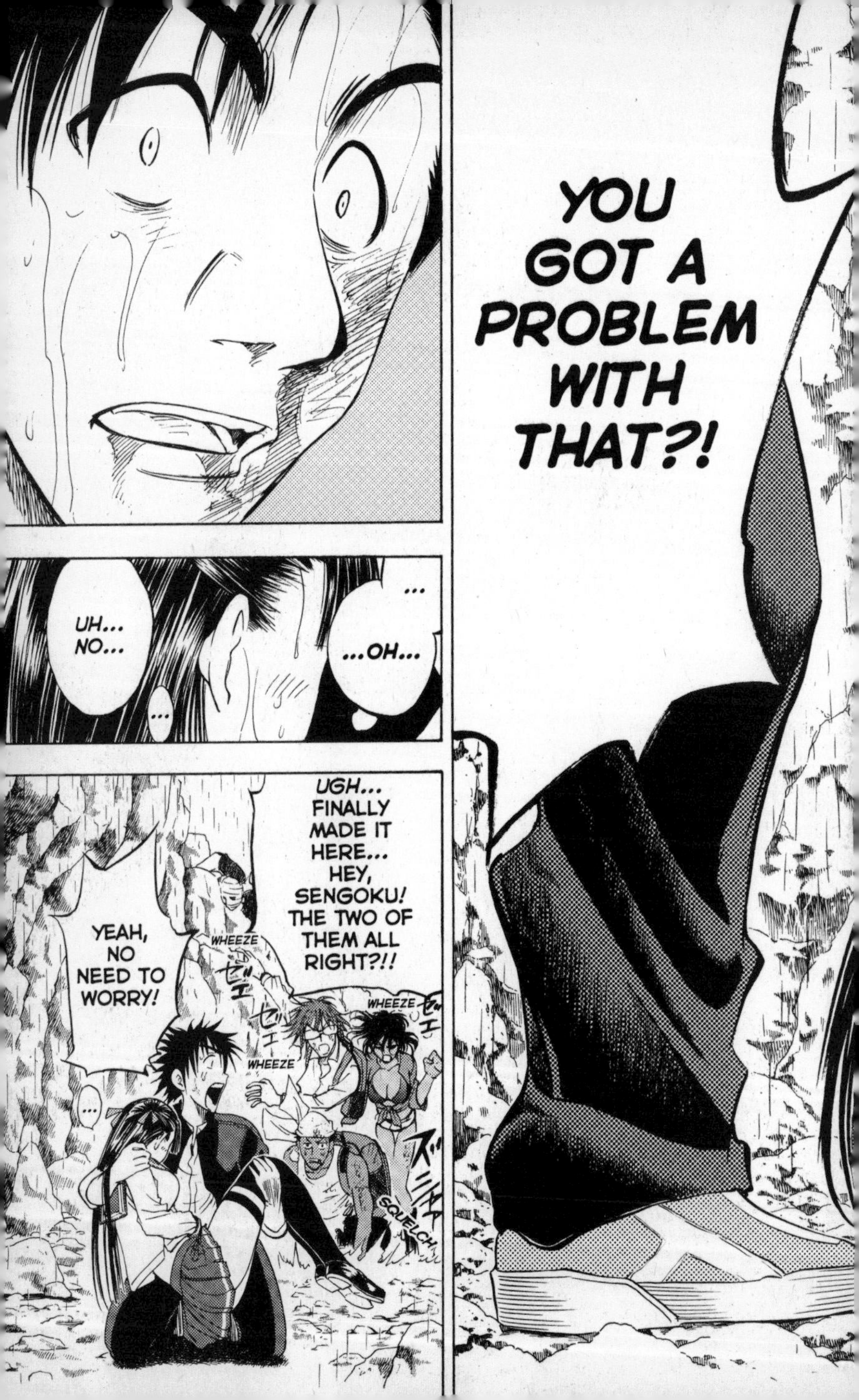
YOU GOT A PROBLEM WITH THAT?!
...
...OH...
UH... NO...
...
UGH... FINALLY MADE IT HERE... HEY, SENGOKU! THE TWO OF THEM ALL RIGHT?!!
WHEEZE
WHEEZE
WHEEZE
YEAH, NO NEED TO WORRY!
SQUELCH
...

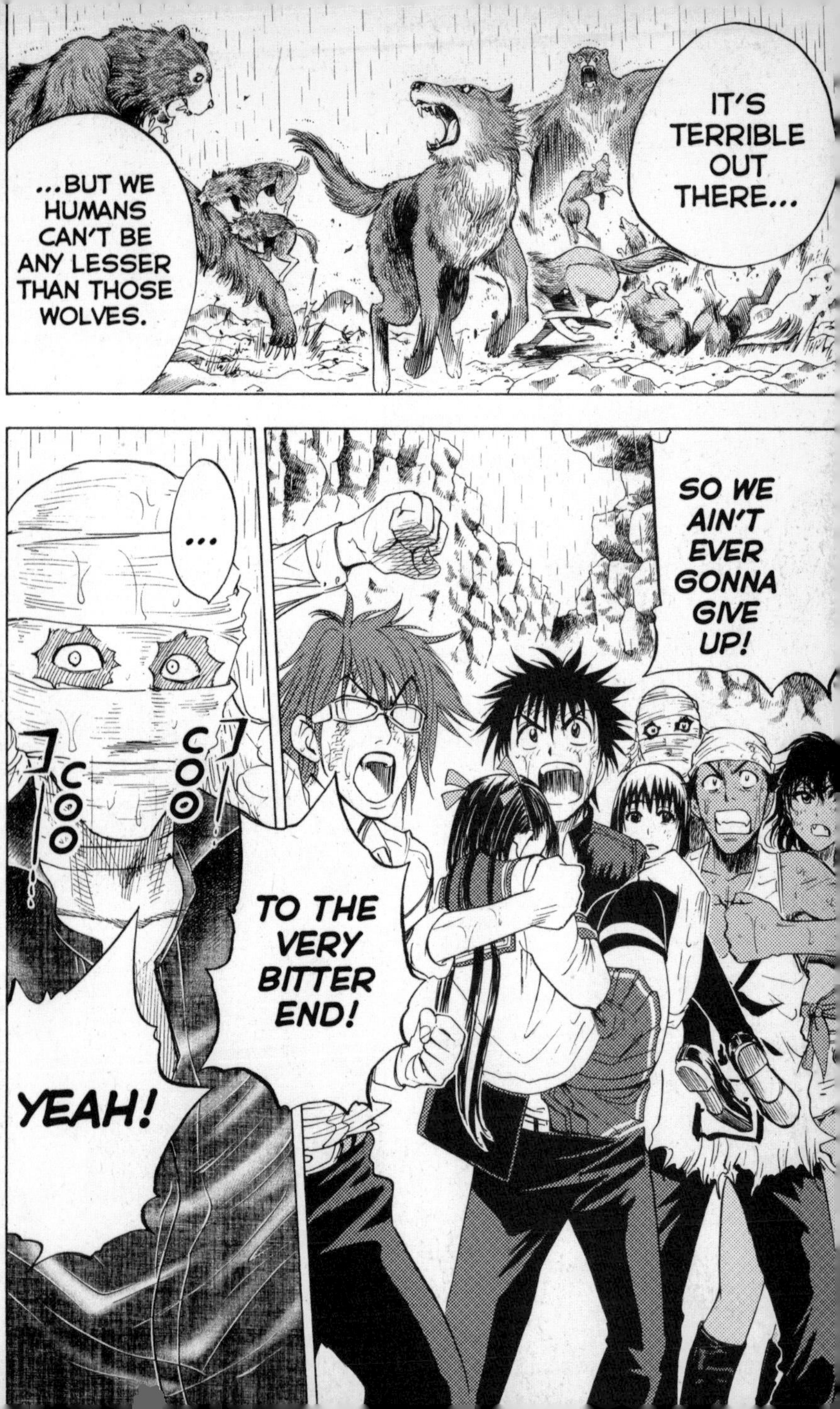
IT'S TERRIBLE OUT THERE...
...BUT WE HUMANS CAN'T BE ANY LESSER THAN THOSE WOLVES.
SO WE AIN'T EVER GONNA GIVE UP!
TO THE VERY BITTER END!
YEAH!
...
COO
COO

Episode 45 Means of Escape

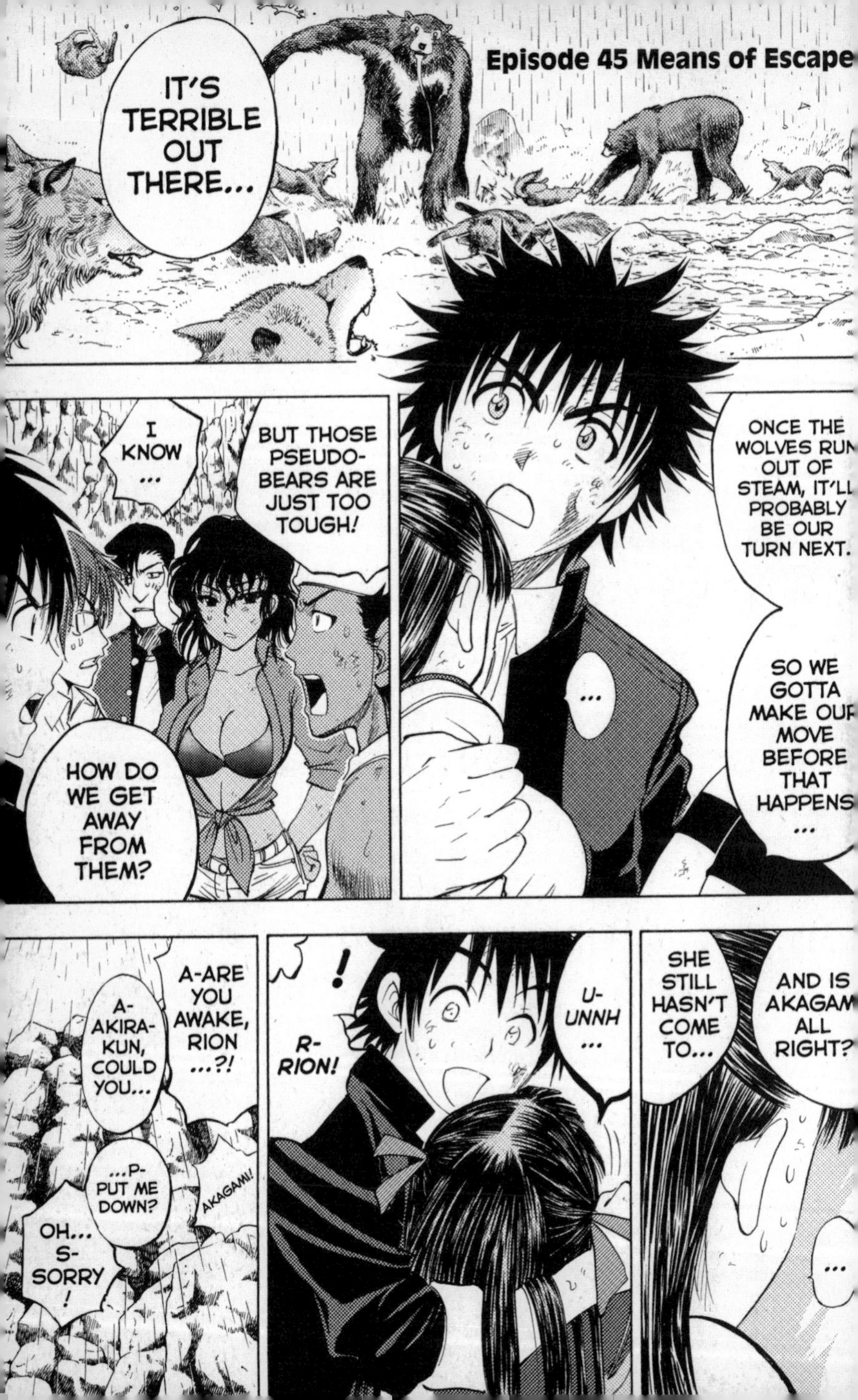

IT'S TERRIBLE OUT THERE...
ONCE THE WOLVES RUN OUT OF STEAM, IT'LL PROBABLY BE OUR TURN NEXT.
SO WE GOTTA MAKE OUR MOVE BEFORE THAT HAPPENS...
...
BUT THOSE PSEUDO-BEARS ARE JUST TOO TOUGH!
I KNOW...
HOW DO WE GET AWAY FROM THEM?
AND IS AKAGAM ALL RIGHT?
SHE STILL HASN'T COME TO...
...
U-UNNH...
!
R-RION!
A-ARE YOU AWAKE, RION...?!
A-AKIRA-KUN, COULD YOU...
...P-PUT ME DOWN?
AKAGAMI!
OH... S-SORRY!

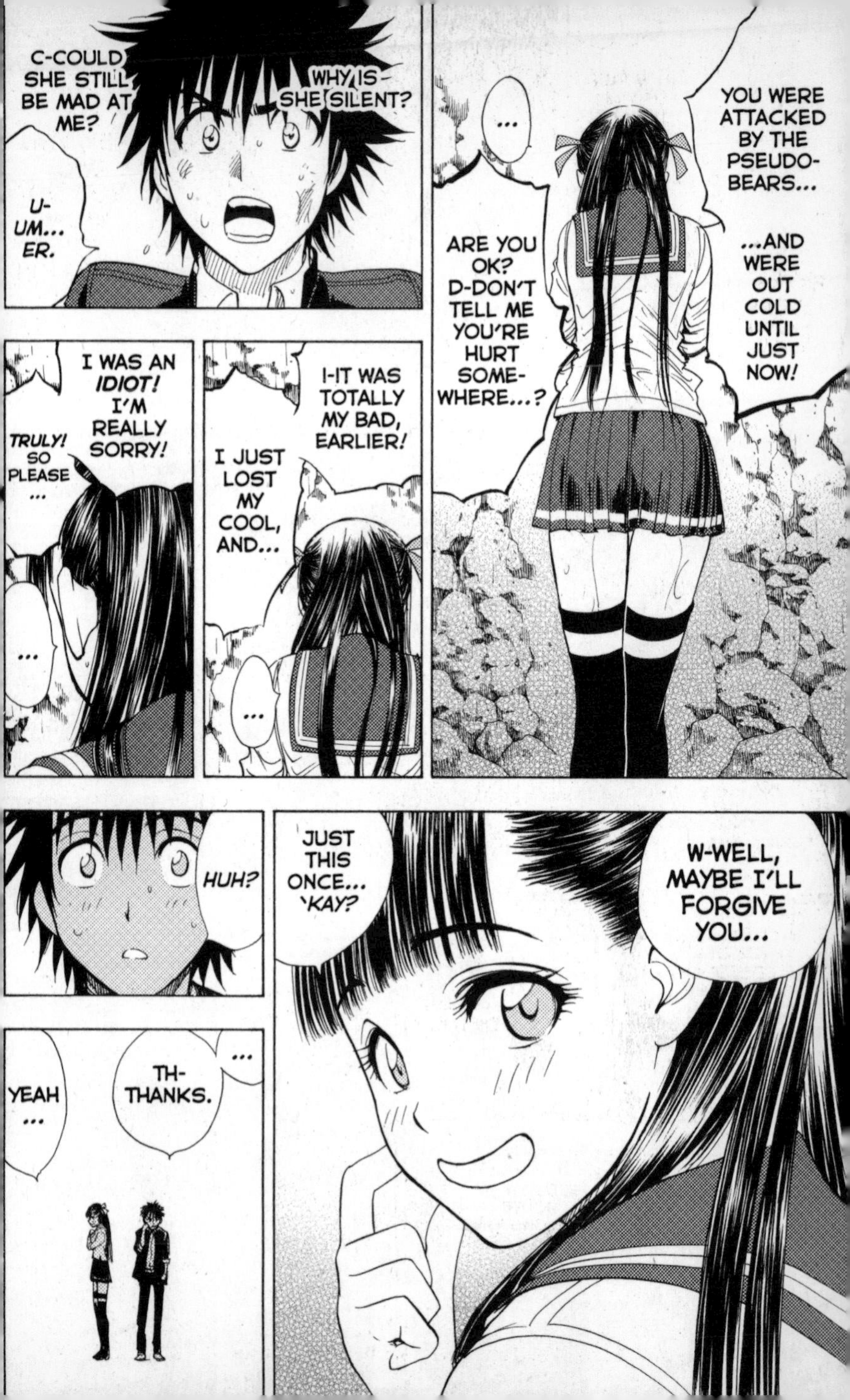
YOU WERE ATTACKED BY THE PSEUDO-BEARS...
...AND WERE OUT COLD UNTIL JUST NOW!
ARE YOU OK? D-DON'T TELL ME YOU'RE HURT SOME-WHERE...?
...
WHY IS SHE SILENT?
C-COULD SHE STILL BE MAD AT ME?
U-UM... ER.
I-IT WAS TOTALLY MY BAD, EARLIER!
I JUST LOST MY COOL, AND...
...
I WAS AN *IDIOT!* I'M REALLY SORRY!
TRULY! SO PLEASE...
...
W-WELL, MAYBE I'LL FORGIVE YOU...
JUST THIS ONCE... 'KAY?
HUH?
...
TH-THANKS.
YEAH...

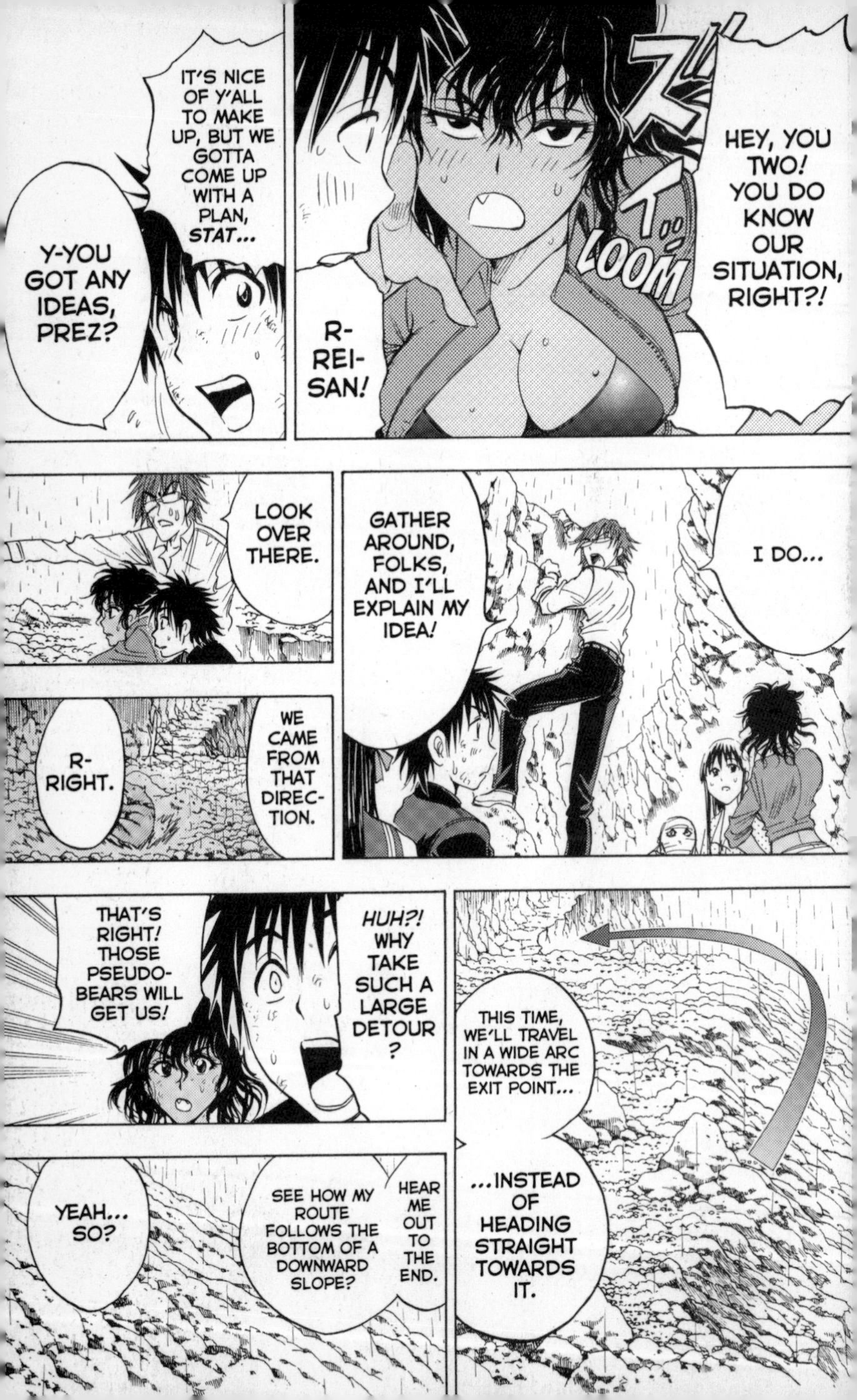
HEY, YOU TWO! YOU DO KNOW OUR SITUATION, RIGHT?!
LOOM
R-REI-SAN!
IT'S NICE OF Y'ALL TO MAKE UP, BUT WE GOTTA COME UP WITH A PLAN, *STAT*...
Y-YOU GOT ANY IDEAS, PREZ?
I DO...
GATHER AROUND, FOLKS, AND I'LL EXPLAIN MY IDEA!
LOOK OVER THERE.
WE CAME FROM THAT DIREC-TION.
R-RIGHT.
THIS TIME, WE'LL TRAVEL IN A WIDE ARC TOWARDS THE EXIT POINT...
...INSTEAD OF HEADING STRAIGHT TOWARDS IT.
HUH?! WHY TAKE SUCH A LARGE DETOUR?
THAT'S RIGHT! THOSE PSEUDO-BEARS WILL GET US!
HEAR ME OUT TO THE END.
SEE HOW MY ROUTE FOLLOWS THE BOTTOM OF A DOWNWARD SLOPE?
YEAH... SO?

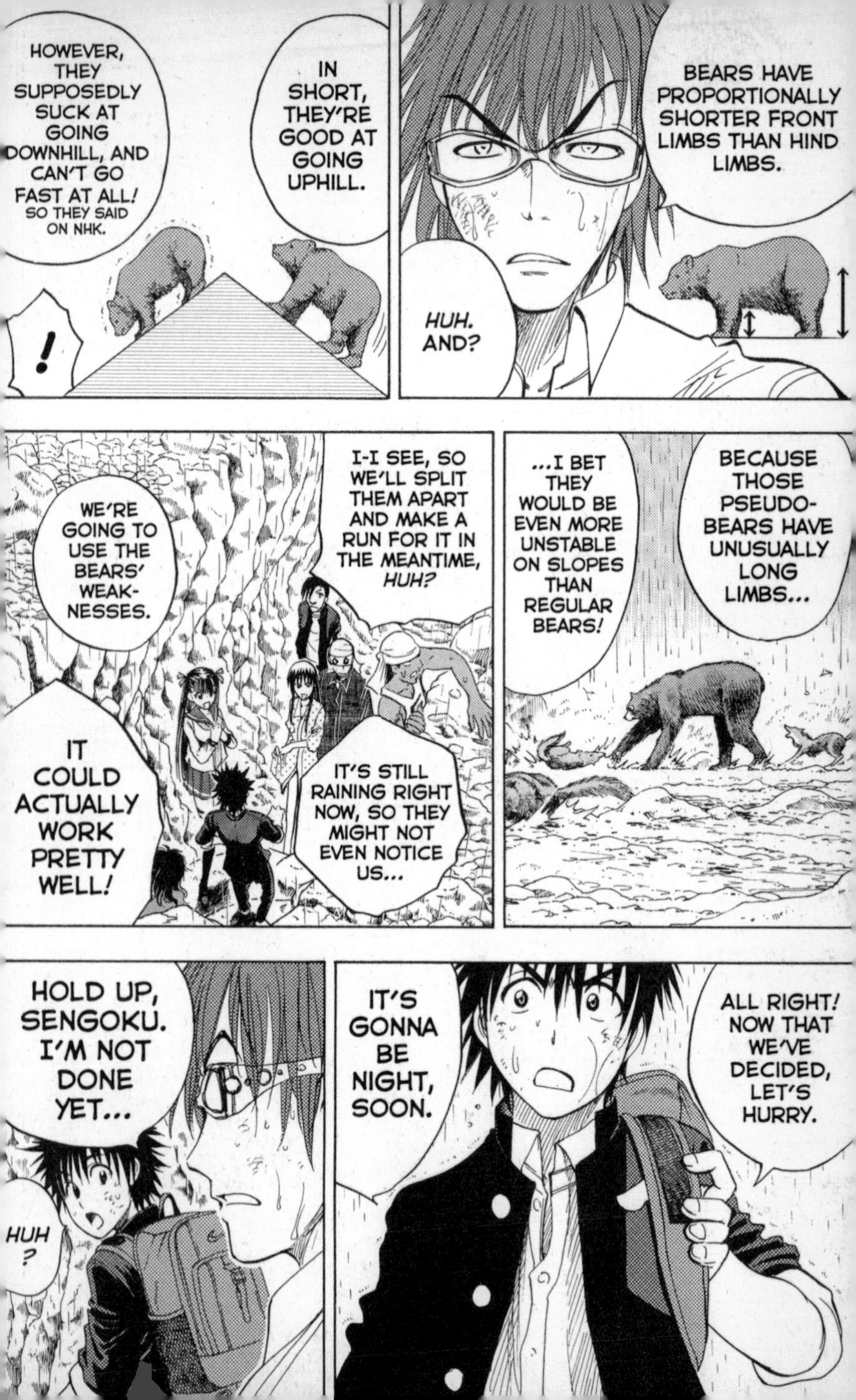
BEARS HAVE PROPORTIONALLY SHORTER FRONT LIMBS THAN HIND LIMBS.
HUH. AND?
IN SHORT, THEY'RE GOOD AT GOING UPHILL.
HOWEVER, THEY SUPPOSEDLY SUCK AT GOING DOWNHILL, AND CAN'T GO FAST AT ALL! SO THEY SAID ON NHK.
!
BECAUSE THOSE PSEUDO-BEARS HAVE UNUSUALLY LONG LIMBS...
...I BET THEY WOULD BE EVEN MORE UNSTABLE ON SLOPES THAN REGULAR BEARS!
I-I SEE, SO WE'LL SPLIT THEM APART AND MAKE A RUN FOR IT IN THE MEANTIME, *HUH?*
WE'RE GOING TO USE THE BEARS' WEAKNESSES.
IT'S STILL RAINING RIGHT NOW, SO THEY MIGHT NOT EVEN NOTICE US...
IT COULD ACTUALLY WORK PRETTY WELL!
ALL RIGHT! NOW THAT WE'VE DECIDED, LET'S HURRY.
IT'S GONNA BE NIGHT, SOON.
HOLD UP, SENGOKU. I'M NOT DONE YET...
HUH?

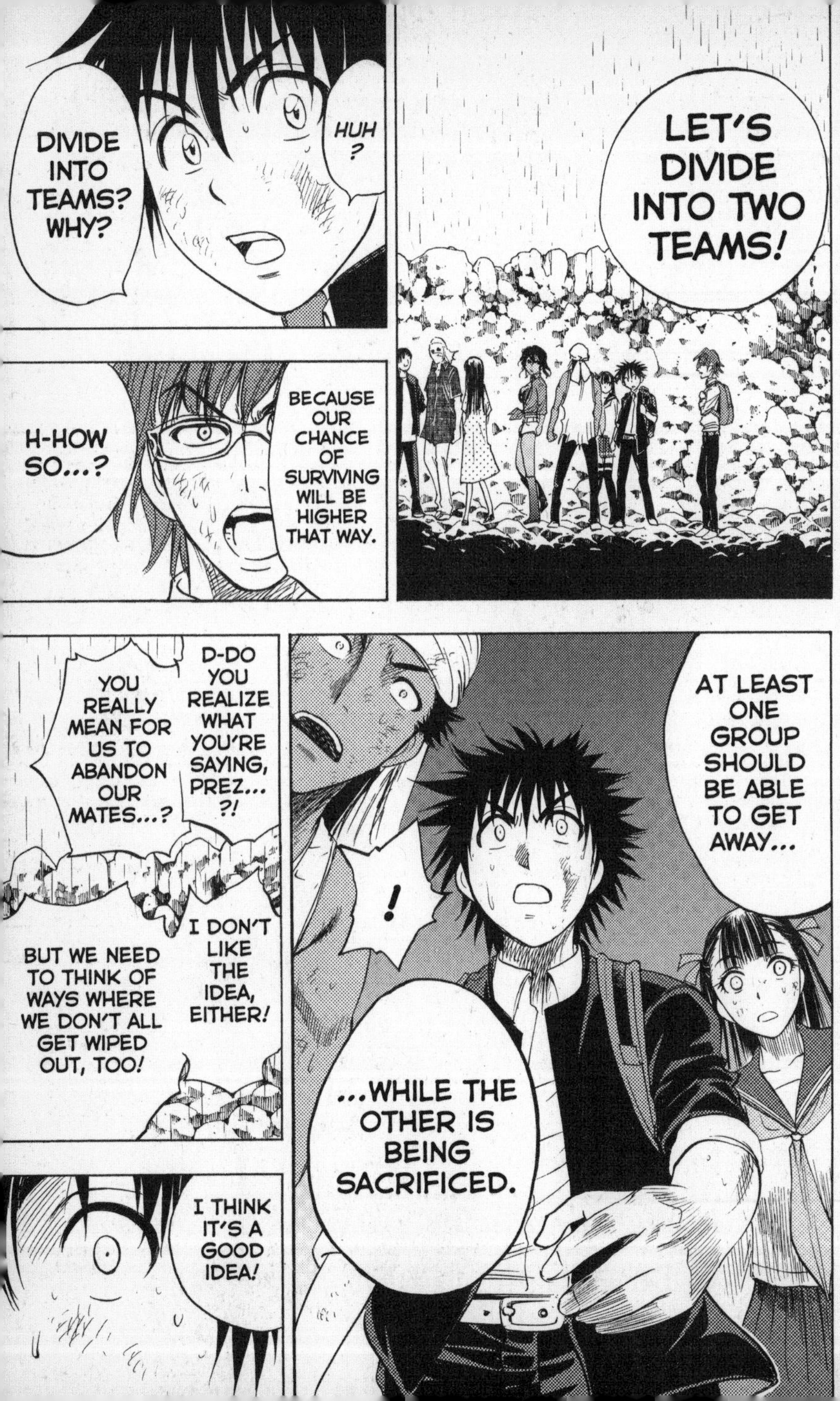
LET'S DIVIDE INTO TWO TEAMS!
HUH?
DIVIDE INTO TEAMS? WHY?
BECAUSE OUR CHANCE OF SURVIVING WILL BE HIGHER THAT WAY.
H-HOW SO...?
AT LEAST ONE GROUP SHOULD BE ABLE TO GET AWAY...
!
...WHILE THE OTHER IS BEING SACRIFICED.
D-DO YOU REALIZE WHAT YOU'RE SAYING, PREZ...?!
YOU REALLY MEAN FOR US TO ABANDON OUR MATES...?
I DON'T LIKE THE IDEA, EITHER!
BUT WE NEED TO THINK OF WAYS WHERE WE DON'T ALL GET WIPED OUT, TOO!
I THINK IT'S A GOOD IDEA!

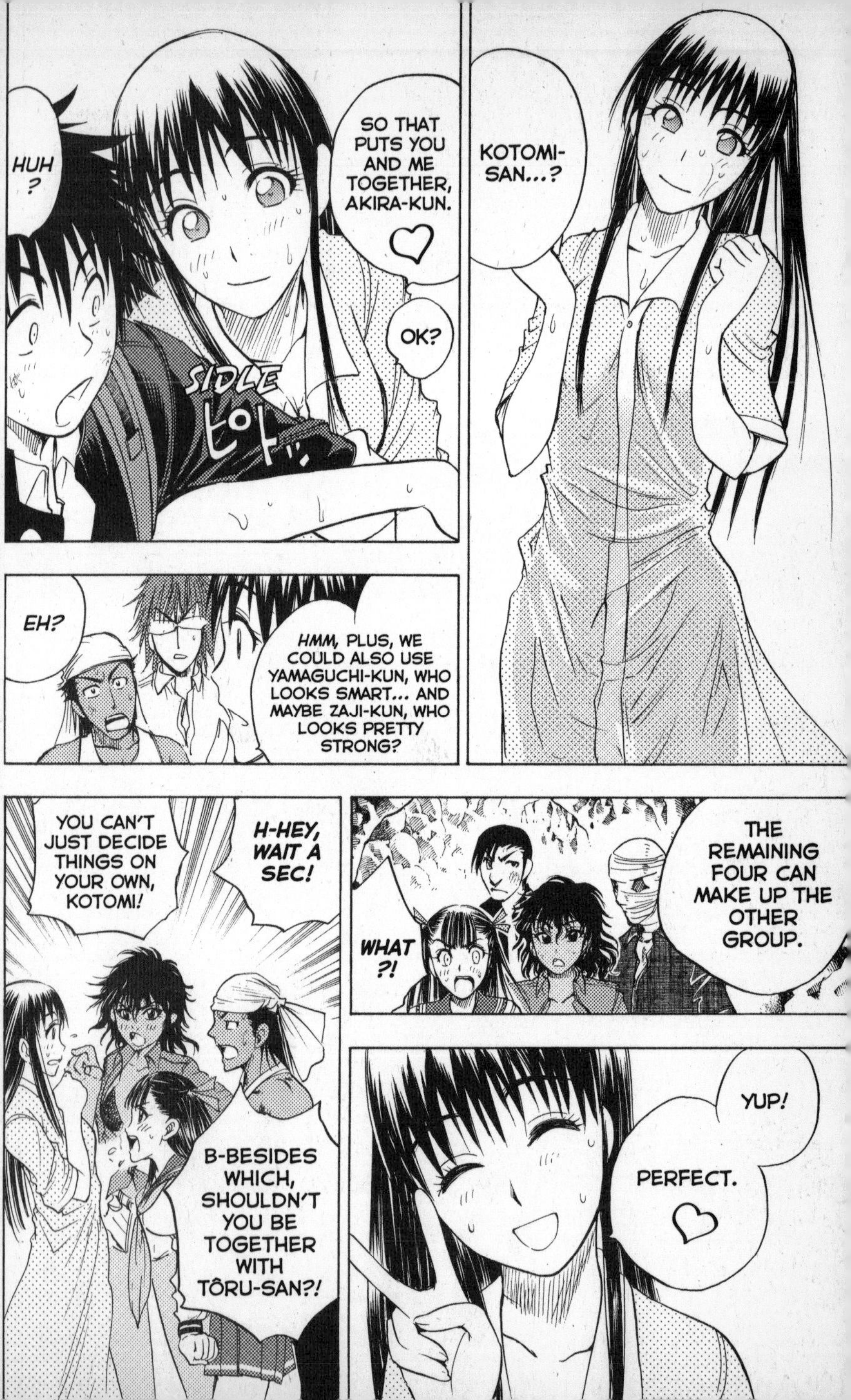
KOTOMI-SAN...?
SO THAT PUTS YOU AND ME TOGETHER, AKIRA-KUN.
OK?
HUH?
SIDLE
HMM, PLUS, WE COULD ALSO USE YAMAGUCHI-KUN, WHO LOOKS SMART... AND MAYBE ZAJI-KUN, WHO LOOKS PRETTY STRONG?
EH?
THE REMAINING FOUR CAN MAKE UP THE OTHER GROUP.
WHAT?!
YUP!
PERFECT.
H-HEY, WAIT A SEC!
YOU CAN'T JUST DECIDE THINGS ON YOUR OWN, KOTOMI!
B-BESIDES WHICH, SHOULDN'T YOU BE TOGETHER WITH TÔRU-SAN?!

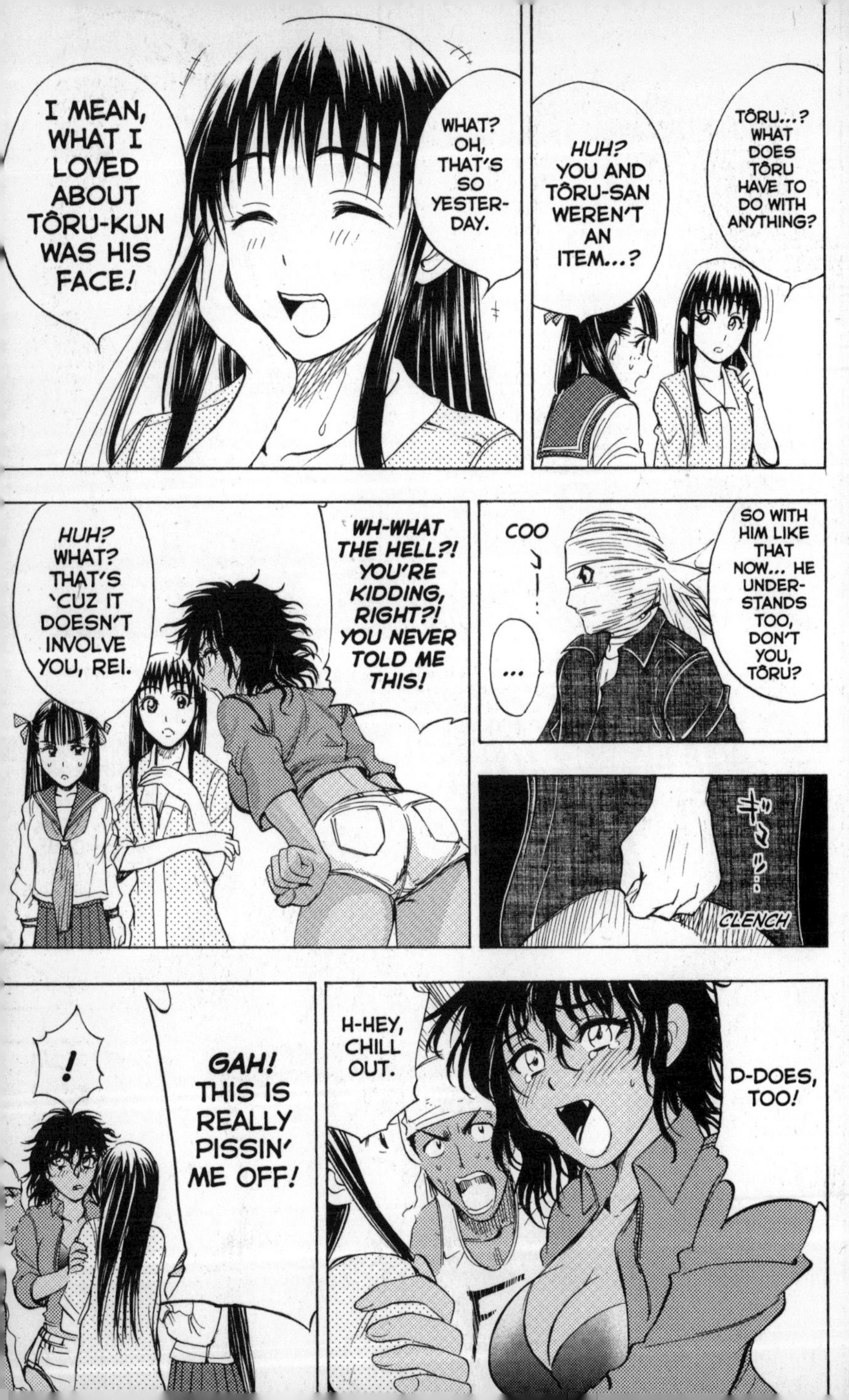
TÔRU...? WHAT DOES TÔRU HAVE TO DO WITH ANYTHING?
HUH? YOU AND TÔRU-SAN WEREN'T AN ITEM...?
WHAT? OH, THAT'S SO YESTER-DAY.
I MEAN, WHAT I LOVED ABOUT TÔRU-KUN WAS HIS FACE!
SO WITH HIM LIKE THAT NOW... HE UNDER-STANDS TOO, DON'T YOU, TÔRU?
COO
...
CLENCH
WH-WHAT THE HELL?! YOU'RE KIDDING, RIGHT?! YOU NEVER TOLD ME THIS!
HUH? WHAT? THAT'S 'CUZ IT DOESN'T INVOLVE YOU, REI.
D-DOES, TOO!
H-HEY, CHILL OUT.
GAH! THIS IS REALLY PISSIN' ME OFF!
!

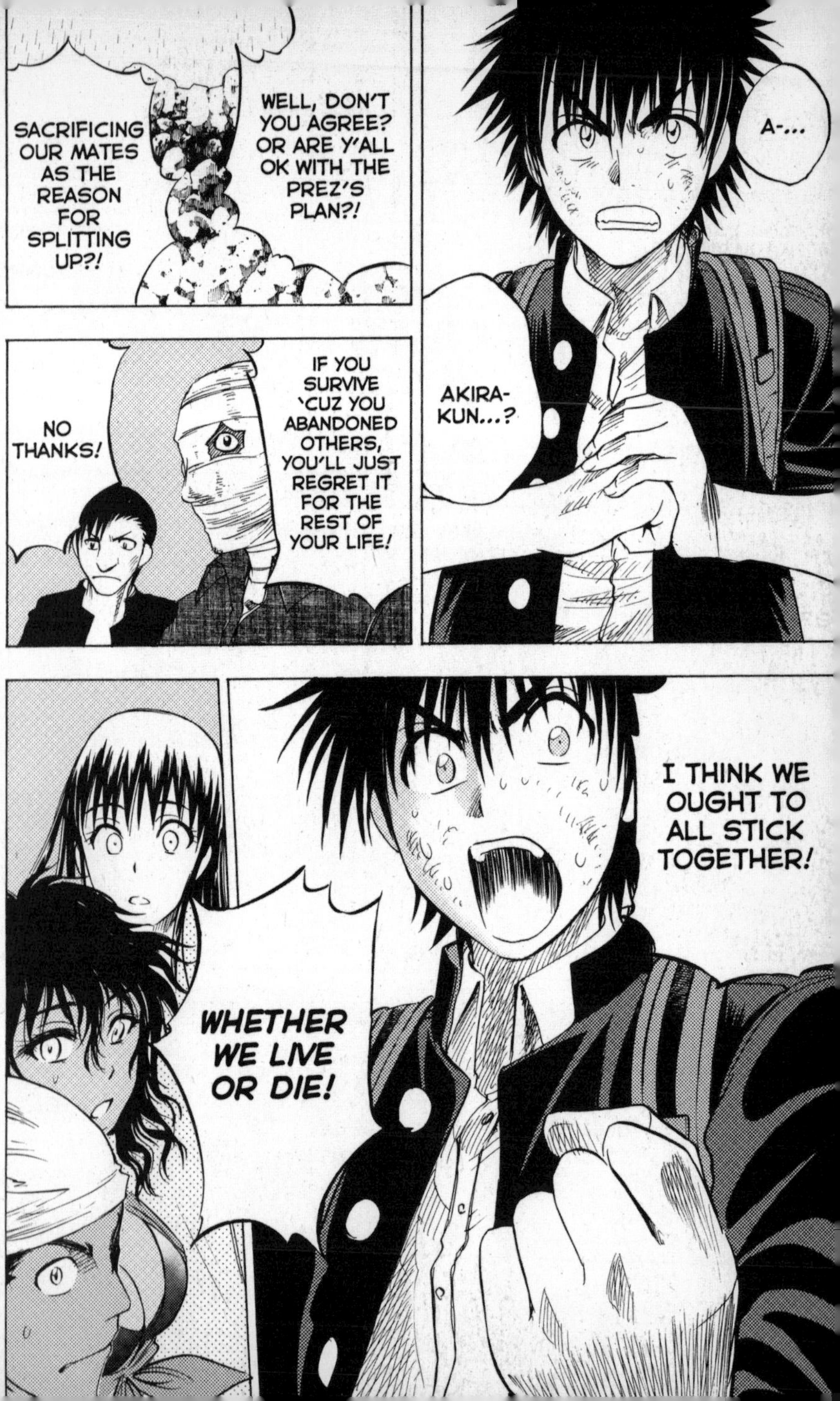
A-...
AKIRA-KUN...?
WELL, DON'T YOU AGREE? OR ARE Y'ALL OK WITH THE PREZ'S PLAN?!
SACRIFICING OUR MATES AS THE REASON FOR SPLITTING UP?!
IF YOU SURVIVE 'CUZ YOU ABANDONED OTHERS, YOU'LL JUST REGRET IT FOR THE REST OF YOUR LIFE!
NO THANKS!
I THINK WE OUGHT TO ALL STICK TOGETHER!
WHETHER WE LIVE OR DIE!

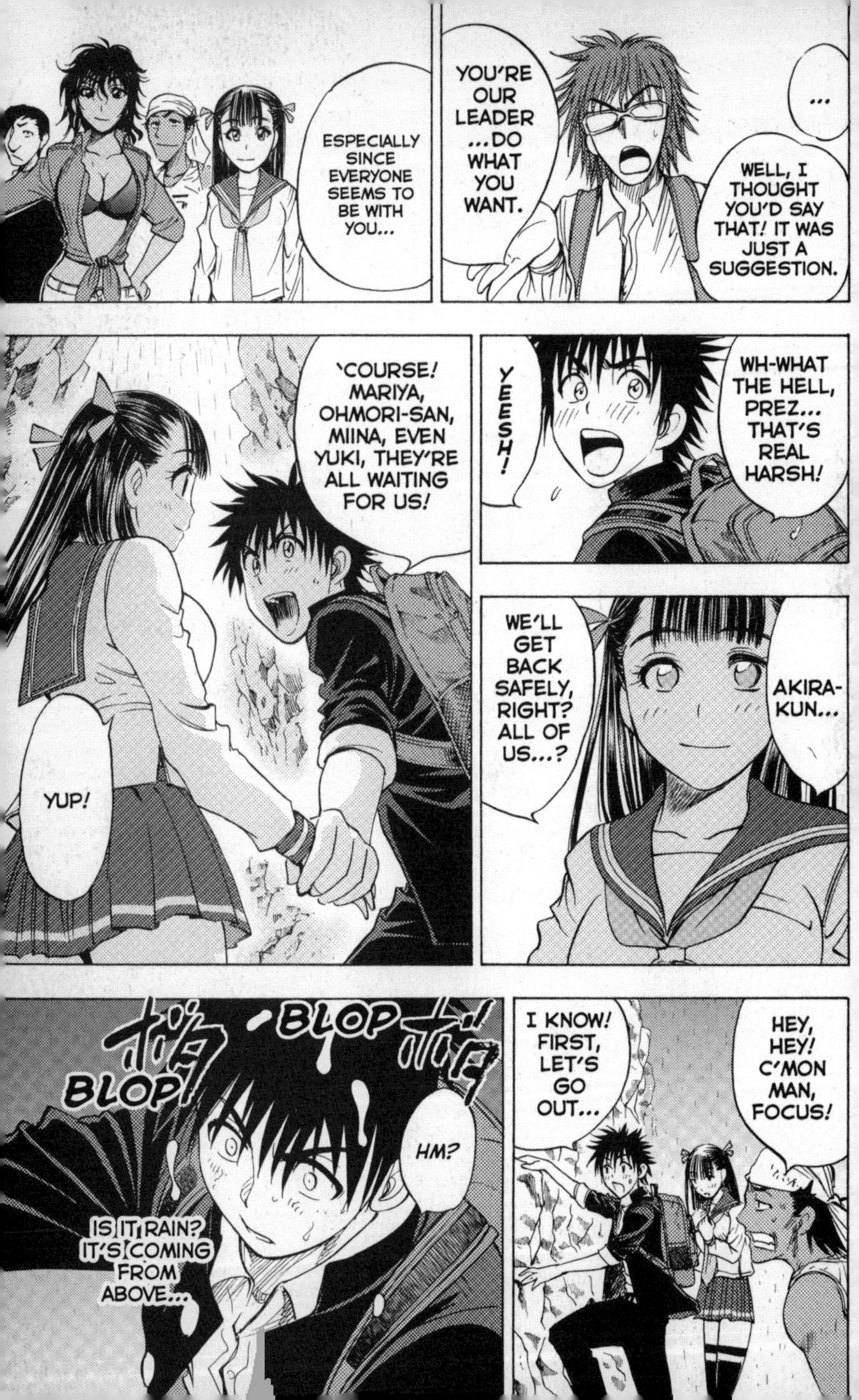
...
WELL, I THOUGHT YOU'D SAY THAT! IT WAS JUST A SUGGESTION.
YOU'RE OUR LEADER ...DO WHAT YOU WANT.
ESPECIALLY SINCE EVERYONE SEEMS TO BE WITH YOU...
WH-WHAT THE HELL, PREZ... THAT'S REAL HARSH!
YEESH!
AKIRA-KUN...
WE'LL GET BACK SAFELY, RIGHT? ALL OF US...?
'COURSE! MARIYA, OHMORI-SAN, MIINA, EVEN YUKI, THEY'RE ALL WAITING FOR US!
YUP!
HEY, HEY! C'MON MAN, FOCUS!
I KNOW! FIRST, LET'S GO OUT...
BLOP
BLOP
HM?
IS IT RAIN? IT'S COMING FROM ABOVE...

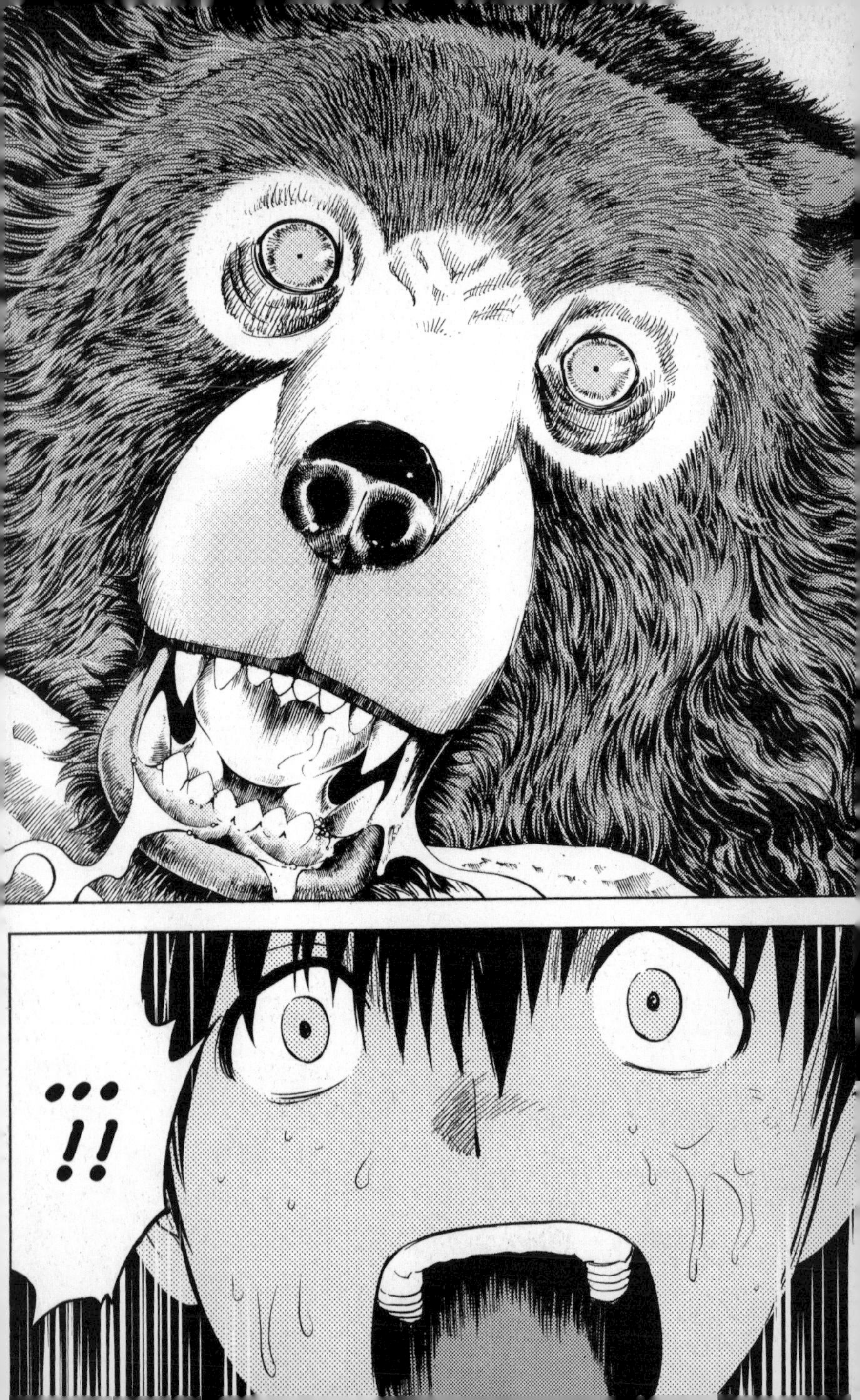
..!!

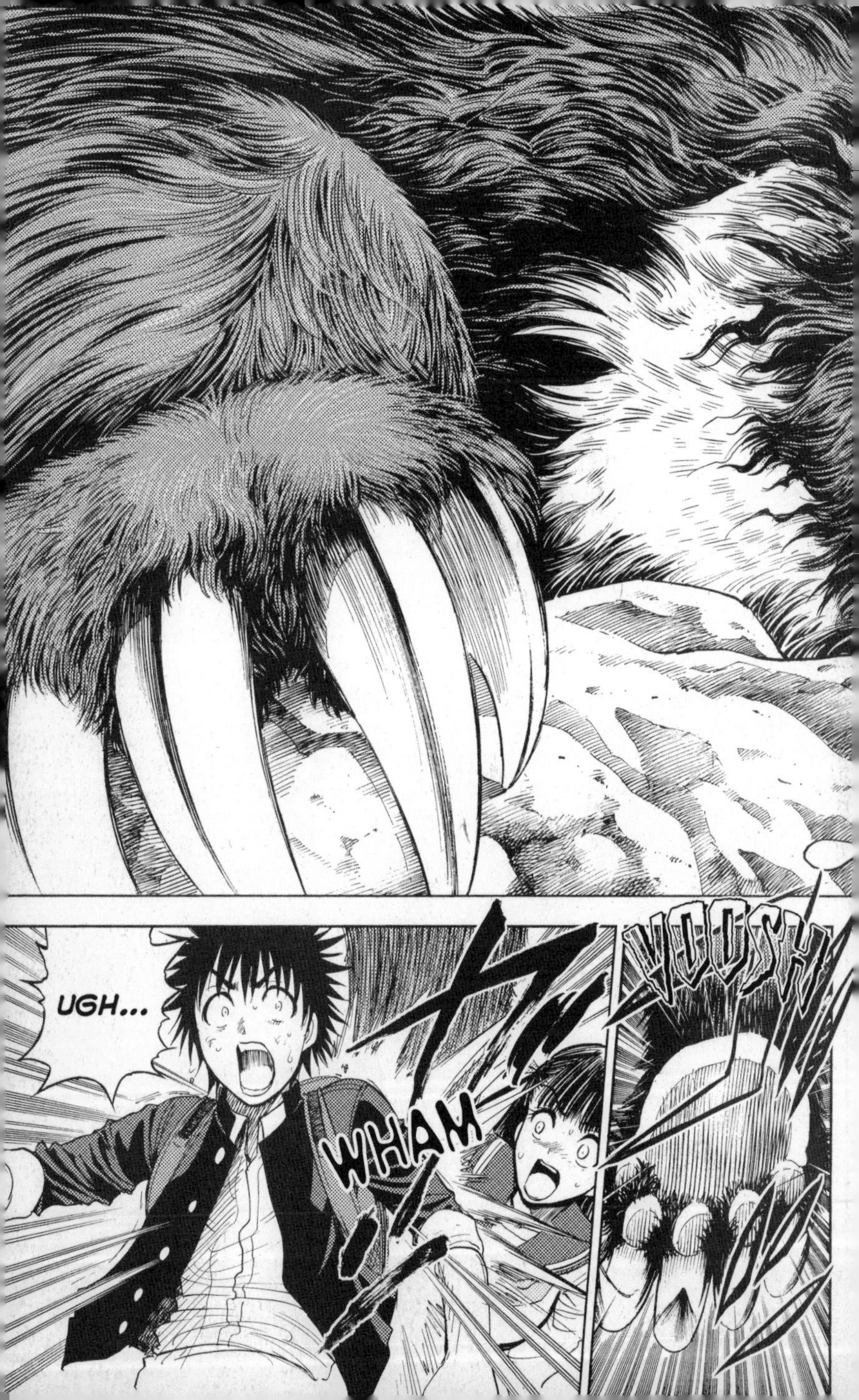
VOOSH
UGH...
WHAM

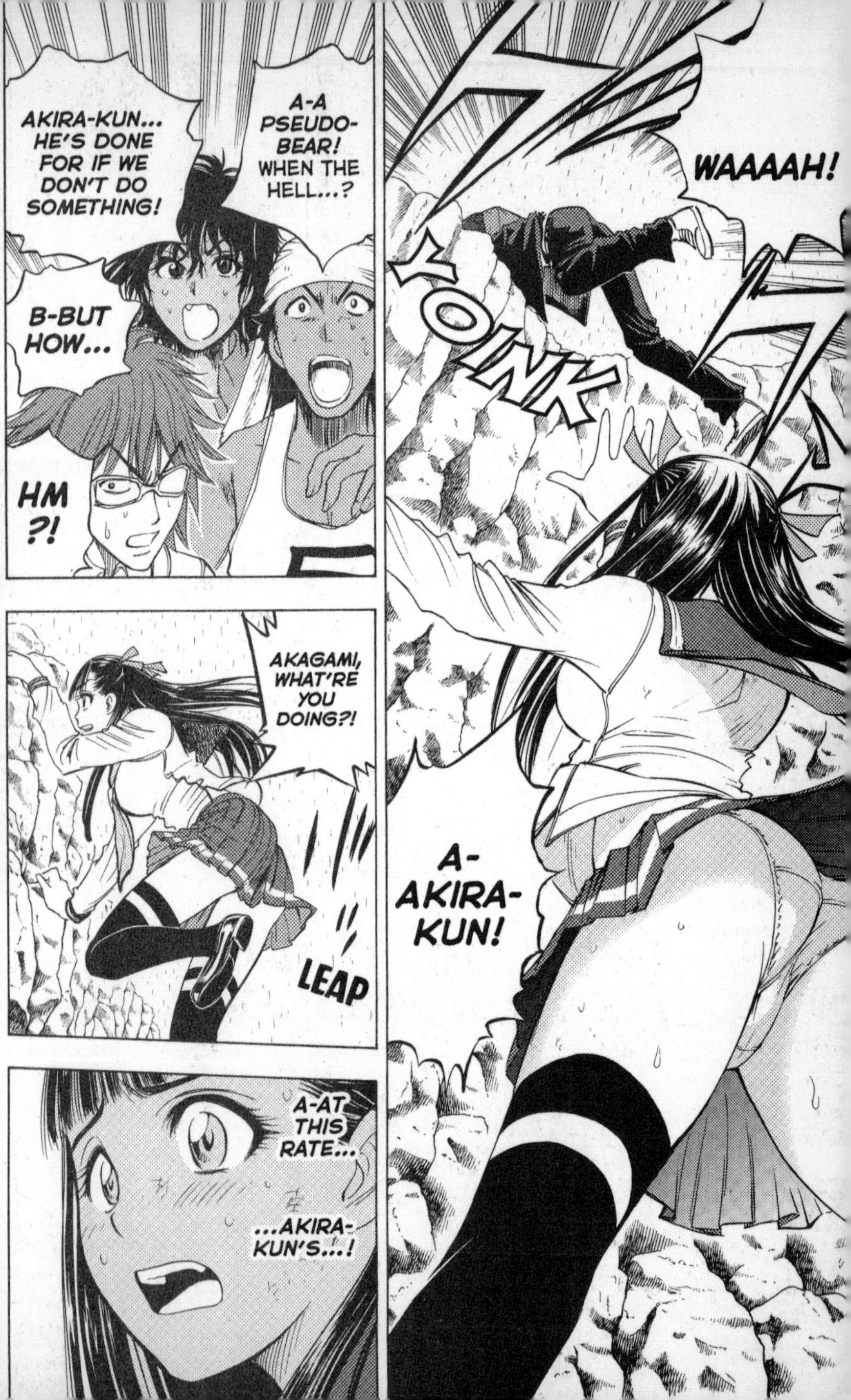
WAAAAH!
YOINK
A-AKIRA-KUN!
A-A PSEUDO-BEAR! WHEN THE HELL...?
AKIRA-KUN... HE'S DONE FOR IF WE DON'T DO SOMETHING!
B-BUT HOW...
HM ?!
AKAGAMI, WHAT'RE YOU DOING?!
LEAP
A-AT THIS RATE...
...AKIRA-KUN'S...!

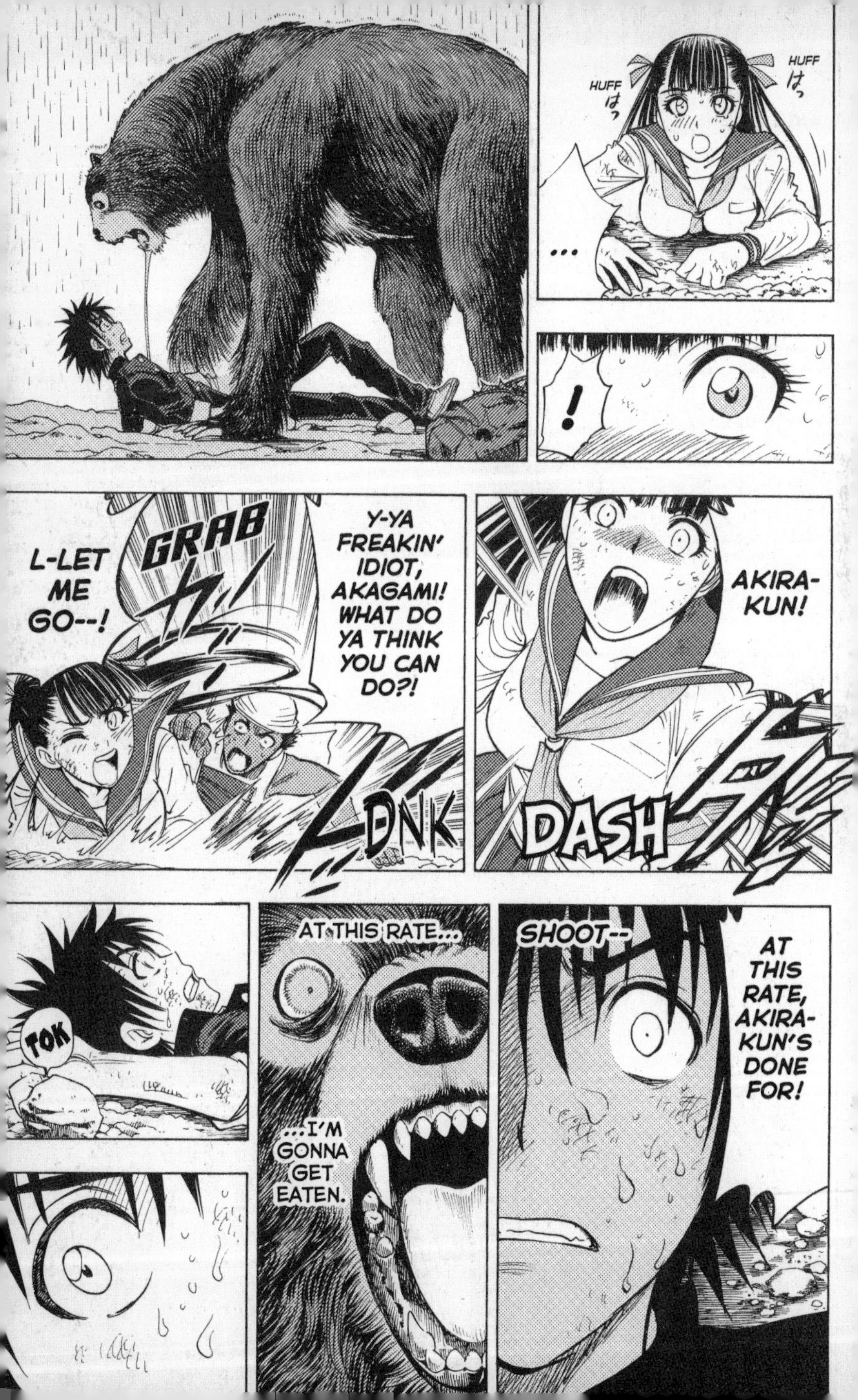
HUFF
はっ
HUFF
はっ
...
!
AKIRA-KUN!
DASH
Y-YA FREAKIN' IDIOT, AKAGAMI! WHAT DO YA THINK YOU CAN DO?!
GRAB
L-LET ME GO--!
DNK
SHOOT--
AT THIS RATE, AKIRA-KUN'S DONE FOR!
AT THIS RATE...
...I'M GONNA GET EATEN.
TOK

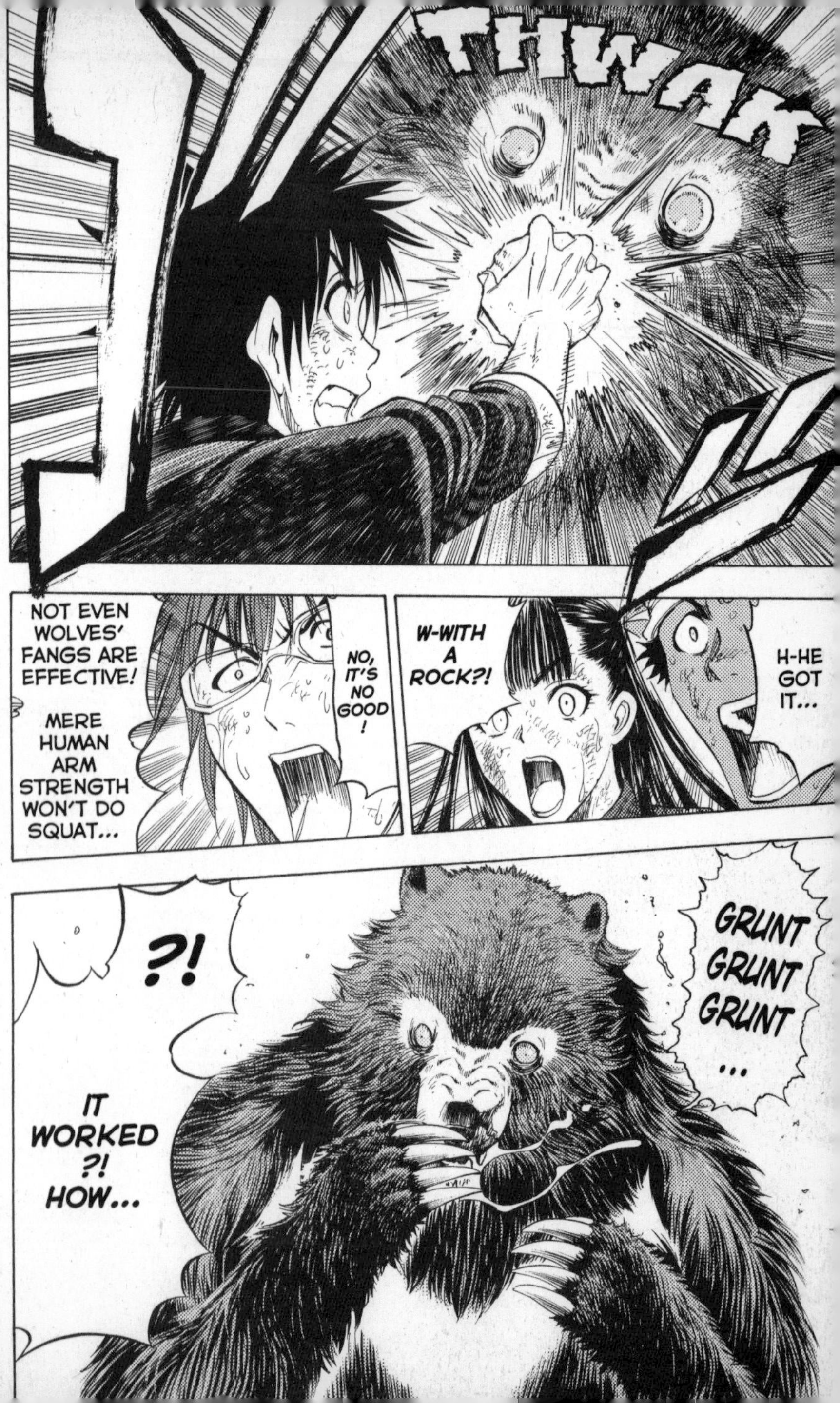
THWAK
H-HE GOT IT...
W-WITH A ROCK?!
NO, IT'S NO GOOD!
NOT EVEN WOLVES' FANGS ARE EFFECTIVE!
MERE HUMAN ARM STRENGTH WON'T DO SQUAT...
GRUNT GRUNT GRUNT...
?!
IT WORKED?! HOW...

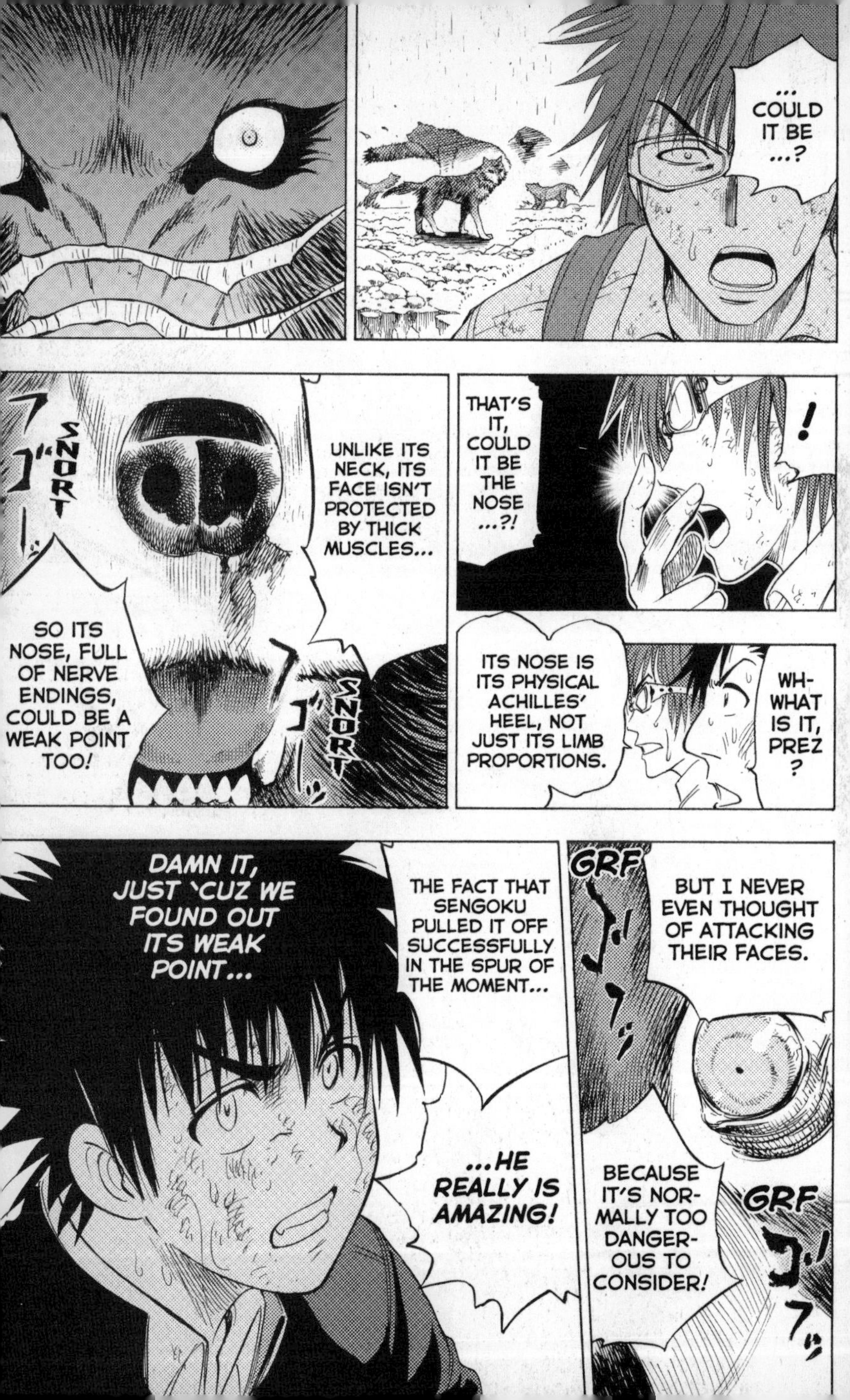
...COULD IT BE ...?
!
THAT'S IT, COULD IT BE THE NOSE ...?!
WH- WHAT IS IT, PREZ ?
ITS NOSE IS ITS PHYSICAL ACHILLES' HEEL, NOT JUST ITS LIMB PROPORTIONS.
UNLIKE ITS NECK, ITS FACE ISN'T PROTECTED BY THICK MUSCLES...
SNORT
SO ITS NOSE, FULL OF NERVE ENDINGS, COULD BE A WEAK POINT TOO!
SNORT
GRF
BUT I NEVER EVEN THOUGHT OF ATTACKING THEIR FACES.
BECAUSE IT'S NORMALLY TOO DANGEROUS TO CONSIDER!
GRF
THE FACT THAT SENGOKU PULLED IT OFF SUCCESSFULLY IN THE SPUR OF THE MOMENT...
DAMN IT, JUST 'CUZ WE FOUND OUT ITS WEAK POINT...
...HE REALLY IS AMAZING!

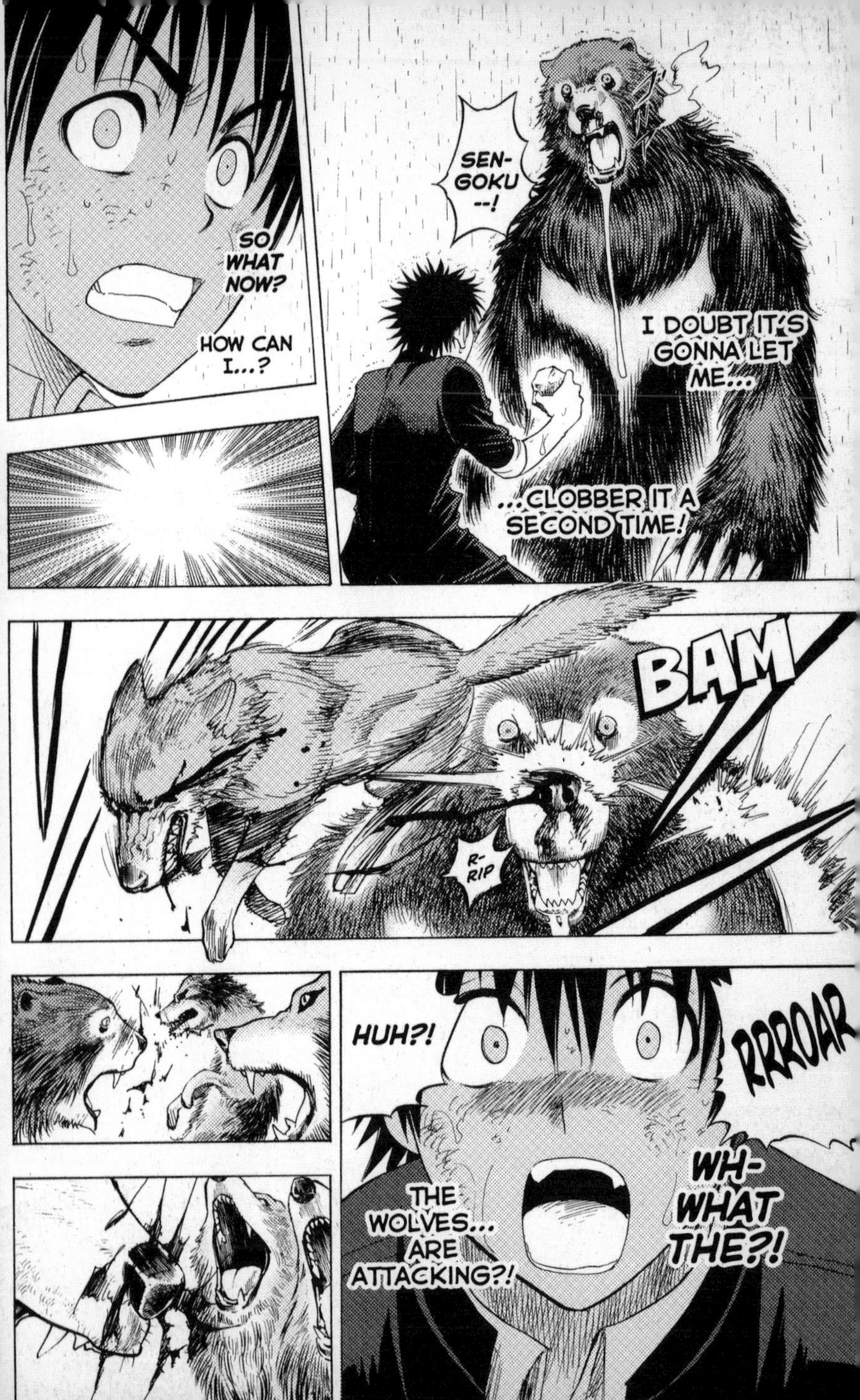
SEN-GOKU--!
I DOUBT IT'S GONNA LET ME...
...CLOBBER IT A SECOND TIME!
SO WHAT NOW?
HOW CAN I...?
BAM
R-RIP
RRROAR
HUH?!
WH-WHAT THE?!
THE WOLVES... ARE ATTACKING?!

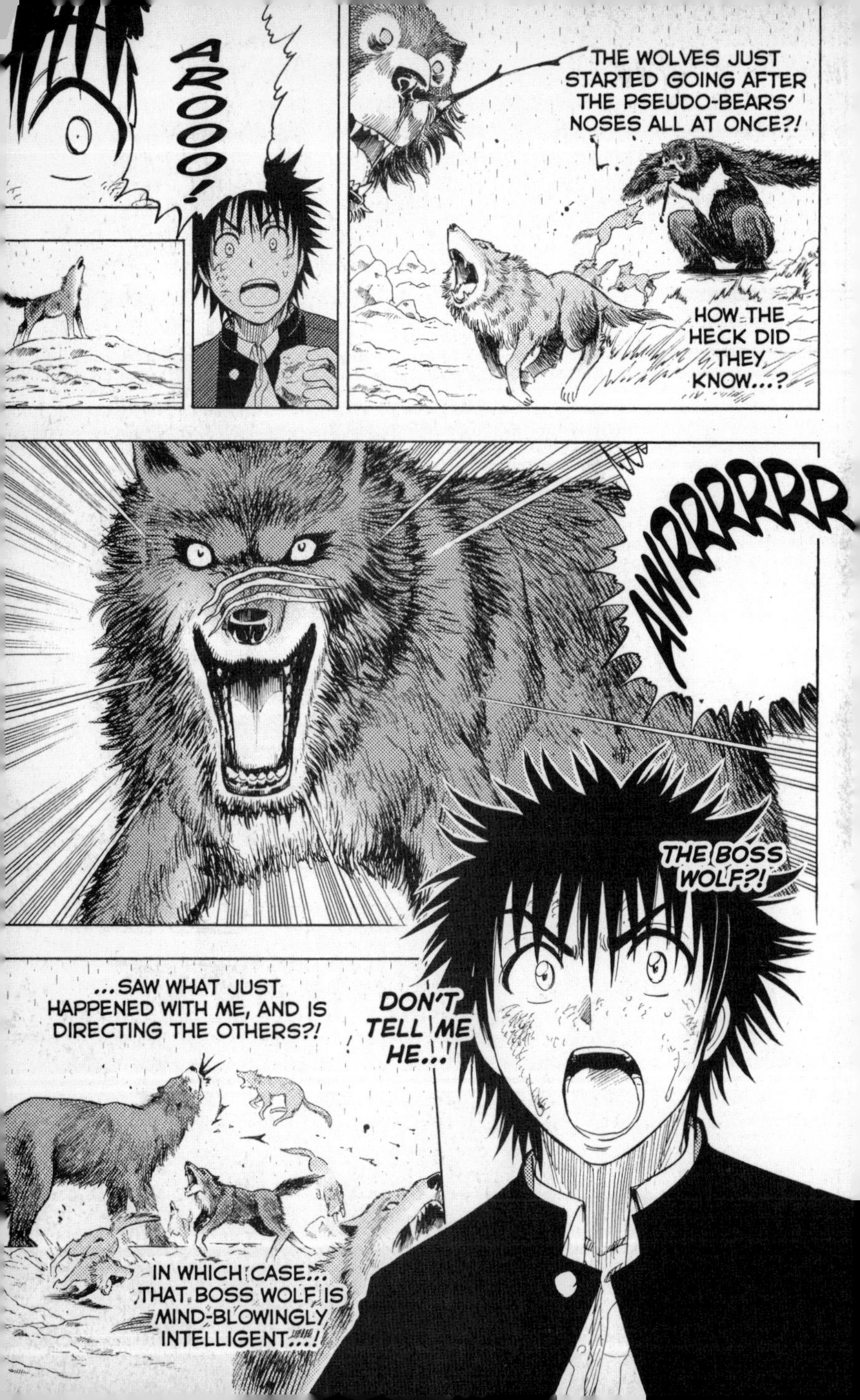
THE WOLVES JUST STARTED GOING AFTER THE PSEUDO-BEARS' NOSES ALL AT ONCE?!
HOW THE HECK DID THEY KNOW...?
AROOO!
AWRRRRRR
THE BOSS WOLF?!
DON'T TELL ME HE...
...SAW WHAT JUST HAPPENED WITH ME, AND IS DIRECTING THE OTHERS?!
IN WHICH CASE... THAT BOSS WOLF IS MIND-BLOWINGLY INTELLIGENT...!

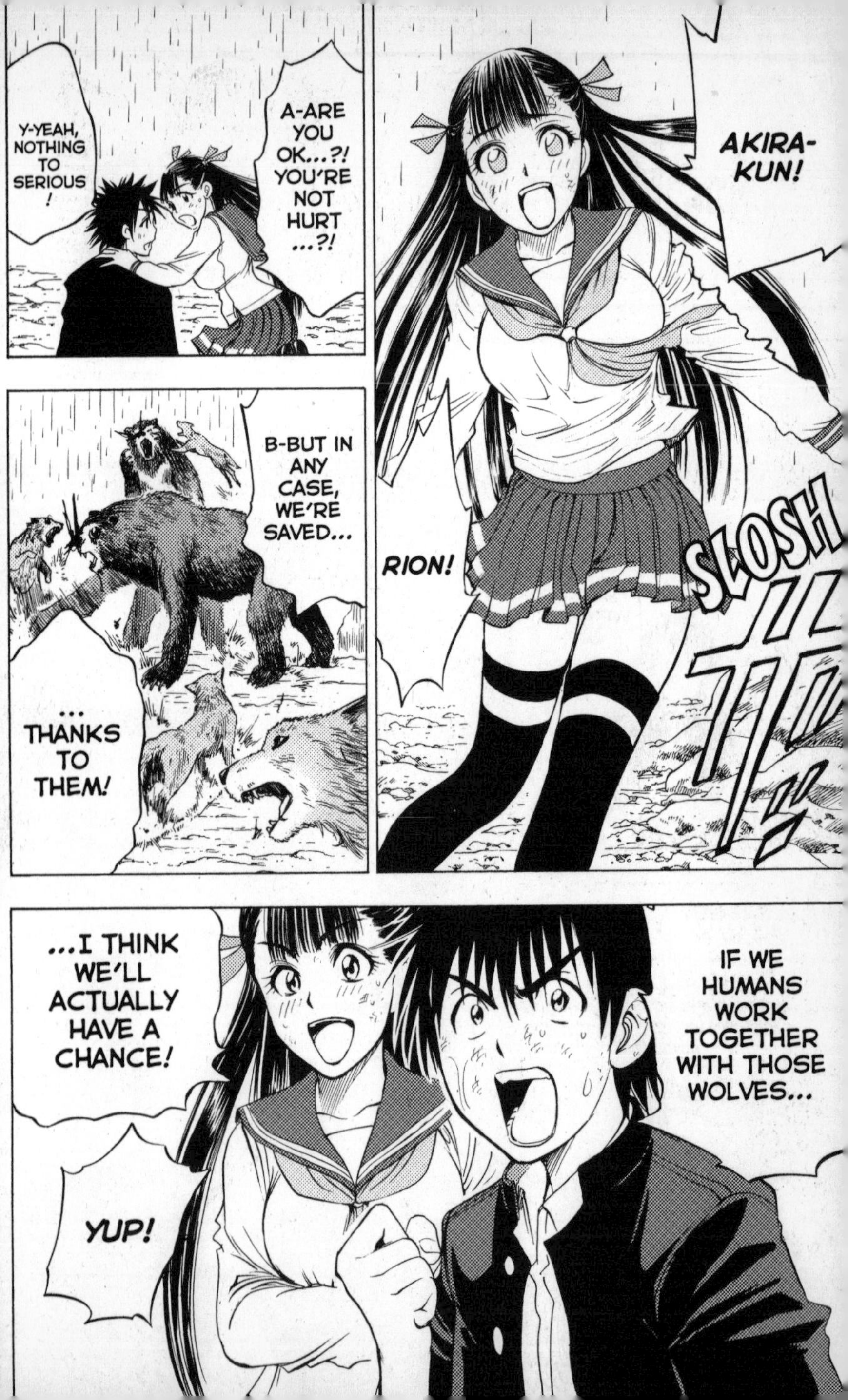
AKIRA-KUN!
SLOSH
RION!
A-ARE YOU OK...?! YOU'RE NOT HURT ...?!
Y-YEAH, NOTHING TO SERIOUS!
B-BUT IN ANY CASE, WE'RE SAVED...
... THANKS TO THEM!
IF WE HUMANS WORK TOGETHER WITH THOSE WOLVES...
...I THINK WE'LL ACTUALLY HAVE A CHANCE!
YUP!

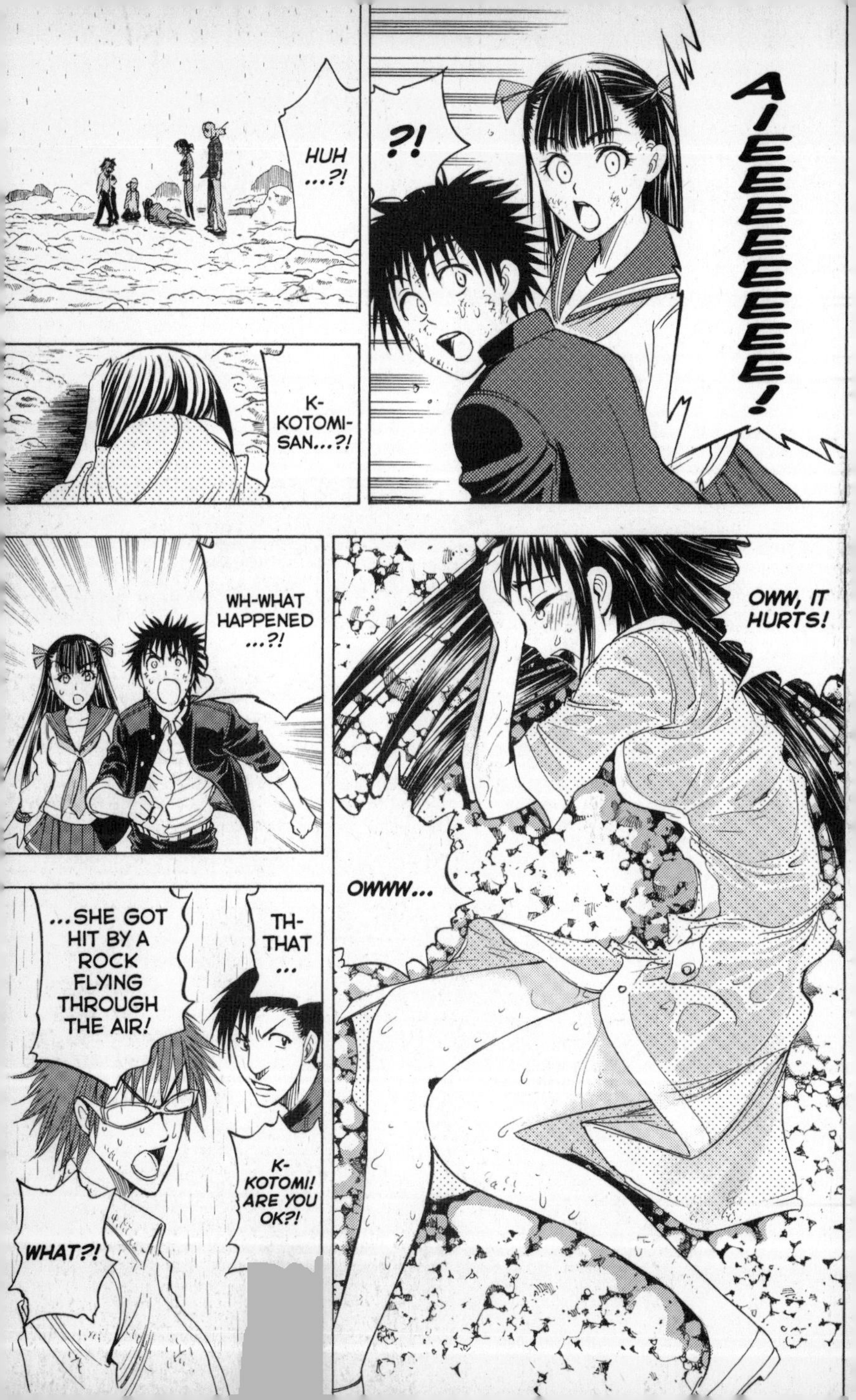
AIEEEEEEEEE!
?!
HUH ...?!
K-KOTOMI-SAN...?!
OWW, IT HURTS!
OWWW...
WH-WHAT HAPPENED ...?!
TH-THAT ...
...SHE GOT HIT BY A ROCK FLYING THROUGH THE AIR!
K-KOTOMI! ARE YOU OK?!
WHAT?!

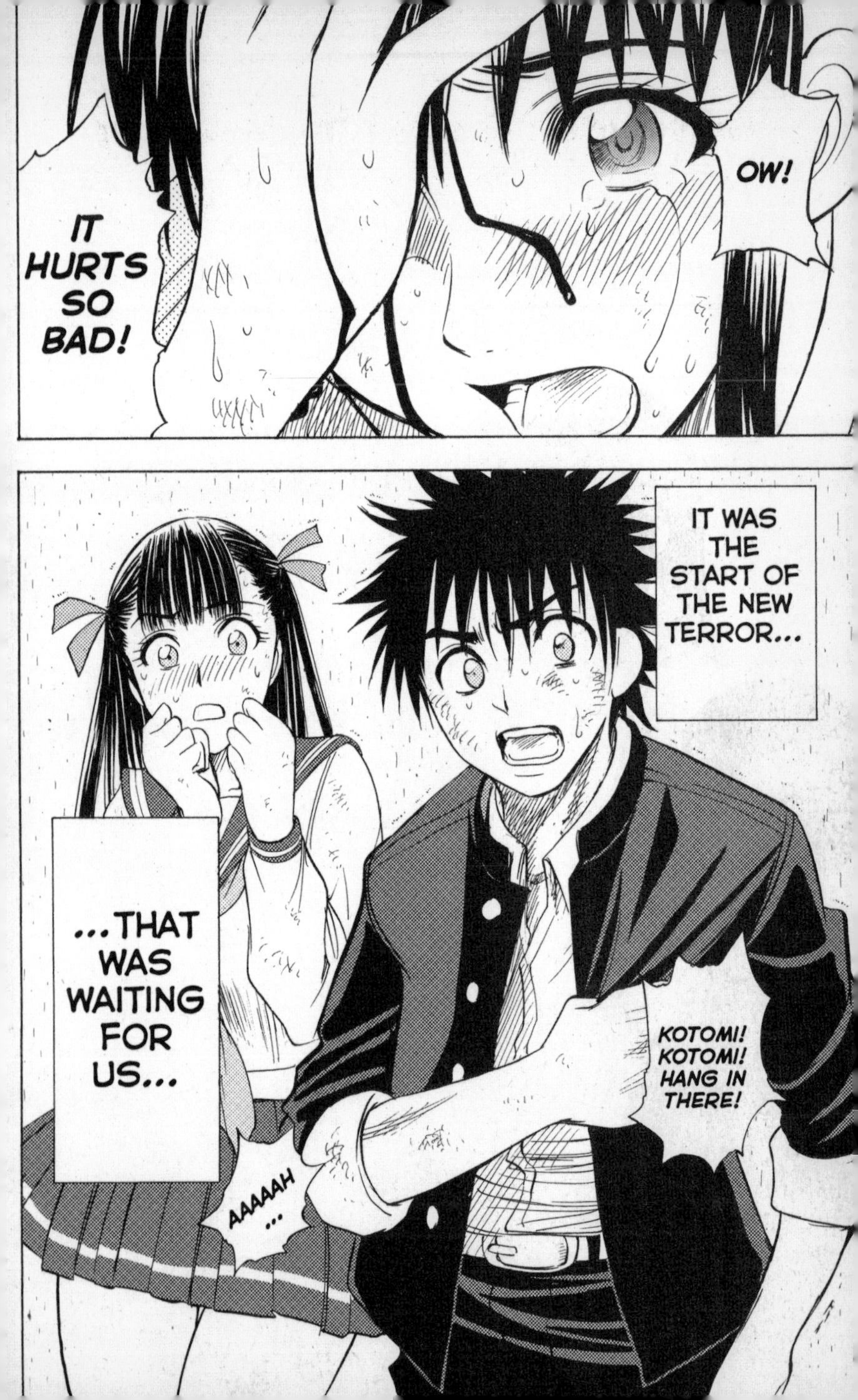
OW!
IT HURTS SO BAD!
IT WAS THE START OF THE NEW TERROR...
KOTOMI! KOTOMI! HANG IN THERE!
...THAT WAS WAITING FOR US...
AAAAAH...

Episode 46: Bridge Over Troubled Water

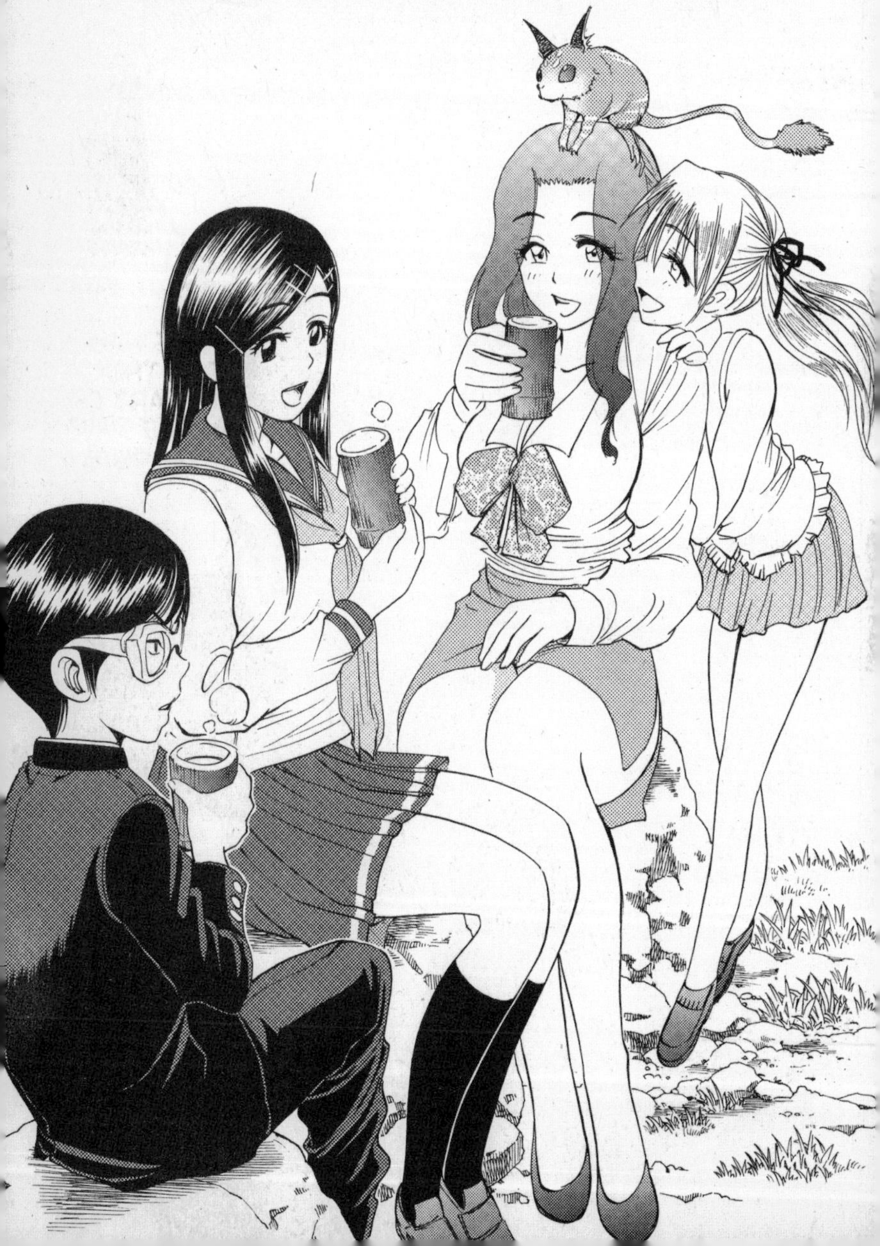

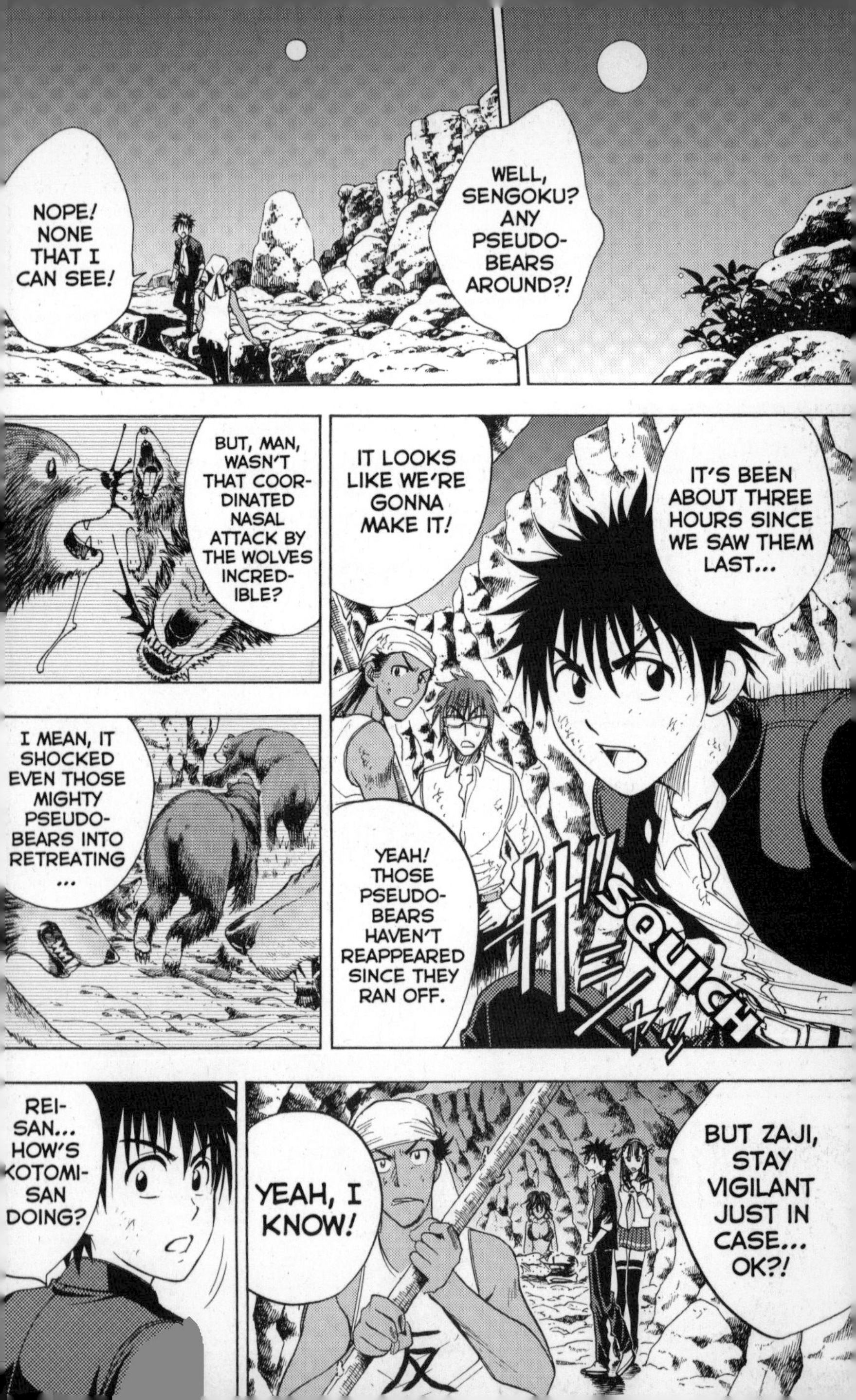
WELL, SENGOKU? ANY PSEUDO-BEARS AROUND?!
NOPE! NONE THAT I CAN SEE!
IT'S BEEN ABOUT THREE HOURS SINCE WE SAW THEM LAST...
IT LOOKS LIKE WE'RE GONNA MAKE IT!
YEAH! THOSE PSEUDO-BEARS HAVEN'T REAPPEARED SINCE THEY RAN OFF.
SQUICH
BUT, MAN, WASN'T THAT COORDINATED NASAL ATTACK BY THE WOLVES INCREDIBLE?
I MEAN, IT SHOCKED EVEN THOSE MIGHTY PSEUDO-BEARS INTO RETREATING...
BUT ZAJI, STAY VIGILANT JUST IN CASE... OK?!
YEAH, I KNOW!
REI-SAN... HOW'S KOTOMI-SAN DOING?

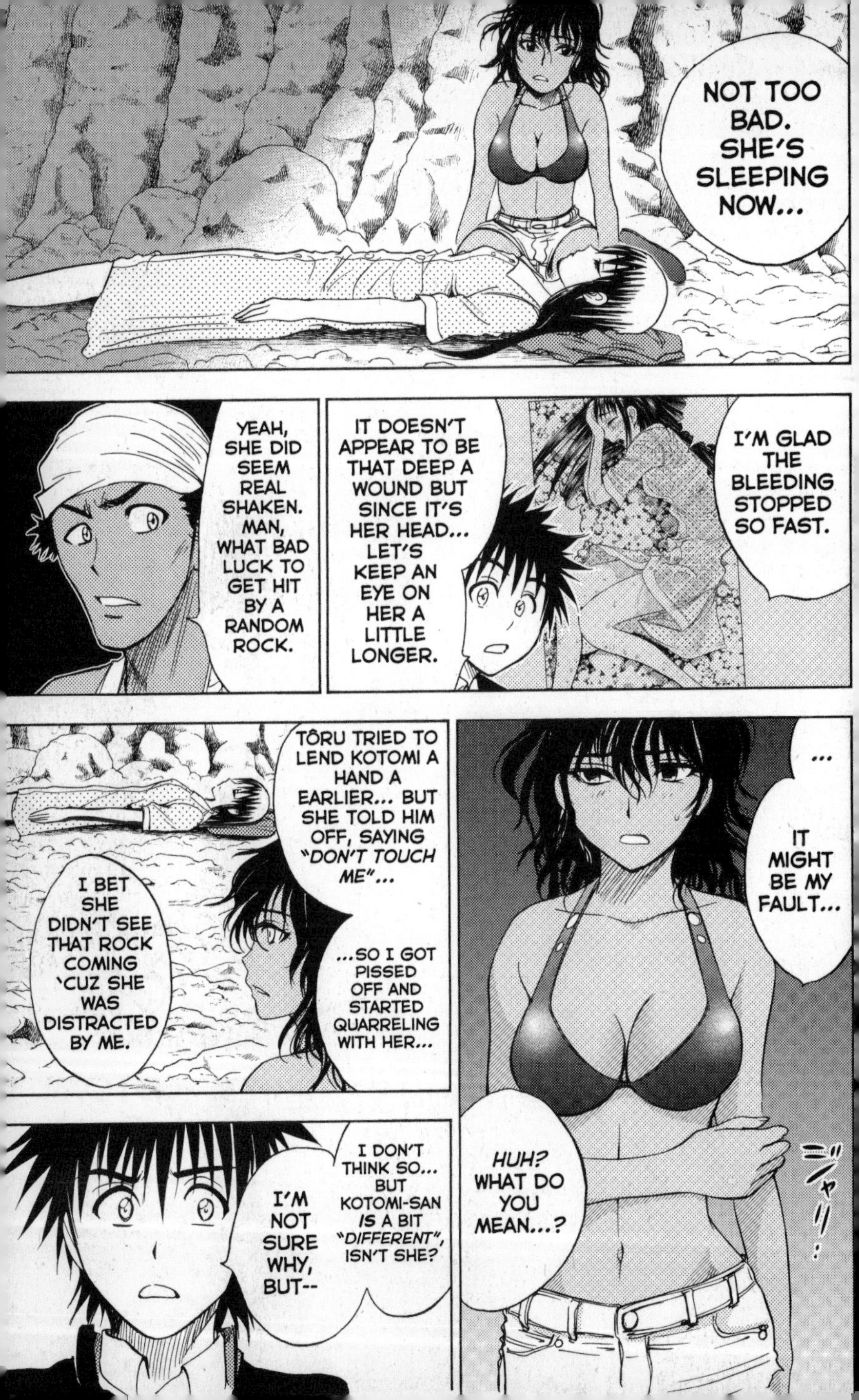
NOT TOO BAD. SHE'S SLEEPING NOW...
I'M GLAD THE BLEEDING STOPPED SO FAST.
IT DOESN'T APPEAR TO BE THAT DEEP A WOUND BUT SINCE IT'S HER HEAD... LET'S KEEP AN EYE ON HER A LITTLE LONGER.
YEAH, SHE DID SEEM REAL SHAKEN. MAN, WHAT BAD LUCK TO GET HIT BY A RANDOM ROCK.
...
IT MIGHT BE MY FAULT...
ジャリ‥
HUH? WHAT DO YOU MEAN...?
TÔRU TRIED TO LEND KOTOMI A HAND A EARLIER... BUT SHE TOLD HIM OFF, SAYING "DON'T TOUCH ME"...
...SO I GOT PISSED OFF AND STARTED QUARRELING WITH HER...
I BET SHE DIDN'T SEE THAT ROCK COMING 'CUZ SHE WAS DISTRACTED BY ME.
I DON'T THINK SO... BUT KOTOMI-SAN IS A BIT "DIFFERENT", ISN'T SHE?
I'M NOT SURE WHY, BUT--

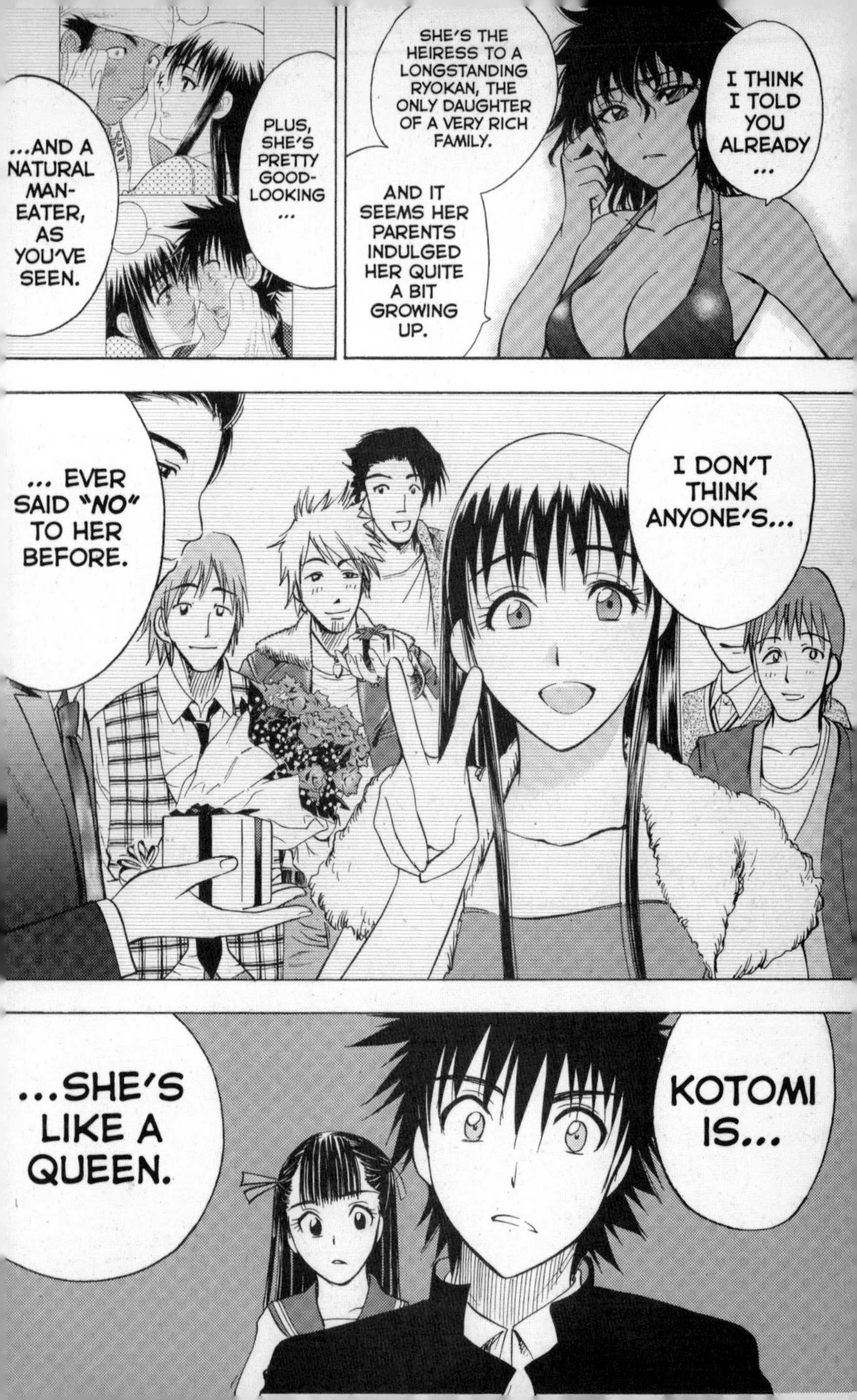
I THINK I TOLD YOU ALREADY...
SHE'S THE HEIRESS TO A LONGSTANDING RYOKAN, THE ONLY DAUGHTER OF A VERY RICH FAMILY.
AND IT SEEMS HER PARENTS INDULGED HER QUITE A BIT GROWING UP.
PLUS, SHE'S PRETTY GOOD-LOOKING...
...AND A NATURAL MAN-EATER, AS YOU'VE SEEN.
I DON'T THINK ANYONE'S...
... EVER SAID "NO" TO HER BEFORE.
KOTOMI IS...
...SHE'S LIKE A QUEEN.

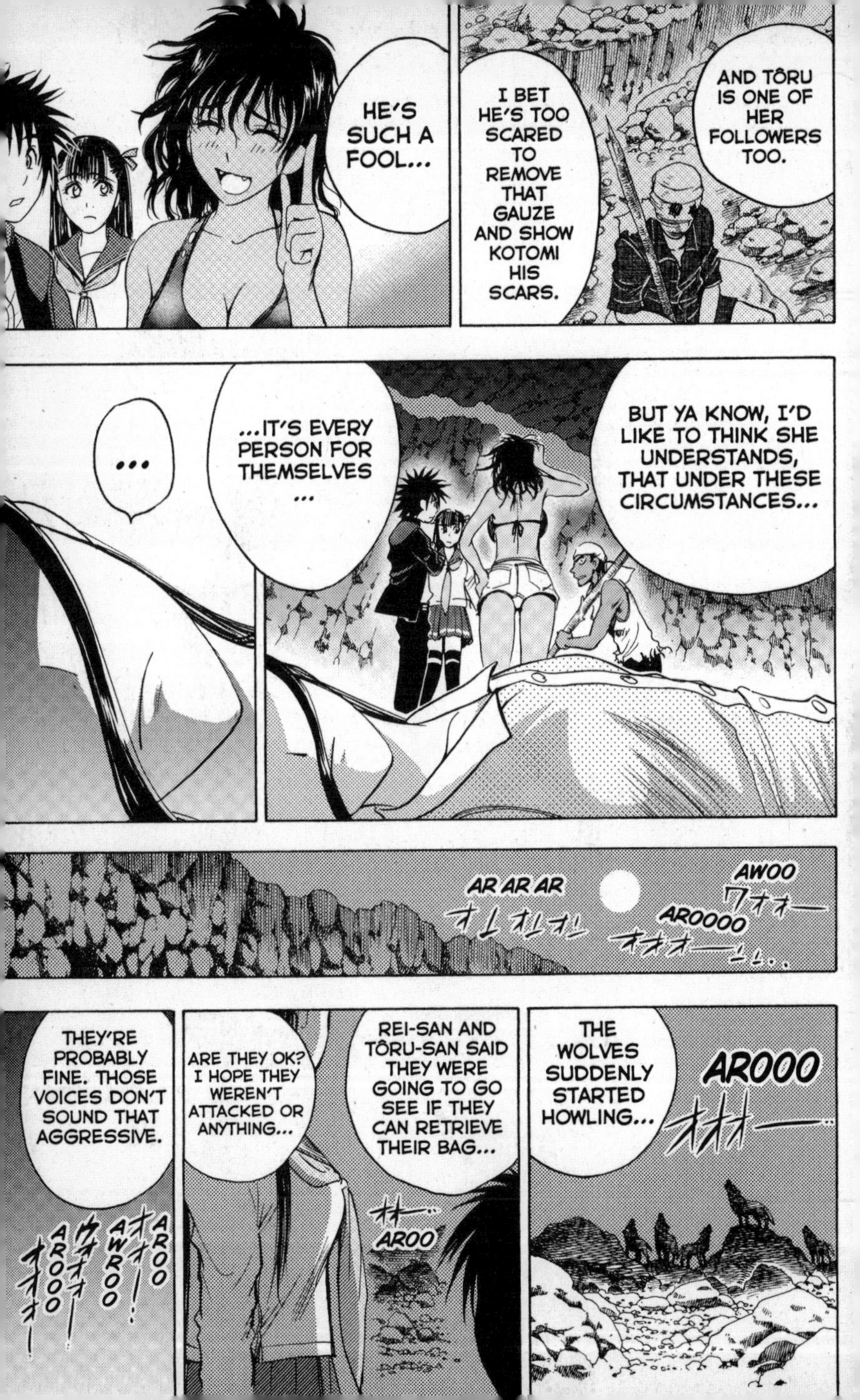
AND TÔRU IS ONE OF HER FOLLOWERS TOO.
I BET HE'S TOO SCARED TO REMOVE THAT GAUZE AND SHOW KOTOMI HIS SCARS.
HE'S SUCH A FOOL...
BUT YA KNOW, I'D LIKE TO THINK SHE UNDERSTANDS, THAT UNDER THESE CIRCUMSTANCES...
...IT'S EVERY PERSON FOR THEMSELVES...
...
AWOO
ワオー
AROOOO
AR AR AR
THE WOLVES SUDDENLY STARTED HOWLING...
AROOO
オオオー
REI-SAN AND TÔRU-SAN SAID THEY WERE GOING TO GO SEE IF THEY CAN RETRIEVE THEIR BAG...
ARE THEY OK? I HOPE THEY WEREN'T ATTACKED OR ANYTHING...
AROO
THEY'RE PROBABLY FINE. THOSE VOICES DON'T SOUND THAT AGGRESSIVE.
AROO
AWROO
AROOO

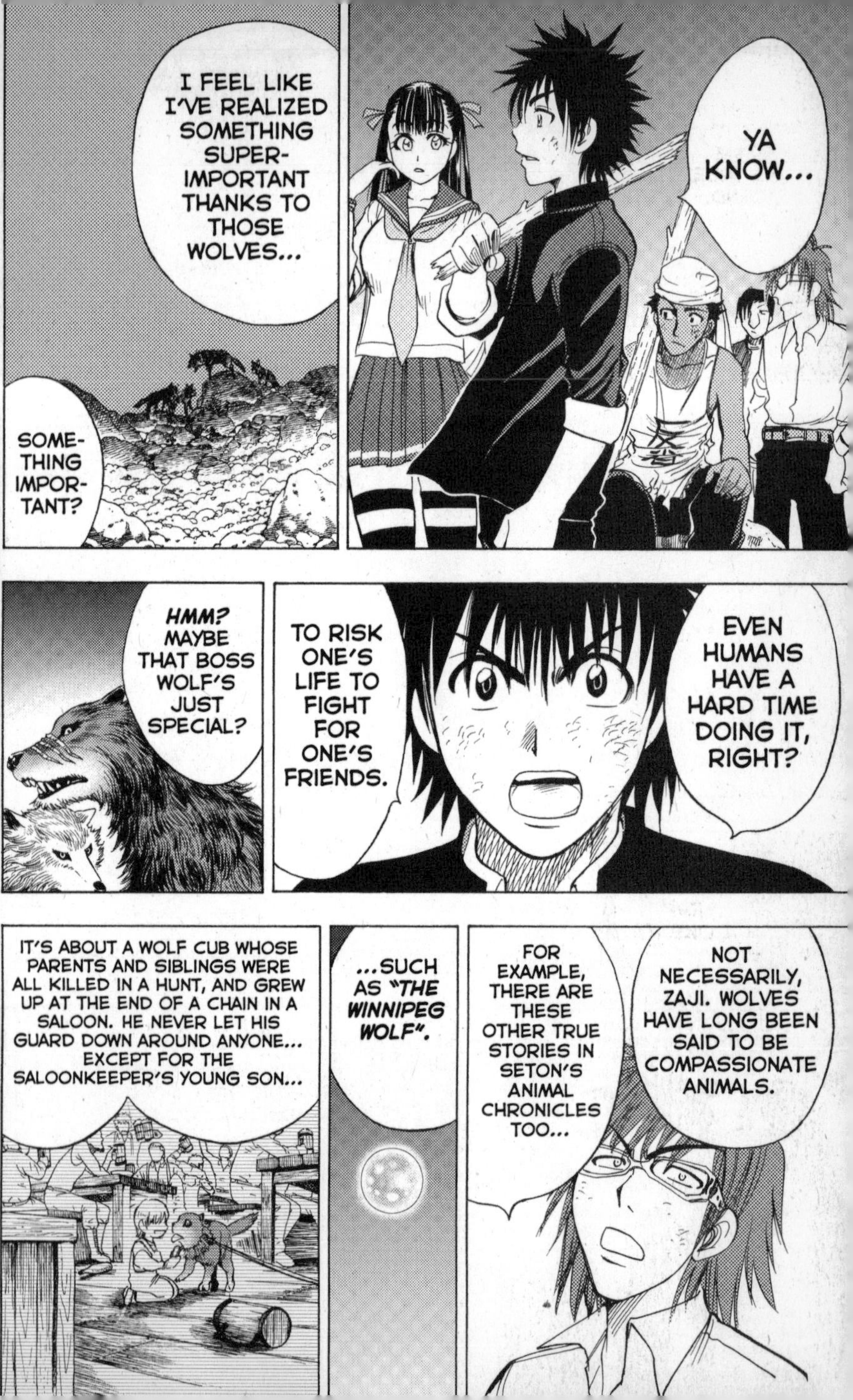
YA KNOW...
I FEEL LIKE I'VE REALIZED SOMETHING SUPER-IMPORTANT THANKS TO THOSE WOLVES...
SOME-THING IMPOR-TANT?
EVEN HUMANS HAVE A HARD TIME DOING IT, RIGHT?
TO RISK ONE'S LIFE TO FIGHT FOR ONE'S FRIENDS.
HMM? MAYBE THAT BOSS WOLF'S JUST SPECIAL?
NOT NECESSARILY, ZAJI. WOLVES HAVE LONG BEEN SAID TO BE COMPASSIONATE ANIMALS.
FOR EXAMPLE, THERE ARE THESE OTHER TRUE STORIES IN SETON'S ANIMAL CHRONICLES TOO...
...SUCH AS *"THE WINNIPEG WOLF"*.
IT'S ABOUT A WOLF CUB WHOSE PARENTS AND SIBLINGS WERE ALL KILLED IN A HUNT, AND GREW UP AT THE END OF A CHAIN IN A SALOON. HE NEVER LET HIS GUARD DOWN AROUND ANYONE... EXCEPT FOR THE SALOONKEEPER'S YOUNG SON...

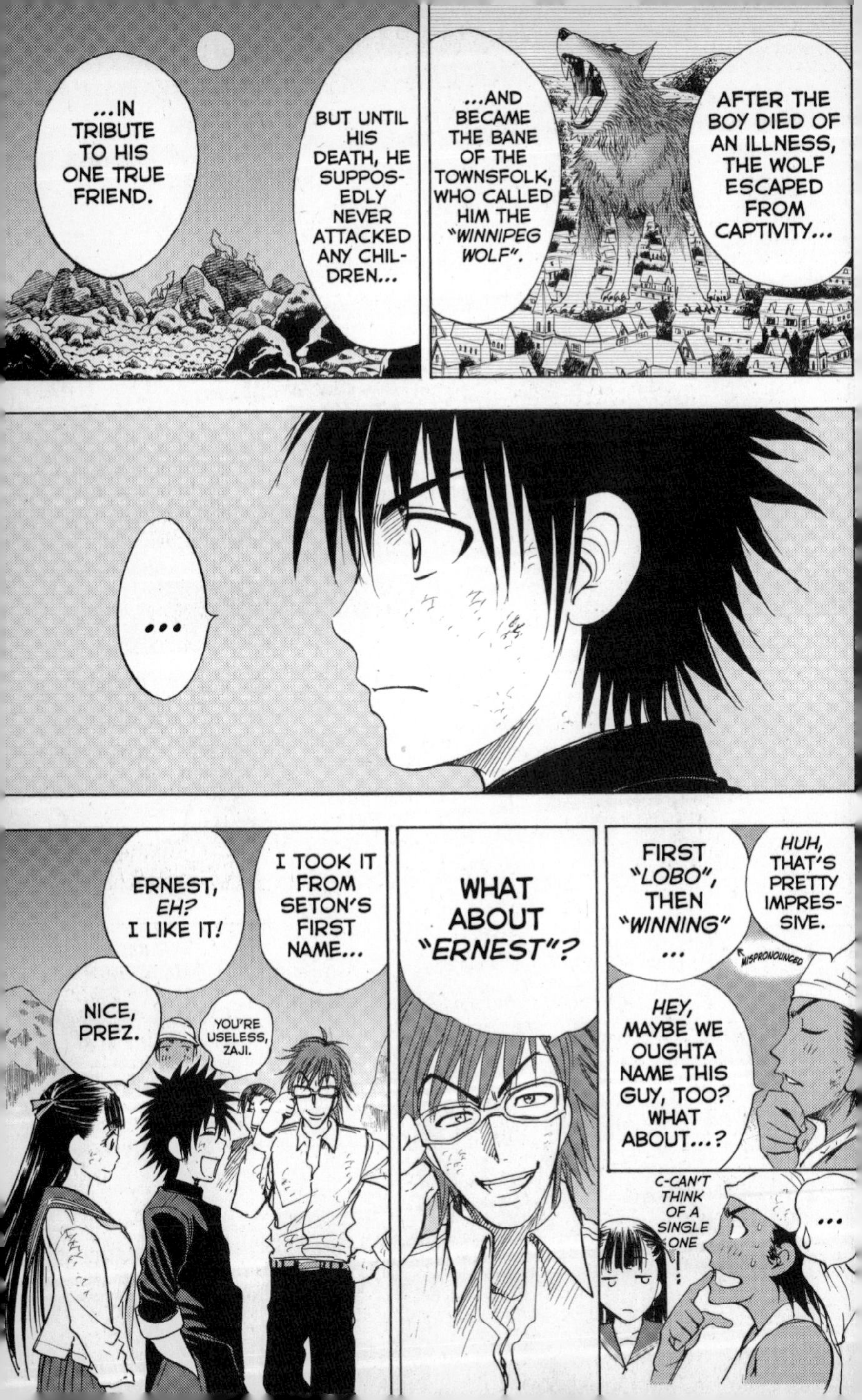
AFTER THE BOY DIED OF AN ILLNESS, THE WOLF ESCAPED FROM CAPTIVITY...
...AND BECAME THE BANE OF THE TOWNSFOLK, WHO CALLED HIM THE "WINNIPEG WOLF".
BUT UNTIL HIS DEATH, HE SUPPOSEDLY NEVER ATTACKED ANY CHILDREN...
...IN TRIBUTE TO HIS ONE TRUE FRIEND.
...
HUH, THAT'S PRETTY IMPRESSIVE.
FIRST "LOBO", THEN "WINNING"...
MISPRONOUNCED
HEY, MAYBE WE OUGHTA NAME THIS GUY, TOO? WHAT ABOUT...?
...
C-CAN'T THINK OF A SINGLE ONE!
WHAT ABOUT "ERNEST"?
I TOOK IT FROM SETON'S FIRST NAME...
ERNEST, EH? I LIKE IT!
YOU'RE USELESS, ZAJI.
NICE, PREZ.

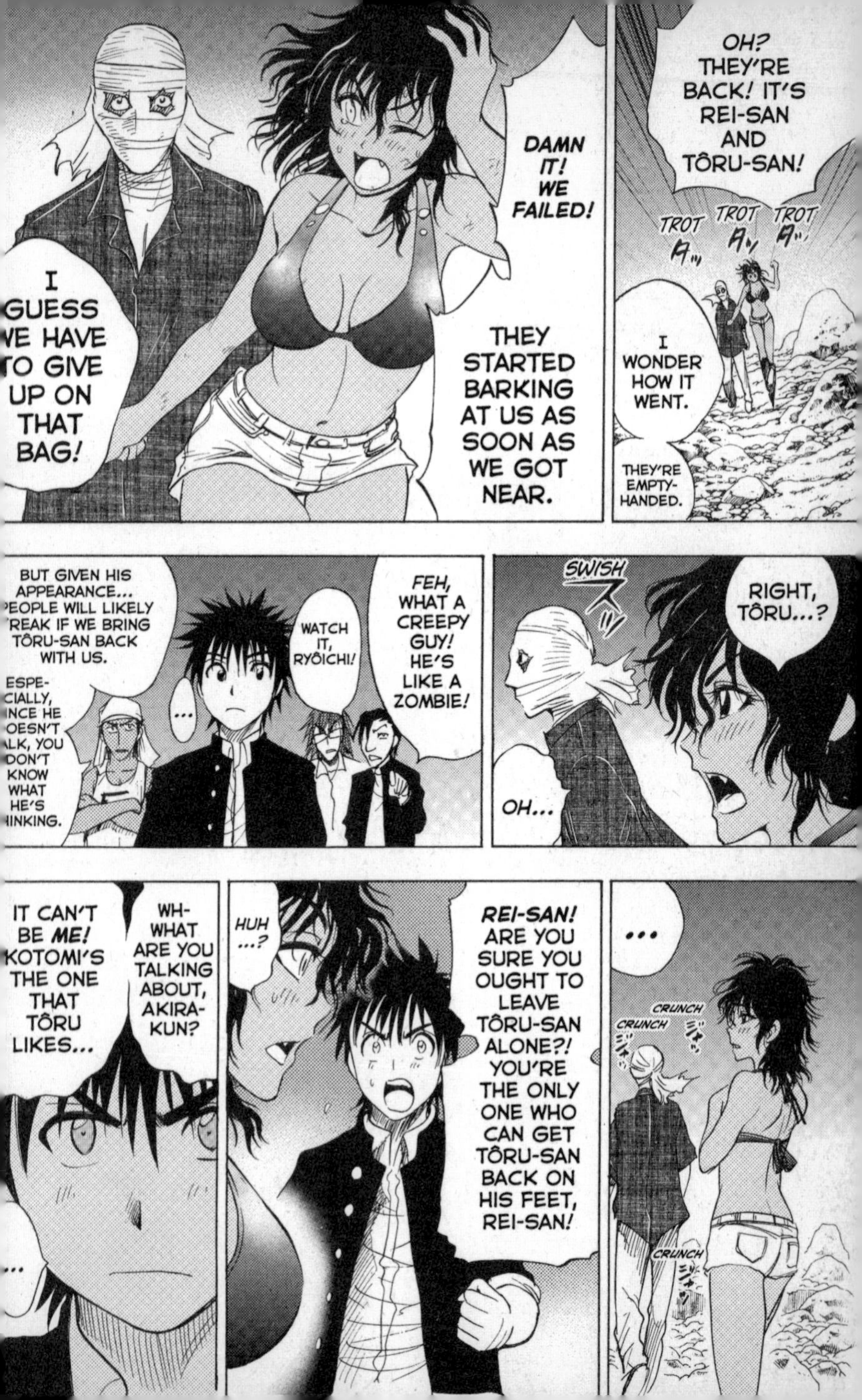
OH? THEY'RE BACK! IT'S REI-SAN AND TÔRU-SAN!
TROT TROT TROT
I WONDER HOW IT WENT.
THEY'RE EMPTY-HANDED.
DAMN IT! WE FAILED!
THEY STARTED BARKING AT US AS SOON AS WE GOT NEAR.
I GUESS WE HAVE TO GIVE UP ON THAT BAG!
SWISH
RIGHT, TÔRU...?
OH...
FEH, WHAT A CREEPY GUY! HE'S LIKE A ZOMBIE!
WATCH IT, RYÔICHI!
BUT GIVEN HIS APPEARANCE... PEOPLE WILL LIKELY FREAK IF WE BRING TÔRU-SAN BACK WITH US.
...
ESPECIALLY, SINCE HE DOESN'T TALK, YOU DON'T KNOW WHAT HE'S THINKING.
...
CRUNCH
CRUNCH
CRUNCH
REI-SAN! ARE YOU SURE YOU OUGHT TO LEAVE TÔRU-SAN ALONE?! YOU'RE THE ONLY ONE WHO CAN GET TÔRU-SAN BACK ON HIS FEET, REI-SAN!
HUH...?
WH-WHAT ARE YOU TALKING ABOUT, AKIRA-KUN?
IT CAN'T BE ME! KOTOMI'S THE ONE THAT TÔRU LIKES...
...

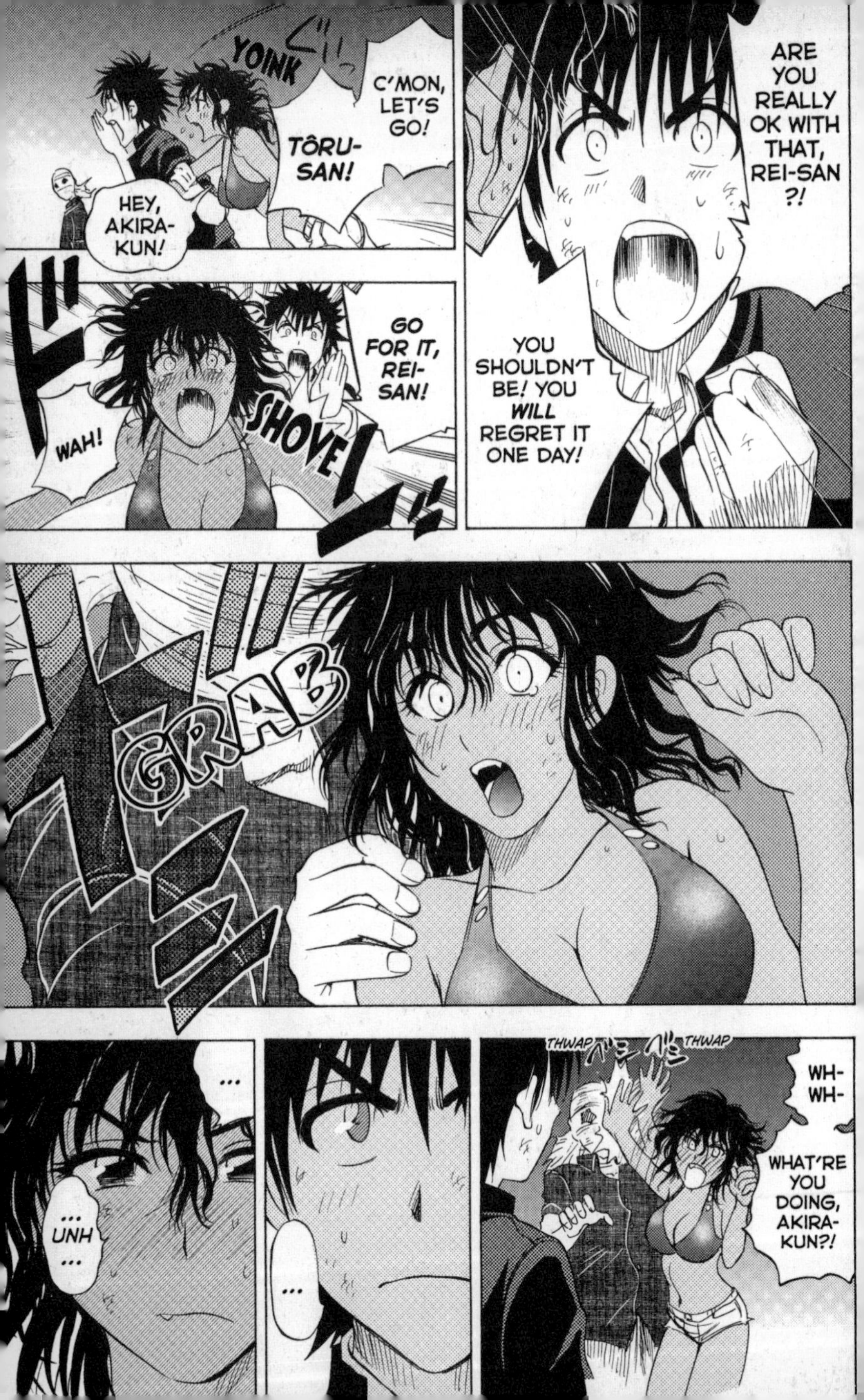
ARE YOU REALLY OK WITH THAT, REI-SAN?!
YOU SHOULDN'T BE! YOU WILL REGRET IT ONE DAY!
YOINK
C'MON, LET'S GO!
TÔRU-SAN!
HEY, AKIRA-KUN!
GO FOR IT, REI-SAN!
SHOVE
WAH!
GRAB
THWAP
THWAP
WH-WH-
WHAT'RE YOU DOING, AKIRA-KUN?!
...
...
... UNH ...

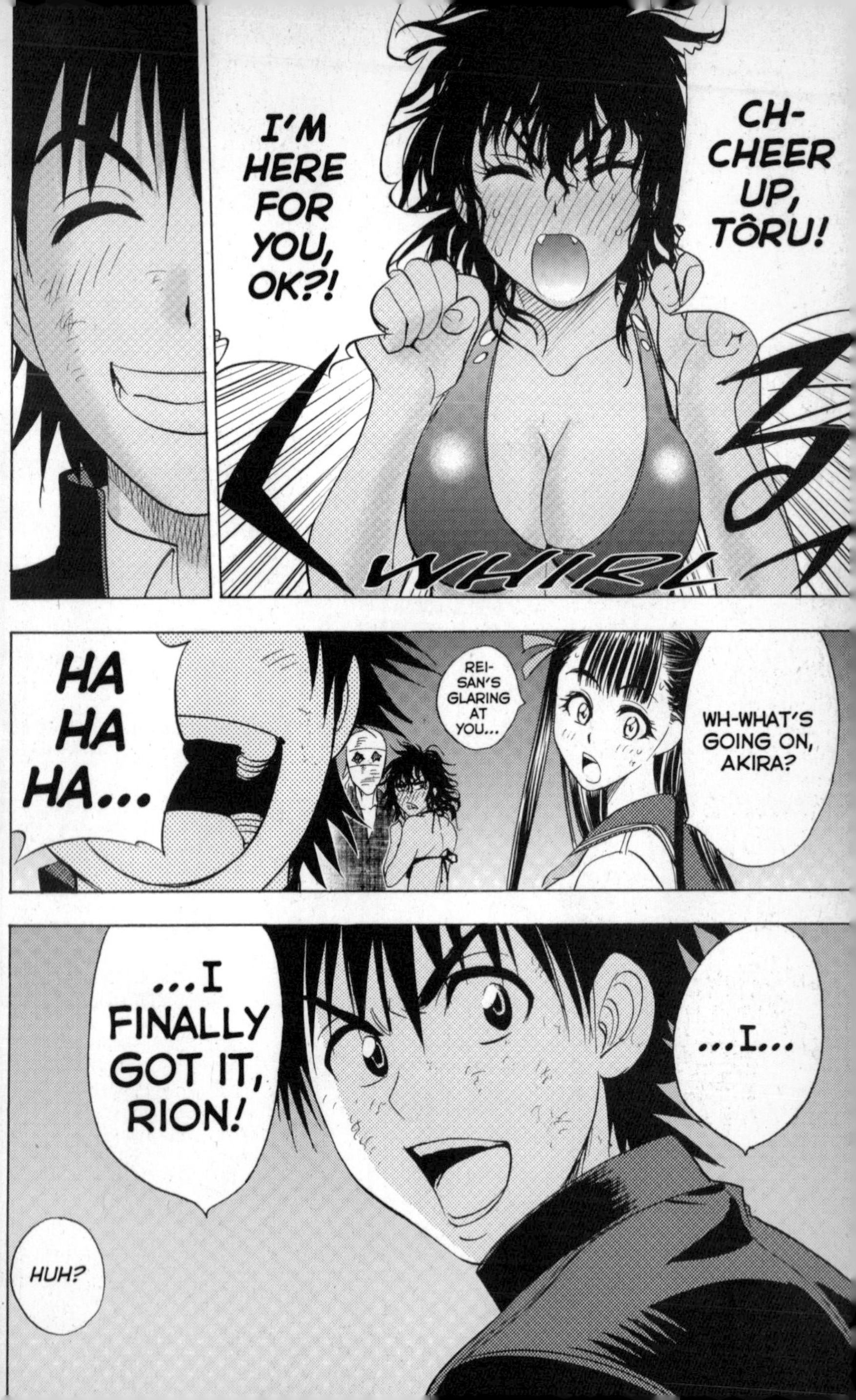
CH-CHEER UP, TÔRU!
I'M HERE FOR YOU, OK?!
WHIRL
WH-WHAT'S GOING ON, AKIRA?
REI-SAN'S GLARING AT YOU...
HA HA HA...
...I...
...I FINALLY GOT IT, RION!
HUH?

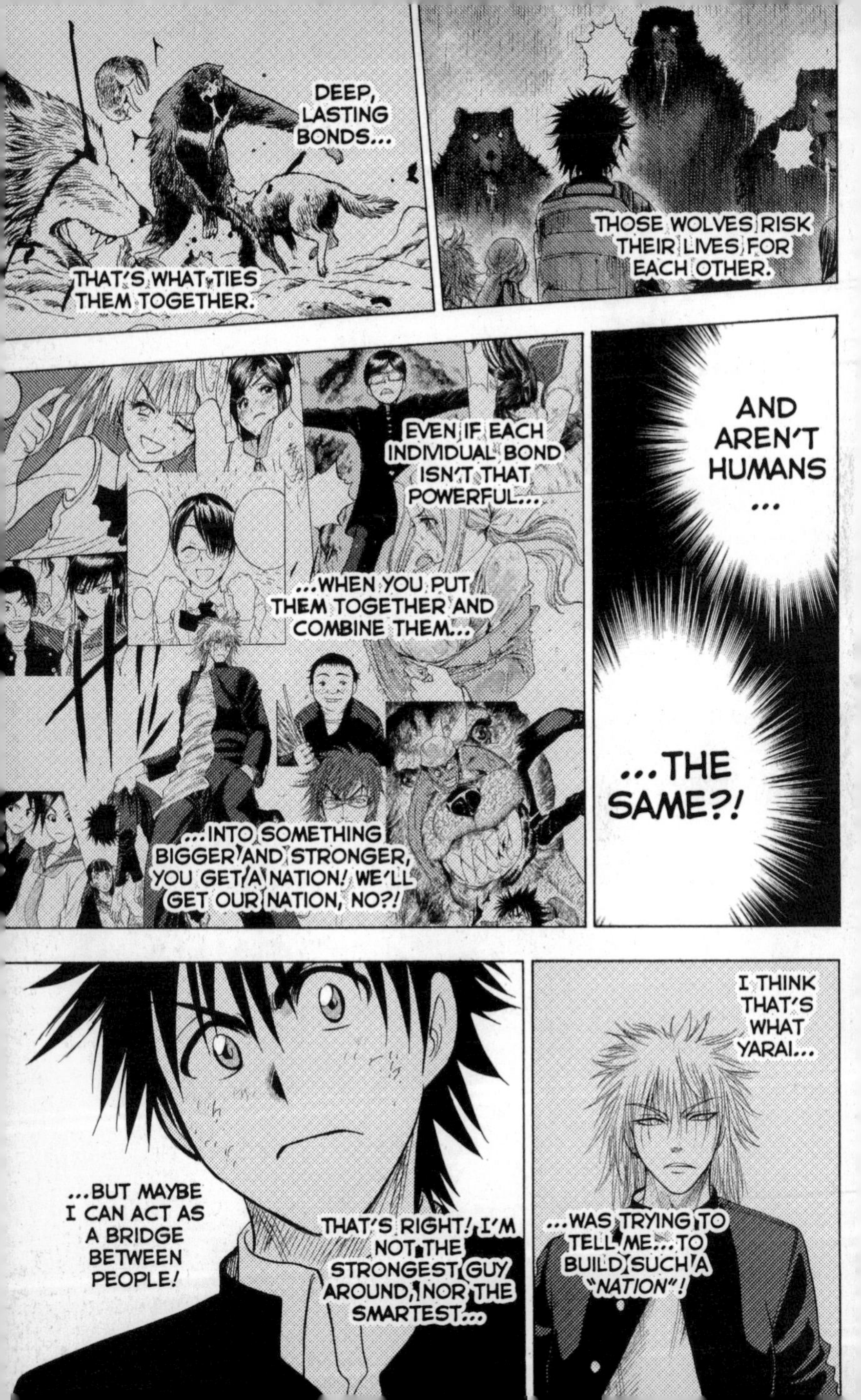
THOSE WOLVES RISK THEIR LIVES FOR EACH OTHER.
DEEP, LASTING BONDS...
THAT'S WHAT TIES THEM TOGETHER.
AND AREN'T HUMANS ...
...THE SAME?!
EVEN IF EACH INDIVIDUAL BOND ISN'T THAT POWERFUL...
...WHEN YOU PUT THEM TOGETHER AND COMBINE THEM...
...INTO SOMETHING BIGGER AND STRONGER, YOU GET A NATION! WE'LL GET OUR NATION, NO?!
I THINK THAT'S WHAT YARAI...
...WAS TRYING TO TELL ME... TO BUILD SUCH A "NATION"!
THAT'S RIGHT! I'M NOT THE STRONGEST GUY AROUND, NOR THE SMARTEST...
...BUT MAYBE I CAN ACT AS A BRIDGE BETWEEN PEOPLE!

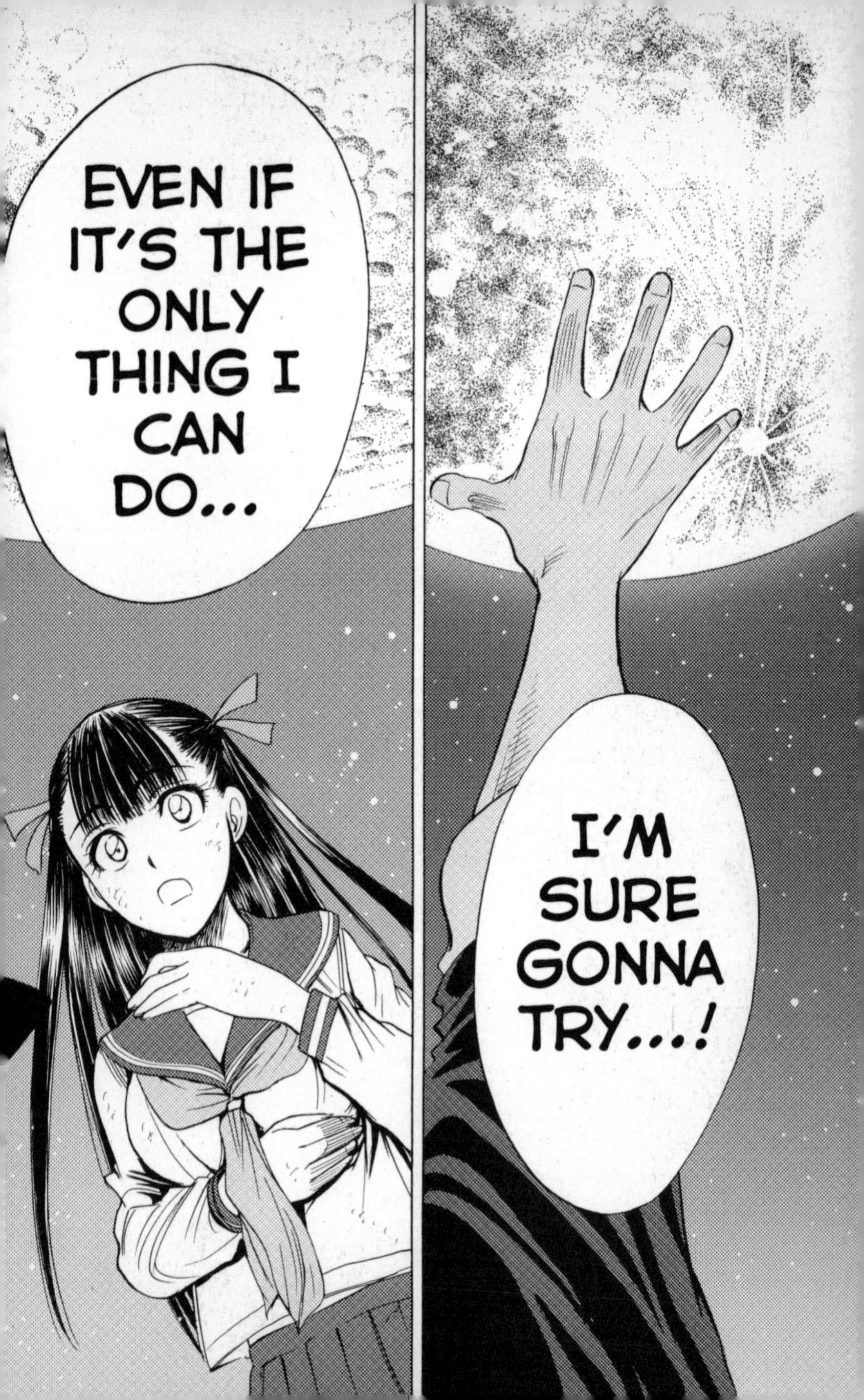
I'M SURE GONNA TRY...!
EVEN IF IT'S THE ONLY THING I CAN DO...

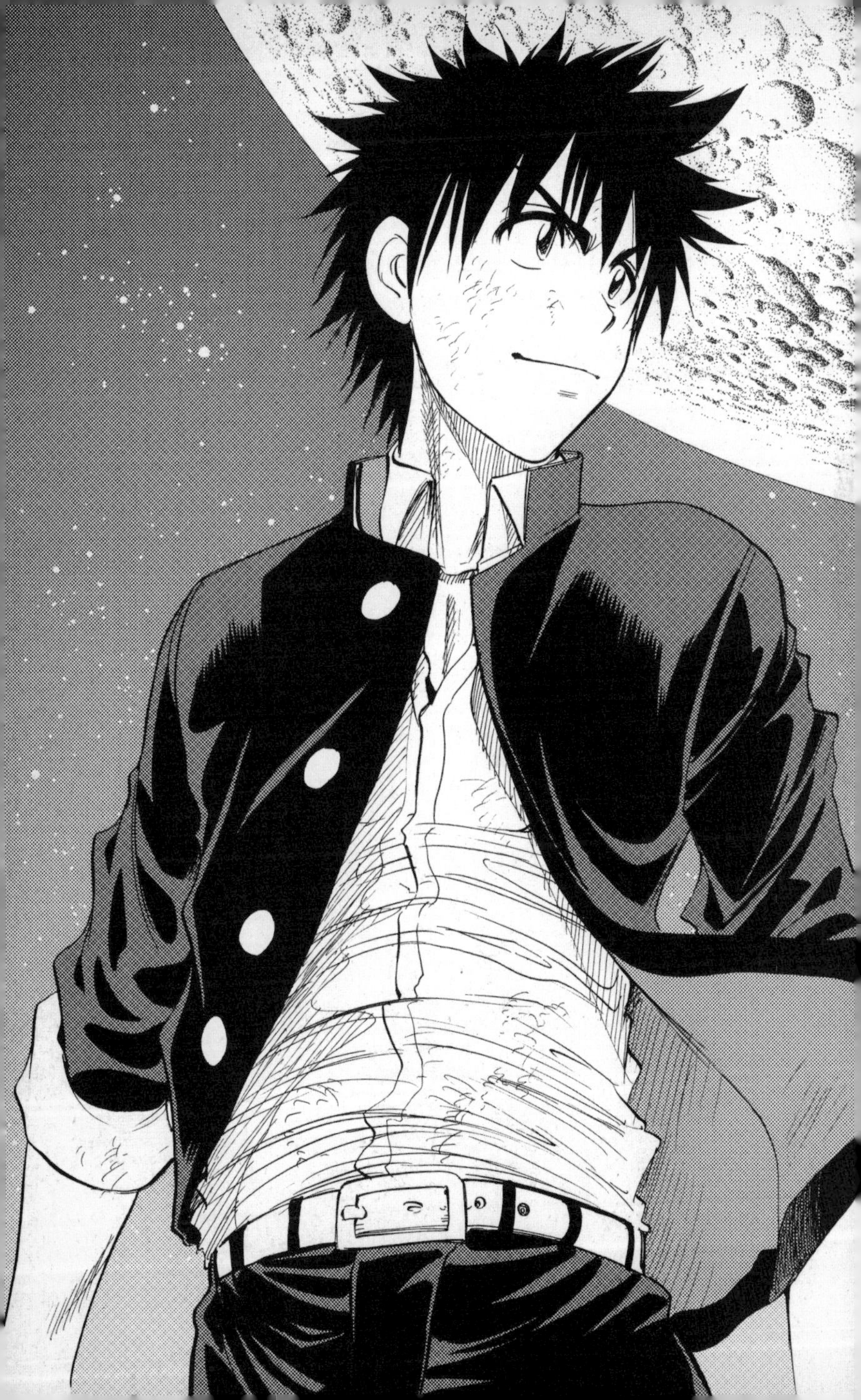

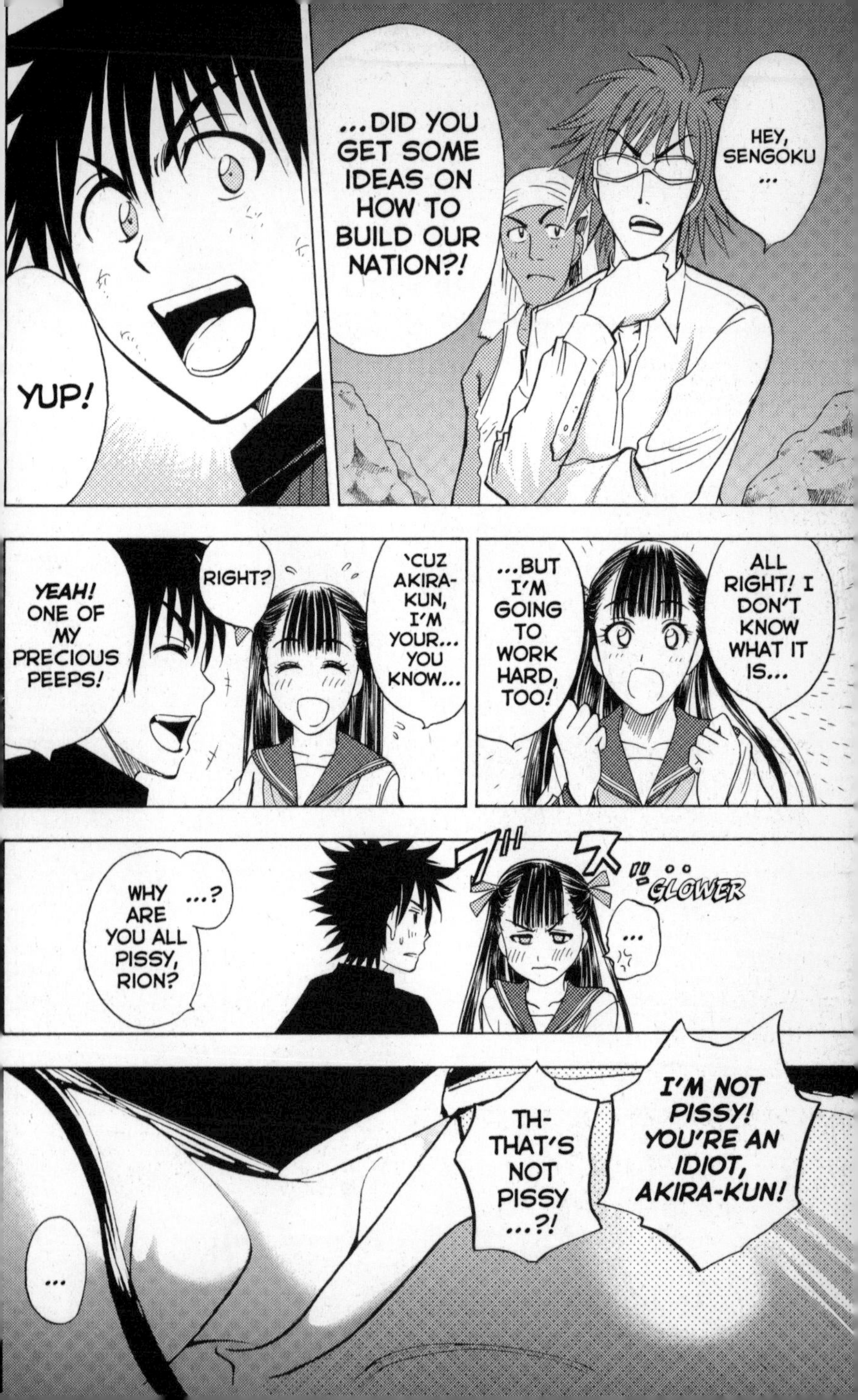
HEY, SENGOKU ...
...DID YOU GET SOME IDEAS ON HOW TO BUILD OUR NATION?!
YUP!
ALL RIGHT! I DON'T KNOW WHAT IT IS...
...BUT I'M GOING TO WORK HARD, TOO!
'CUZ AKIRA-KUN, I'M YOUR... YOU KNOW...
RIGHT?
YEAH! ONE OF MY PRECIOUS PEEPS!
GLOWER
...
WHY ARE YOU ALL PISSY, RION?
...?
I'M NOT PISSY! YOU'RE AN IDIOT, AKIRA-KUN!
TH- THAT'S NOT PISSY ...?!
...

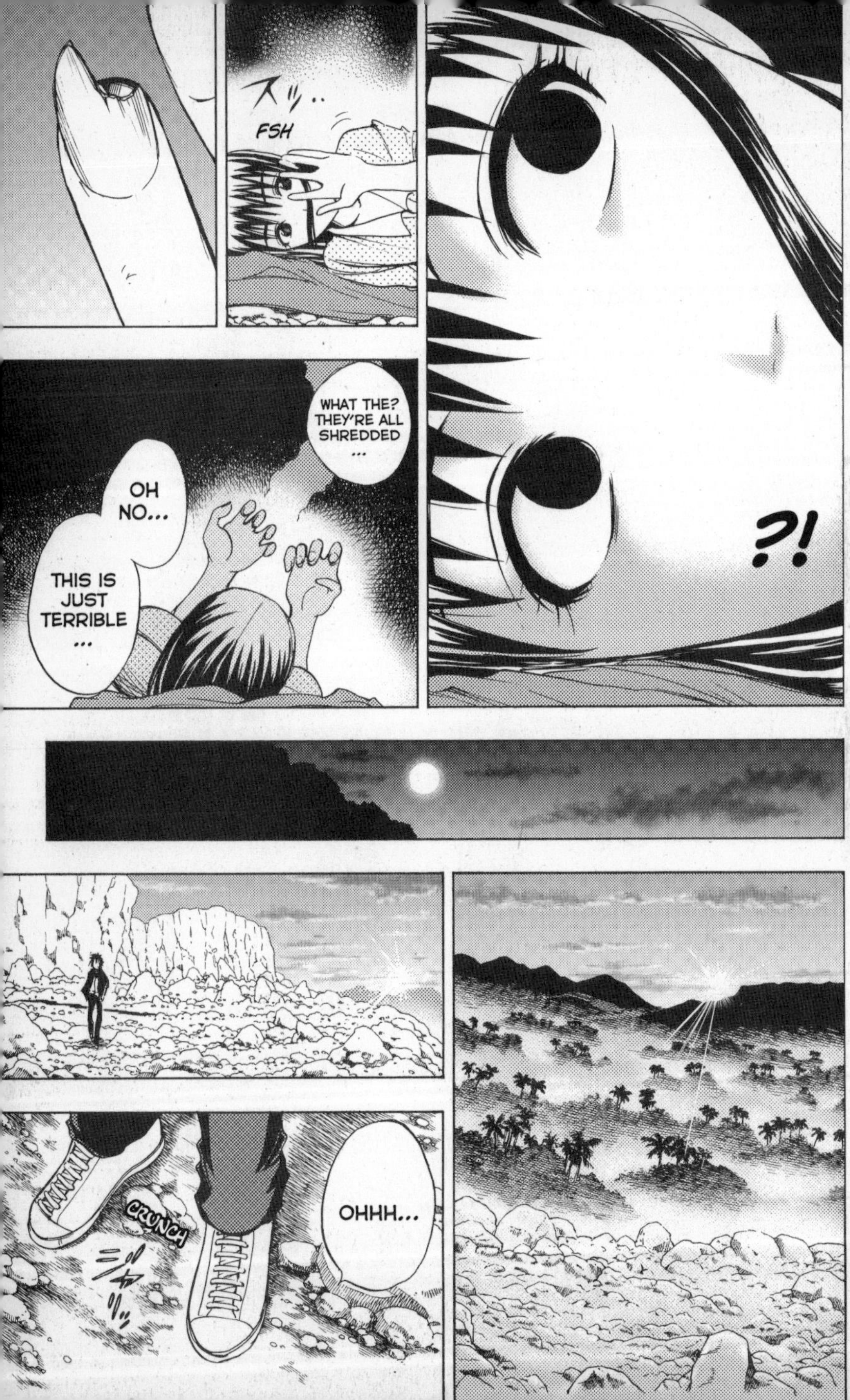
?!
スッ..
FSH
WHAT THE? THEY'RE ALL SHREDDED ...
OH NO...
THIS IS JUST TERRIBLE ...
OHHH...
CRUNCH

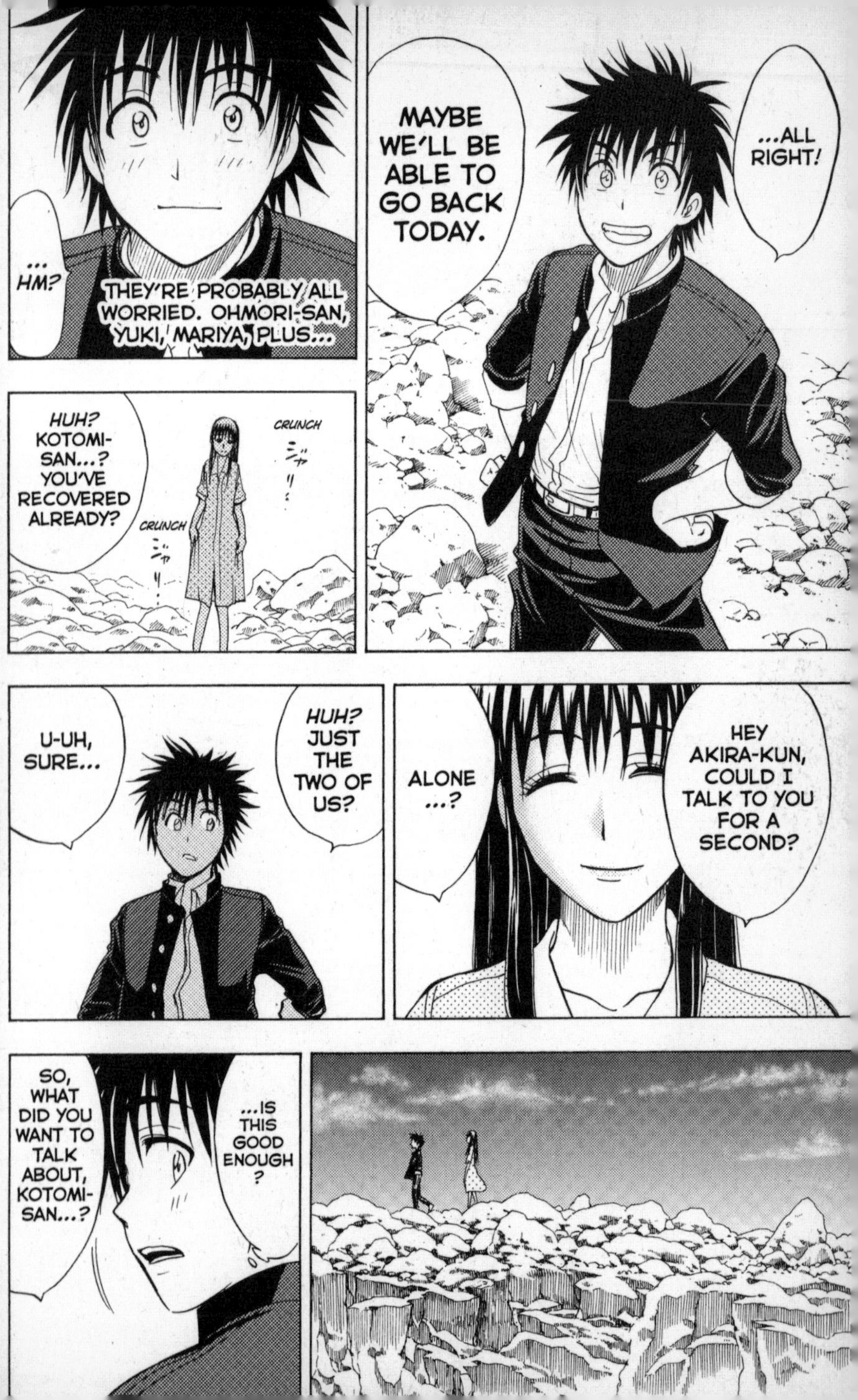
...ALL RIGHT!
MAYBE WE'LL BE ABLE TO GO BACK TODAY.
THEY'RE PROBABLY ALL WORRIED. OHMORI-SAN, YUKI, MARIYA, PLUS...
... HM?
CRUNCH
HUH? KOTOMI-SAN...? YOU'VE RECOVERED ALREADY?
CRUNCH
HEY AKIRA-KUN, COULD I TALK TO YOU FOR A SECOND?
ALONE ...?
HUH? JUST THE TWO OF US?
U-UH, SURE...
...IS THIS GOOD ENOUGH ?
SO, WHAT DID YOU WANT TO TALK ABOUT, KOTOMI-SAN...?

WHA ?! *WHIRL*

HEY, AKIRA-KUN, DO IT WITH ME.

FSSH

?!

WH-WHAT IS SHE SAYING? WHERE'D THIS COME FROM? WHAT IF RION SEES US!...

N-N-N-N-N-NO WAY, I, UH...

I-I'M SORRY, BUT I CAN'T! PLEASE PUT YOUR CLOTHES BACK ON!

...

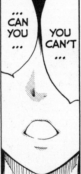

...CAN YOU...

YOU CAN'T...

KOTOMI-SAN...?!

HUH ?

UGH?!

GRAB

SUNOVABITCH! YOU REALLY CAN'T DO IT, CAN YOU?!

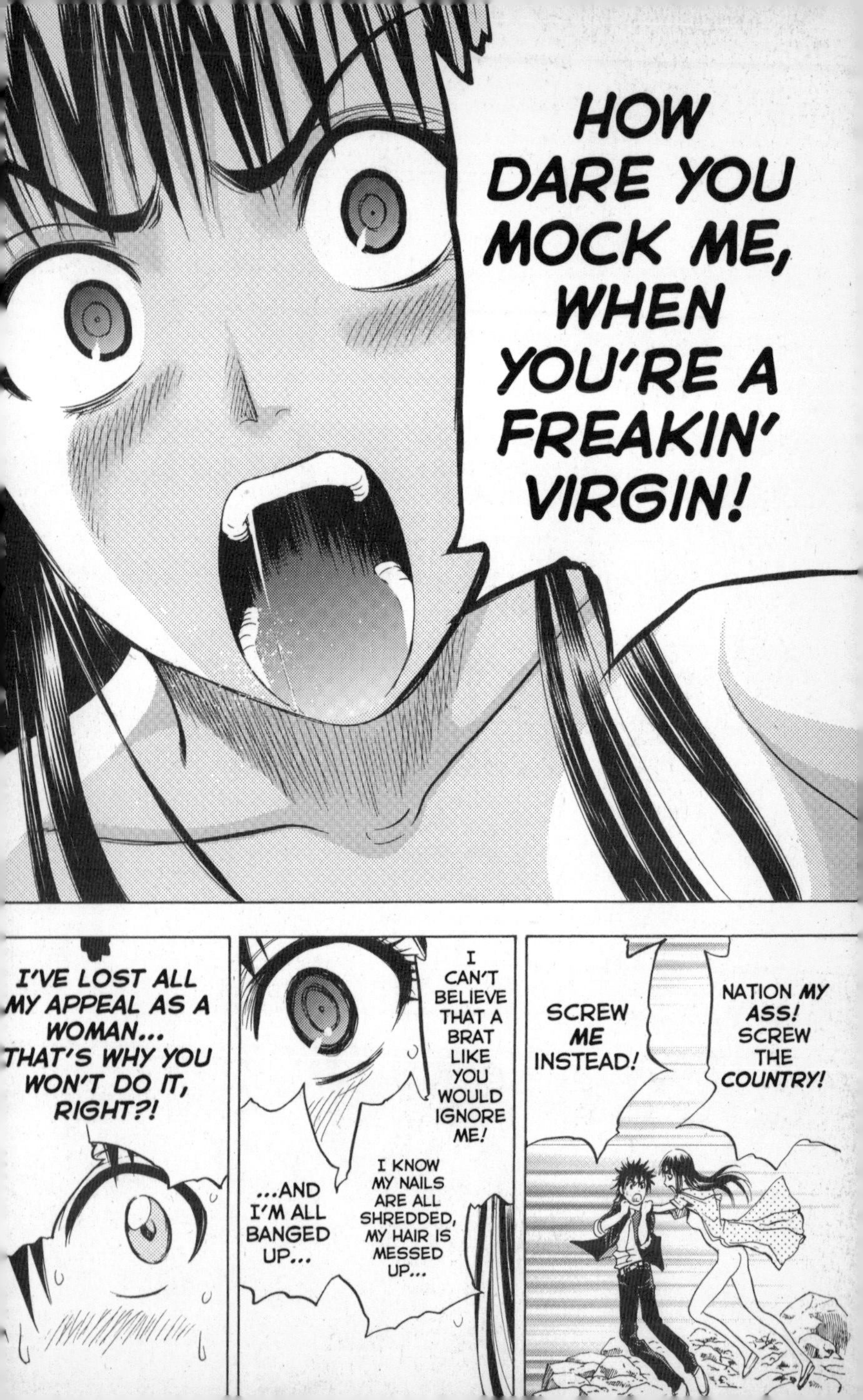
HOW DARE YOU MOCK ME, WHEN YOU'RE A FREAKIN' VIRGIN!
NATION MY ASS! SCREW THE COUNTRY!
SCREW ME INSTEAD!
I CAN'T BELIEVE THAT A BRAT LIKE YOU WOULD IGNORE ME!
I KNOW MY NAILS ARE ALL SHREDDED, MY HAIR IS MESSED UP...
...AND I'M ALL BANGED UP...
I'VE LOST ALL MY APPEAL AS A WOMAN... THAT'S WHY YOU WON'T DO IT, RIGHT?!

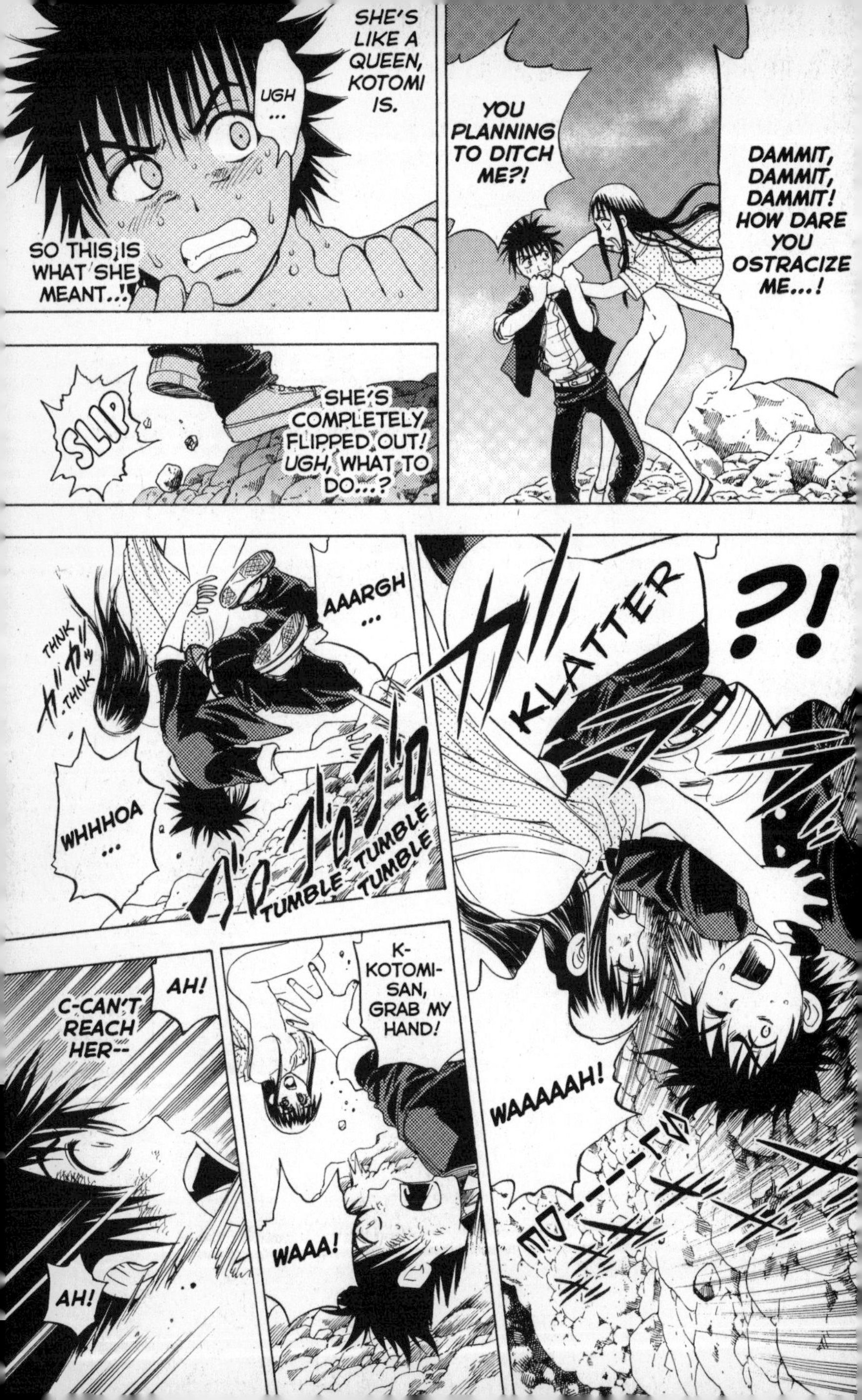
DAMMIT, DAMMIT, DAMMIT! HOW DARE YOU OSTRACIZE ME...!
YOU PLANNING TO DITCH ME?!
SHE'S LIKE A QUEEN, KOTOMI IS.
UGH ...
SO THIS IS WHAT SHE MEANT..!
SHE'S COMPLETELY FLIPPED OUT! UGH, WHAT TO DO...?
SLIP
?!
KLATTER
WAAAAAH!
AAARGH ...
THNK THNK
WHHHOA ...
TUMBLE TUMBLE TUMBLE
K-KOTOMI-SAN, GRAB MY HAND!
WAAA!
AH!
C-CAN'T REACH HER--
AH!

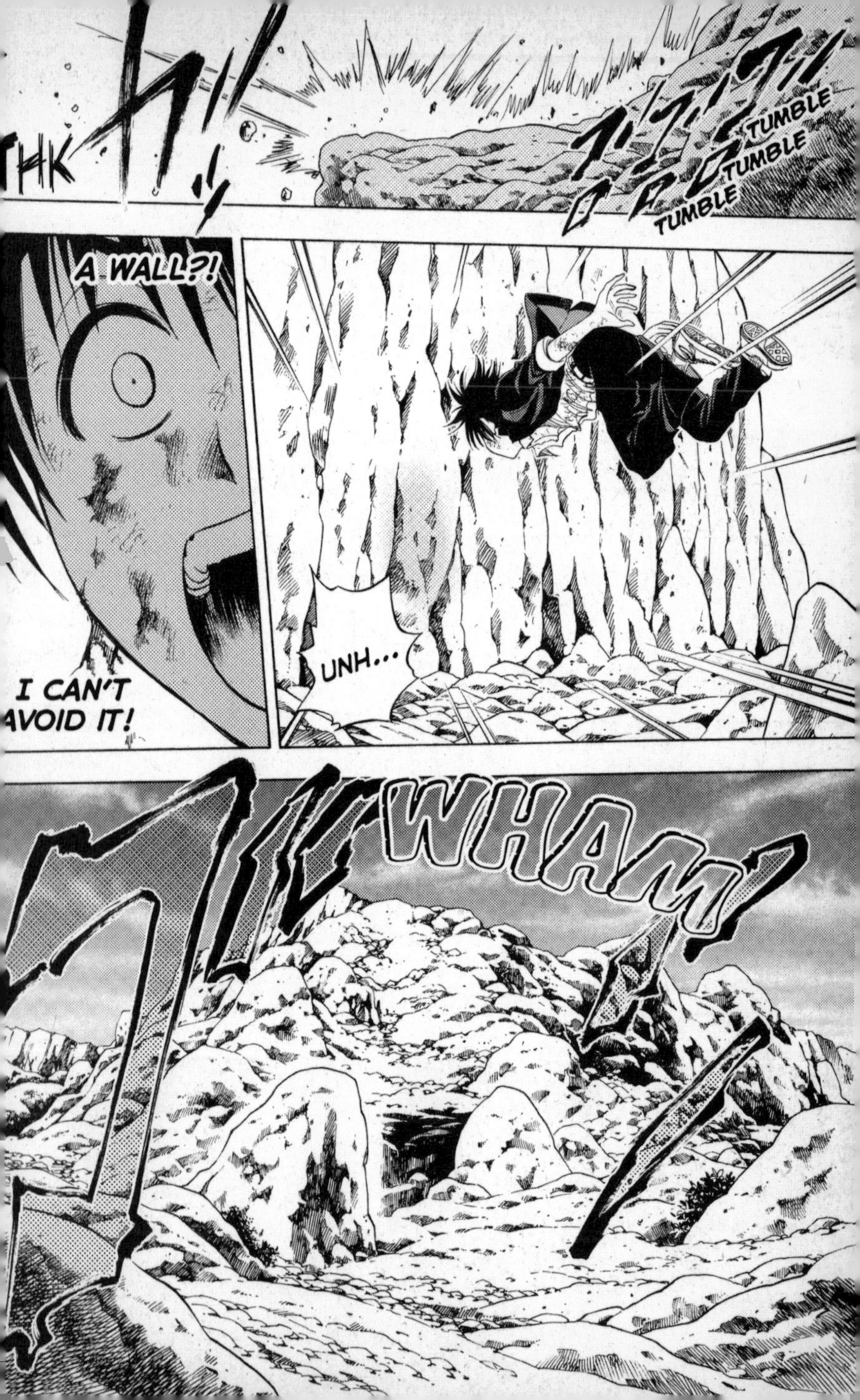
TUMBLE
TUMBLE
TUMBLE
THK
UNH...
A WALL?!
I CAN'T AVOID IT!
WHAM

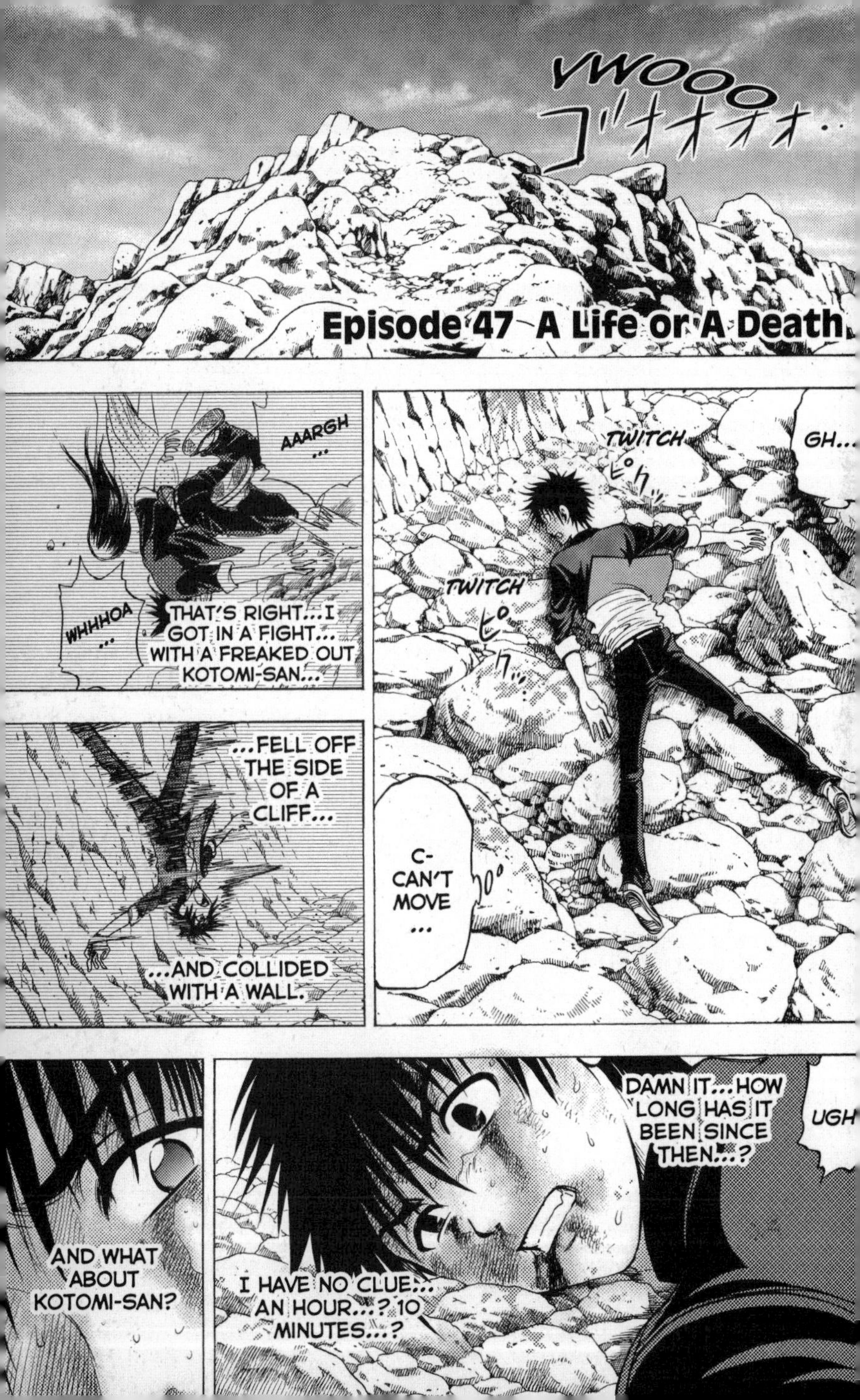
VWOOOO
ゴオオオオ…
Episode 47 A Life or A Death
GH...
TWITCH
ピクッ
TWITCH
ピクッ
C- CAN'T MOVE ...
AAARGH ...
WHHHOA ...
THAT'S RIGHT...I GOT IN A FIGHT... WITH A FREAKED OUT KOTOMI-SAN...
...FELL OFF THE SIDE OF A CLIFF...
...AND COLLIDED WITH A WALL.
UGH
DAMN IT... HOW LONG HAS IT BEEN SINCE THEN...?
I HAVE NO CLUE... AN HOUR...? 10 MINUTES...?
AND WHAT ABOUT KOTOMI-SAN?

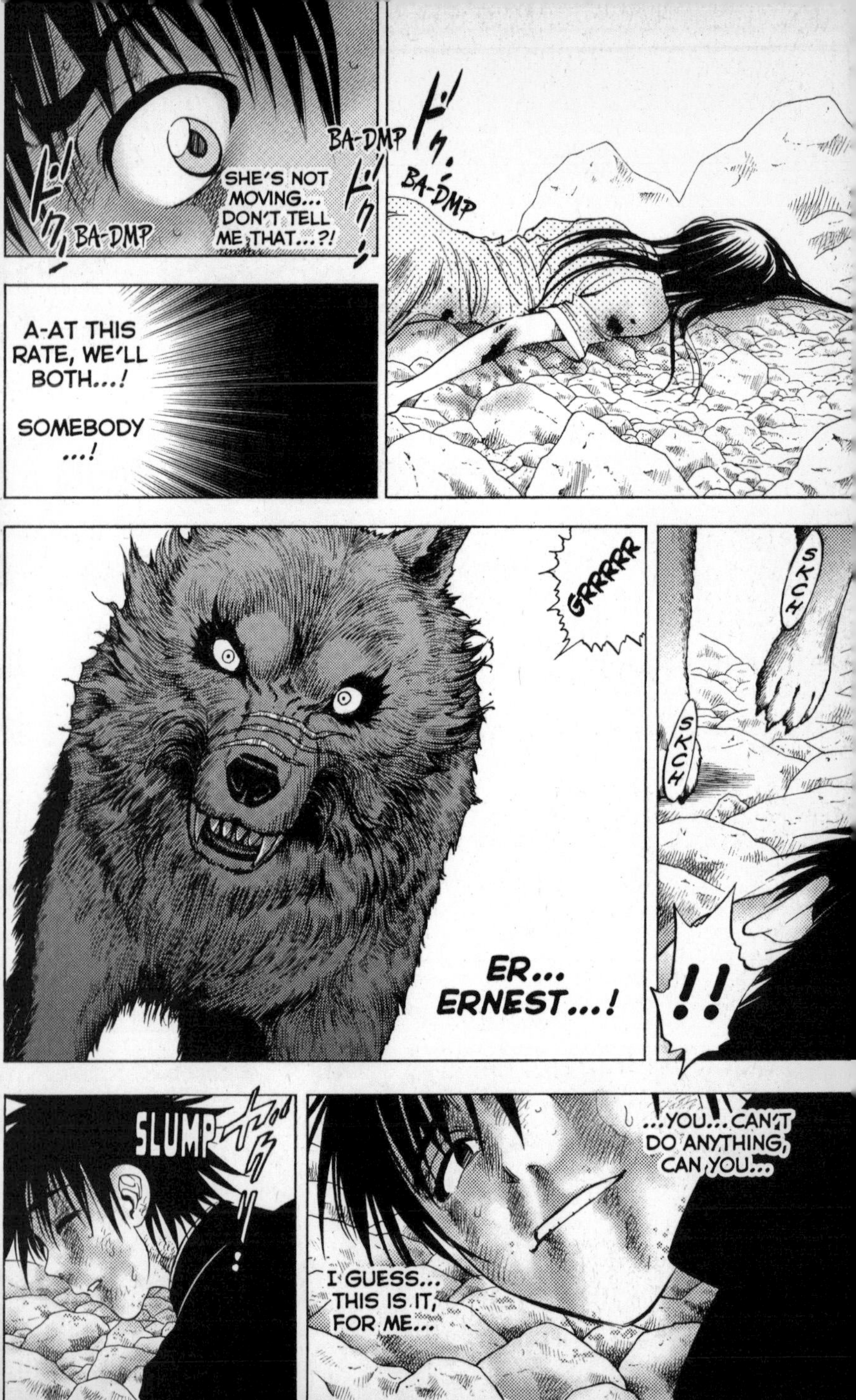
BA-DMP
BA-DMP
SHE'S NOT MOVING... DON'T TELL ME THAT...?!
BA-DMP
A-AT THIS RATE, WE'LL BOTH...!
SOMEBODY ...!
SKCH
SKCH
!!
GRRRRR
ER... ERNEST...!
...YOU... CAN'T DO ANYTHING, CAN YOU...
I GUESS... THIS IS IT, FOR ME...
SLUMP

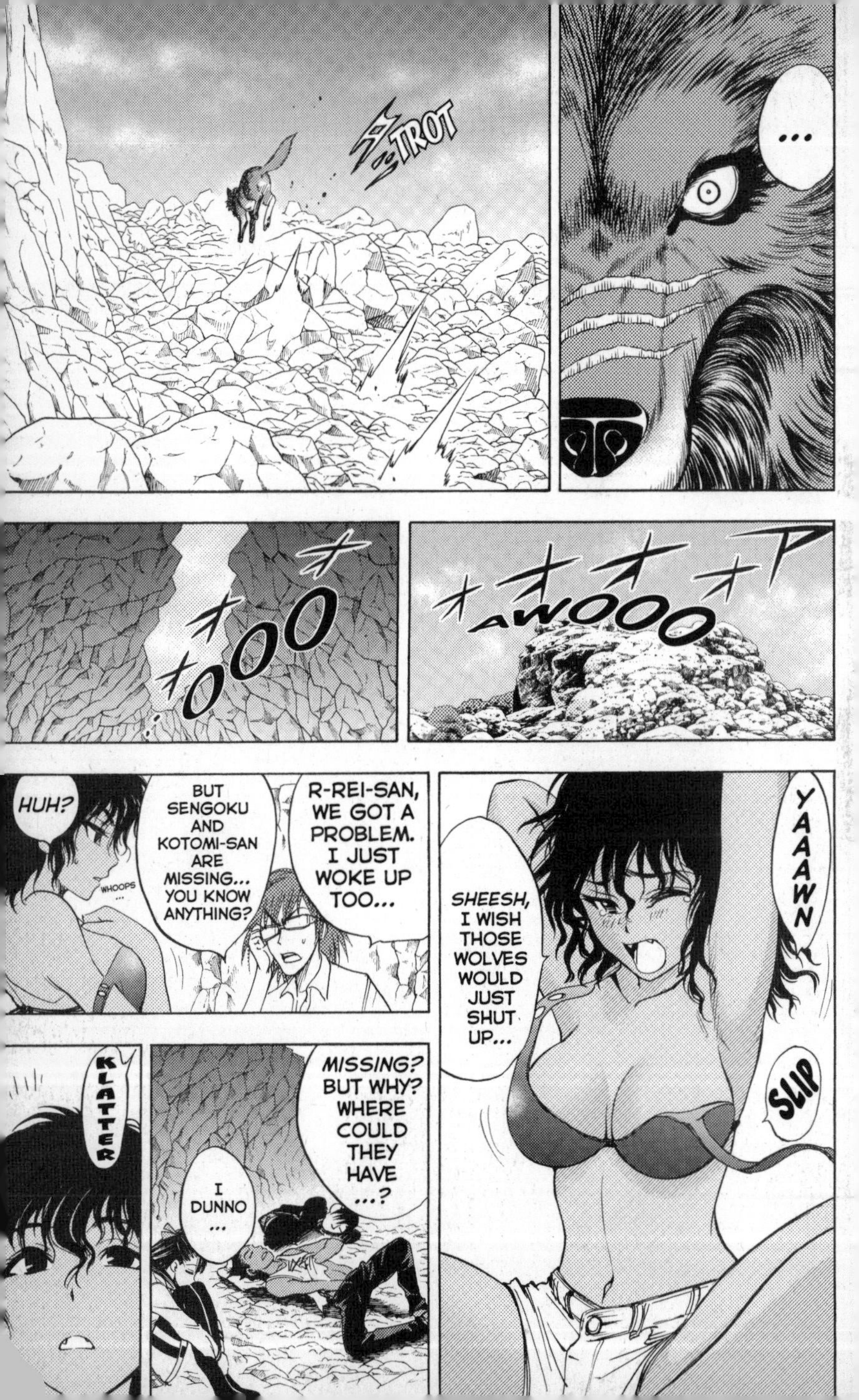
...
TROT
AWOOO
OOO
YAAAWN
SHEESH, I WISH THOSE WOLVES WOULD JUST SHUT UP...
SLIP
R-REI-SAN, WE GOT A PROBLEM. I JUST WOKE UP TOO...
BUT SENGOKU AND KOTOMI-SAN ARE MISSING... YOU KNOW ANYTHING?
HUH?
WHOOPS ...
MISSING? BUT WHY? WHERE COULD THEY HAVE ...?
I DUNNO ...
KLATTER

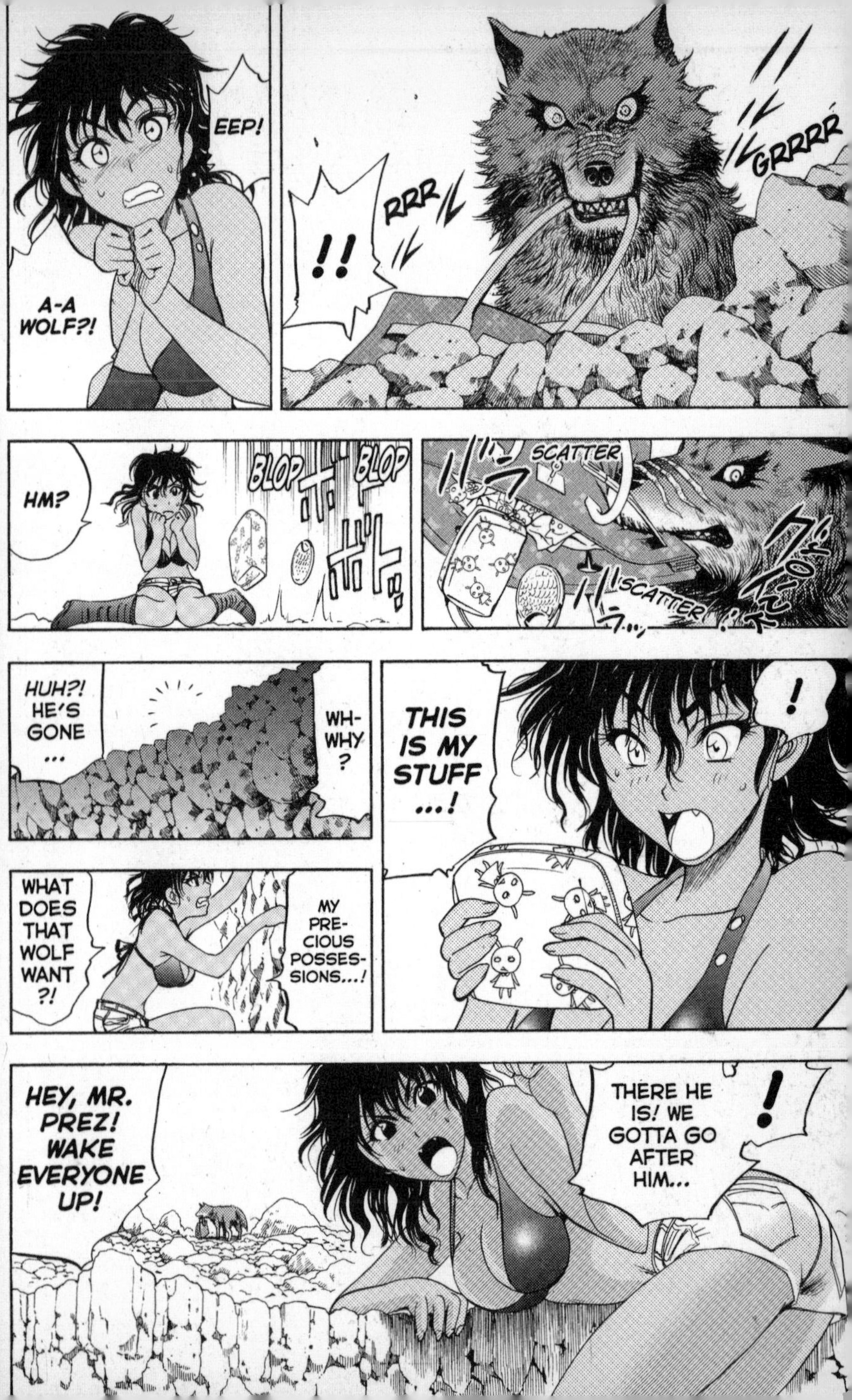
GRRRR
RRR
!!
EEP!
A-A WOLF?!
SCATTER
SCATTER
BLOP BLOP
HM?
!
THIS IS MY STUFF ...!
WH-WHY?
HUH?! HE'S GONE ...
MY PRECIOUS POSSESSIONS...!
WHAT DOES THAT WOLF WANT?!
!
THERE HE IS! WE GOTTA GO AFTER HIM...
HEY, MR. PREZ! WAKE EVERYONE UP!

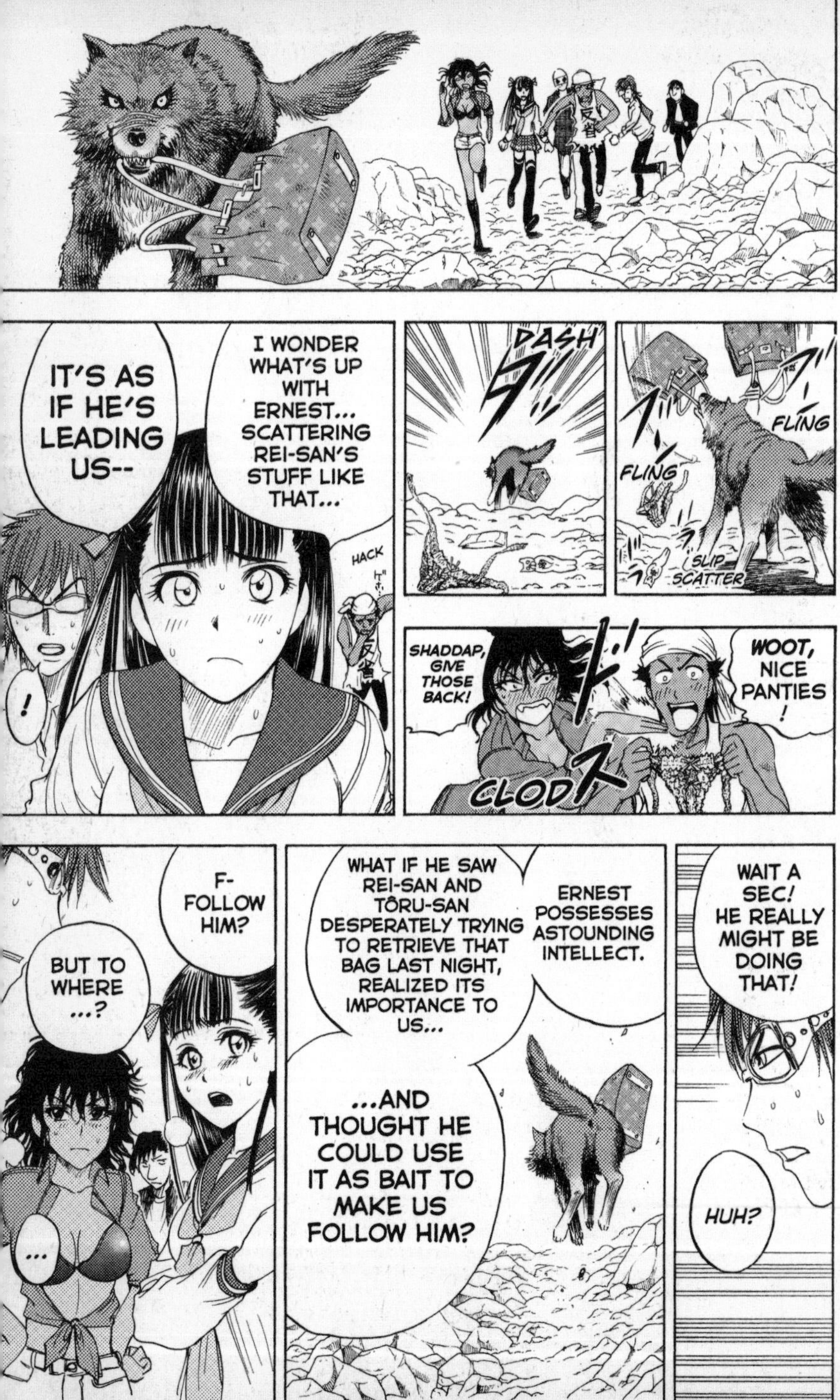
FLING
FLING
SLIP
SCATTER
DASH
WOOT, NICE PANTIES!
SHADDAP, GIVE THOSE BACK!
CLOD
I WONDER WHAT'S UP WITH ERNEST... SCATTERING REI-SAN'S STUFF LIKE THAT...
IT'S AS IF HE'S LEADING US--
HACK
!
WAIT A SEC! HE REALLY MIGHT BE DOING THAT!
HUH?
ERNEST POSSESSES ASTOUNDING INTELLECT.
WHAT IF HE SAW REI-SAN AND TÔRU-SAN DESPERATELY TRYING TO RETRIEVE THAT BAG LAST NIGHT, REALIZED ITS IMPORTANCE TO US...
...AND THOUGHT HE COULD USE IT AS BAIT TO MAKE US FOLLOW HIM?
F- FOLLOW HIM?
BUT TO WHERE ...?
...

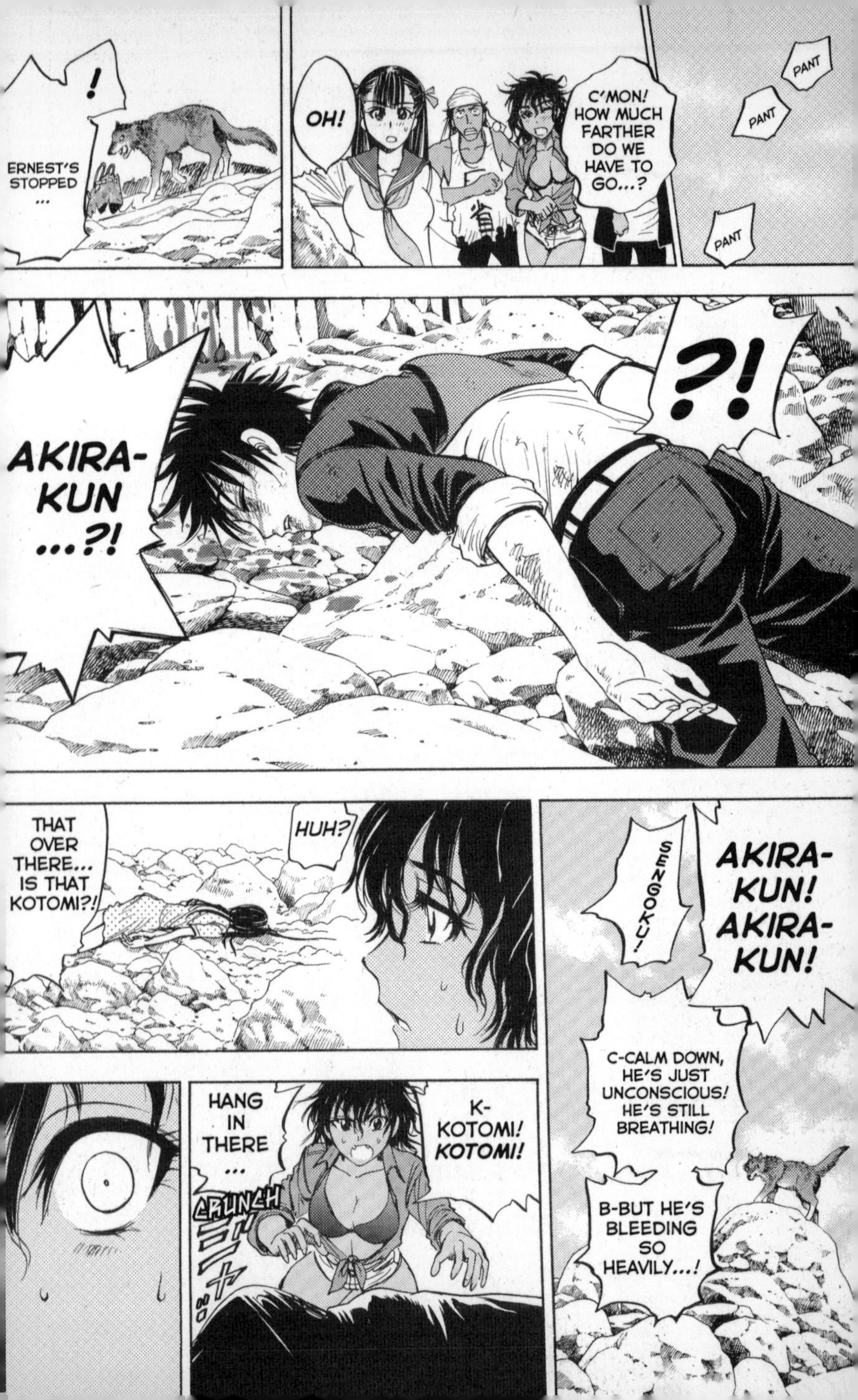
PANT
PANT
PANT
C'MON! HOW MUCH FARTHER DO WE HAVE TO GO...?
OH!
!
ERNEST'S STOPPED ...
?!
AKIRA-KUN ...?!
AKIRA-KUN! AKIRA-KUN!
SENGOKU!
C-CALM DOWN, HE'S JUST UNCONSCIOUS! HE'S STILL BREATHING!
B-BUT HE'S BLEEDING SO HEAVILY...!
HUH?
THAT OVER THERE... IS THAT KOTOMI?!
K-KOTOMI! KOTOMI!
HANG IN THERE ...
CRUNCH

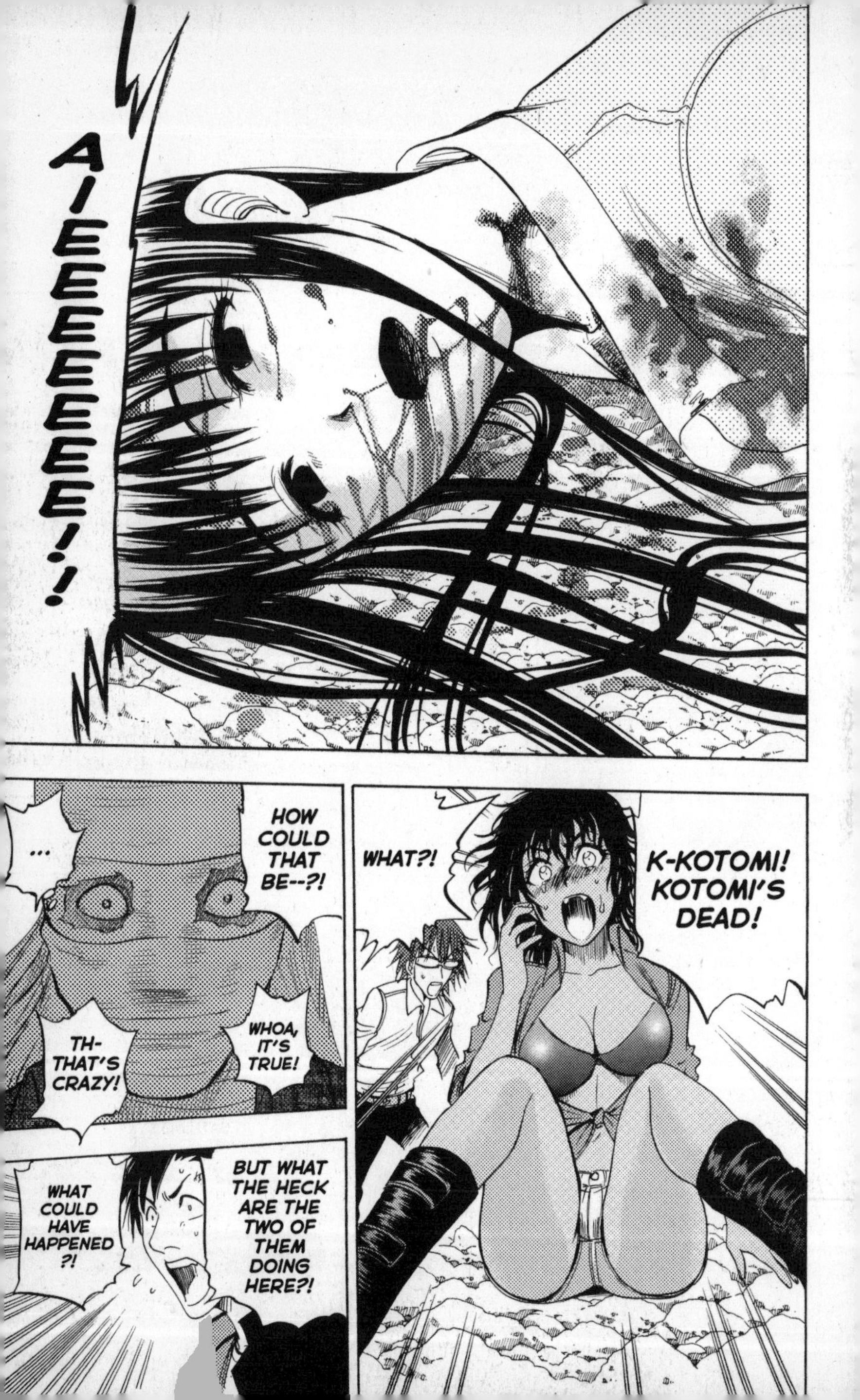
AIEEEEEEE!!
K-KOTOMI! KOTOMI'S DEAD!
WHAT?!
HOW COULD THAT BE--?!
...
WHOA, IT'S TRUE!
TH-THAT'S CRAZY!
BUT WHAT THE HECK ARE THE TWO OF THEM DOING HERE?!
WHAT COULD HAVE HAPPENED?!

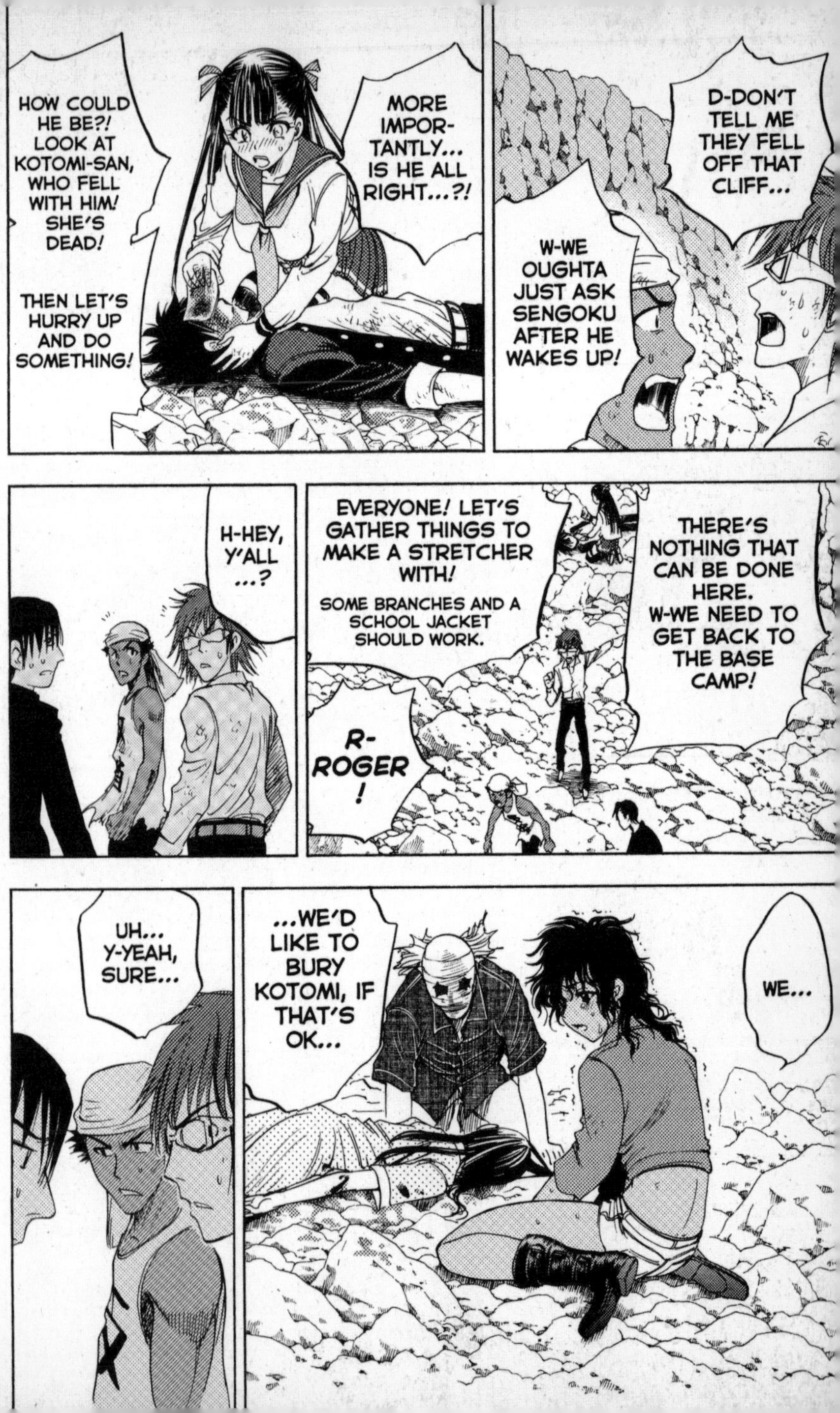
D-DON'T TELL ME THEY FELL OFF THAT CLIFF...
W-WE OUGHTA JUST ASK SENGOKU AFTER HE WAKES UP!
MORE IMPORTANTLY... IS HE ALL RIGHT...?!
HOW COULD HE BE?! LOOK AT KOTOMI-SAN, WHO FELL WITH HIM! SHE'S DEAD!
THEN LET'S HURRY UP AND DO SOMETHING!
THERE'S NOTHING THAT CAN BE DONE HERE. W-WE NEED TO GET BACK TO THE BASE CAMP!
EVERYONE! LET'S GATHER THINGS TO MAKE A STRETCHER WITH!
SOME BRANCHES AND A SCHOOL JACKET SHOULD WORK.
R-ROGER!
H-HEY, Y'ALL ...?
WE...
...WE'D LIKE TO BURY KOTOMI, IF THAT'S OK...
UH... Y-YEAH, SURE...

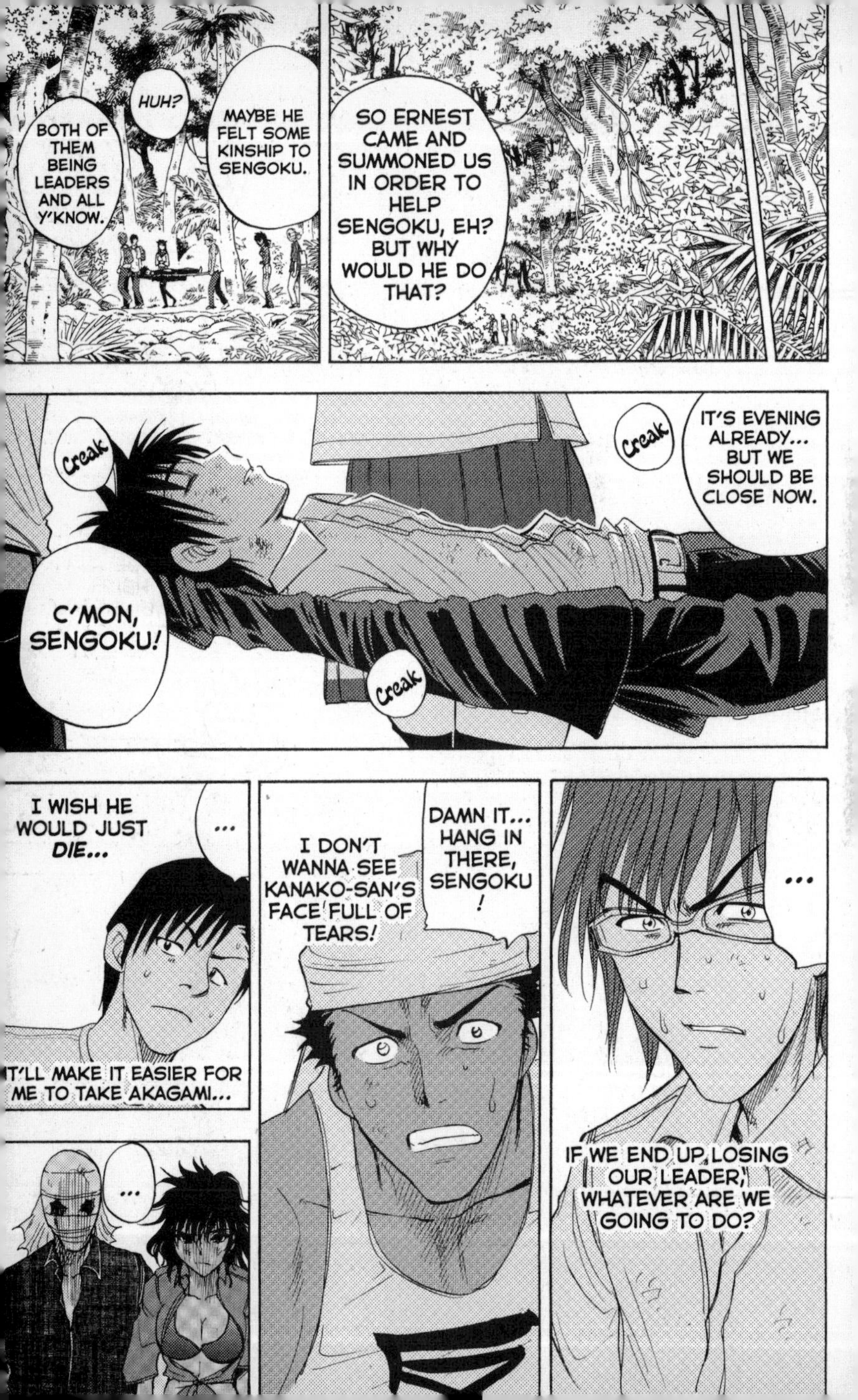
SO ERNEST CAME AND SUMMONED US IN ORDER TO HELP SENGOKU, EH? BUT WHY WOULD HE DO THAT?
MAYBE HE FELT SOME KINSHIP TO SENGOKU.
HUH?
BOTH OF THEM BEING LEADERS AND ALL Y'KNOW.
IT'S EVENING ALREADY... BUT WE SHOULD BE CLOSE NOW.
Creak
Creak
C'MON, SENGOKU!
Creak
...
IF WE END UP LOSING OUR LEADER, WHATEVER ARE WE GOING TO DO?
DAMN IT... HANG IN THERE, SENGOKU!
I DON'T WANNA SEE KANAKO-SAN'S FACE FULL OF TEARS!
...
I WISH HE WOULD JUST *DIE*...
IT'LL MAKE IT EASIER FOR ME TO TAKE AKAGAMI...
...

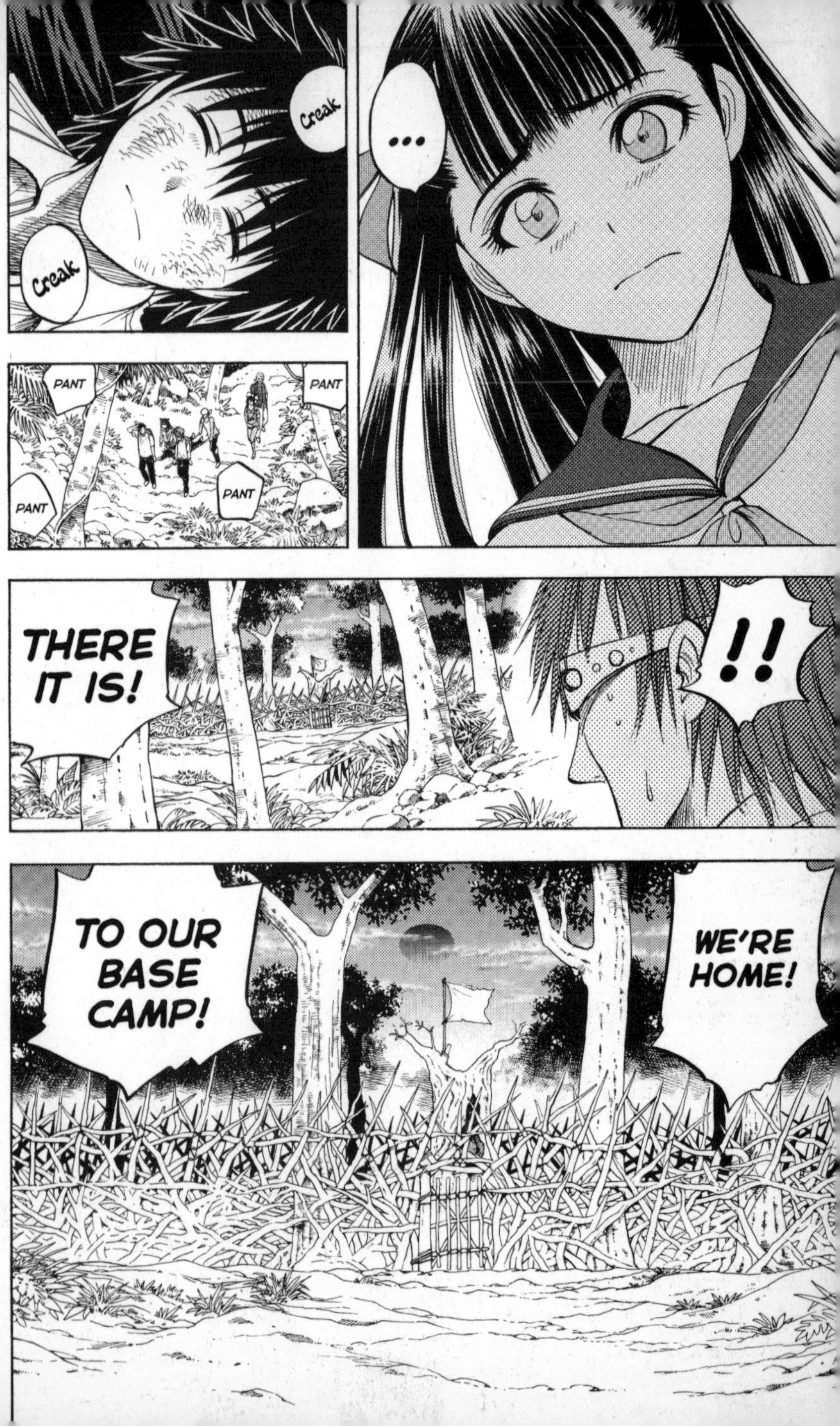
...
Creak
Creak
PANT
PANT
PANT
PANT
!!
THERE IT IS!
WE'RE HOME!
TO OUR BASE CAMP!

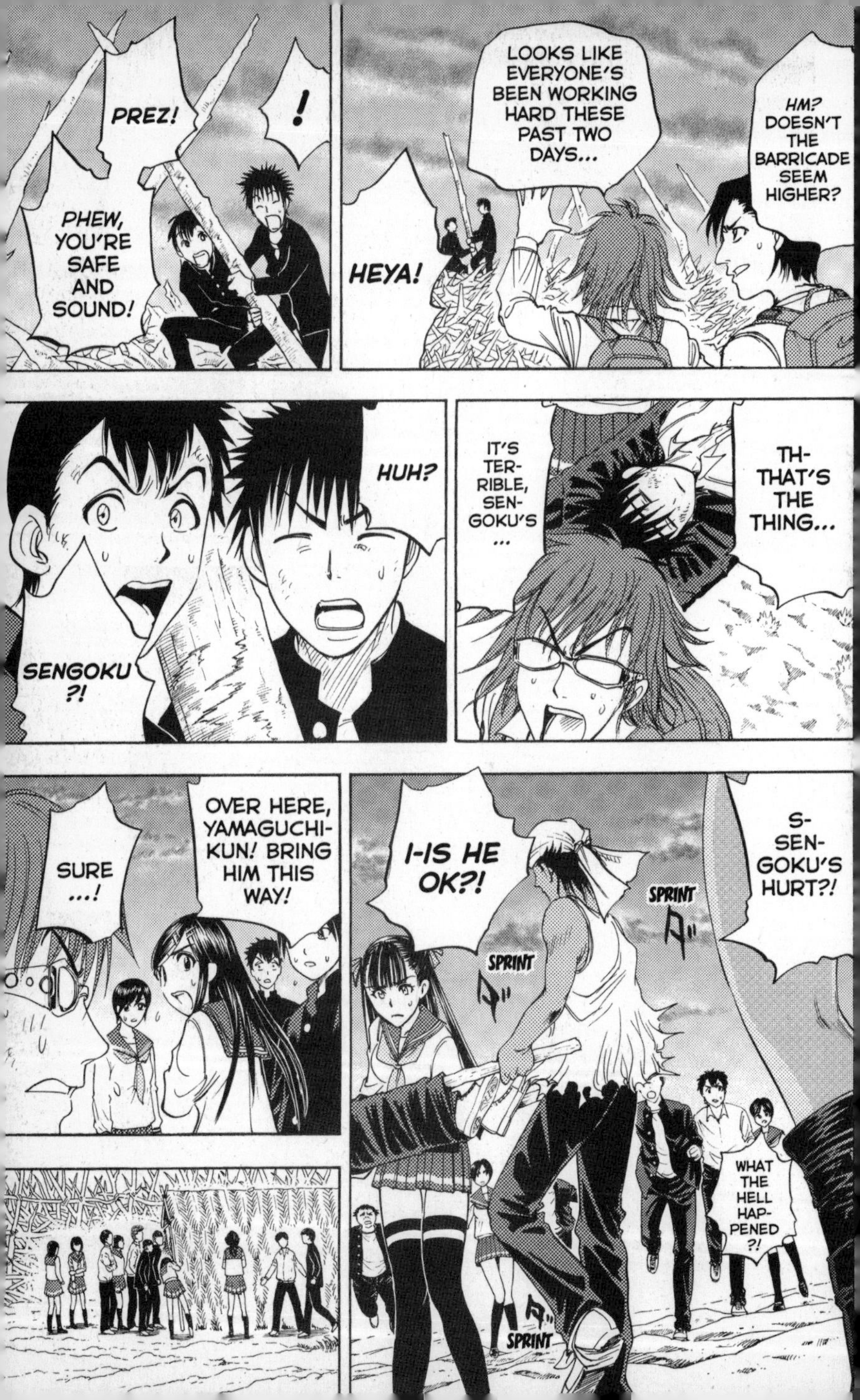
HM? DOESN'T THE BARRICADE SEEM HIGHER?
LOOKS LIKE EVERYONE'S BEEN WORKING HARD THESE PAST TWO DAYS...
HEYA!
!
PREZ!
PHEW, YOU'RE SAFE AND SOUND!
TH-THAT'S THE THING...
IT'S TERRIBLE, SENGOKU'S ...
HUH?
SENGOKU?!
S-SENGOKU'S HURT?!
SPRINT
I-IS HE OK?!
SPRINT
WHAT THE HELL HAPPENED?!
SPRINT
OVER HERE, YAMAGUCHI-KUN! BRING HIM THIS WAY!
SURE ...!

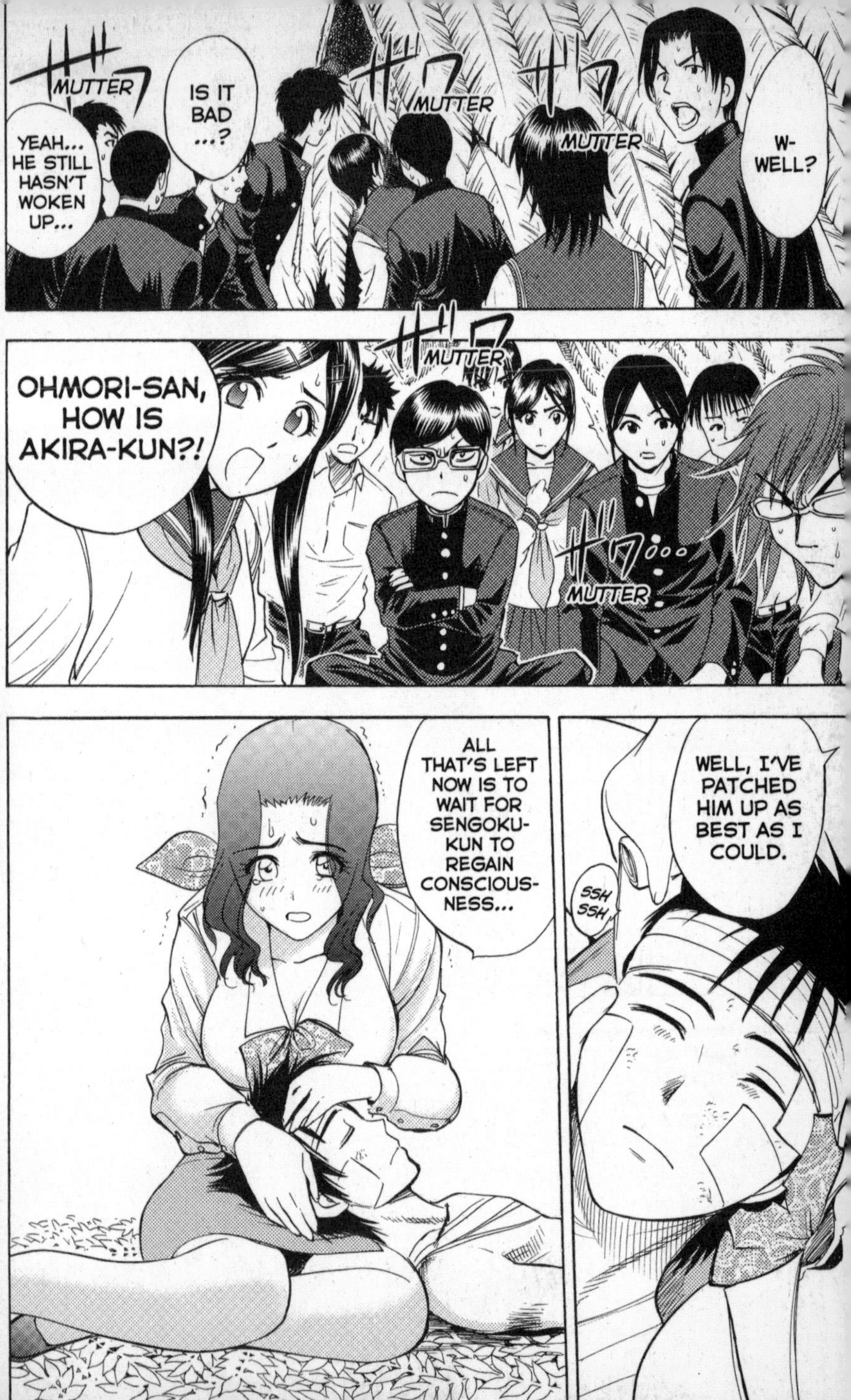
W-WELL?
MUTTER
MUTTER
MUTTER
IS IT BAD ...?
MUTTER
YEAH... HE STILL HASN'T WOKEN UP...
MUTTER
OHMORI-SAN, HOW IS AKIRA-KUN?!
MUTTER
WELL, I'VE PATCHED HIM UP AS BEST AS I COULD.
SSH SSH
ALL THAT'S LEFT NOW IS TO WAIT FOR SENGOKU-KUN TO REGAIN CONSCIOUS-NESS...

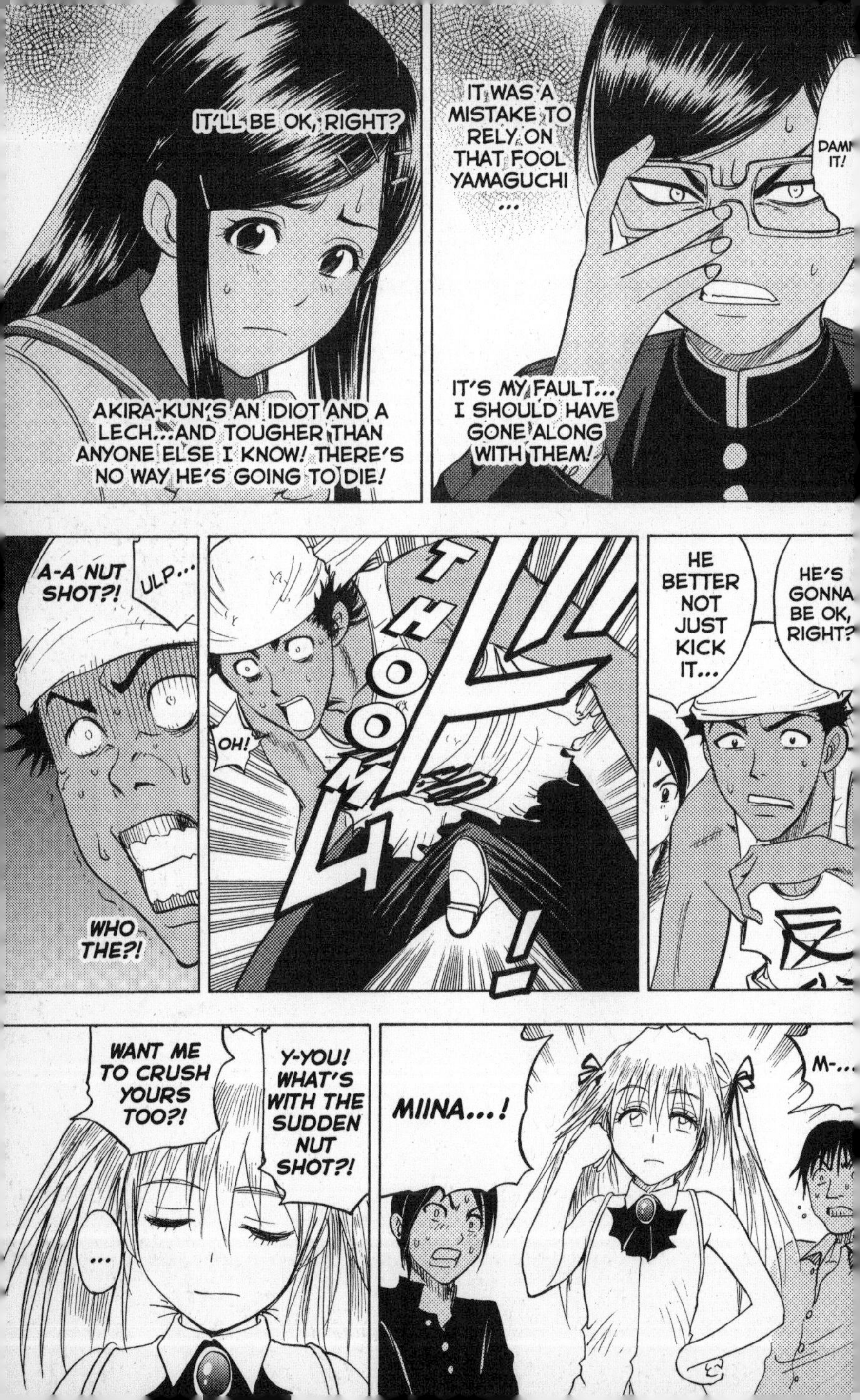
DAMN IT!
IT WAS A MISTAKE TO RELY ON THAT FOOL YAMAGUCHI ...
IT'S MY FAULT... I SHOULD HAVE GONE ALONG WITH THEM!
IT'LL BE OK, RIGHT?
AKIRA-KUN'S AN IDIOT AND A LECH...AND TOUGHER THAN ANYONE ELSE I KNOW! THERE'S NO WAY HE'S GOING TO DIE!
HE'S GONNA BE OK, RIGHT?
HE BETTER NOT JUST KICK IT...
THOOMP!
OH!
ULP...
A-A NUT SHOT?!
WHO THE?!
M-...
MIINA...!
Y-YOU! WHAT'S WITH THE SUDDEN NUT SHOT?!
WANT ME TO CRUSH YOURS TOO?!
...

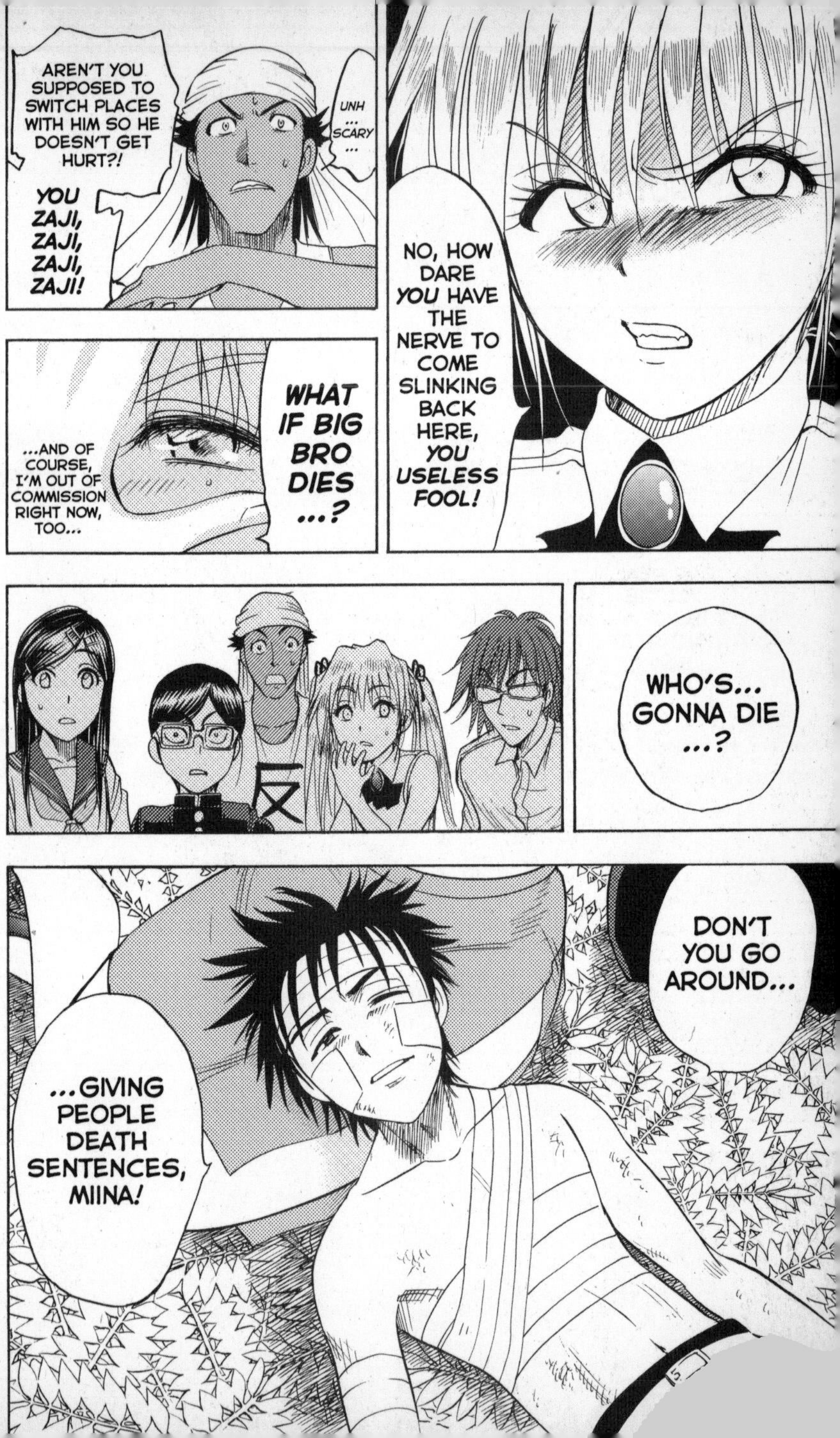
NO, HOW DARE YOU HAVE THE NERVE TO COME SLINKING BACK HERE, YOU USELESS FOOL!
UNH ... SCARY ...
AREN'T YOU SUPPOSED TO SWITCH PLACES WITH HIM SO HE DOESN'T GET HURT?!
YOU ZAJI, ZAJI, ZAJI, ZAJI!
WHAT IF BIG BRO DIES ...?
...AND OF COURSE, I'M OUT OF COMMISSION RIGHT NOW, TOO...
WHO'S... GONNA DIE ...?
DON'T YOU GO AROUND...
...GIVING PEOPLE DEATH SENTENCES, MIINA!

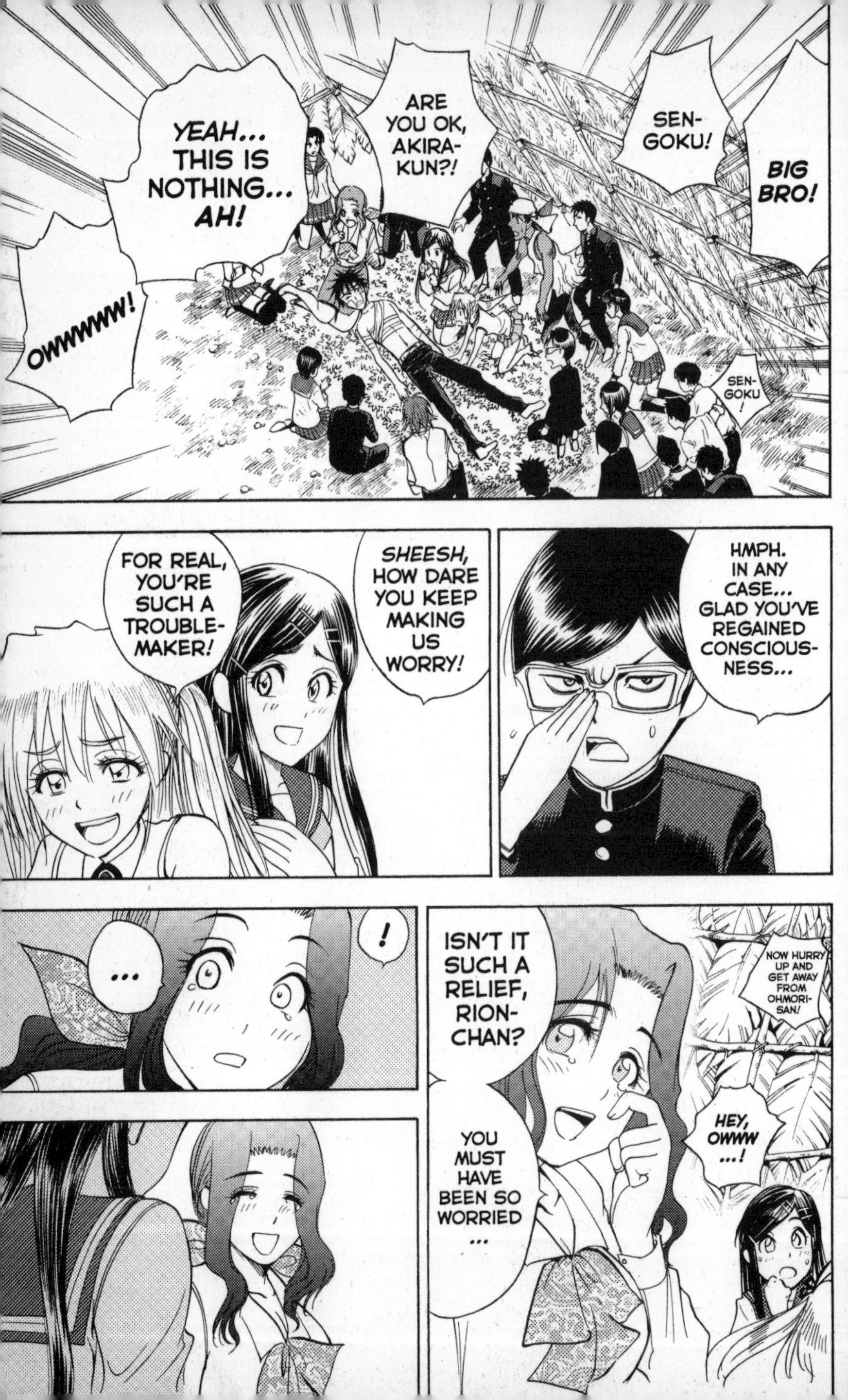
BIG BRO!
SEN-GOKU!
SEN-GOKU!
ARE YOU OK, AKIRA-KUN?!
YEAH... THIS IS NOTHING... AH!
OWWWWW!
HMPH. IN ANY CASE... GLAD YOU'VE REGAINED CONSCIOUS-NESS...
SHEESH, HOW DARE YOU KEEP MAKING US WORRY!
FOR REAL, YOU'RE SUCH A TROUBLE-MAKER!
NOW HURRY UP AND GET AWAY FROM OHMORI-SAN!
ISN'T IT SUCH A RELIEF, RION-CHAN?
HEY, OWWW ...!
YOU MUST HAVE BEEN SO WORRIED ...
!
...

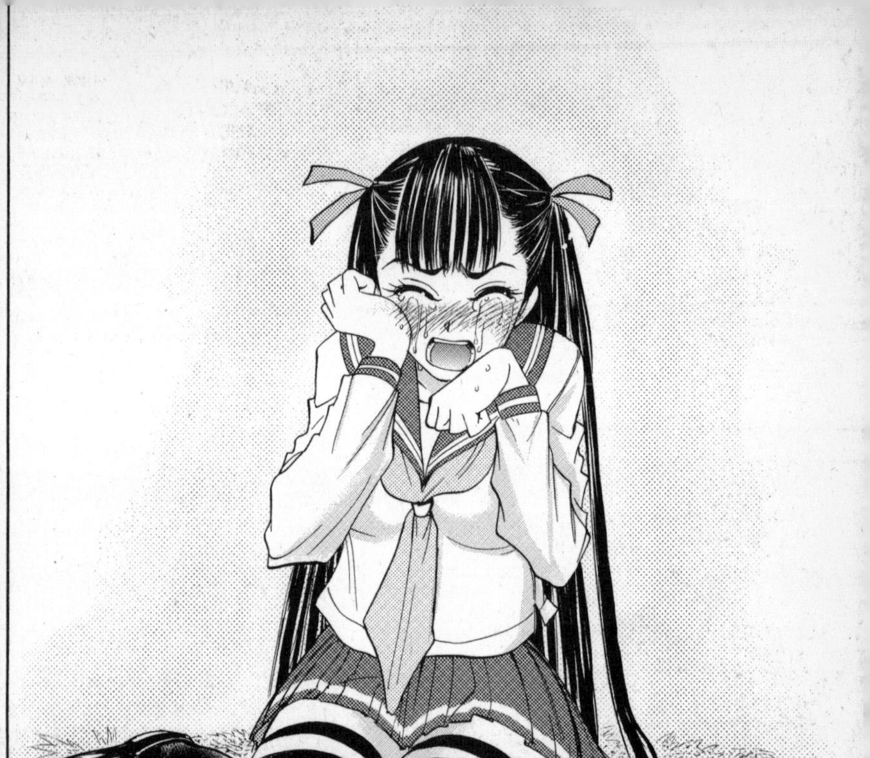

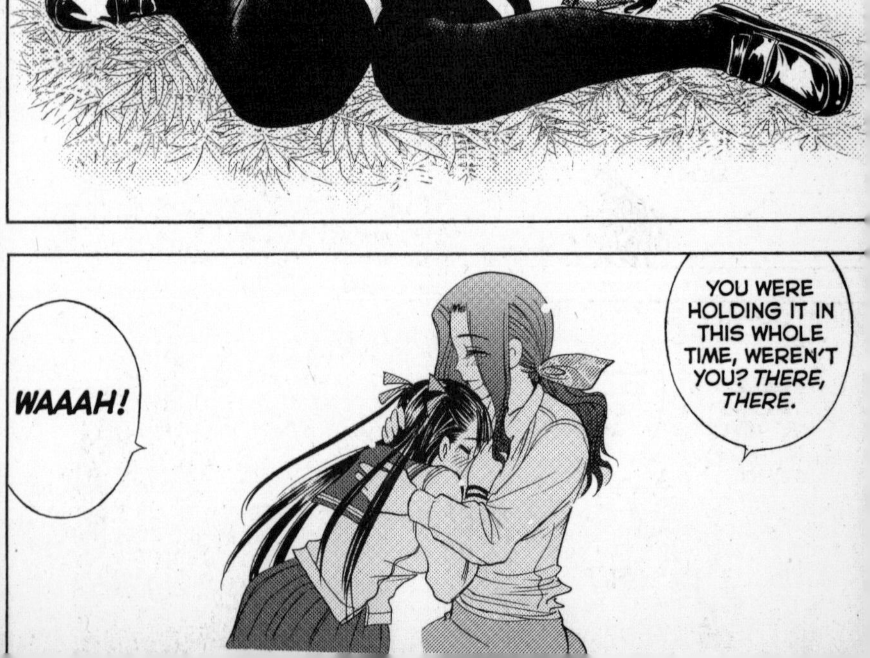
YOU WERE HOLDING IT IN THIS WHOLE TIME, WEREN'T YOU? *THERE, THERE.*
WAAAH!

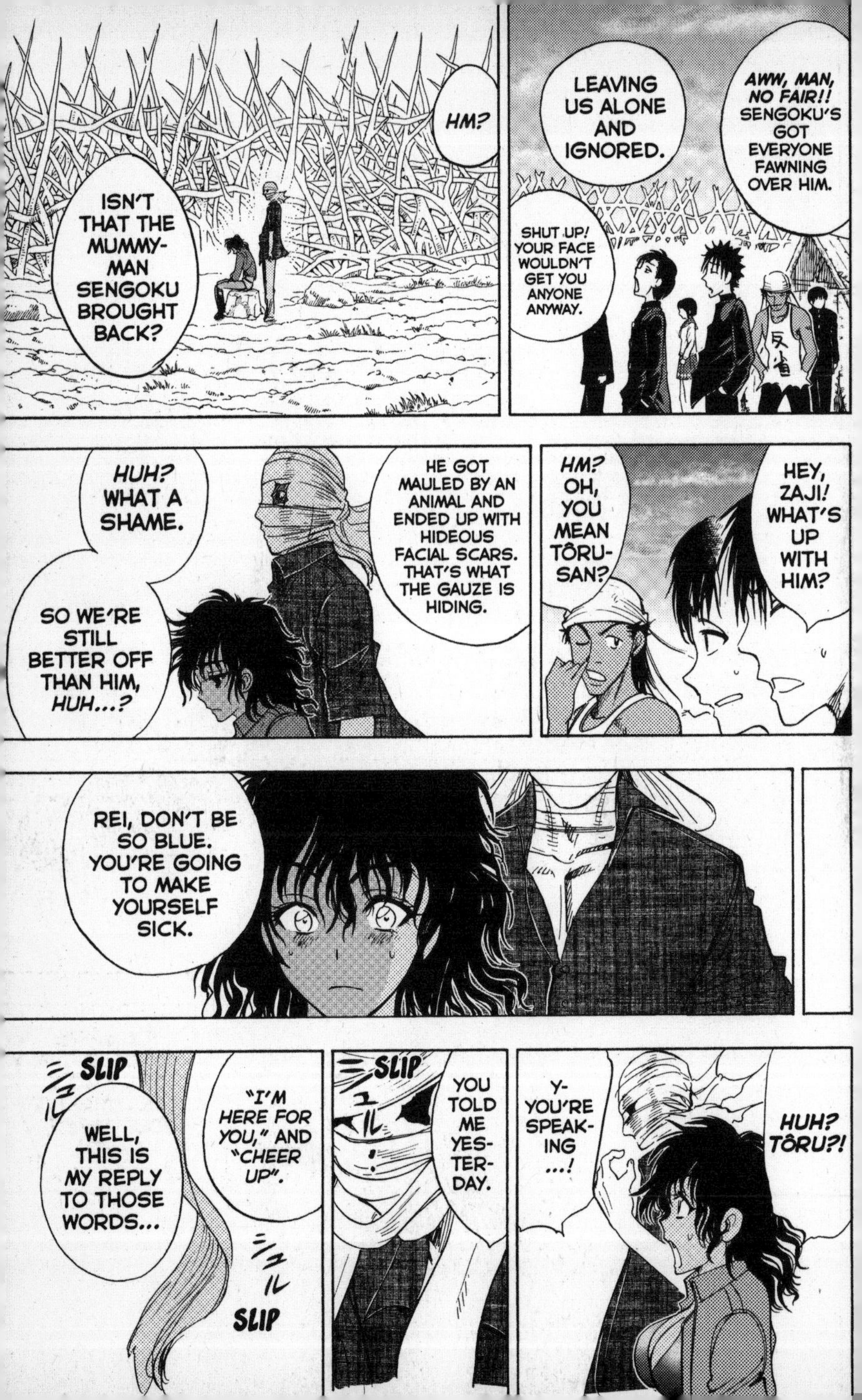
AWW, MAN, NO FAIR!! SENGOKU'S GOT EVERYONE FAWNING OVER HIM.
LEAVING US ALONE AND IGNORED.
SHUT UP! YOUR FACE WOULDN'T GET YOU ANYONE ANYWAY.
HM?
ISN'T THAT THE MUMMY-MAN SENGOKU BROUGHT BACK?
HEY, ZAJI! WHAT'S UP WITH HIM?
HM? OH, YOU MEAN TÔRU-SAN?
HE GOT MAULED BY AN ANIMAL AND ENDED UP WITH HIDEOUS FACIAL SCARS. THAT'S WHAT THE GAUZE IS HIDING.
HUH? WHAT A SHAME.
SO WE'RE STILL BETTER OFF THAN HIM, HUH...?
REI, DON'T BE SO BLUE. YOU'RE GOING TO MAKE YOURSELF SICK.
HUH? TÔRU?!
Y-YOU'RE SPEAK-ING...!
SLIP
YOU TOLD ME YES-TER-DAY.
SLIP
"I'M HERE FOR YOU," AND "CHEER UP".
WELL, THIS IS MY REPLY TO THOSE WORDS...
SLIP

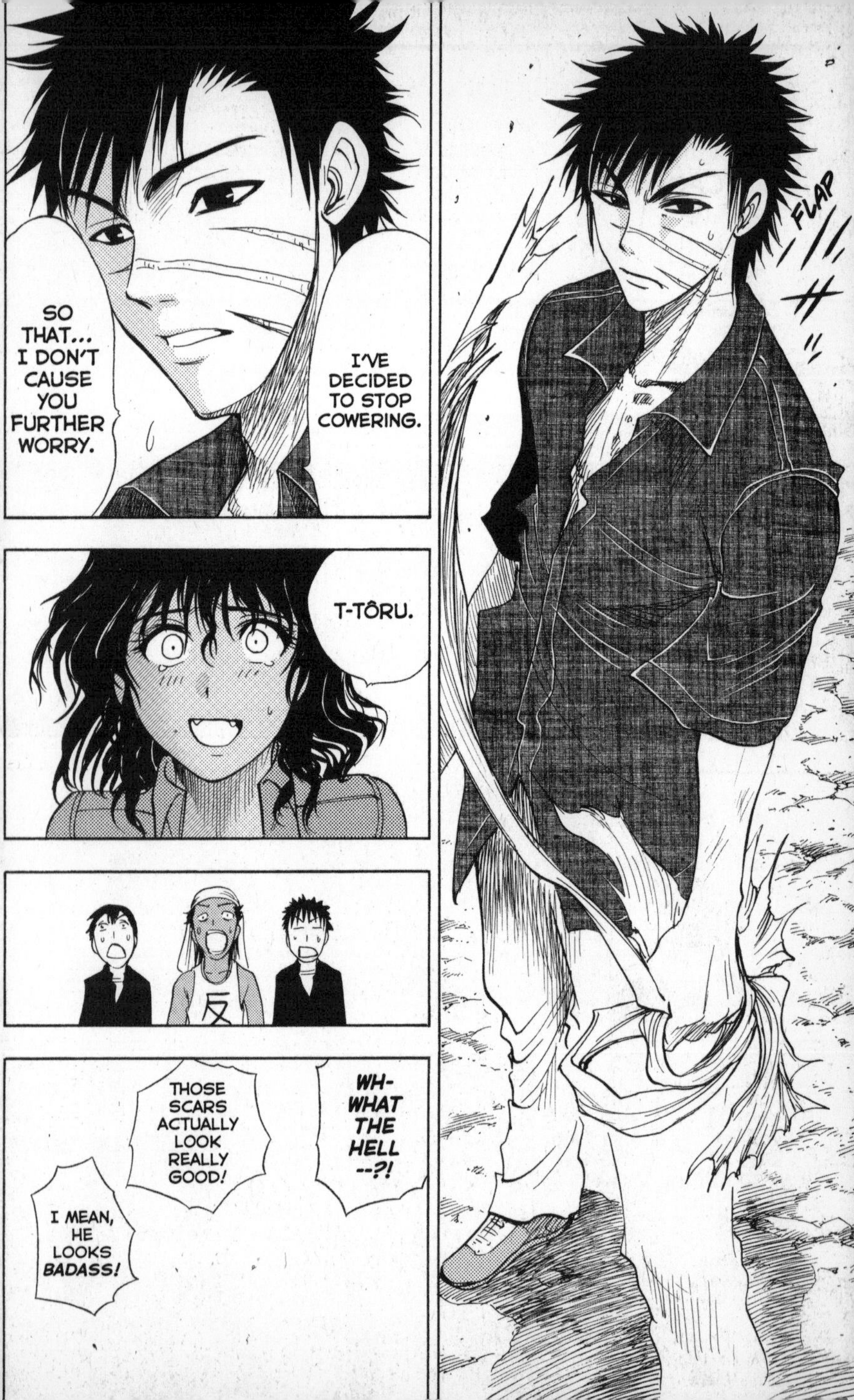
FLAP
I'VE DECIDED TO STOP COWERING.
SO THAT... I DON'T CAUSE YOU FURTHER WORRY.
T-TÔRU.
WH-WHAT THE HELL--?!
THOSE SCARS ACTUALLY LOOK REALLY GOOD!
I MEAN, HE LOOKS BADASS!

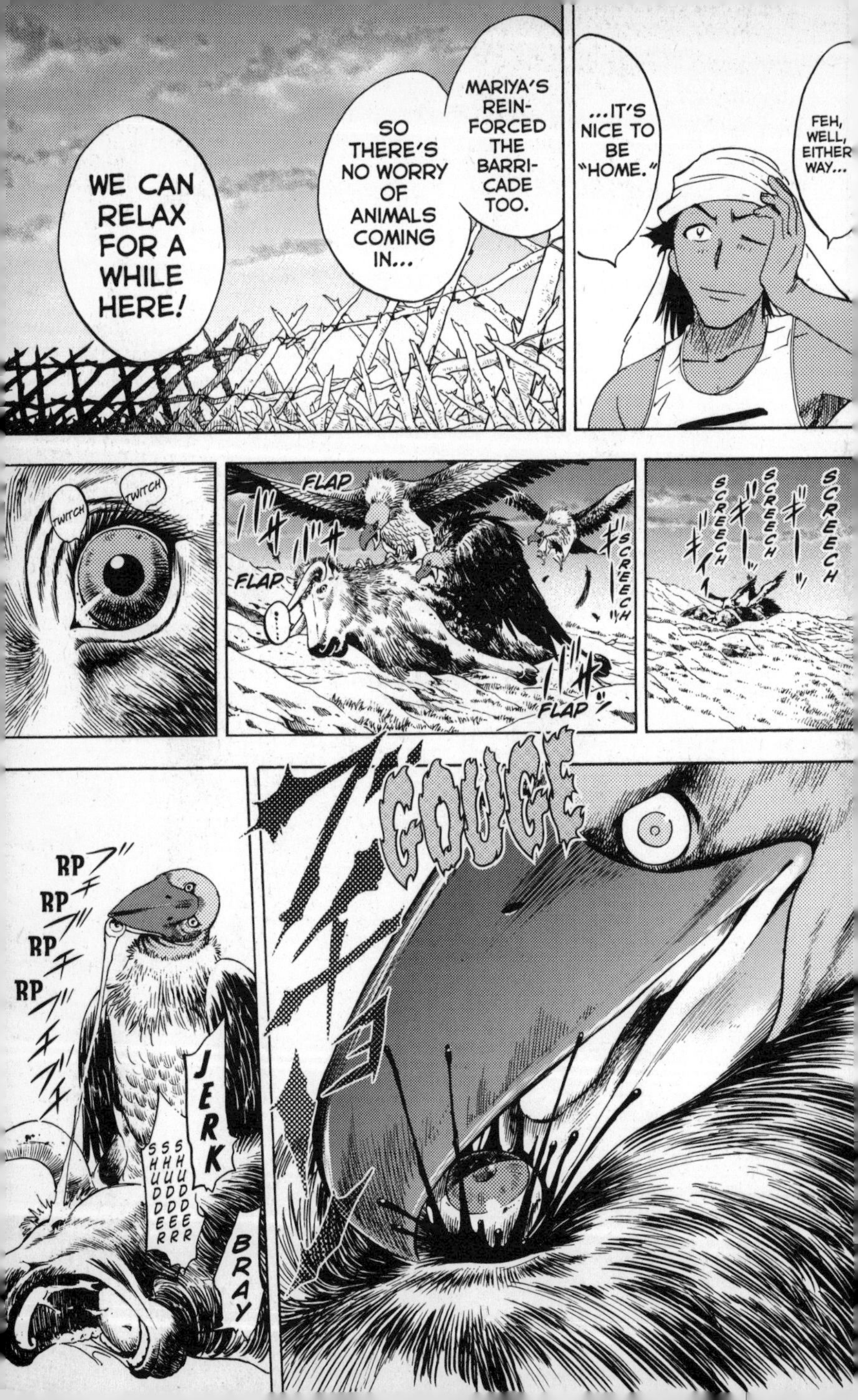
FEH, WELL, EITHER WAY...
...IT'S NICE TO BE "HOME."
MARIYA'S REIN-FORCED THE BARRI-CADE TOO.
SO THERE'S NO WORRY OF ANIMALS COMING IN...
WE CAN RELAX FOR A WHILE HERE!
SCREECH
SCREECH
SCREECH
FLAP
SCREECH
FLAP
...
FLAP
TWITCH
TWITCH
GOUGE
RP
RP
RP
RP
JERK
SHUDDER
SHUDDER
BRAY

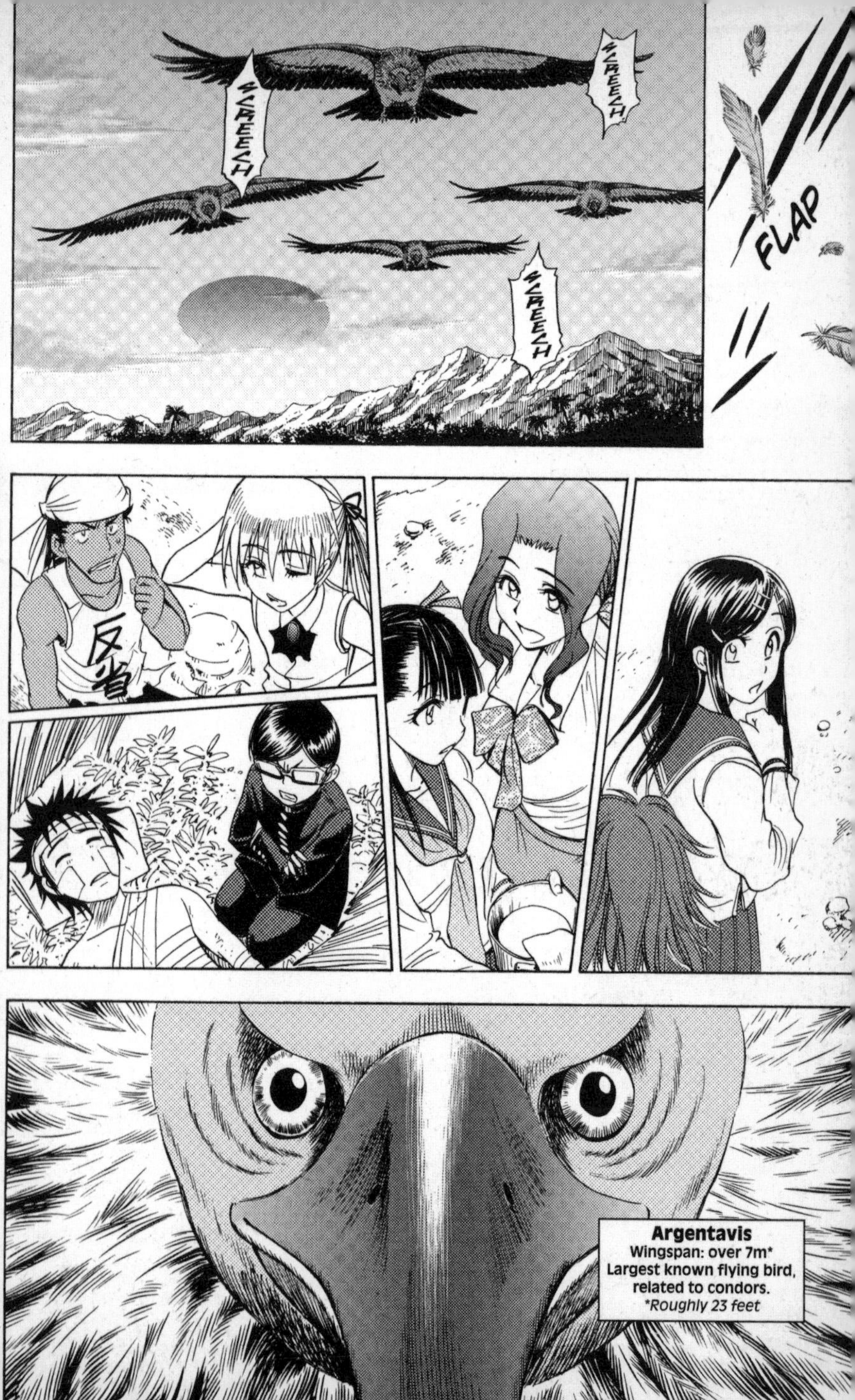
FLAP
SCREECH
SCREECH
SCREECH
反省
Argentavis
Wingspan: over 7m*
Largest known flying bird, related to condors.
*Roughly 23 feet

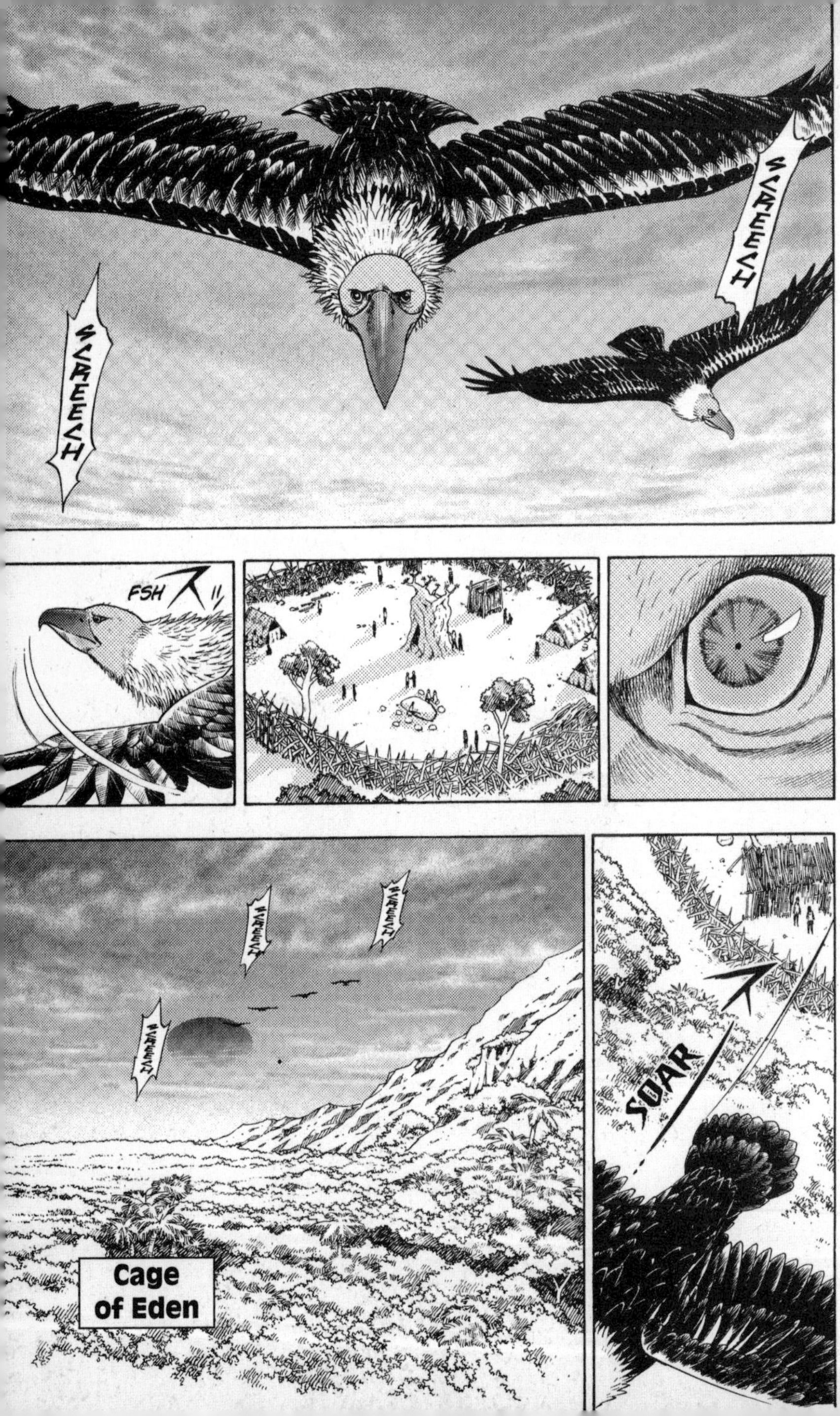
SCREECH
SCREECH
FSH
SOAR
SCREECH
SCREECH
SCREECH
Cage of Eden

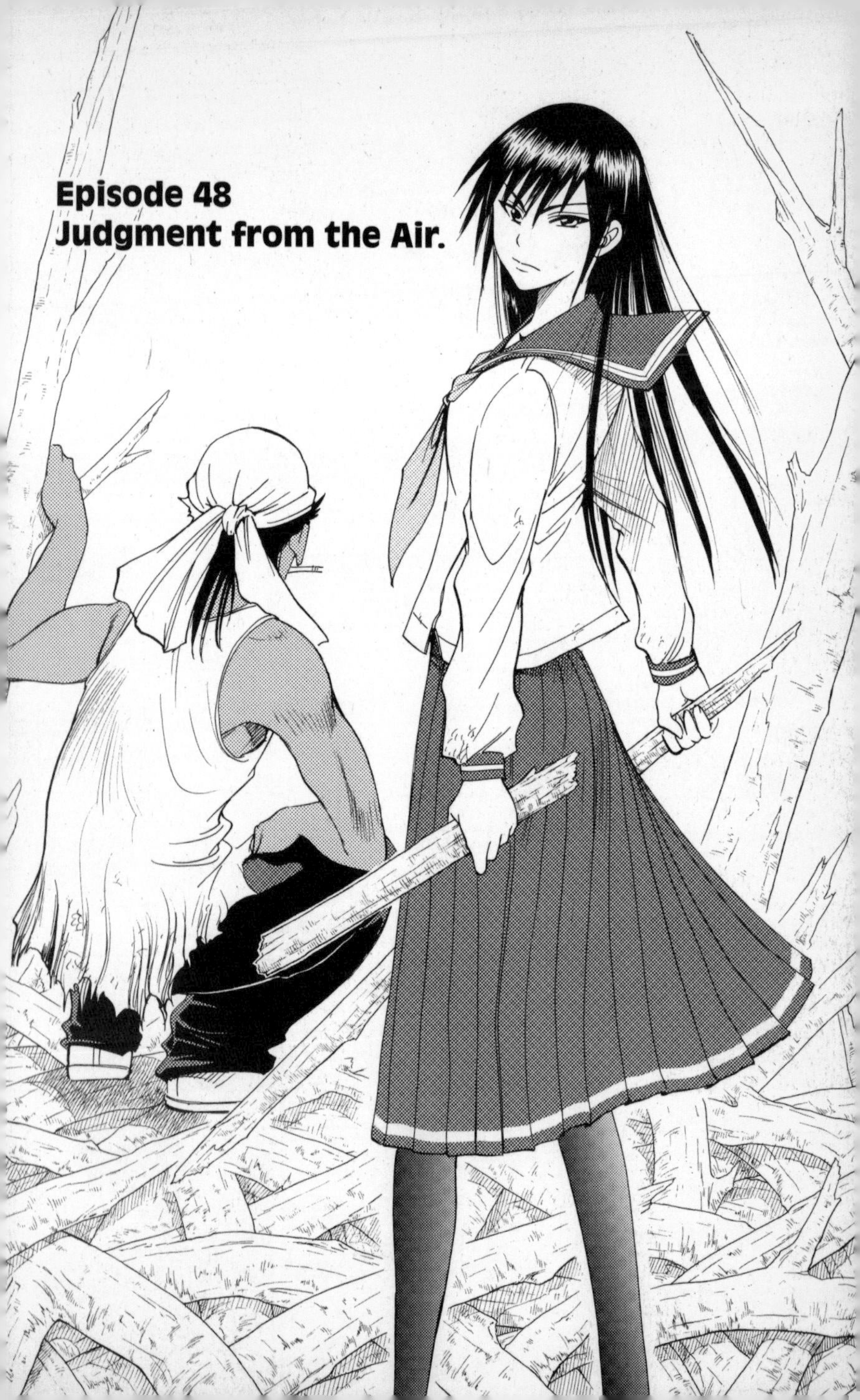
Episode 48
Judgment from the Air.

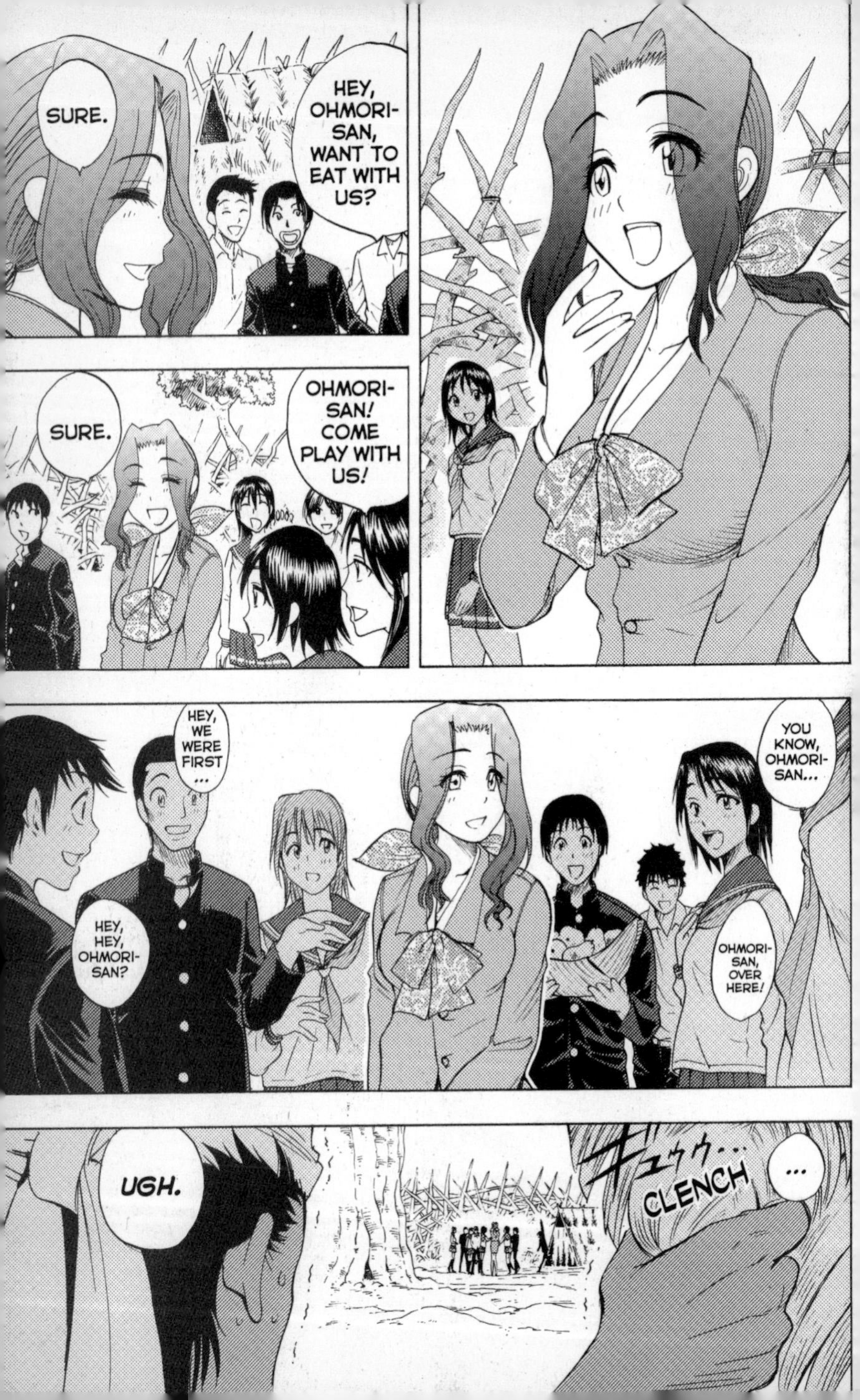
HEY, OHMORI-SAN, WANT TO EAT WITH US?
SURE.
OHMORI-SAN! COME PLAY WITH US!
SURE.
YOU KNOW, OHMORI-SAN...
OHMORI-SAN, OVER HERE!
HEY, WE WERE FIRST ...
HEY, HEY, OHMORI-SAN?
...
ギュウウ...
CLENCH
UGH.

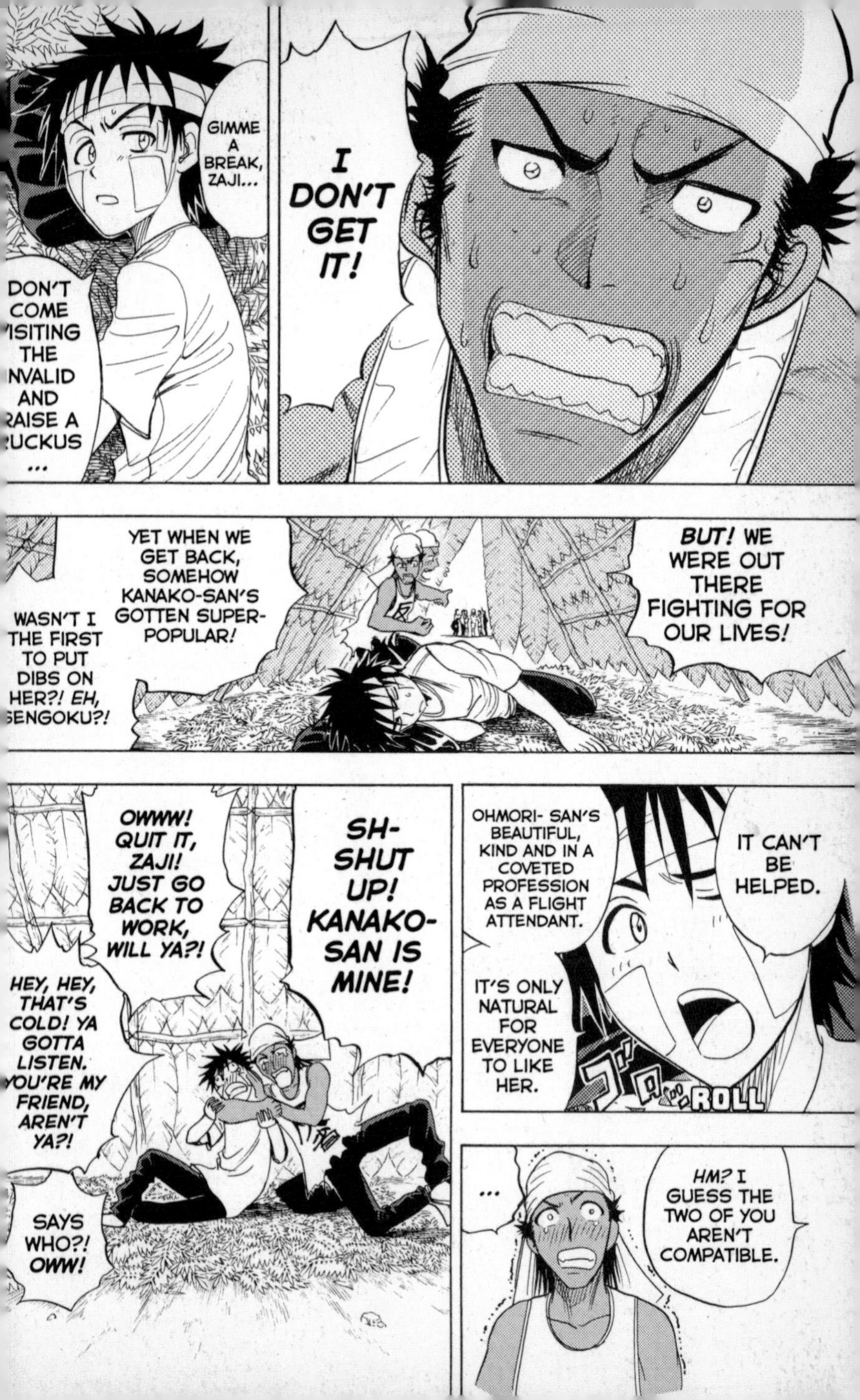
I DON'T GET IT!
GIMME A BREAK, ZAJI...
DON'T COME VISITING THE INVALID AND RAISE A RUCKUS ...
BUT! WE WERE OUT THERE FIGHTING FOR OUR LIVES!
YET WHEN WE GET BACK, SOMEHOW KANAKO-SAN'S GOTTEN SUPER-POPULAR!
WASN'T I THE FIRST TO PUT DIBS ON HER?! EH, SENGOKU?!
IT CAN'T BE HELPED.
OHMORI- SAN'S BEAUTIFUL, KIND AND IN A COVETED PROFESSION AS A FLIGHT ATTENDANT.
IT'S ONLY NATURAL FOR EVERYONE TO LIKE HER.
ROLL
HM? I GUESS THE TWO OF YOU AREN'T COMPATIBLE.
...
SH-SHUT UP! KANAKO-SAN IS MINE!
OWWW! QUIT IT, ZAJI! JUST GO BACK TO WORK, WILL YA?!
HEY, HEY, THAT'S COLD! YA GOTTA LISTEN. YOU'RE MY FRIEND, AREN'T YA?!
SAYS WHO?! OWW!

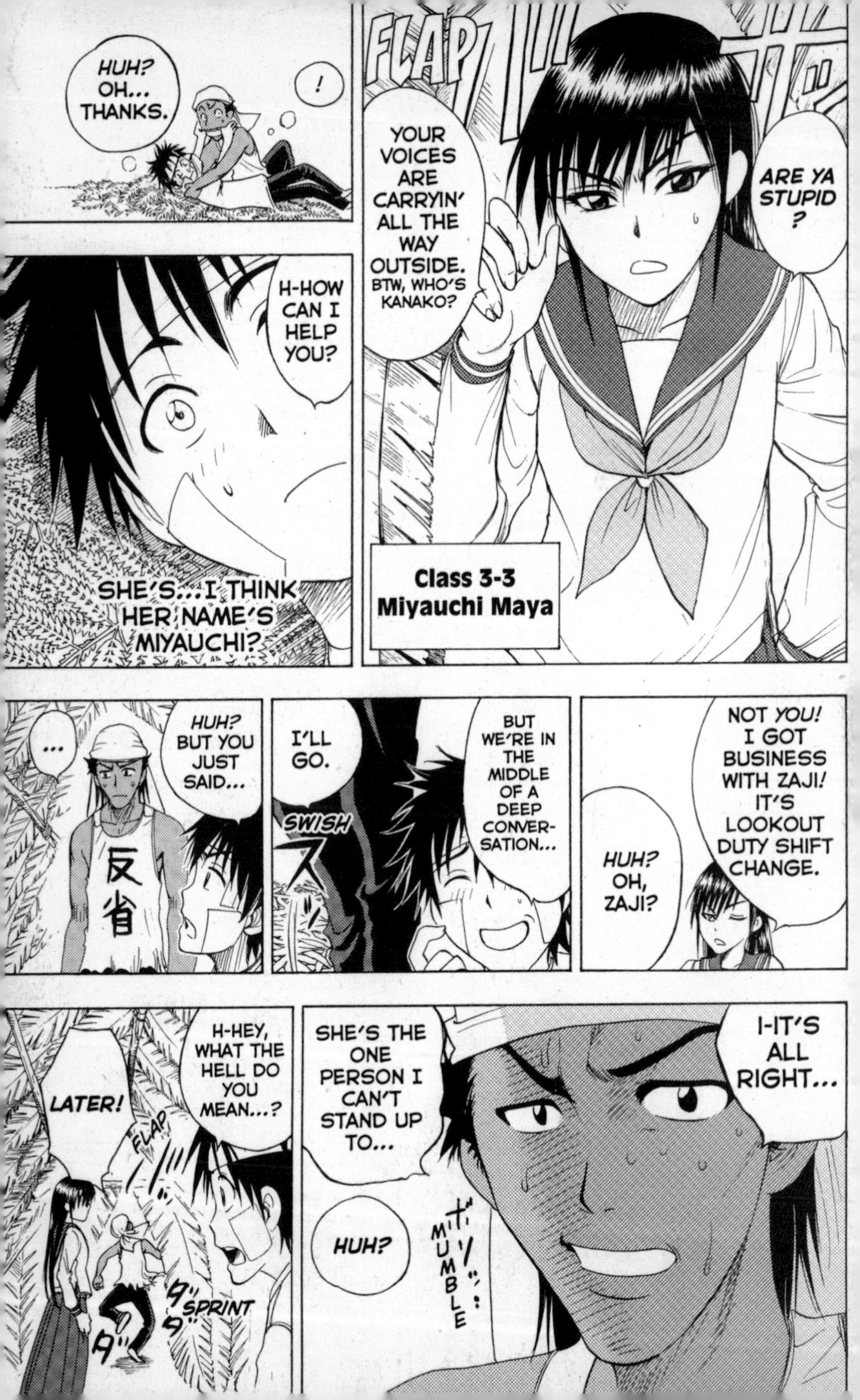
FLAP
ARE YA STUPID?
YOUR VOICES ARE CARRYIN' ALL THE WAY OUTSIDE. BTW, WHO'S KANAKO?
Class 3-3
Miyauchi Maya
!
HUH? OH... THANKS.
H-HOW CAN I HELP YOU?
SHE'S... I THINK HER NAME'S MIYAUCHI?
NOT YOU! I GOT BUSINESS WITH ZAJI! IT'S LOOKOUT DUTY SHIFT CHANGE.
HUH? OH, ZAJI?
BUT WE'RE IN THE MIDDLE OF A DEEP CONVERSATION...
I'LL GO.
SWISH
HUH? BUT YOU JUST SAID...
...
反省
I-IT'S ALL RIGHT...
SHE'S THE ONE PERSON I CAN'T STAND UP TO...
HUH?
MUMBLE
H-HEY, WHAT THE HELL DO YOU MEAN...?
LATER!
FLAP
SPRINT

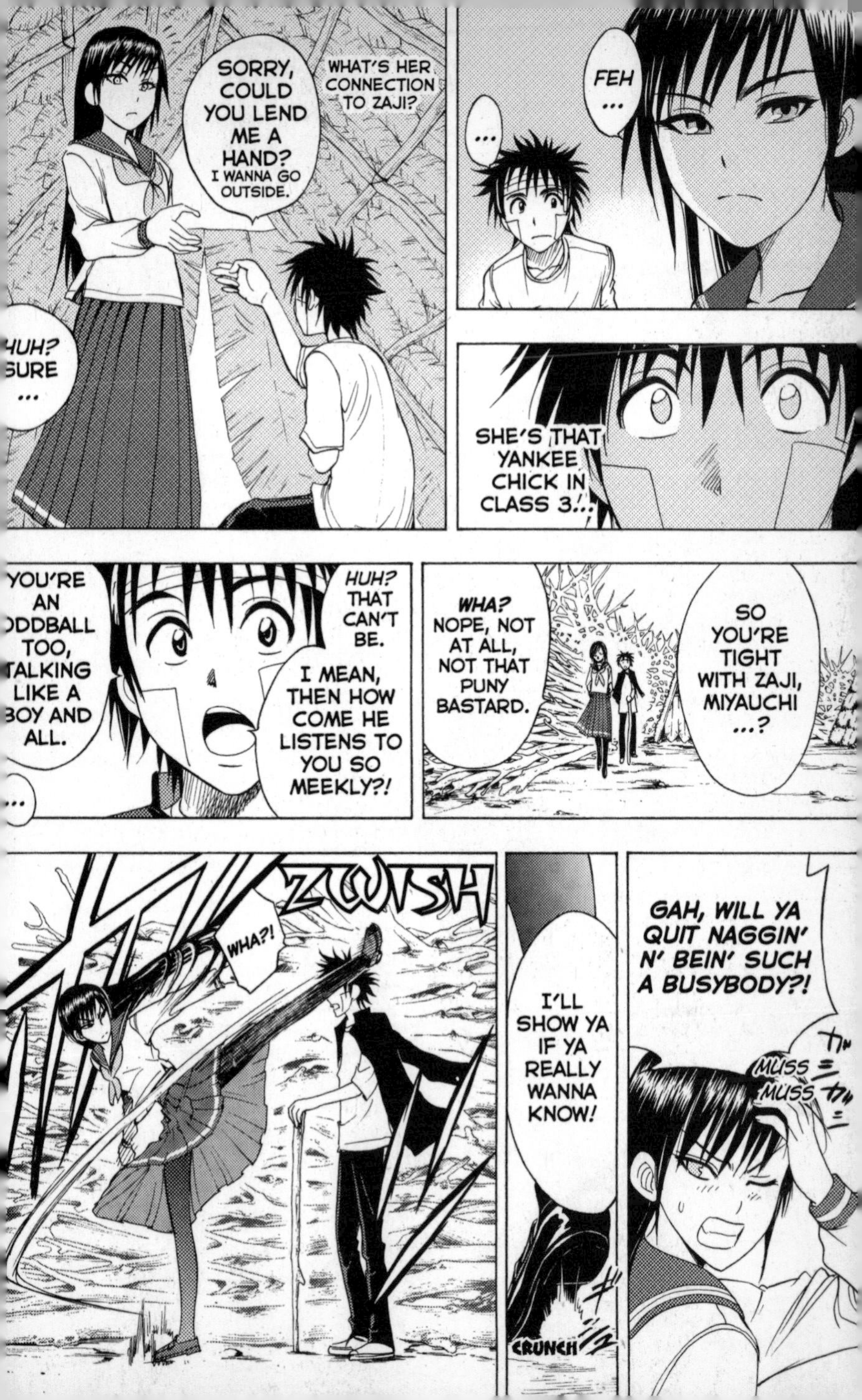
FEH ...
...
SHE'S THAT YANKEE CHICK IN CLASS 3...
SORRY, COULD YOU LEND ME A HAND? I WANNA GO OUTSIDE.
WHAT'S HER CONNECTION TO ZAJI?
HUH? SURE ...
SO YOU'RE TIGHT WITH ZAJI, MIYAUCHI ...?
WHA? NOPE, NOT AT ALL, NOT THAT PUNY BASTARD.
HUH? THAT CAN'T BE.
I MEAN, THEN HOW COME HE LISTENS TO YOU SO MEEKLY?!
YOU'RE AN ODDBALL TOO, TALKING LIKE A BOY AND ALL.
...
GAH, WILL YA QUIT NAGGIN' N' BEIN' SUCH A BUSYBODY?!
MUSS MUSS
I'LL SHOW YA IF YA REALLY WANNA KNOW!
CRUNCH
ZWISH
WHA?!

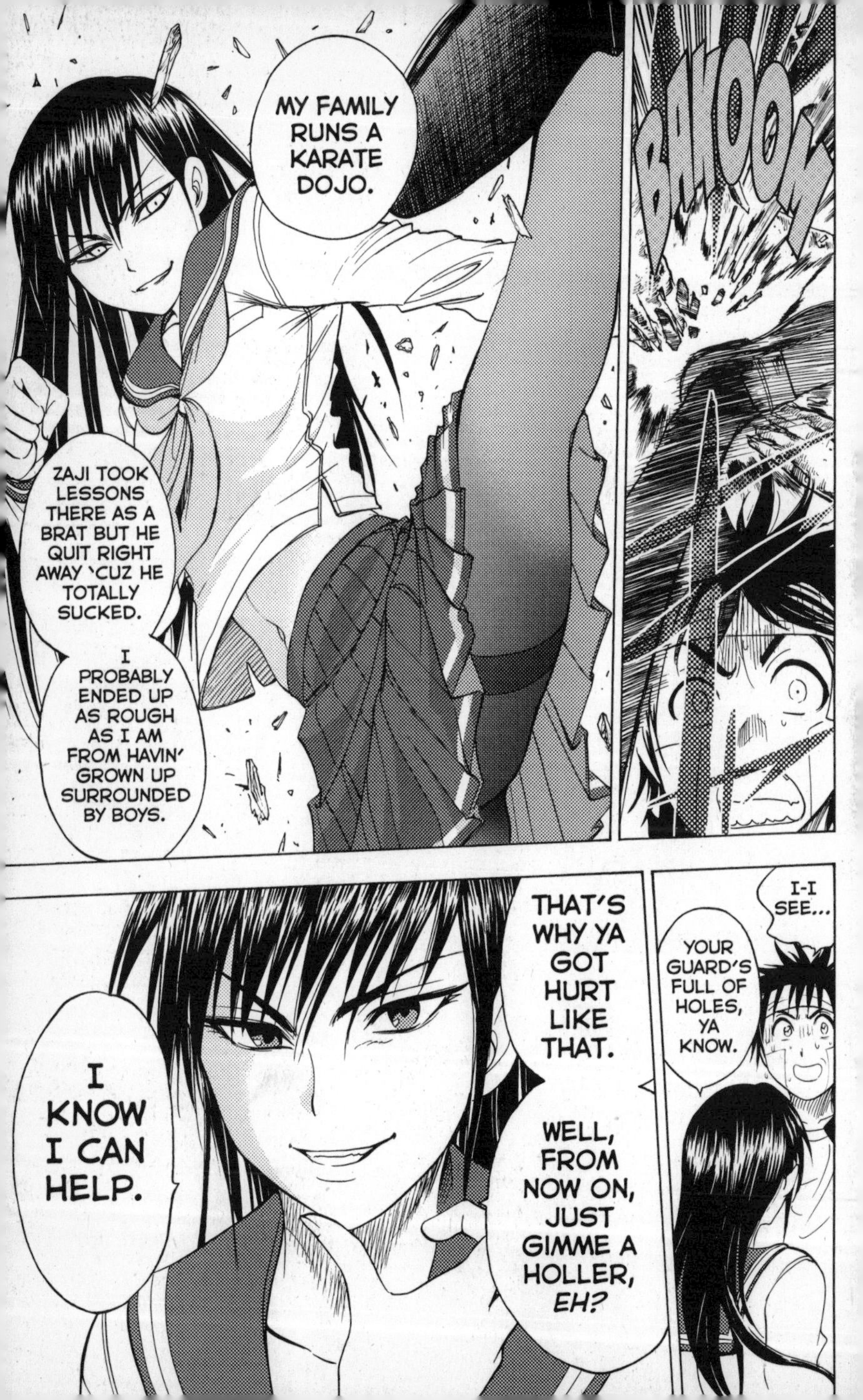
BAKOOM
MY FAMILY RUNS A KARATE DOJO.
ZAJI TOOK LESSONS THERE AS A BRAT BUT HE QUIT RIGHT AWAY 'CUZ HE TOTALLY SUCKED.
I PROBABLY ENDED UP AS ROUGH AS I AM FROM HAVIN' GROWN UP SURROUNDED BY BOYS.
I-I SEE...
YOUR GUARD'S FULL OF HOLES, YA KNOW.
THAT'S WHY YA GOT HURT LIKE THAT.
WELL, FROM NOW ON, JUST GIMME A HOLLER, *EH?*
I KNOW I CAN HELP.

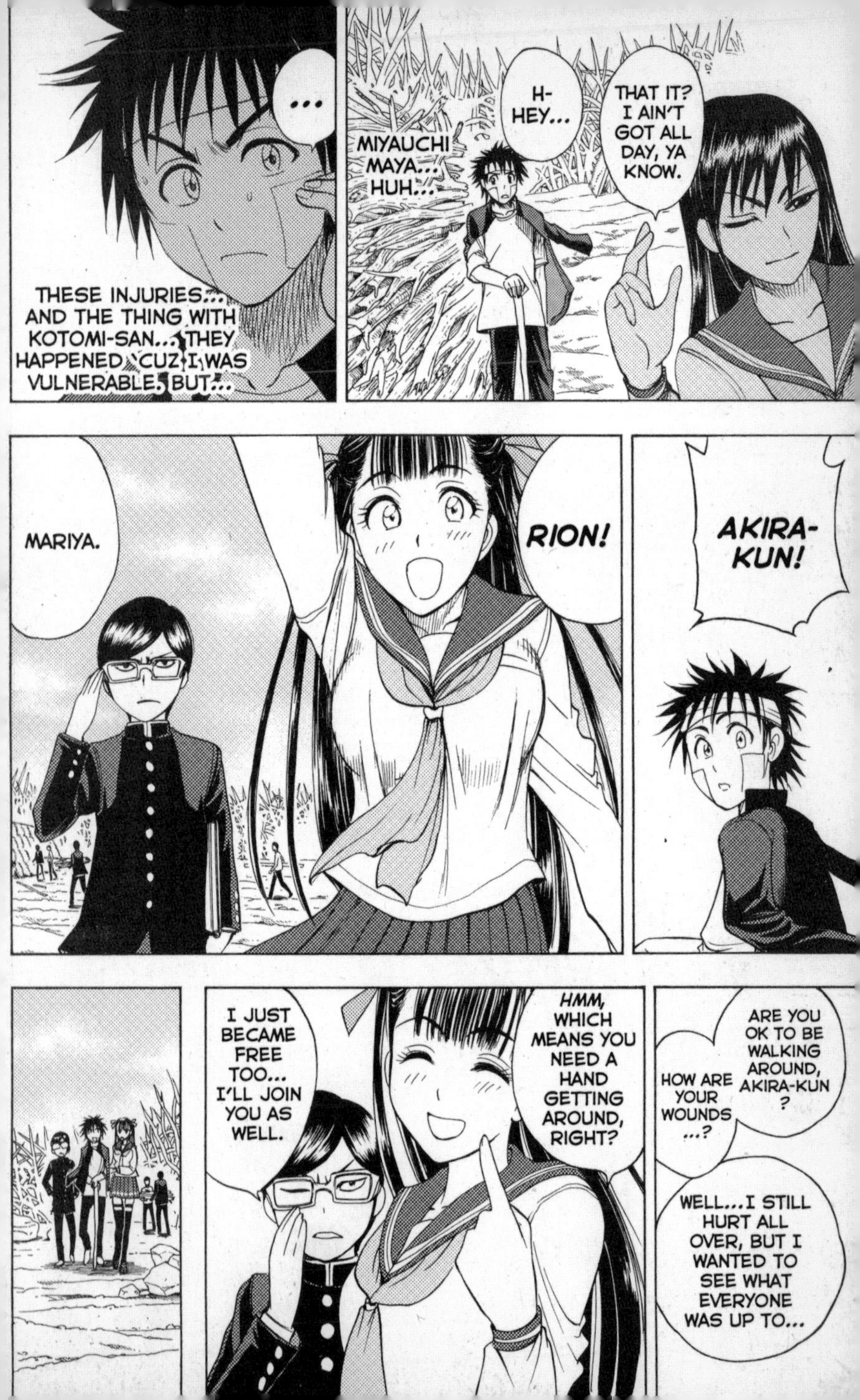
THAT IT? I AIN'T GOT ALL DAY, YA KNOW.
H- HEY...
MIYAUCHI MAYA... HUH...
...
THESE INJURIES... AND THE THING WITH KOTOMI-SAN... THEY HAPPENED 'CUZ I WAS VULNERABLE. BUT...
AKIRA-KUN!
RION!
MARIYA.
ARE YOU OK TO BE WALKING AROUND, AKIRA-KUN?
HOW ARE YOUR WOUNDS...?
WELL...I STILL HURT ALL OVER, BUT I WANTED TO SEE WHAT EVERYONE WAS UP TO...
HMM, WHICH MEANS YOU NEED A HAND GETTING AROUND, RIGHT?
I JUST BECAME FREE TOO... I'LL JOIN YOU AS WELL.

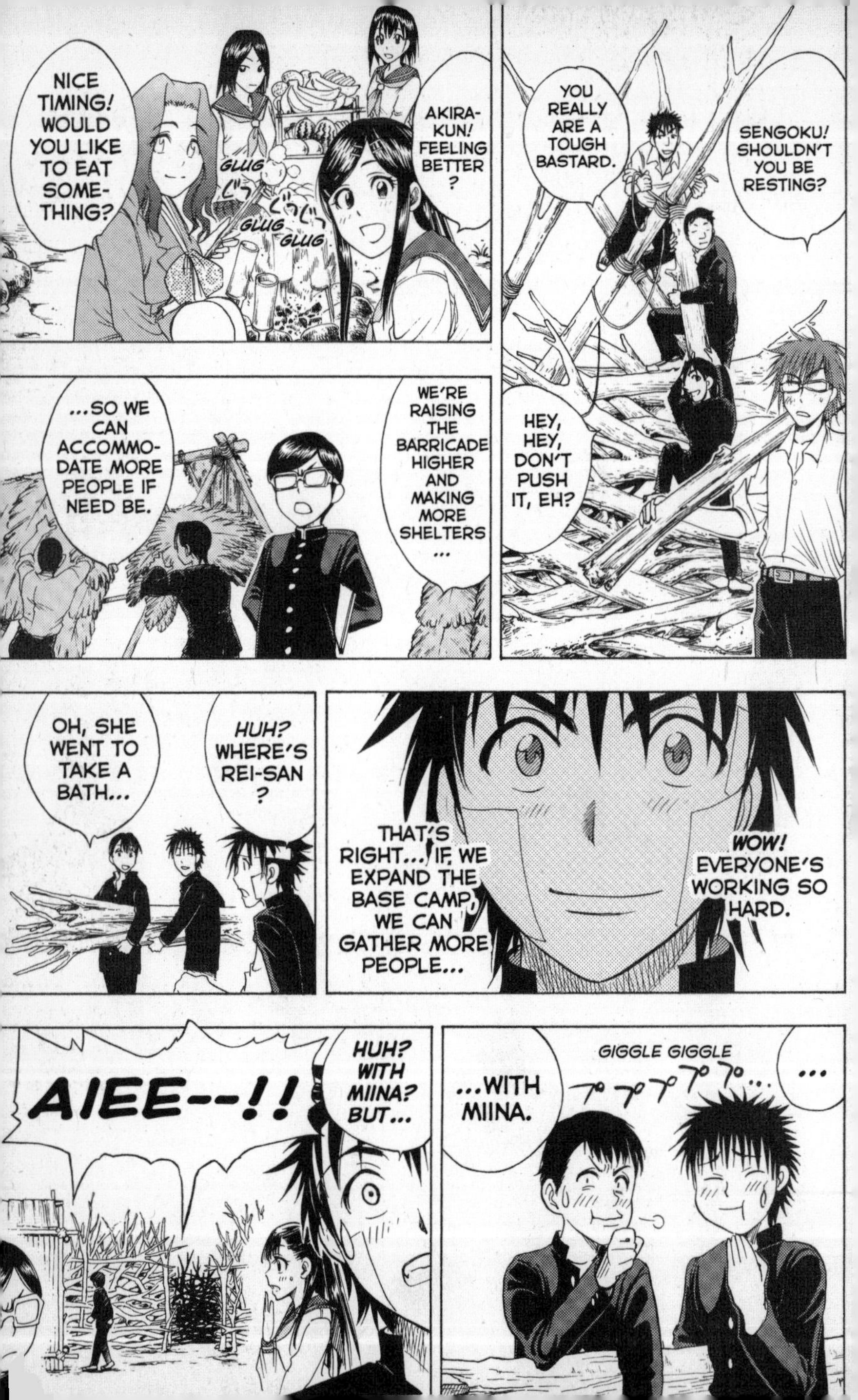
SENGOKU! SHOULDN'T YOU BE RESTING?
YOU REALLY ARE A TOUGH BASTARD.
HEY, HEY, DON'T PUSH IT, EH?
AKIRA-KUN! FEELING BETTER?
NICE TIMING! WOULD YOU LIKE TO EAT SOMETHING?
GLUG GLUG GLUG
WE'RE RAISING THE BARRICADE HIGHER AND MAKING MORE SHELTERS...
...SO WE CAN ACCOMMODATE MORE PEOPLE IF NEED BE.
WOW! EVERYONE'S WORKING SO HARD.
THAT'S RIGHT... IF WE EXPAND THE BASE CAMP, WE CAN GATHER MORE PEOPLE...
HUH? WHERE'S REI-SAN?
OH, SHE WENT TO TAKE A BATH...
...
GIGGLE GIGGLE
...WITH MIINA.
HUH? WITH MIINA? BUT...
AIEE--!!

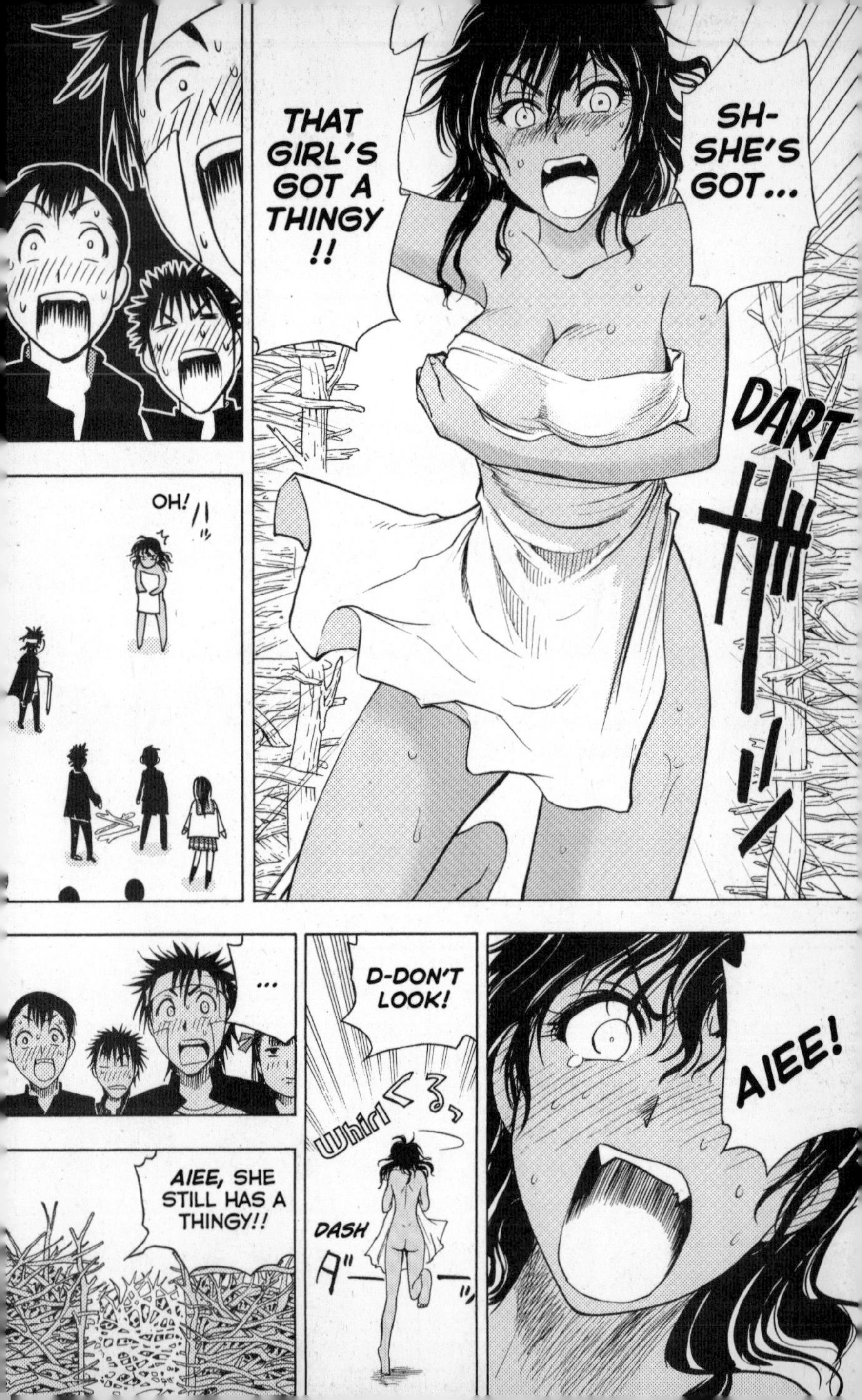

SH- SHE'S GOT...
THAT GIRL'S GOT A THINGY !!
DART
OH!
AIEE!
D-DON'T LOOK!
Whirl
DASH
...
AIEE, SHE STILL HAS A THINGY!!

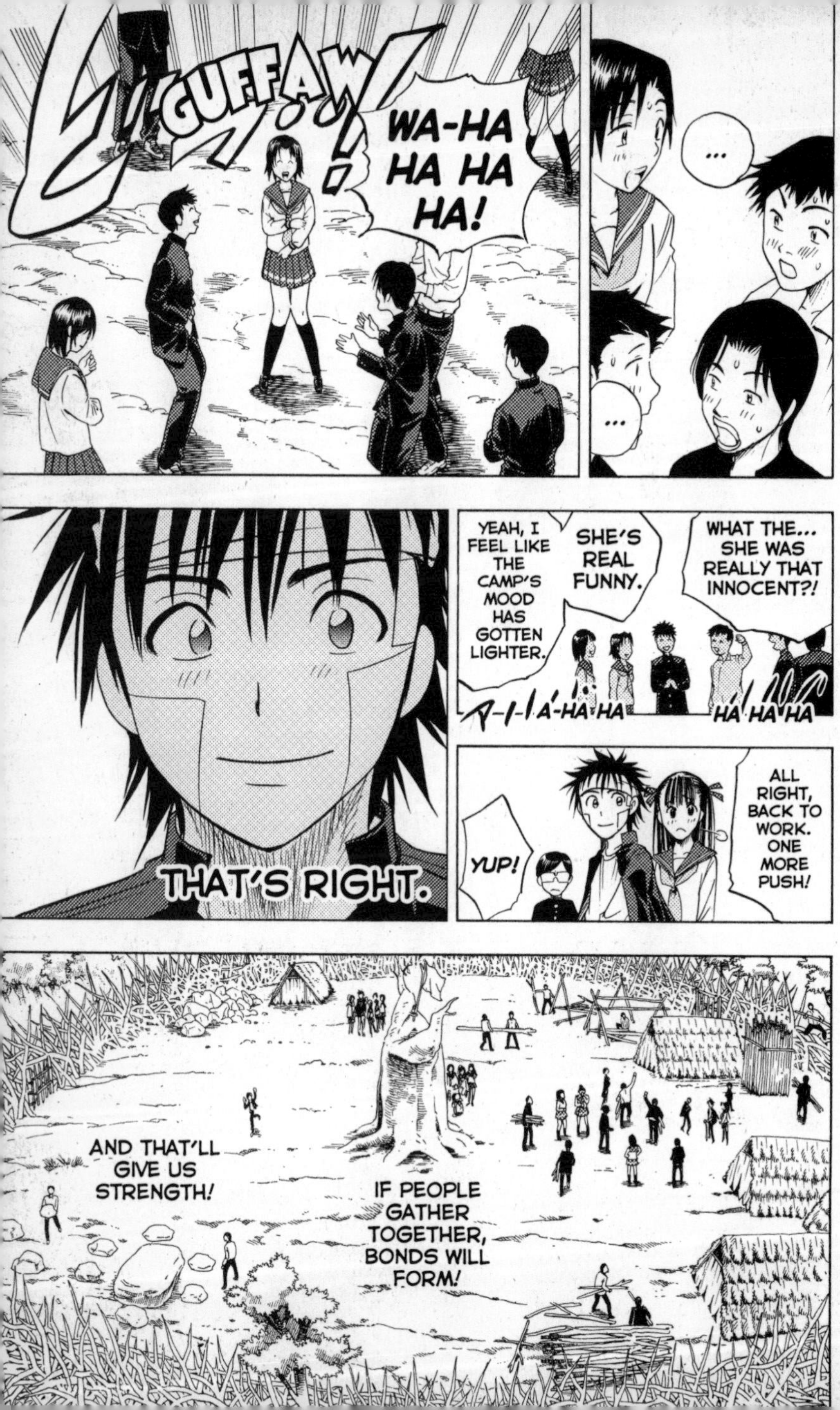
...
...
GUFFAW
WA-HA HA HA HA!
WHAT THE... SHE WAS REALLY THAT INNOCENT?!
SHE'S REAL FUNNY.
YEAH, I FEEL LIKE THE CAMP'S MOOD HAS GOTTEN LIGHTER.
HA HA HA
A-I-I A-HA HA
ALL RIGHT, BACK TO WORK. ONE MORE PUSH!
YUP!
THAT'S RIGHT.
IF PEOPLE GATHER TOGETHER, BONDS WILL FORM!
AND THAT'LL GIVE US STRENGTH!

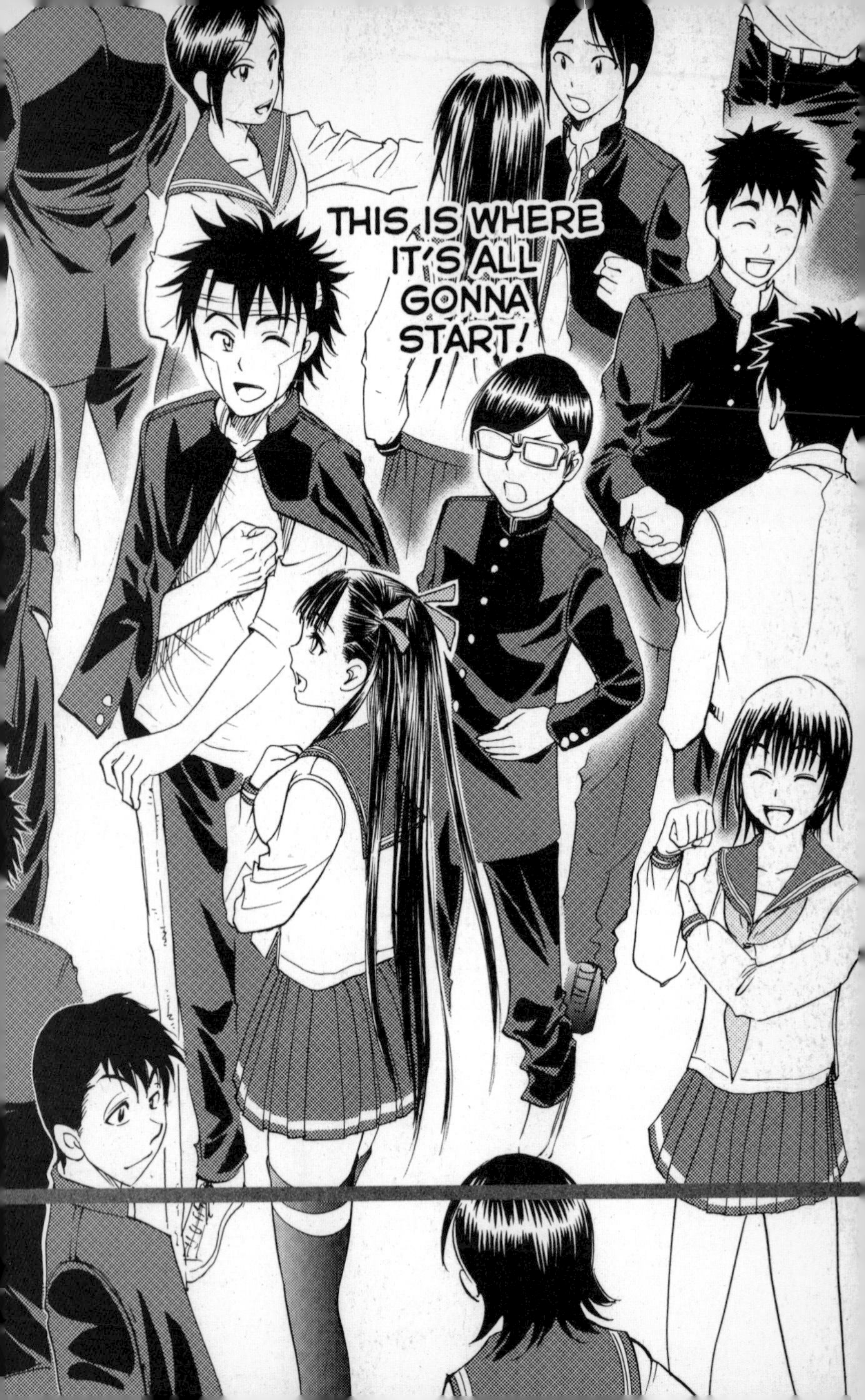
THIS IS WHERE IT'S ALL GONNA START!

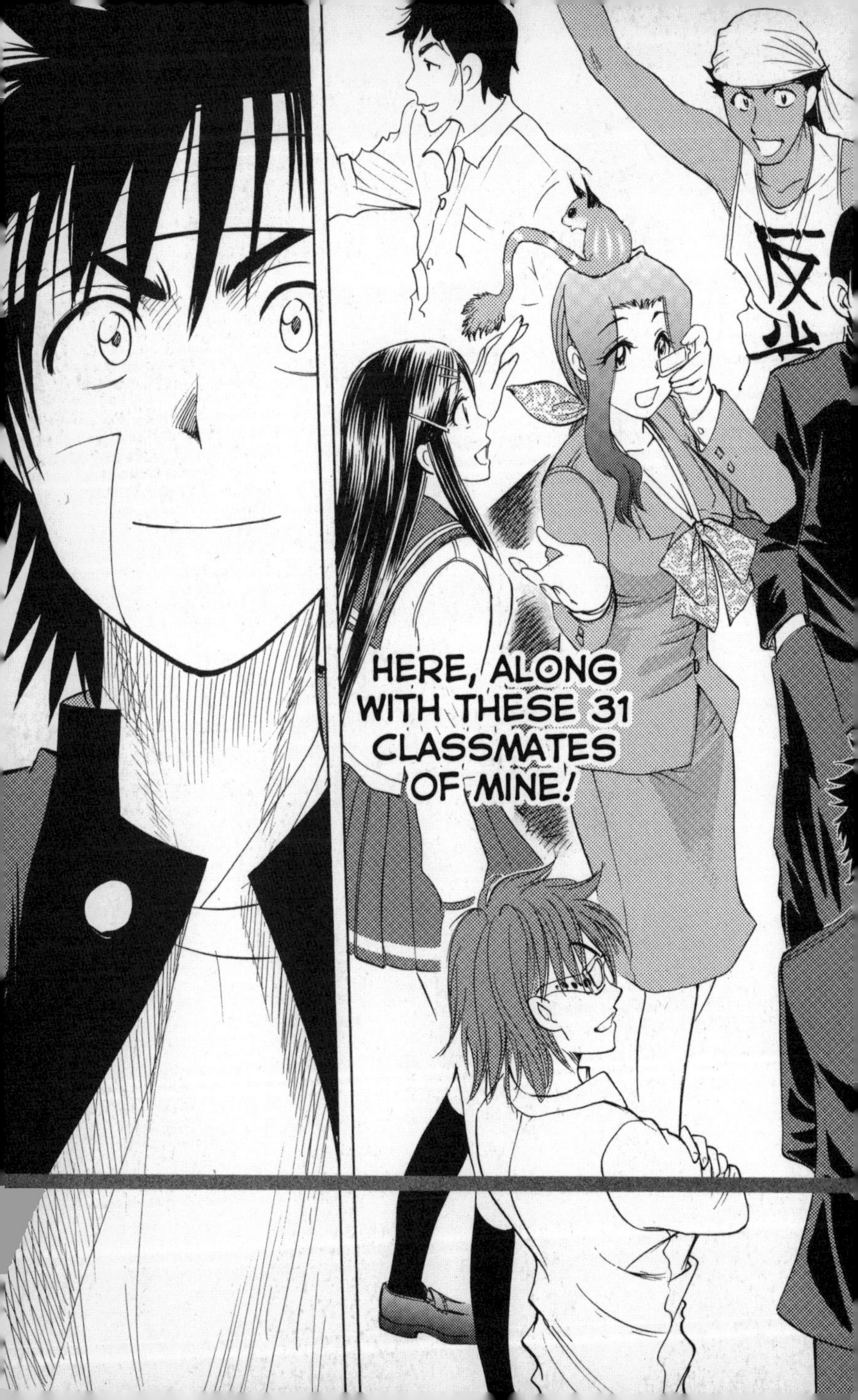
HERE, ALONG WITH THESE 31 CLASSMATES OF MINE!

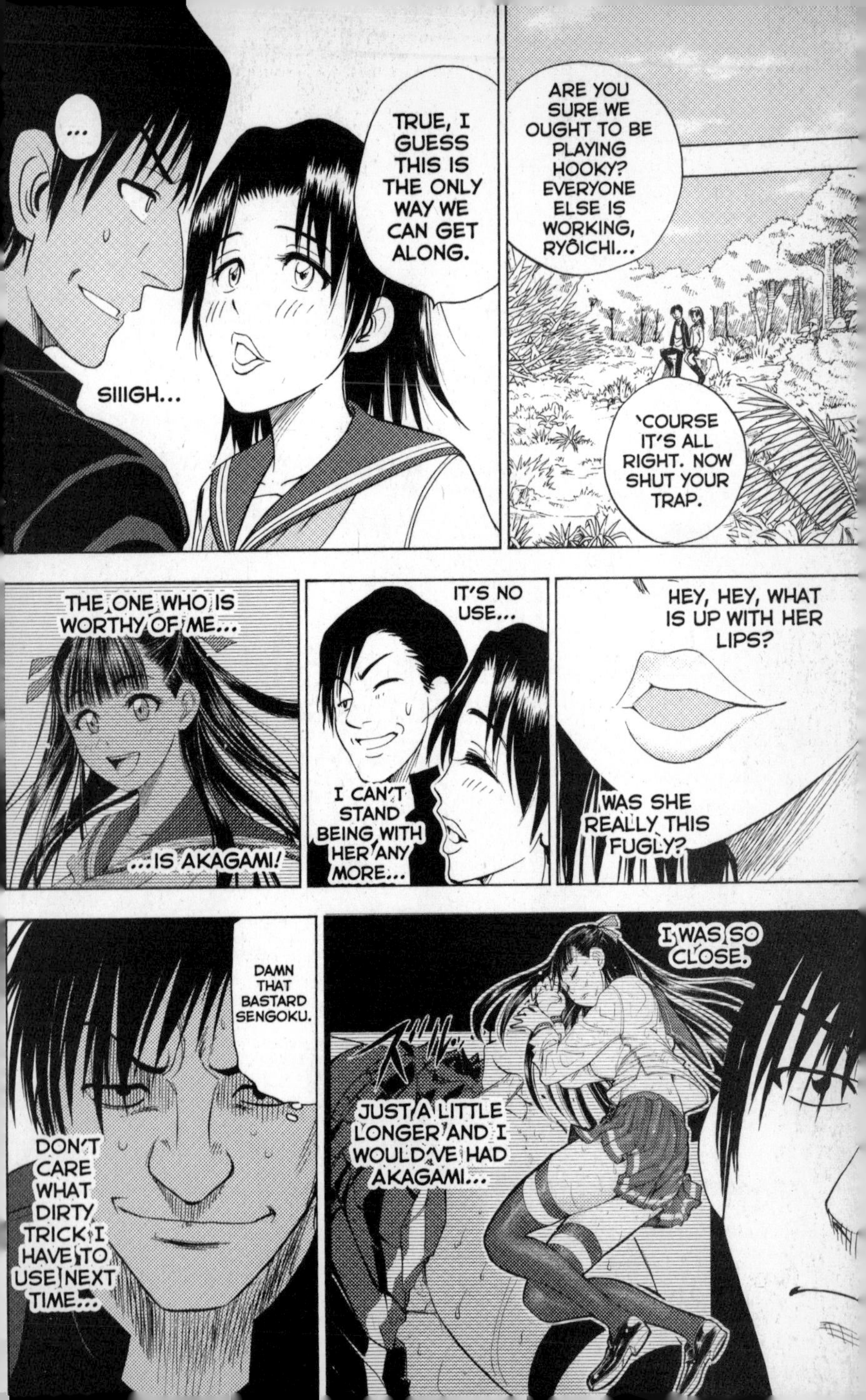
ARE YOU SURE WE OUGHT TO BE PLAYING HOOKY? EVERYONE ELSE IS WORKING, RYÔICHI...
'COURSE IT'S ALL RIGHT. NOW SHUT YOUR TRAP.
TRUE, I GUESS THIS IS THE ONLY WAY WE CAN GET ALONG.
...
SIIIGH...
HEY, HEY, WHAT IS UP WITH HER LIPS?
WAS SHE REALLY THIS FUGLY?
IT'S NO USE...
I CAN'T STAND BEING WITH HER ANY MORE...
THE ONE WHO IS WORTHY OF ME...
...IS AKAGAMI!
I WAS SO CLOSE.
JUST A LITTLE LONGER AND I WOULD'VE HAD AKAGAMI...
DAMN THAT BASTARD SENGOKU.
DON'T CARE WHAT DIRTY TRICK I HAVE TO USE NEXT TIME...

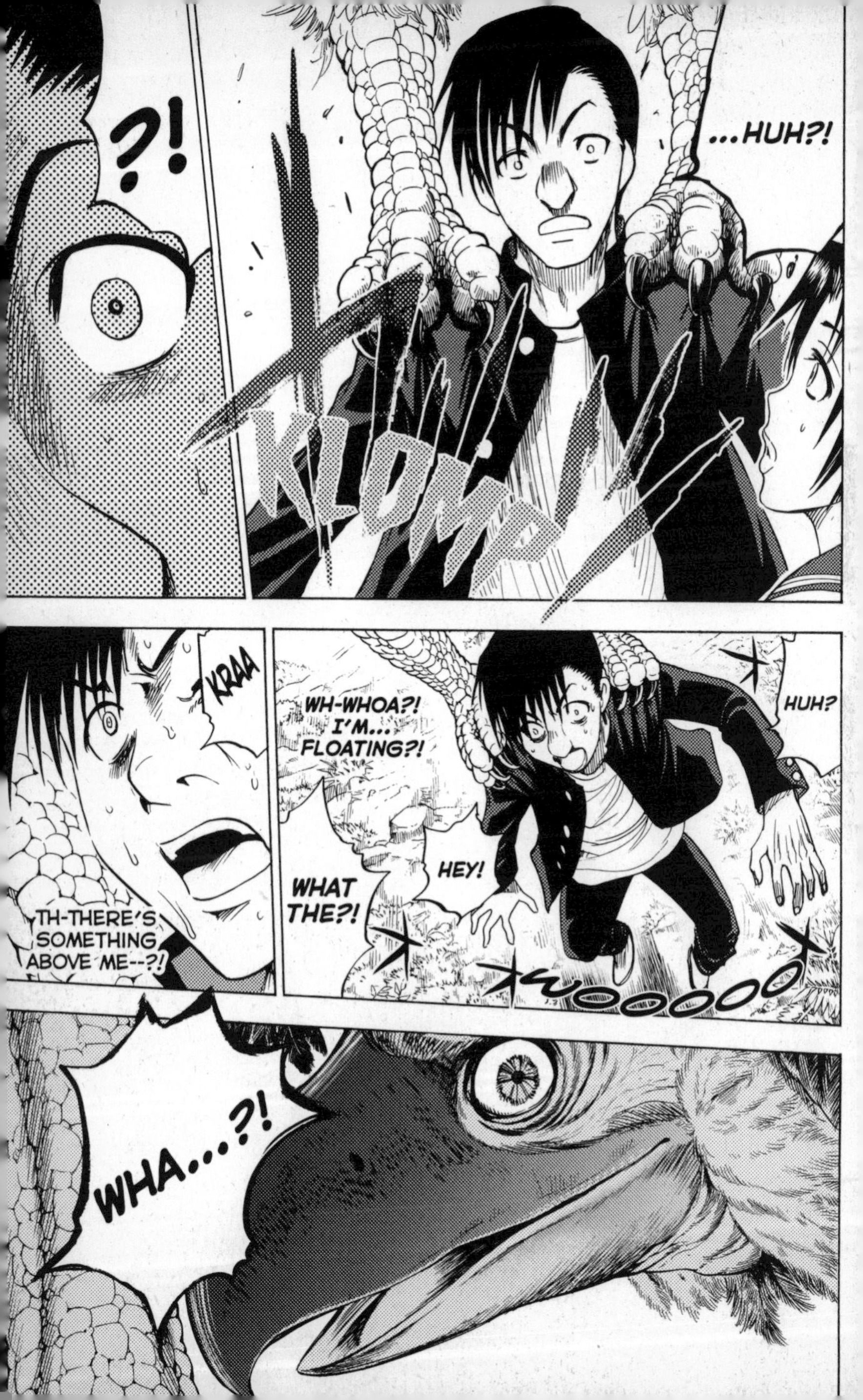
...HUH?!
KLOMP
?!
HUH?
WH-WHOA?! I'M... FLOATING?!
HEY!
WHAT THE?!
WOOOOOO
KRAA
TH-THERE'S SOMETHING ABOVE ME--?!
WHA...?!

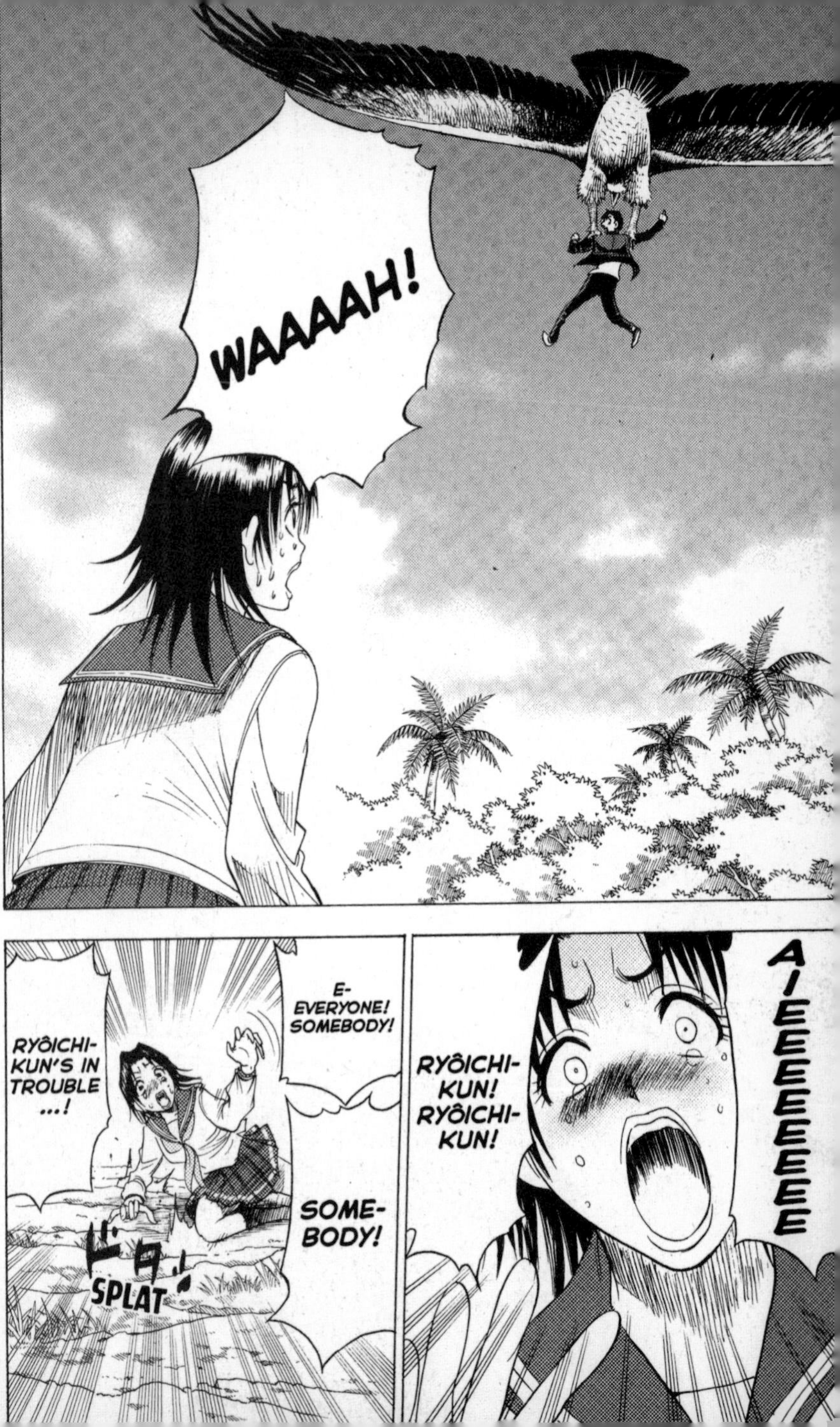
WAAAAH!
AIEEEEEEEE
RYÔICHI-KUN! RYÔICHI-KUN!
E-EVERYONE! SOMEBODY!
RYÔICHI-KUN'S IN TROUBLE ...!
SOME-BODY!
SPLAT

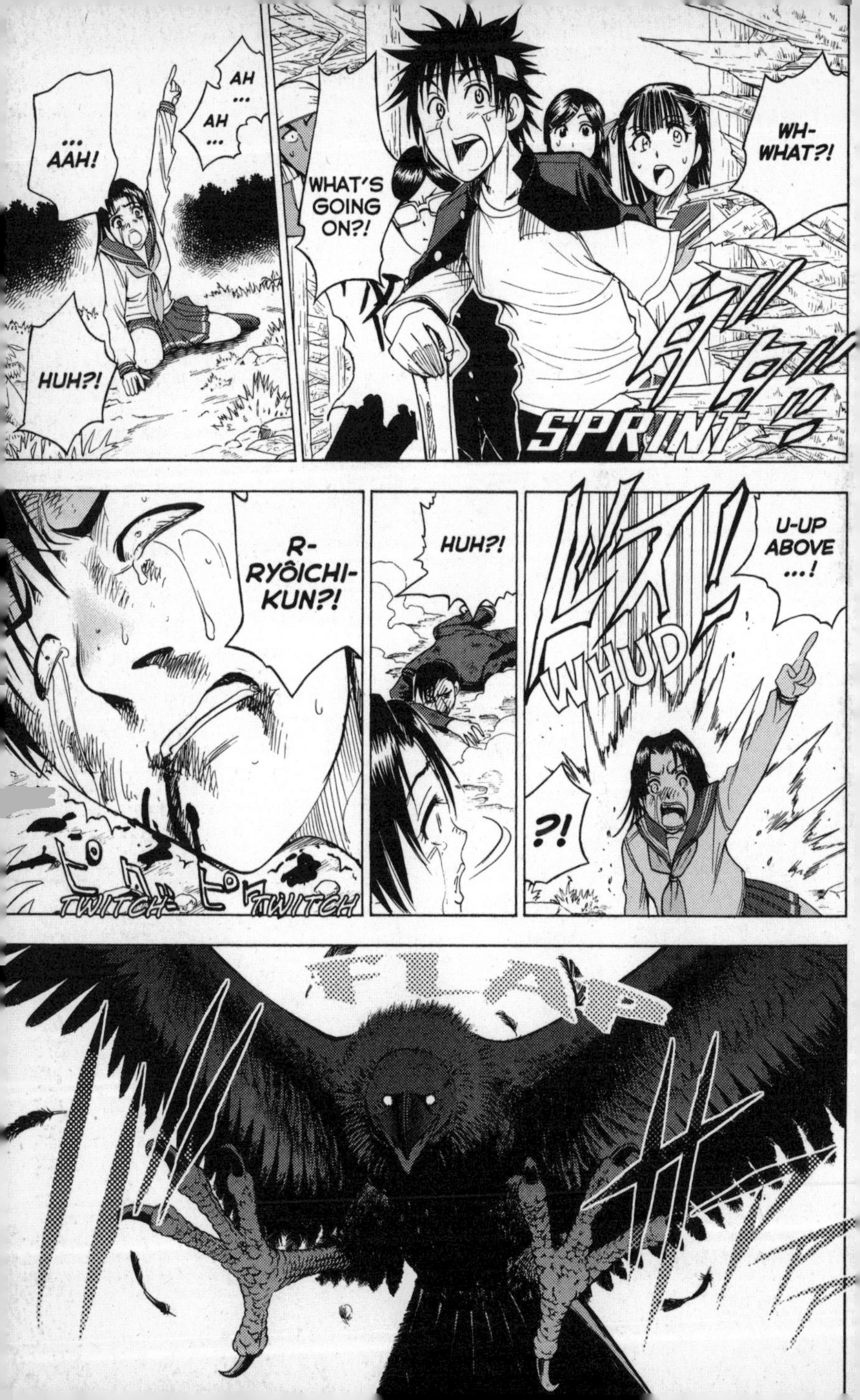
WH-WHAT?!
WHAT'S GOING ON?!
SPRINT
AH ... AH ...
... AAH!
HUH?!
U-UP ABOVE ...!
WHUD
?!
HUH?!
R-RYÔICHI-KUN?!
TWITCH TWITCH
FLAP

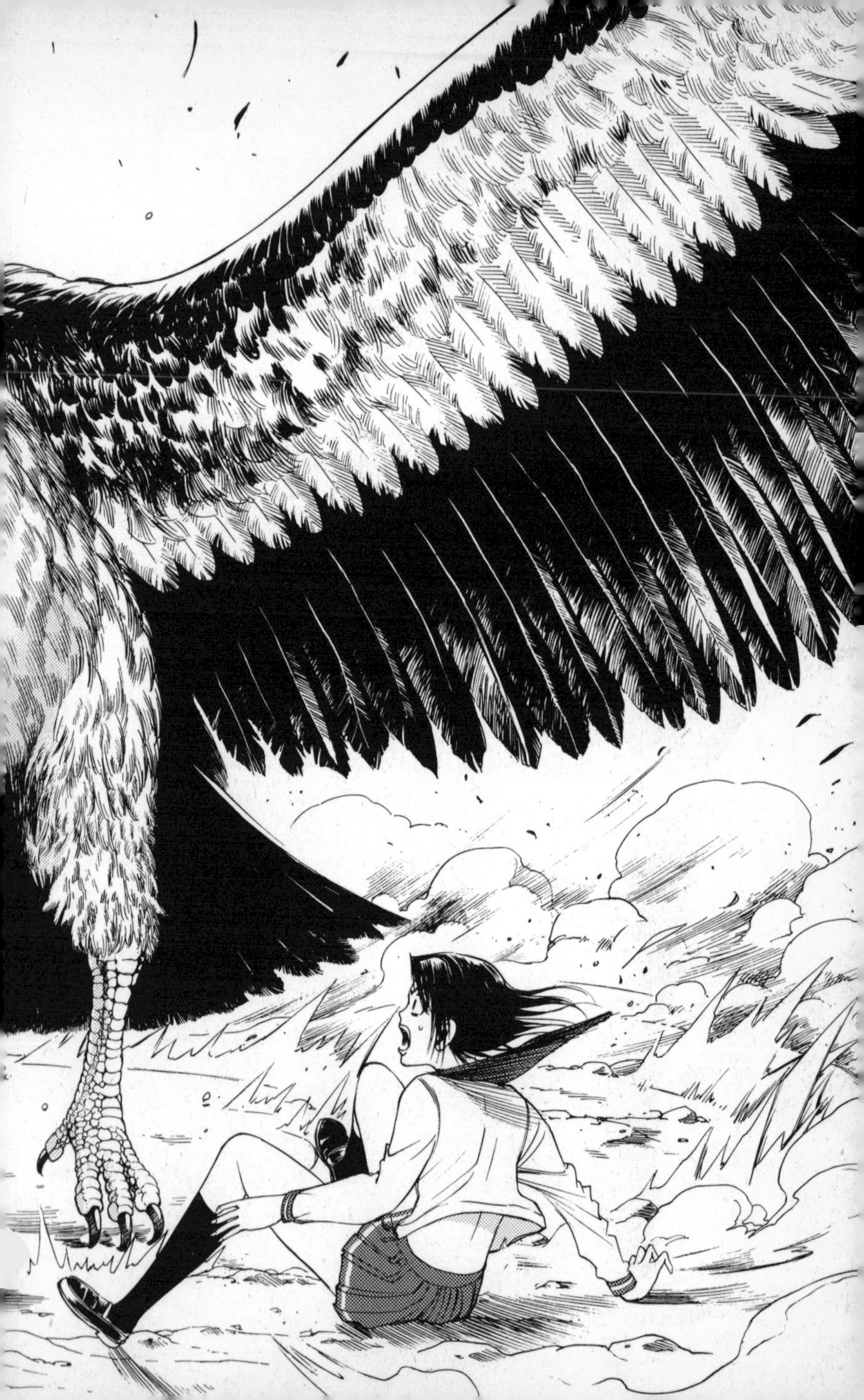

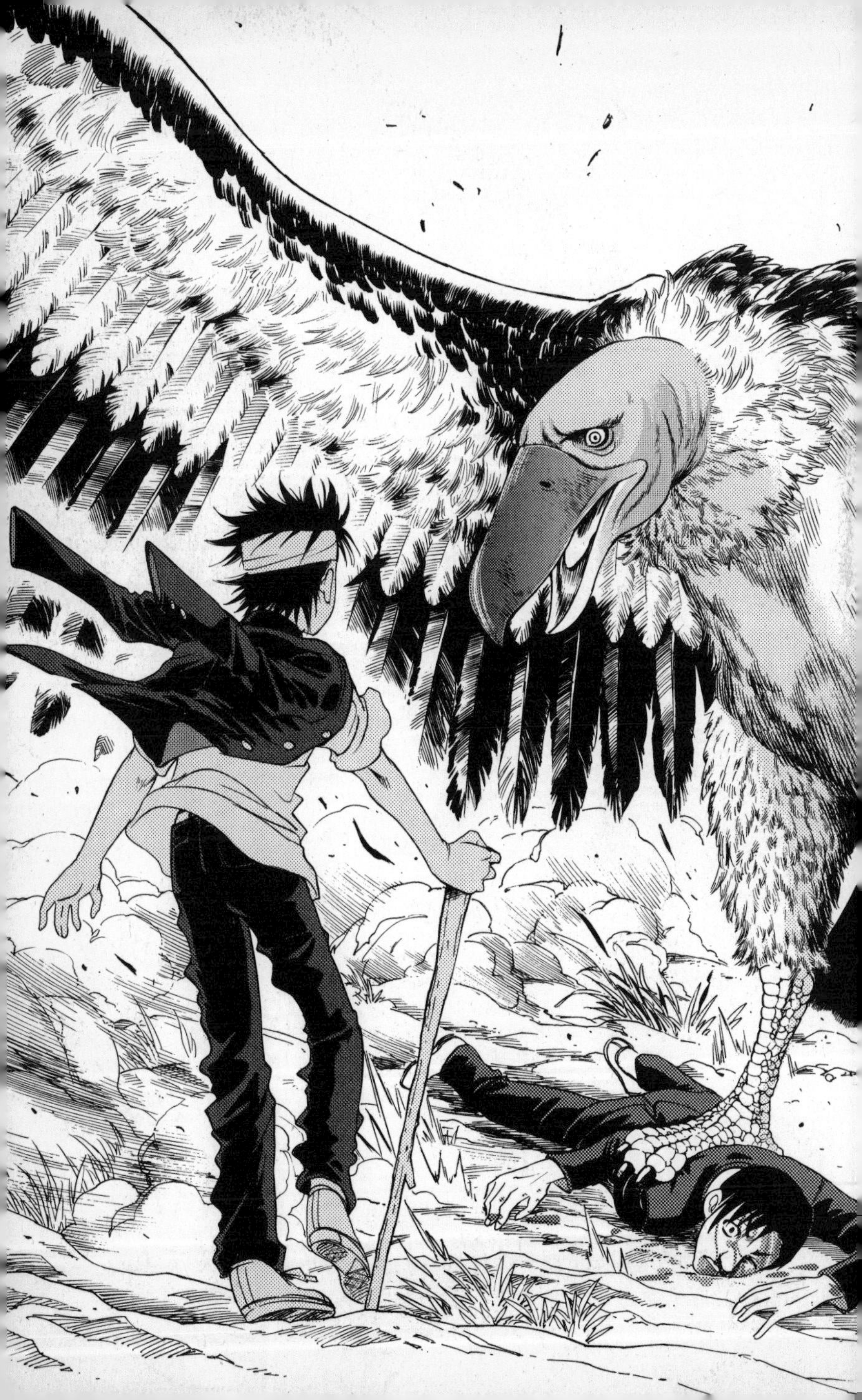

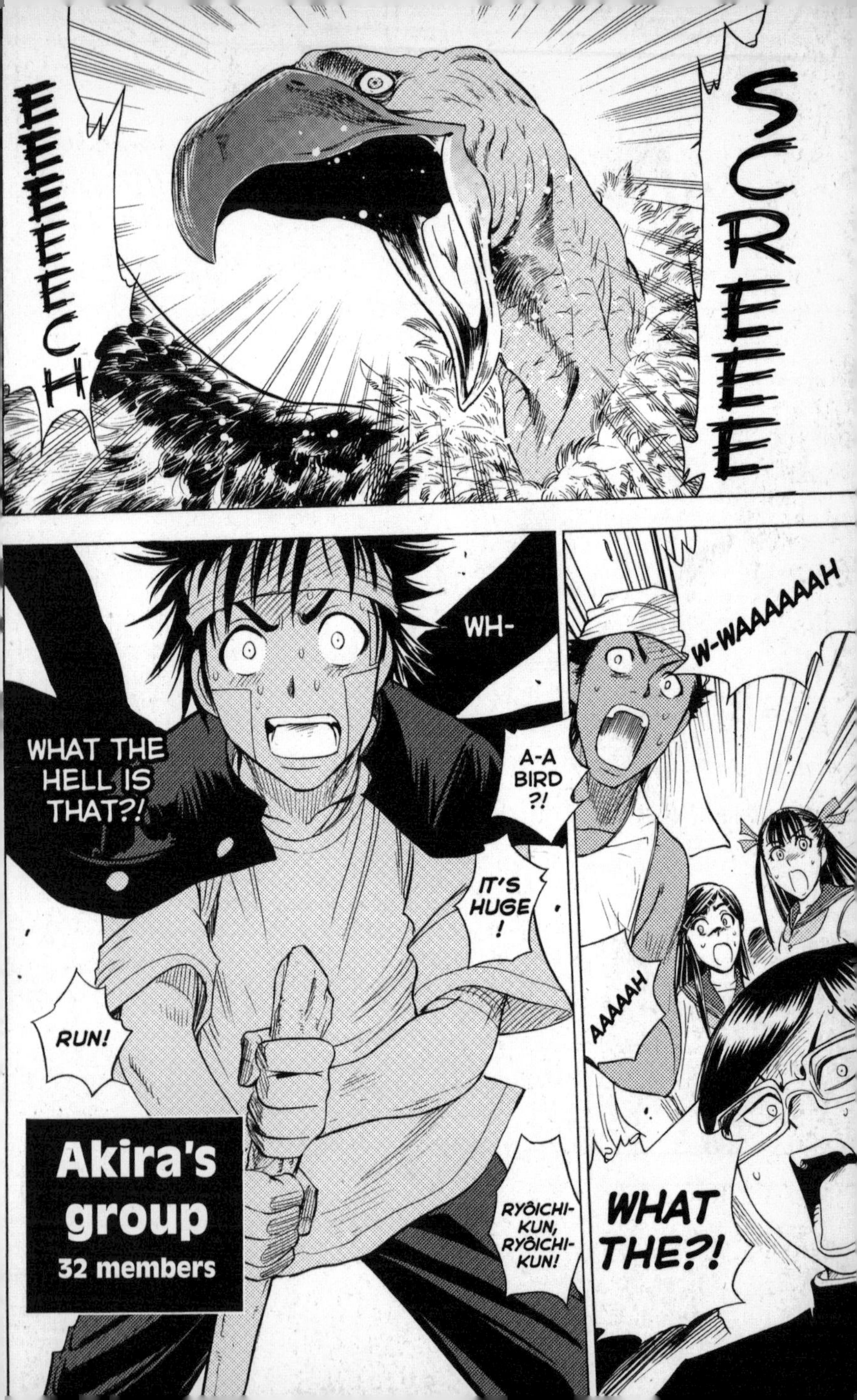
SCREEEE
EEEEEEEECH
W-WAAAAAAH
A-A BIRD?!
IT'S HUGE!
AAAAAH
RYÔICHI-KUN, RYÔICHI-KUN!
WHAT THE?!
WH-
WHAT THE HELL IS THAT?!
RUN!
Akira's group
32 members

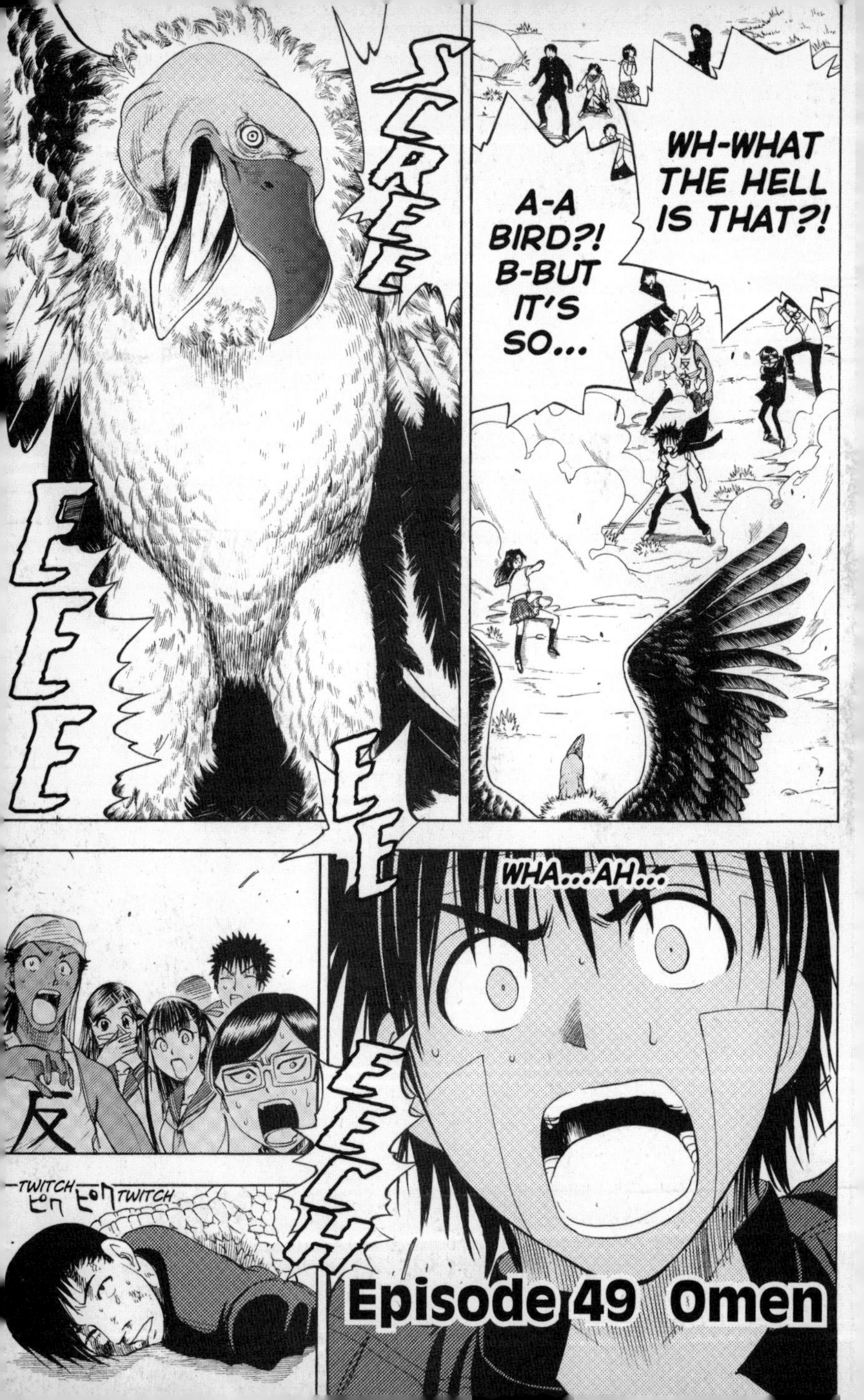
WH-WHAT THE HELL IS THAT?!
A-A BIRD?! B-BUT IT'S SO...
SCREE
EEEE
EEE
WHA...AH...
Episode 49 Omen
EEECH
TWITCH TWITCH

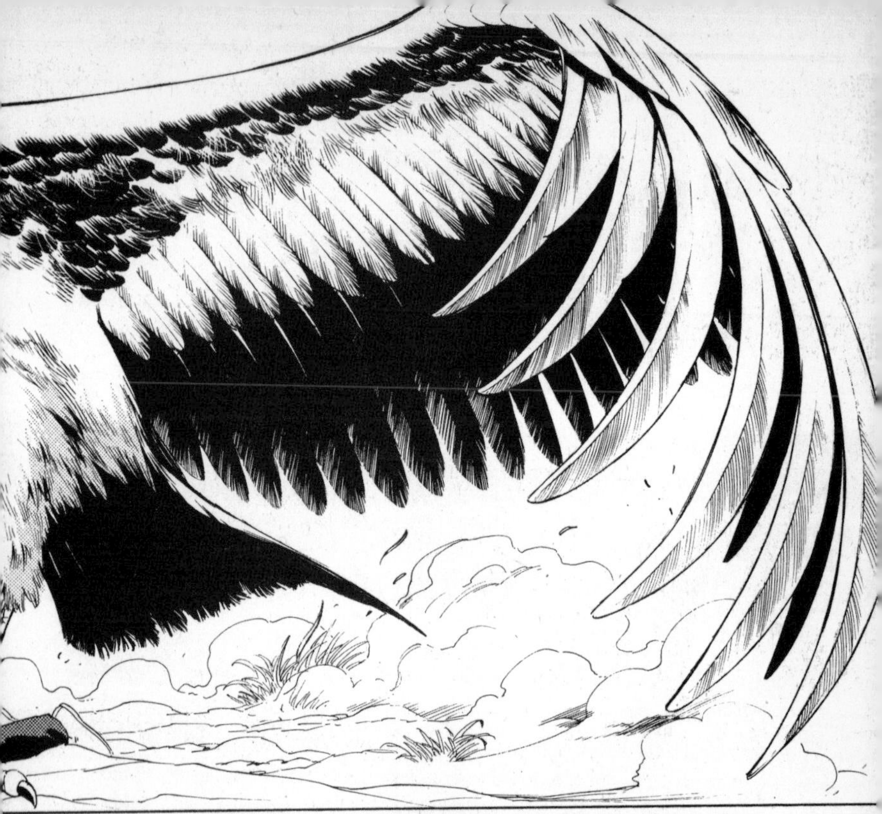

*6 METERS = ROUGHLY 20 FEET, 8 METERS = ROUGHLY 26 FEET

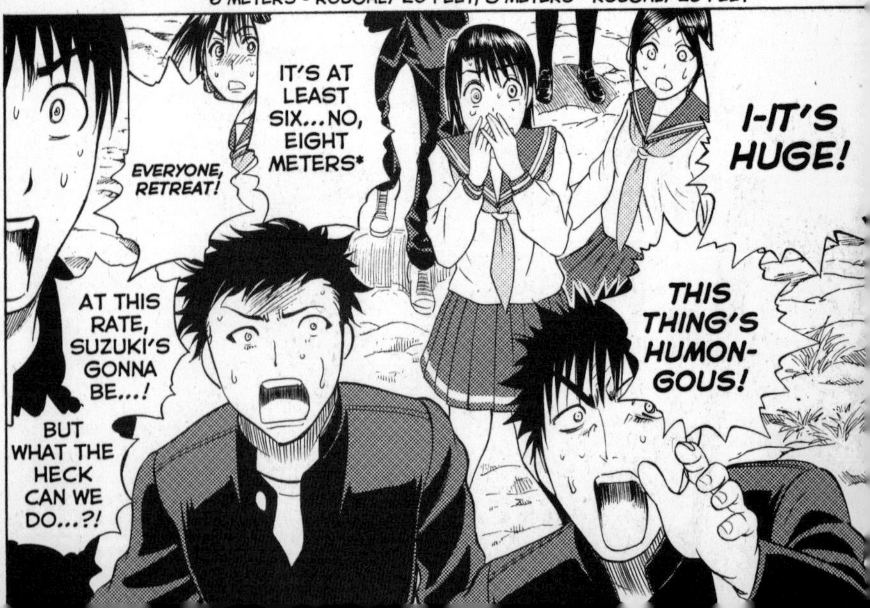
I-IT'S HUGE!
IT'S AT LEAST SIX...NO, EIGHT METERS*
EVERYONE, RETREAT!
THIS THING'S HUMON-GOUS!
AT THIS RATE, SUZUKI'S GONNA BE...!
BUT WHAT THE HECK CAN WE DO...?!

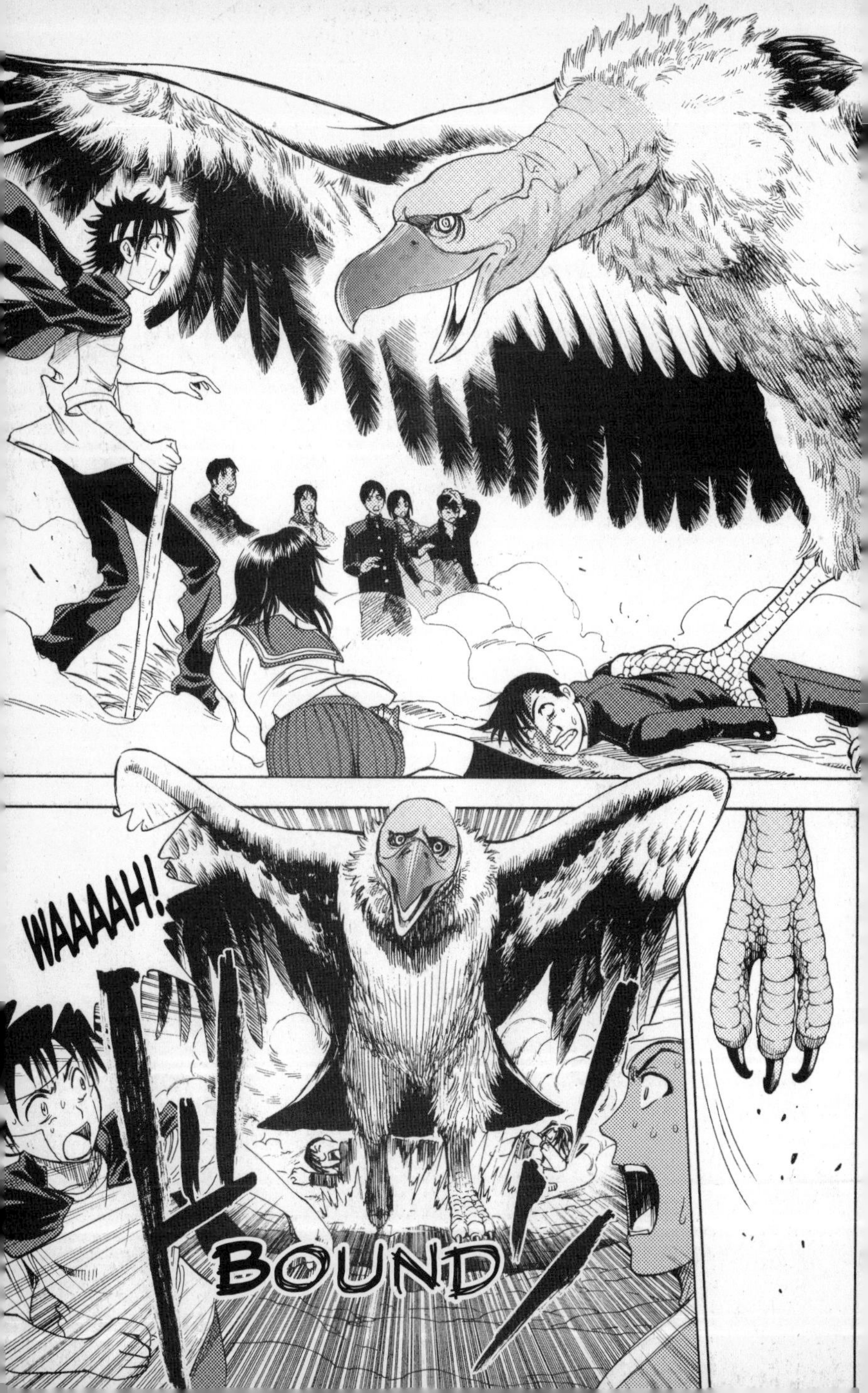
WAAAAH!
BOUND

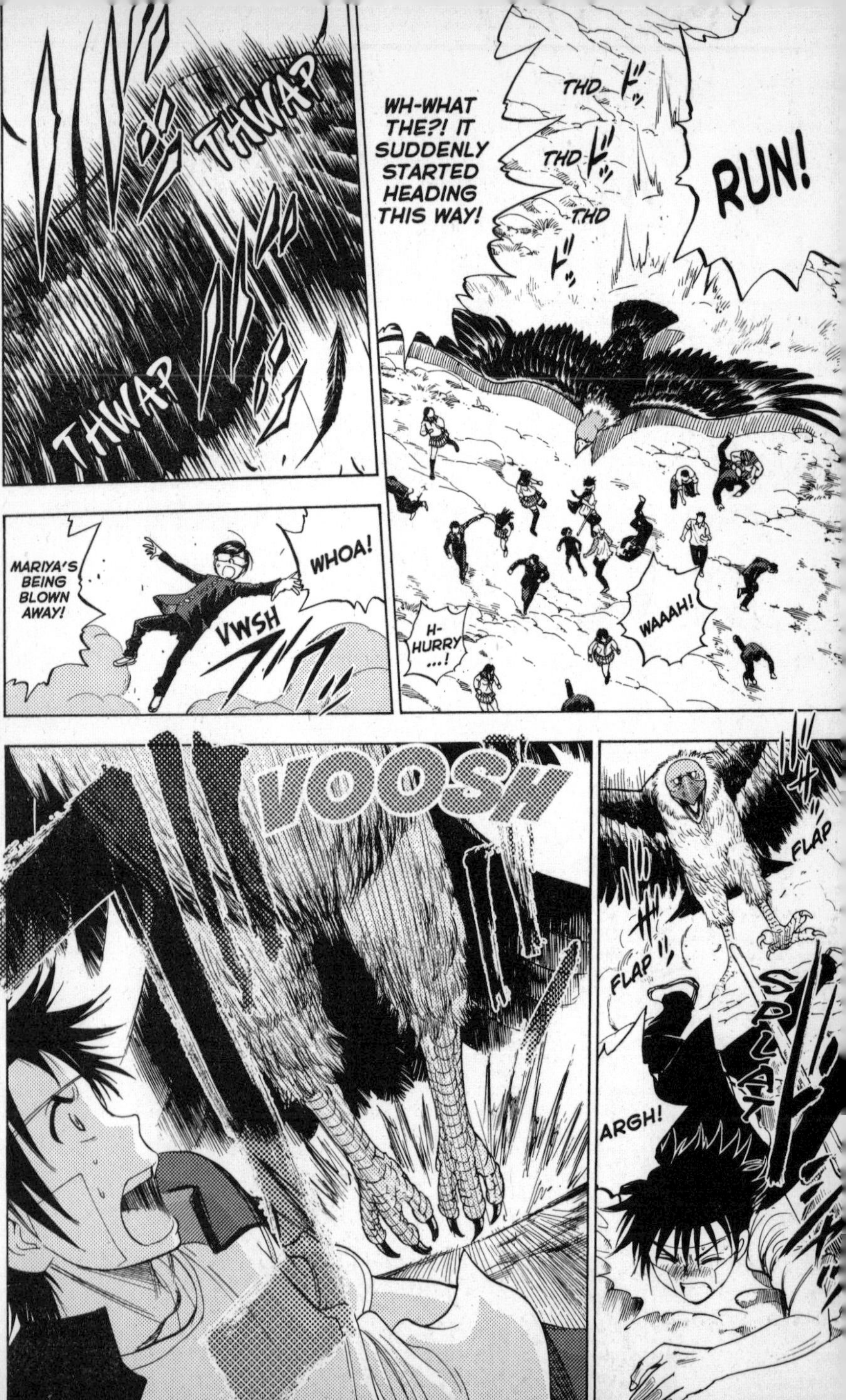
RUN!
THD
THD
THD
WH-WHAT THE?! IT SUDDENLY STARTED HEADING THIS WAY!
WAAAH!
H-HURRY ...!
THWAP
THWAP
WHOA!
MARIYA'S BEING BLOWN AWAY!
VWSH
FLAP
FLAP
SPLAT
ARGH!
VOOSH

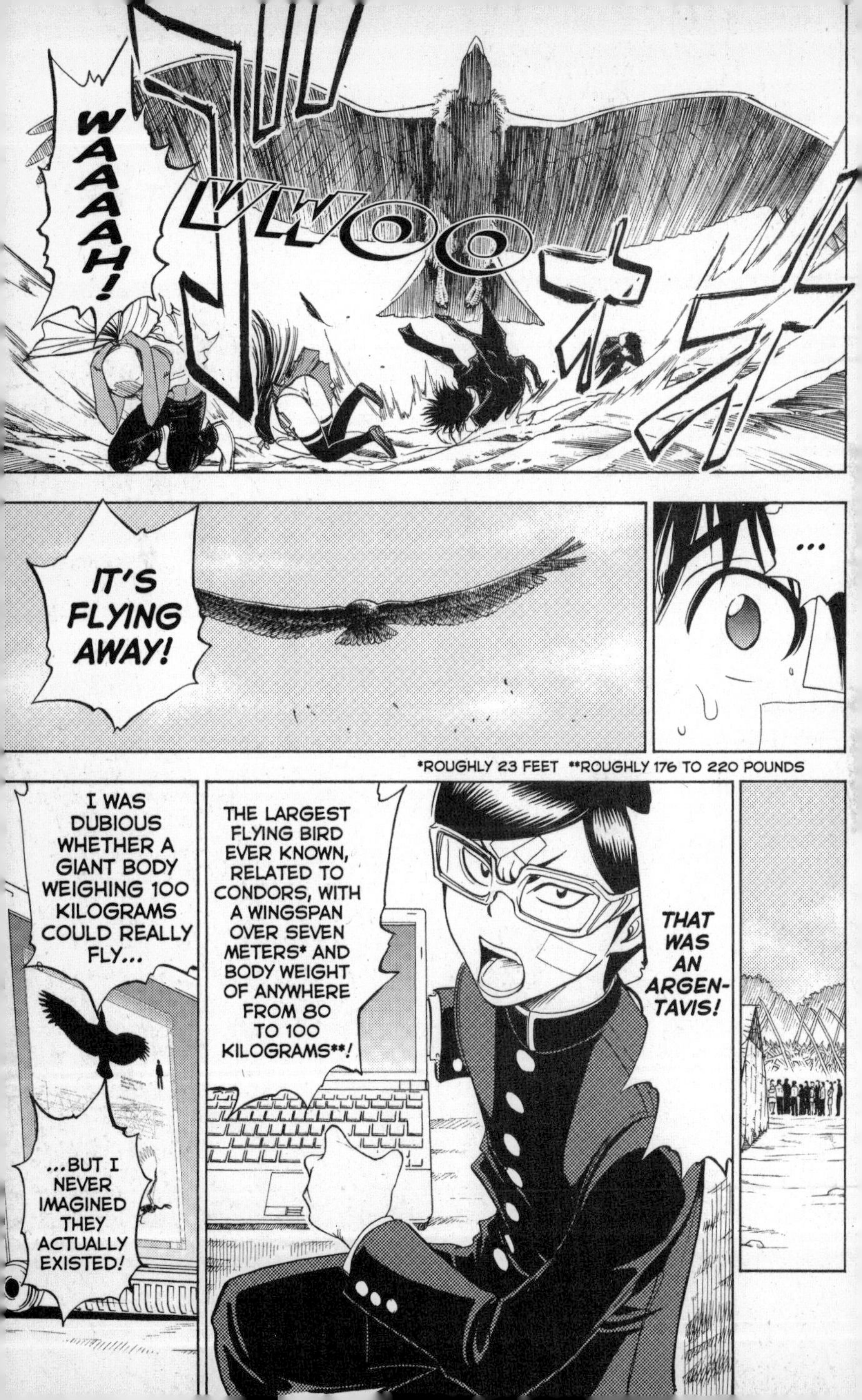
WAAAAAH!
...
IT'S FLYING AWAY!
THAT WAS AN ARGEN-TAVIS!
THE LARGEST FLYING BIRD EVER KNOWN, RELATED TO CONDORS, WITH A WINGSPAN OVER SEVEN METERS* AND BODY WEIGHT OF ANYWHERE FROM 80 TO 100 KILOGRAMS**!
I WAS DUBIOUS WHETHER A GIANT BODY WEIGHING 100 KILOGRAMS COULD REALLY FLY...
...BUT I NEVER IMAGINED THEY ACTUALLY EXISTED!

*ROUGHLY 23 FEET **ROUGHLY 176 TO 220 POUNDS

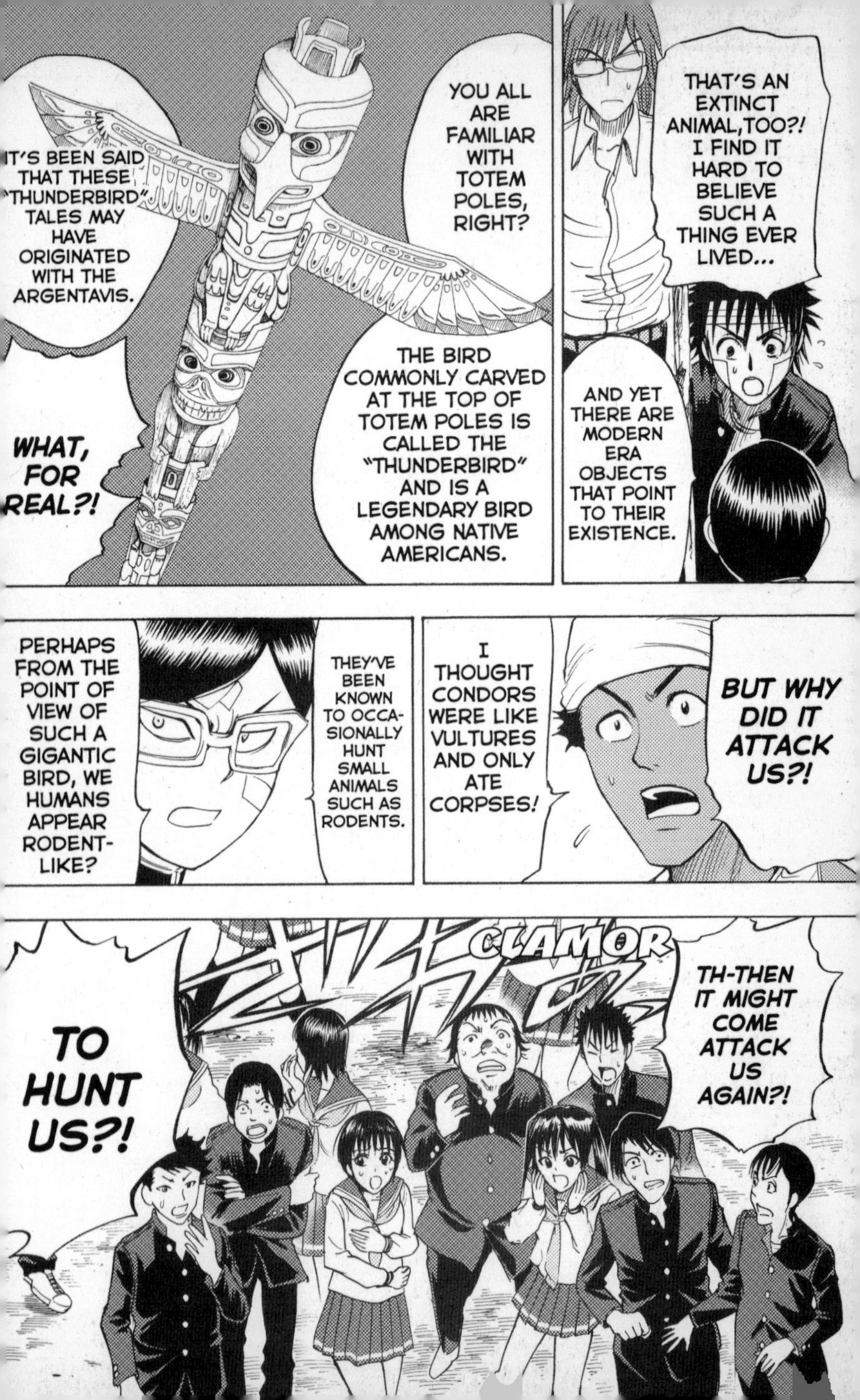
THAT'S AN EXTINCT ANIMAL, TOO?! I FIND IT HARD TO BELIEVE SUCH A THING EVER LIVED...
AND YET THERE ARE MODERN ERA OBJECTS THAT POINT TO THEIR EXISTENCE.
YOU ALL ARE FAMILIAR WITH TOTEM POLES, RIGHT?
THE BIRD COMMONLY CARVED AT THE TOP OF TOTEM POLES IS CALLED THE "THUNDERBIRD" AND IS A LEGENDARY BIRD AMONG NATIVE AMERICANS.
IT'S BEEN SAID THAT THESE "THUNDERBIRD" TALES MAY HAVE ORIGINATED WITH THE ARGENTAVIS.
WHAT, FOR REAL?!
BUT WHY DID IT ATTACK US?!
I THOUGHT CONDORS WERE LIKE VULTURES AND ONLY ATE CORPSES!
THEY'VE BEEN KNOWN TO OCCASIONALLY HUNT SMALL ANIMALS SUCH AS RODENTS.
PERHAPS FROM THE POINT OF VIEW OF SUCH A GIGANTIC BIRD, WE HUMANS APPEAR RODENT-LIKE?
CLAMOR
TH-THEN IT MIGHT COME ATTACK US AGAIN?!
TO HUNT US?!

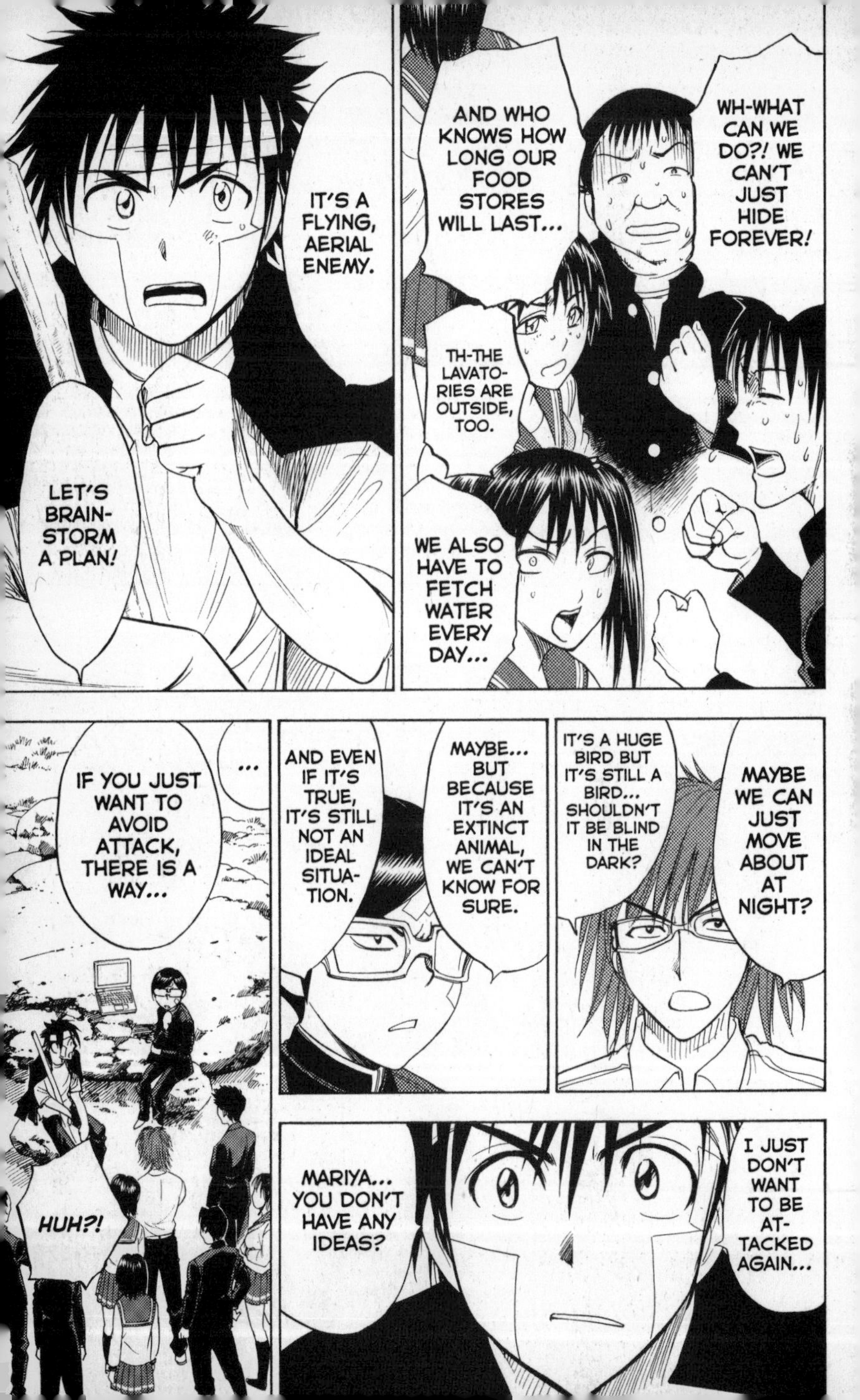
WH-WHAT CAN WE DO?! WE CAN'T JUST HIDE FOREVER!
AND WHO KNOWS HOW LONG OUR FOOD STORES WILL LAST...
TH-THE LAVATORIES ARE OUTSIDE, TOO.
WE ALSO HAVE TO FETCH WATER EVERY DAY...
IT'S A FLYING, AERIAL ENEMY.
LET'S BRAINSTORM A PLAN!
MAYBE WE CAN JUST MOVE ABOUT AT NIGHT?
IT'S A HUGE BIRD BUT IT'S STILL A BIRD... SHOULDN'T IT BE BLIND IN THE DARK?
MAYBE... BUT BECAUSE IT'S AN EXTINCT ANIMAL, WE CAN'T KNOW FOR SURE.
AND EVEN IF IT'S TRUE, IT'S STILL NOT AN IDEAL SITUATION.
I JUST DON'T WANT TO BE ATTACKED AGAIN...
MARIYA... YOU DON'T HAVE ANY IDEAS?
...
IF YOU JUST WANT TO AVOID ATTACK, THERE IS A WAY...
HUH?!

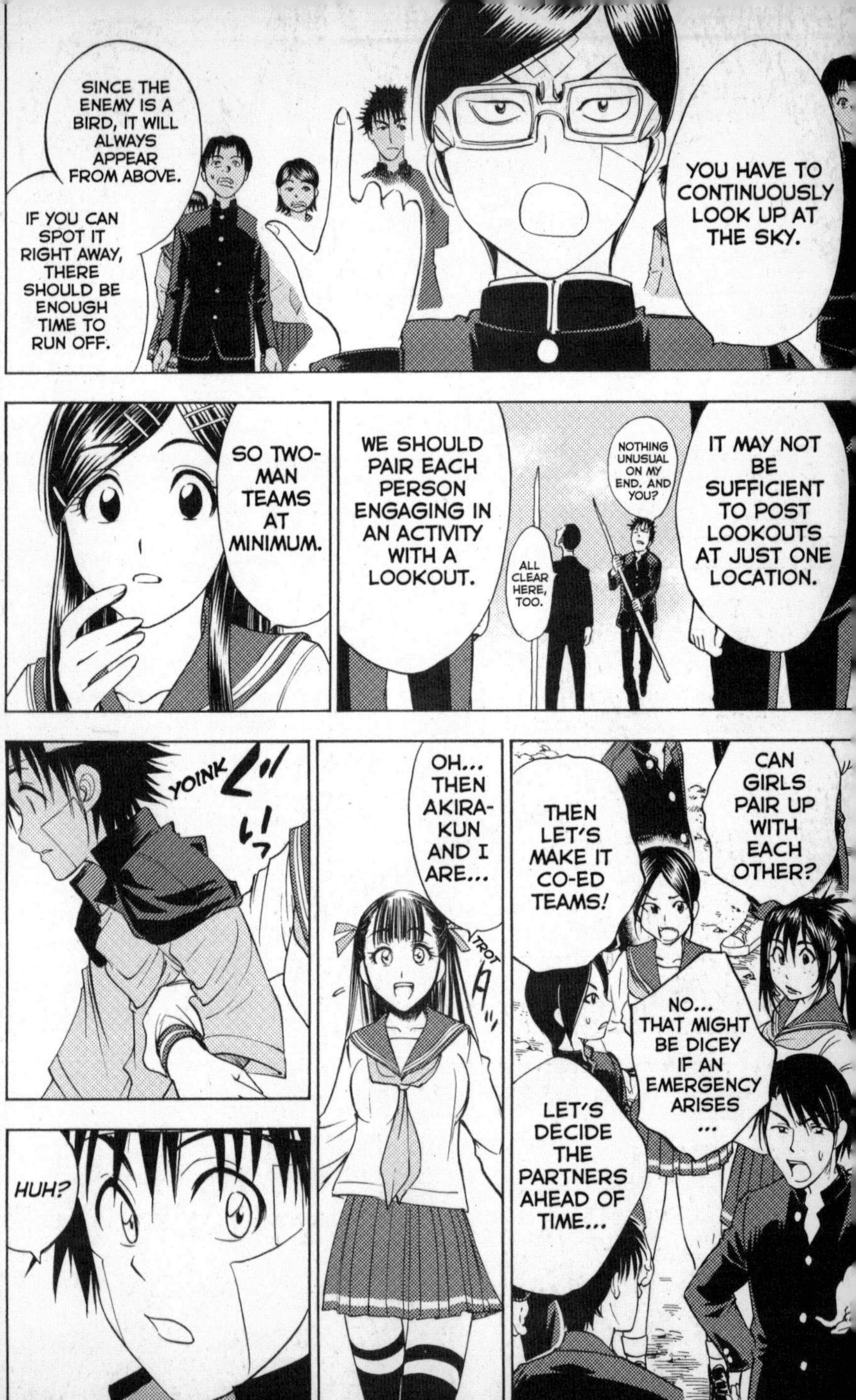
SINCE THE ENEMY IS A BIRD, IT WILL ALWAYS APPEAR FROM ABOVE.
YOU HAVE TO CONTINUOUSLY LOOK UP AT THE SKY.
IF YOU CAN SPOT IT RIGHT AWAY, THERE SHOULD BE ENOUGH TIME TO RUN OFF.
IT MAY NOT BE SUFFICIENT TO POST LOOKOUTS AT JUST ONE LOCATION.
NOTHING UNUSUAL ON MY END. AND YOU?
ALL CLEAR HERE, TOO.
WE SHOULD PAIR EACH PERSON ENGAGING IN AN ACTIVITY WITH A LOOKOUT.
SO TWO-MAN TEAMS AT MINIMUM.
CAN GIRLS PAIR UP WITH EACH OTHER?
NO... THAT MIGHT BE DICEY IF AN EMERGENCY ARISES...
THEN LET'S MAKE IT CO-ED TEAMS!
LET'S DECIDE THE PARTNERS AHEAD OF TIME...
OH... THEN AKIRA-KUN AND I ARE...
TROT
YOINK
HUH?

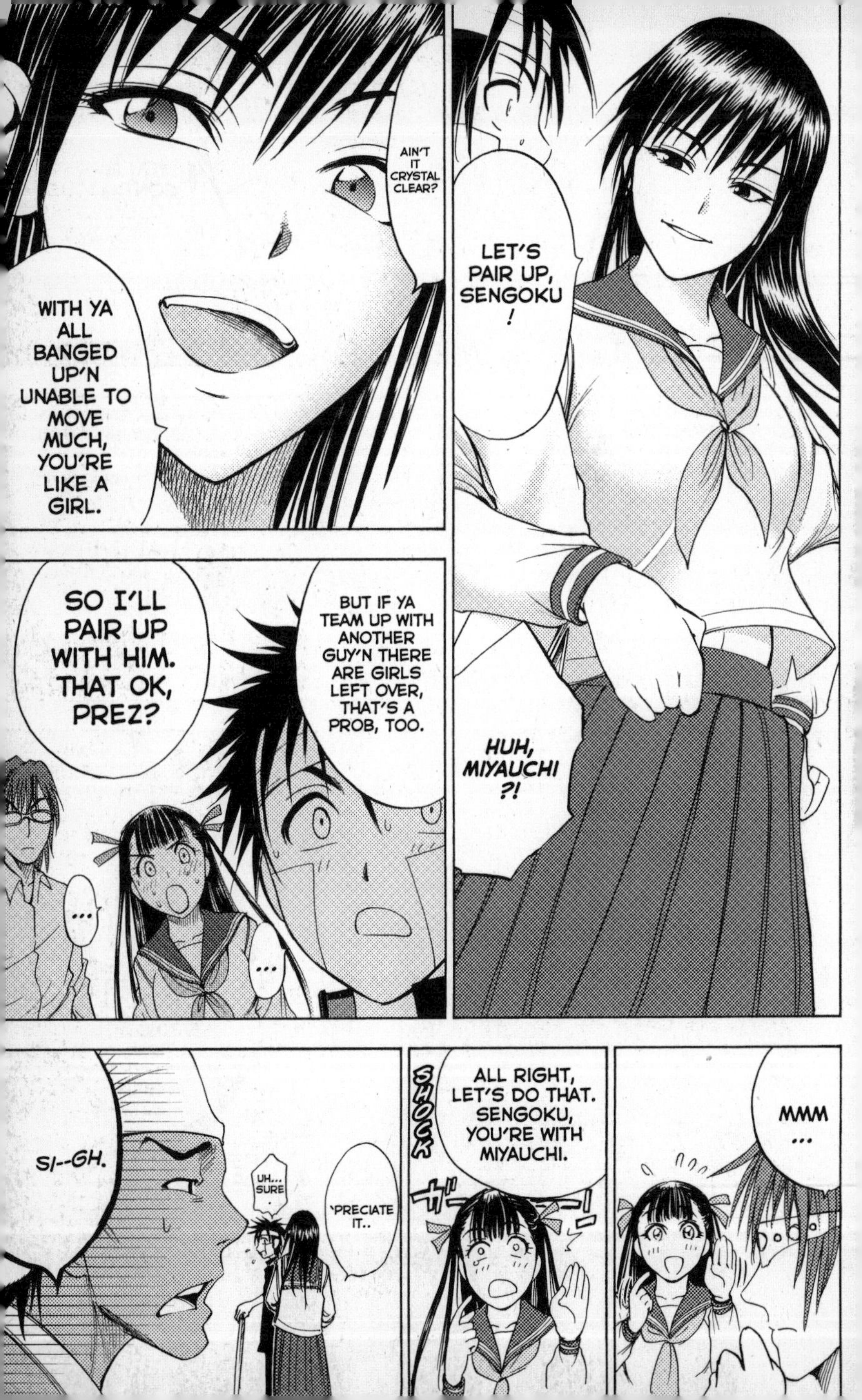
LET'S PAIR UP, SENGOKU!
HUH, MIYAUCHI?!
AIN'T IT CRYSTAL CLEAR?
WITH YA ALL BANGED UP'N UNABLE TO MOVE MUCH, YOU'RE LIKE A GIRL.
BUT IF YA TEAM UP WITH ANOTHER GUY'N THERE ARE GIRLS LEFT OVER, THAT'S A PROB, TOO.
SO I'LL PAIR UP WITH HIM. THAT OK, PREZ?
...
...
MMM...
SHOCK
ALL RIGHT, LET'S DO THAT. SENGOKU, YOU'RE WITH MIYAUCHI.
'PRECIATE IT..
UH... SURE.
SI--GH.

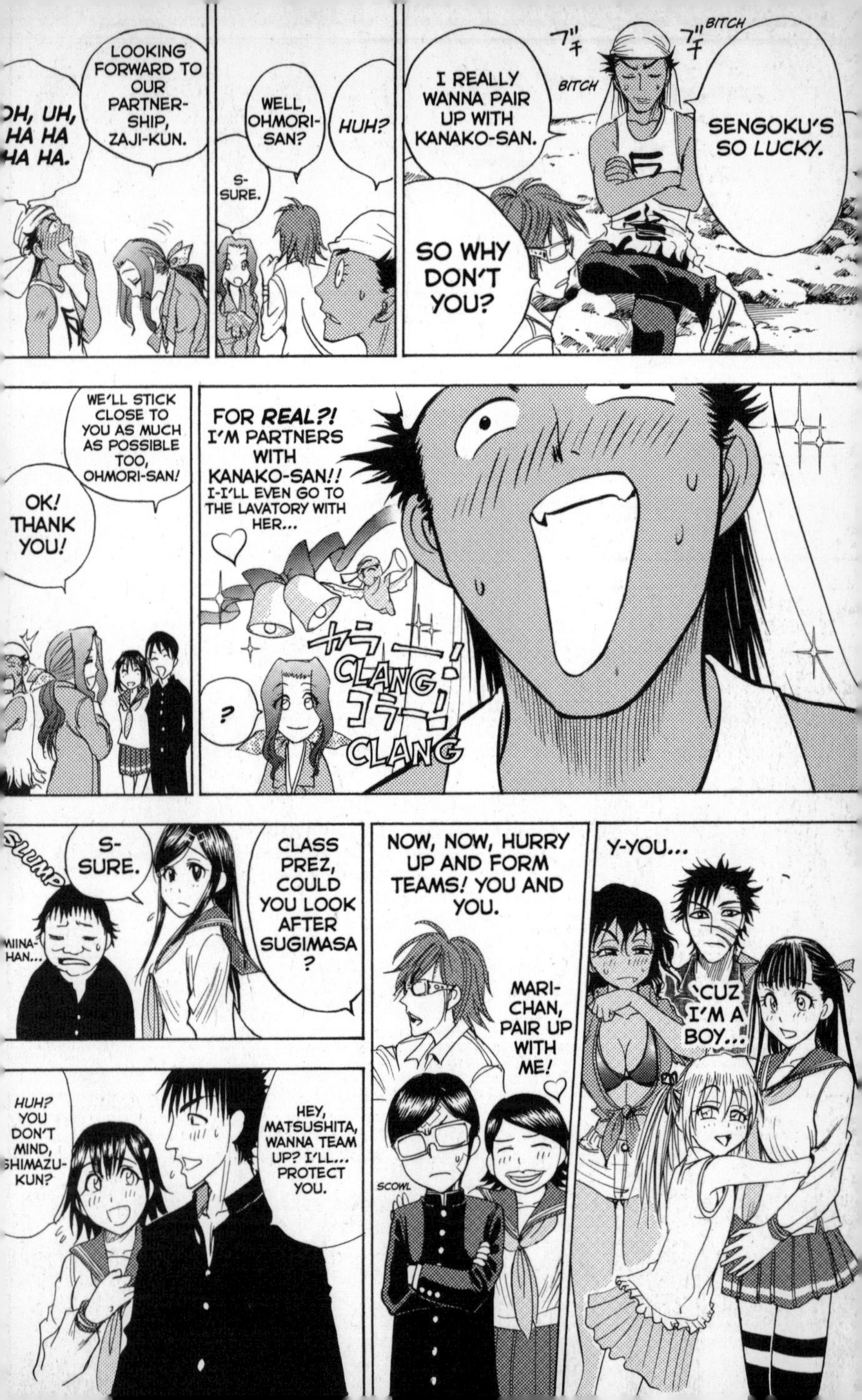
BITCH
BITCH
SENGOKU'S SO LUCKY.
I REALLY WANNA PAIR UP WITH KANAKO-SAN.
SO WHY DON'T YOU?
HUH?
WELL, OHMORI-SAN?
S-SURE.
LOOKING FORWARD TO OUR PARTNERSHIP, ZAJI-KUN.
OH, UH, HA HA HA HA.
FOR REAL?! I'M PARTNERS WITH KANAKO-SAN!! I-I'LL EVEN GO TO THE LAVATORY WITH HER...
CLANG
CLANG
?
WE'LL STICK CLOSE TO YOU AS MUCH AS POSSIBLE TOO, OHMORI-SAN!
OK! THANK YOU!
Y-YOU...
'CUZ I'M A BOY...
NOW, NOW, HURRY UP AND FORM TEAMS! YOU AND YOU.
MARI-CHAN, PAIR UP WITH ME!
SCOWL
CLASS PREZ, COULD YOU LOOK AFTER SUGIMASA?
S-SURE.
SLUMP
MIINA-HAN...
HEY, MATSUSHITA, WANNA TEAM UP? I'LL... PROTECT YOU.
HUH? YOU DON'T MIND, SHIMAZU-KUN?

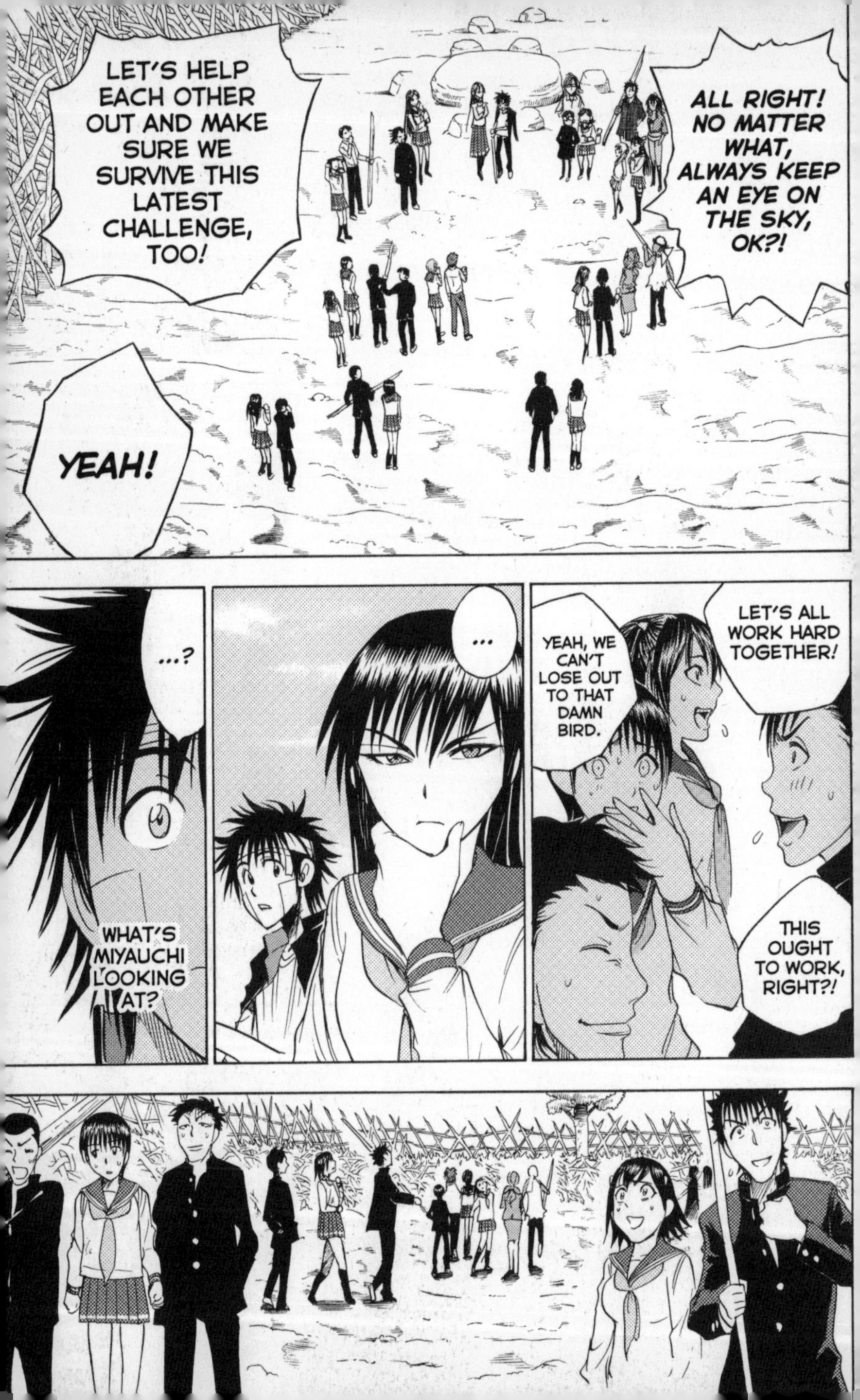
ALL RIGHT! NO MATTER WHAT, ALWAYS KEEP AN EYE ON THE SKY, OK?!
LET'S HELP EACH OTHER OUT AND MAKE SURE WE SURVIVE THIS LATEST CHALLENGE, TOO!
YEAH!
LET'S ALL WORK HARD TOGETHER!
YEAH, WE CAN'T LOSE OUT TO THAT DAMN BIRD.
THIS OUGHT TO WORK, RIGHT?!
...
...?
WHAT'S MIYAUCHI LOOKING AT?

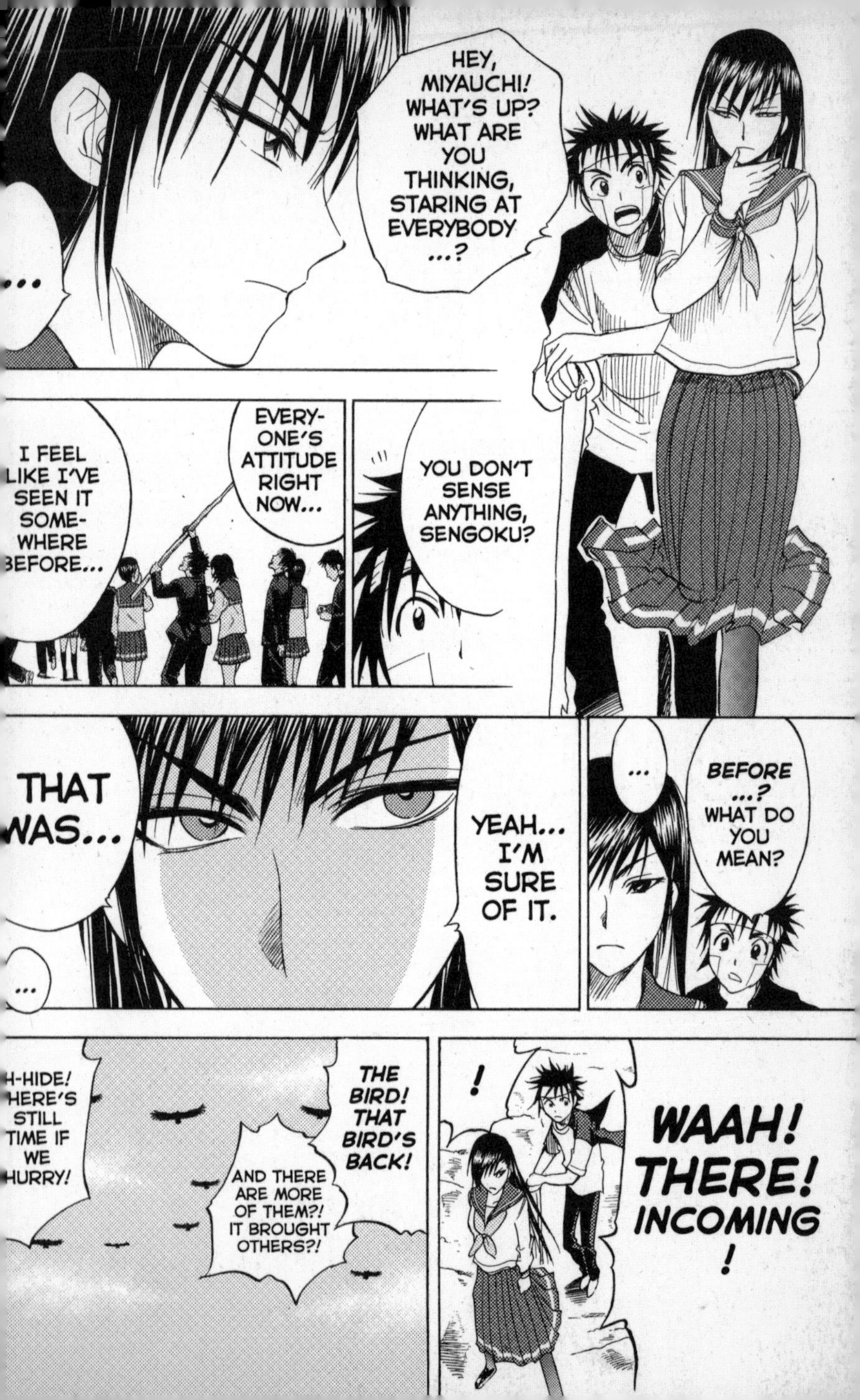
HEY, MIYAUCHI! WHAT'S UP? WHAT ARE YOU THINKING, STARING AT EVERYBODY ...?
...
YOU DON'T SENSE ANYTHING, SENGOKU?
EVERYONE'S ATTITUDE RIGHT NOW...
I FEEL LIKE I'VE SEEN IT SOMEWHERE BEFORE...
BEFORE ...? WHAT DO YOU MEAN?
...
YEAH... I'M SURE OF IT.
THAT WAS...
...
WAAH! THERE! INCOMING!
!
THE BIRD! THAT BIRD'S BACK!
AND THERE ARE MORE OF THEM?! IT BROUGHT OTHERS?!
H-HIDE! HERE'S STILL TIME IF WE HURRY!

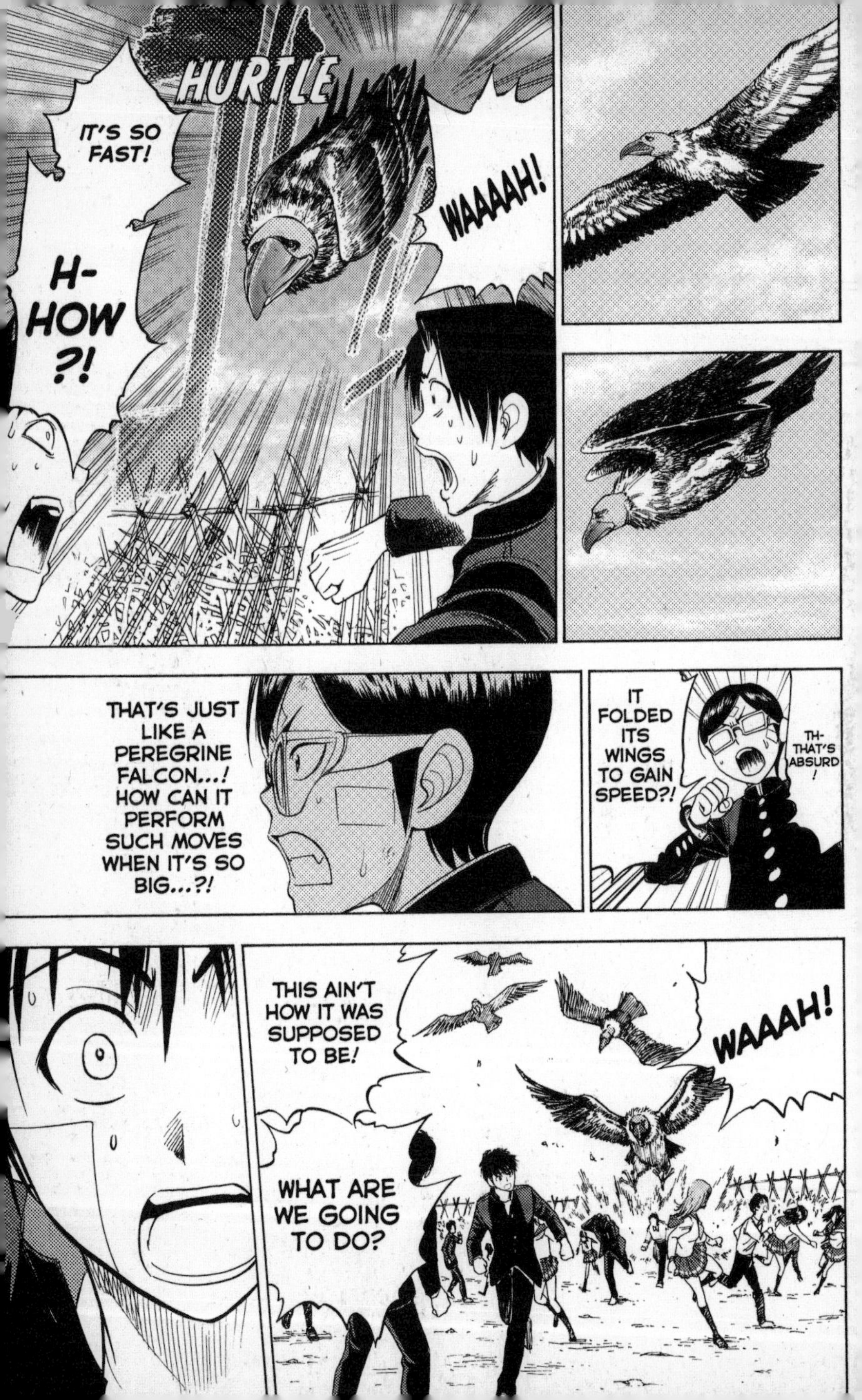
HURTLE
IT'S SO FAST!
WAAAAH!
H-HOW?!
IT FOLDED ITS WINGS TO GAIN SPEED?!
TH-THAT'S ABSURD!
THAT'S JUST LIKE A PEREGRINE FALCON...! HOW CAN IT PERFORM SUCH MOVES WHEN IT'S SO BIG...?!
WAAAH!
THIS AIN'T HOW IT WAS SUPPOSED TO BE!
WHAT ARE WE GOING TO DO?

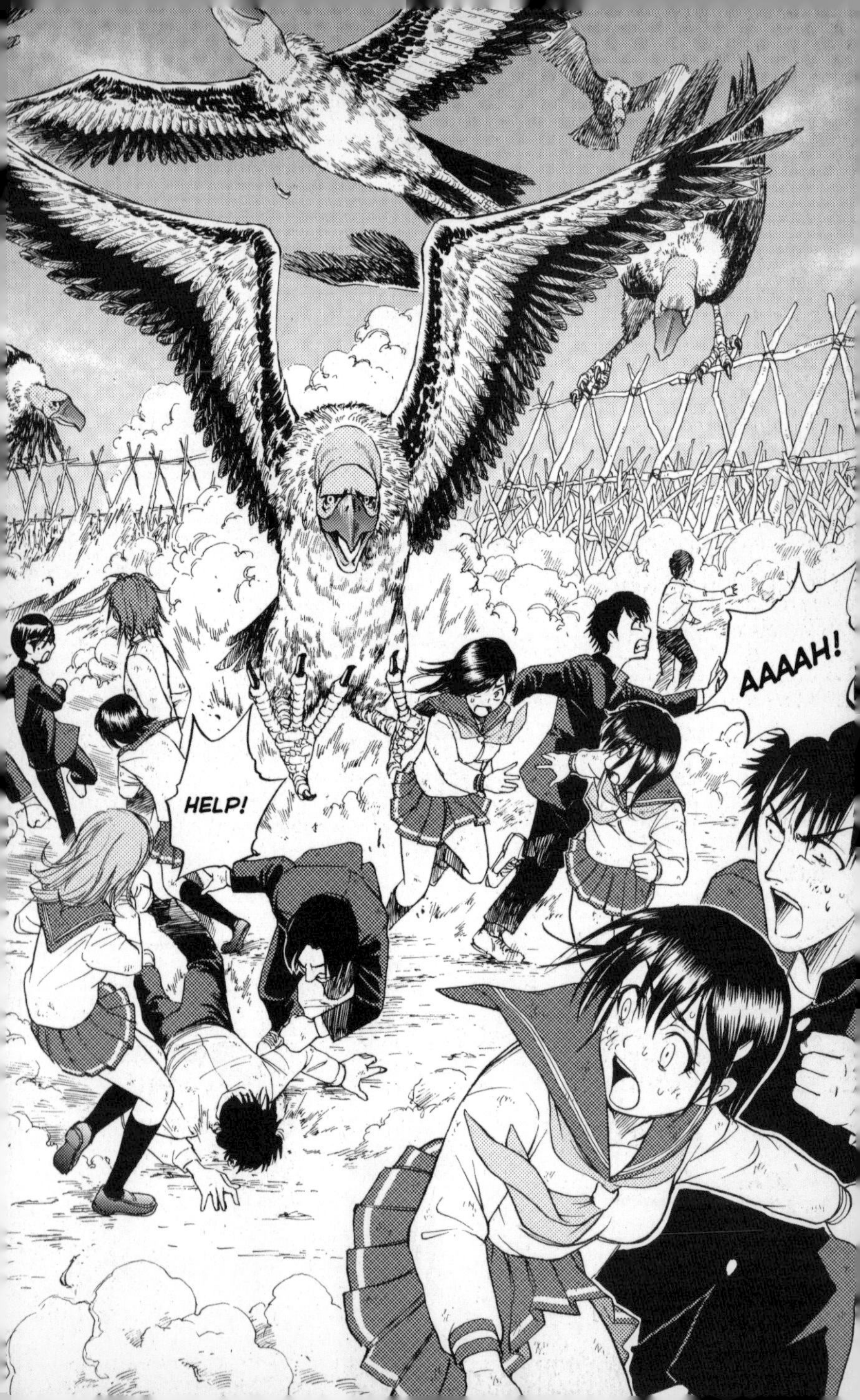
AAAAH!
HELP!

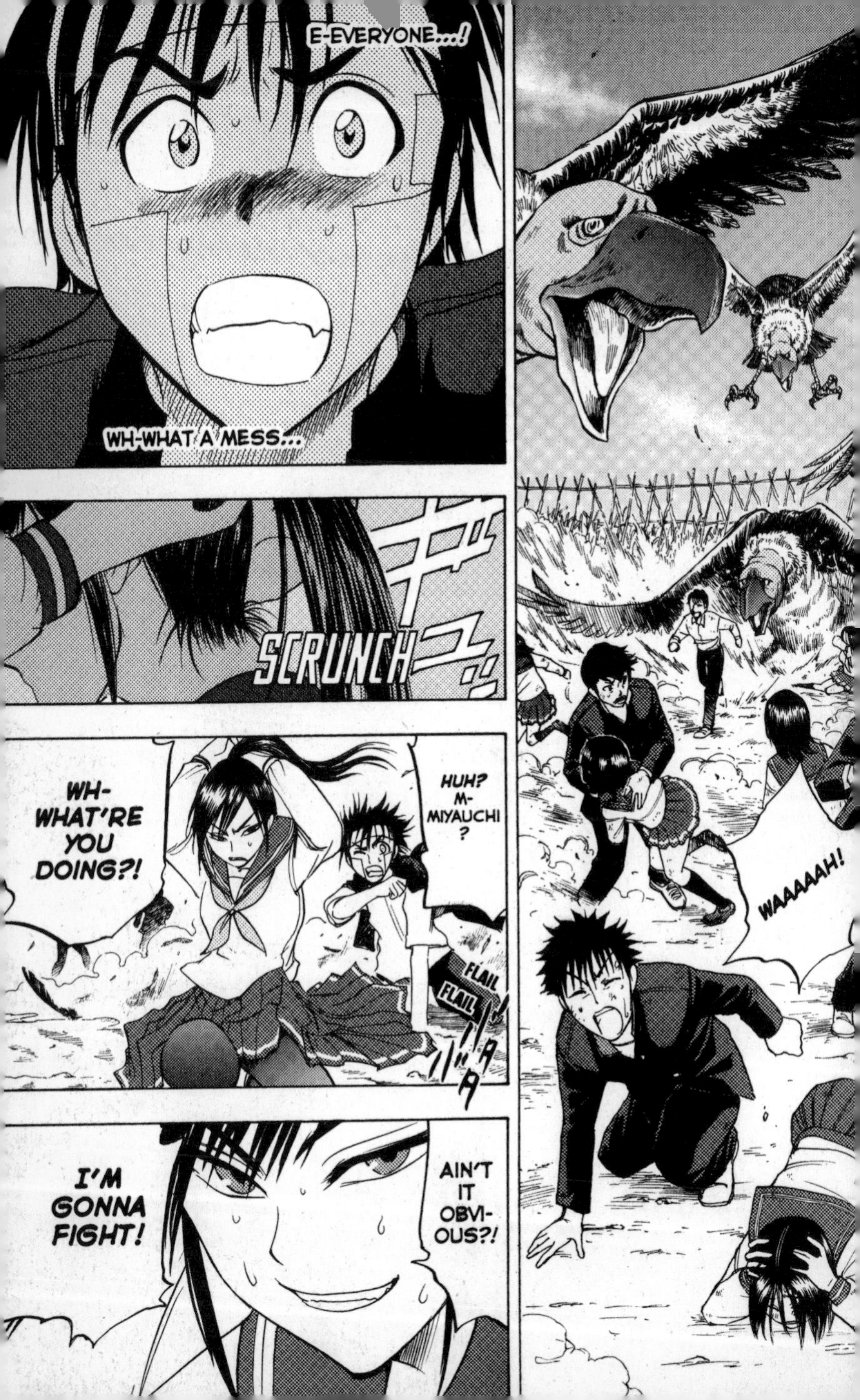
WAAAAAH!
E-EVERYONE...!
WH-WHAT A MESS...
SCRUNCH
HUH? M-MIYAUCHI?
WH-WHAT'RE YOU DOING?!
FLAIL FLAIL
AIN'T IT OBVIOUS?!
I'M GONNA FIGHT!

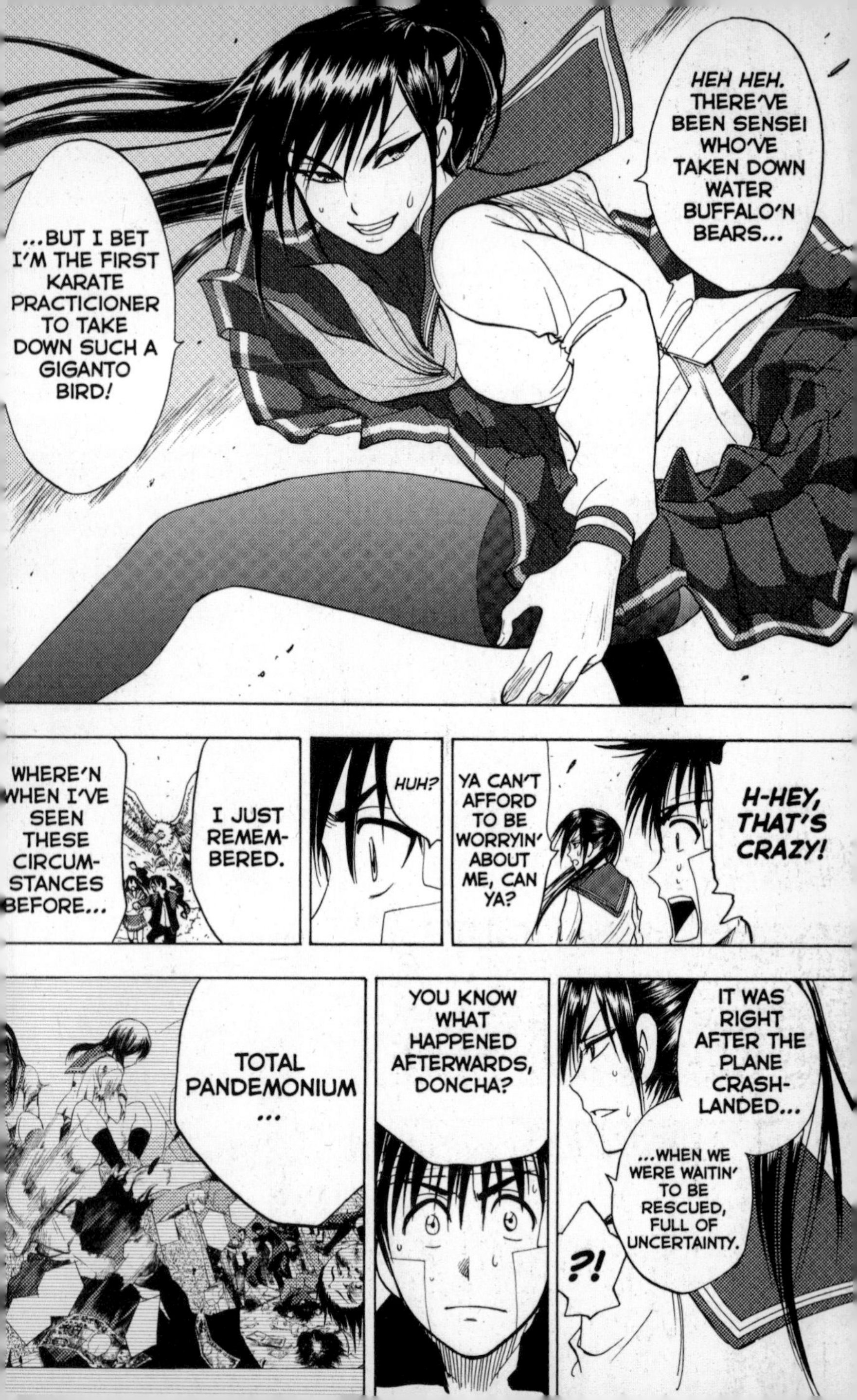
HEH HEH. THERE'VE BEEN SENSEI WHO'VE TAKEN DOWN WATER BUFFALO'N BEARS...
...BUT I BET I'M THE FIRST KARATE PRACTICIONER TO TAKE DOWN SUCH A GIGANTO BIRD!
H-HEY, THAT'S CRAZY!
YA CAN'T AFFORD TO BE WORRYIN' ABOUT ME, CAN YA?
HUH?
I JUST REMEMBERED.
WHERE'N WHEN I'VE SEEN THESE CIRCUMSTANCES BEFORE...
IT WAS RIGHT AFTER THE PLANE CRASH-LANDED...
...WHEN WE WERE WAITIN' TO BE RESCUED, FULL OF UNCERTAINTY.
?!
YOU KNOW WHAT HAPPENED AFTERWARDS, DONCHA?
TOTAL PANDEMONIUM ...

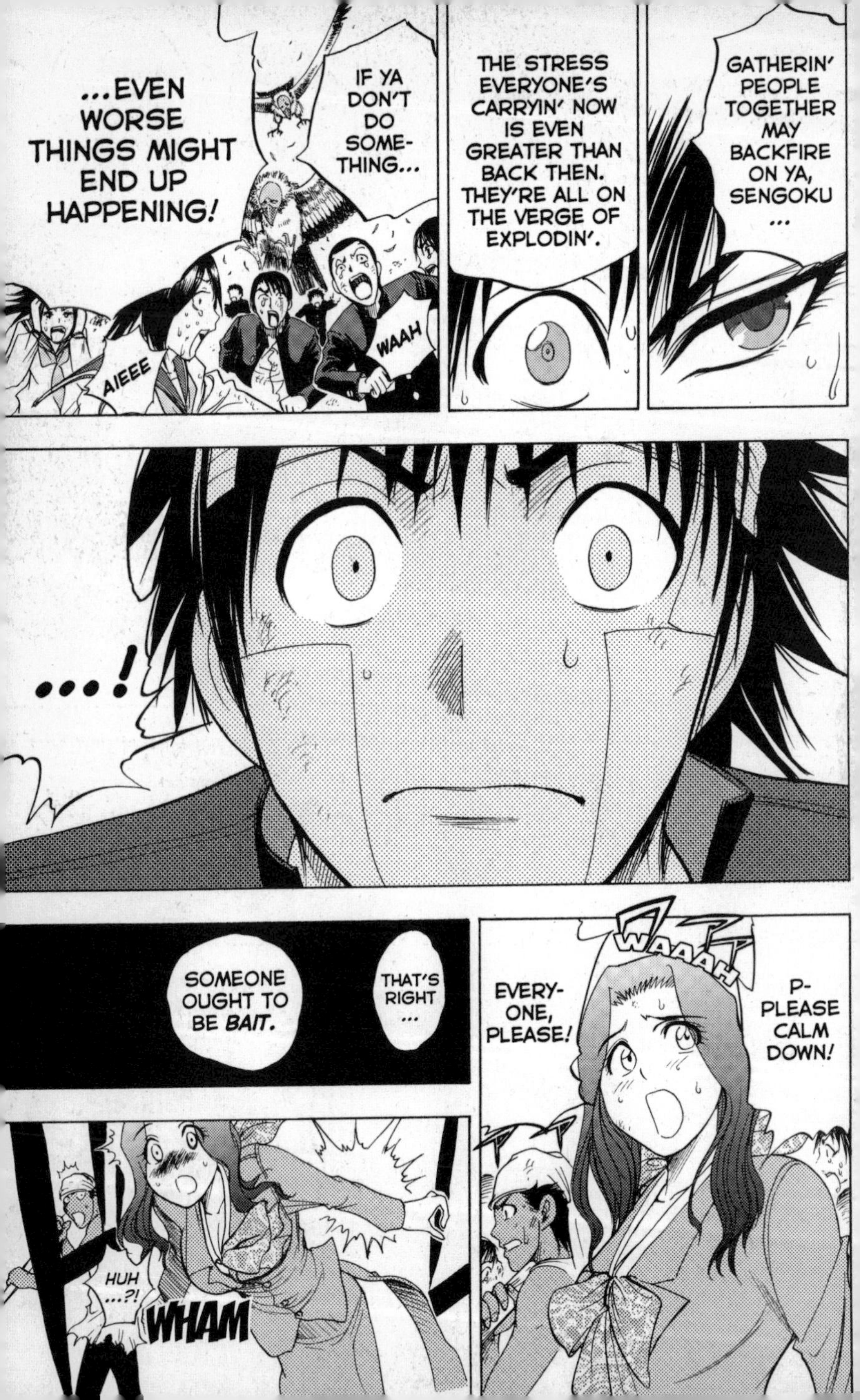
GATHERIN' PEOPLE TOGETHER MAY BACKFIRE ON YA, SENGOKU ...
THE STRESS EVERYONE'S CARRYIN' NOW IS EVEN GREATER THAN BACK THEN. THEY'RE ALL ON THE VERGE OF EXPLODIN'.
IF YA DON'T DO SOME-THING...
...EVEN WORSE THINGS MIGHT END UP HAPPENING!
WAAH
AIEEE
...!
WAAAH
P- PLEASE CALM DOWN!
EVERY-ONE, PLEASE!
THAT'S RIGHT ...
SOMEONE OUGHT TO BE *BAIT*.
HUH ...?!
WHAM

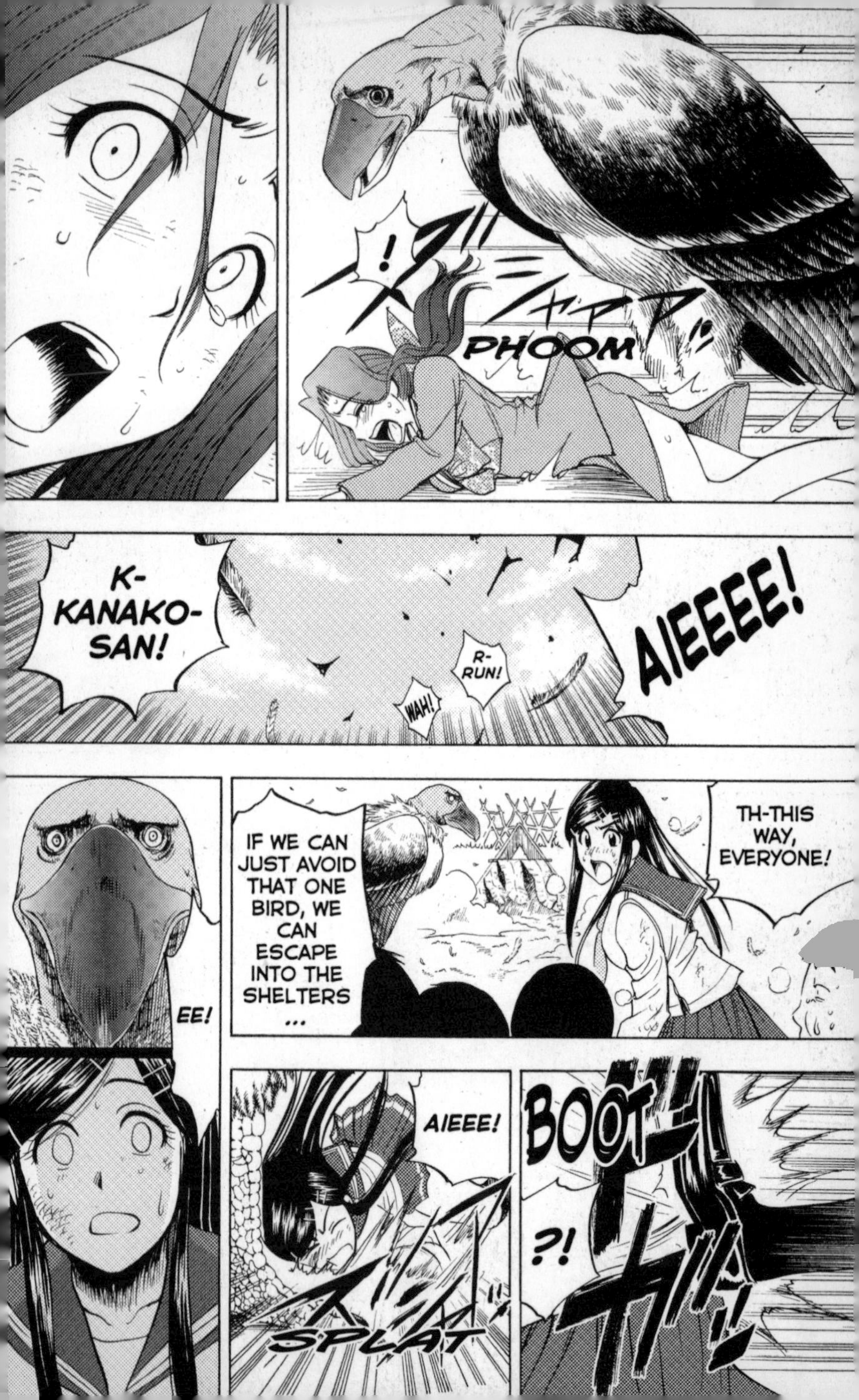
!
PHOOM
AIEEEE!
R-RUN!
WAH!
K-KANAKO-SAN!
TH-THIS WAY, EVERYONE!
IF WE CAN JUST AVOID THAT ONE BIRD, WE CAN ESCAPE INTO THE SHELTERS ...
BOOT
?!
AIEEE!
SPLAT
EE!

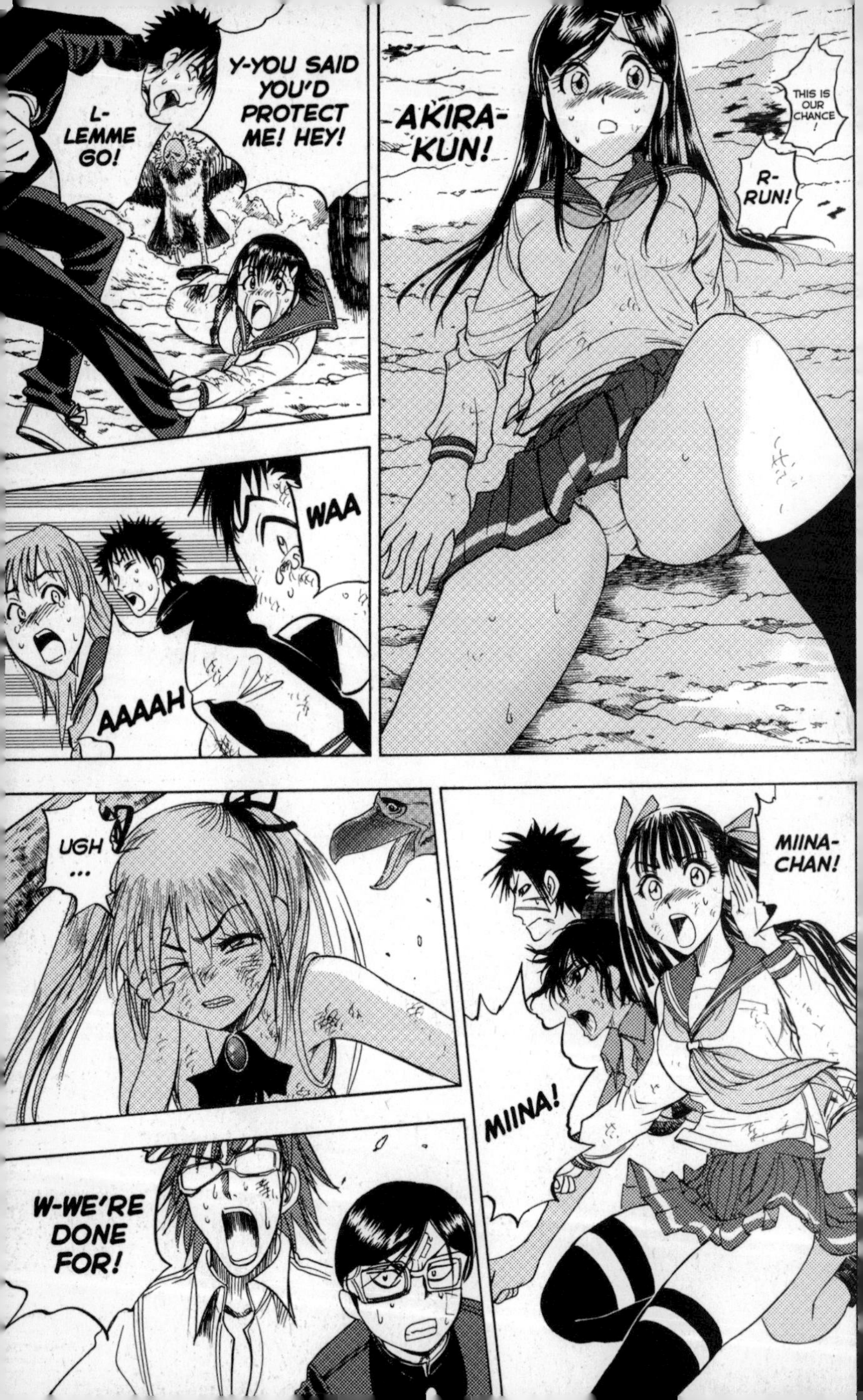
THIS IS OUR CHANCE!
R-RUN!
AKIRA-KUN!
Y-YOU SAID YOU'D PROTECT ME! HEY!
L-LEMME GO!
WAA
AAAAH
MIINA-CHAN!
MIINA!
UGH ...
W-WE'RE DONE FOR!

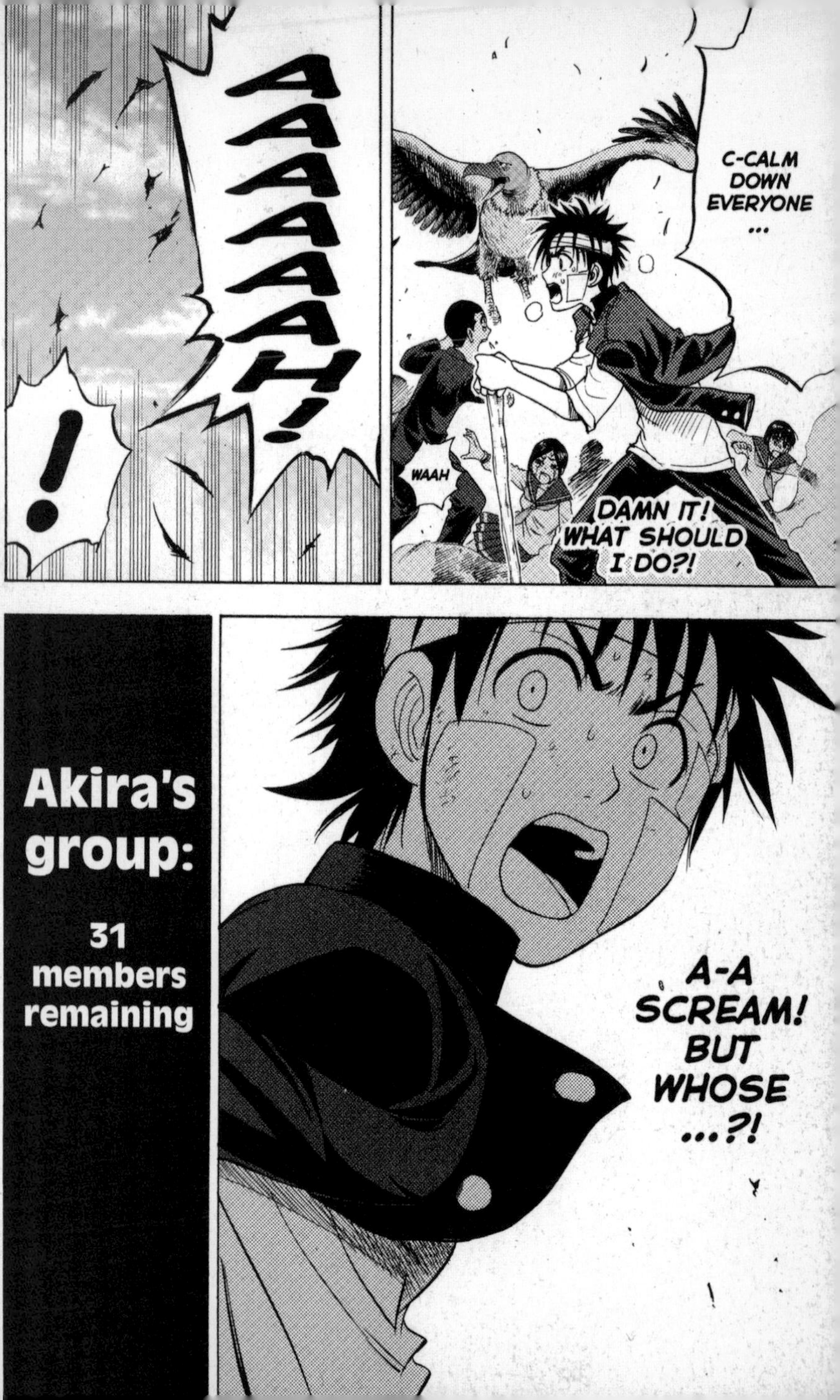
C-CALM DOWN EVERYONE ...
WAAH
DAMN IT! WHAT SHOULD I DO?!
AAAAAH!
!
A-A SCREAM! BUT WHOSE ...?!
Akira's group:
31 members remaining

To Be Continued...

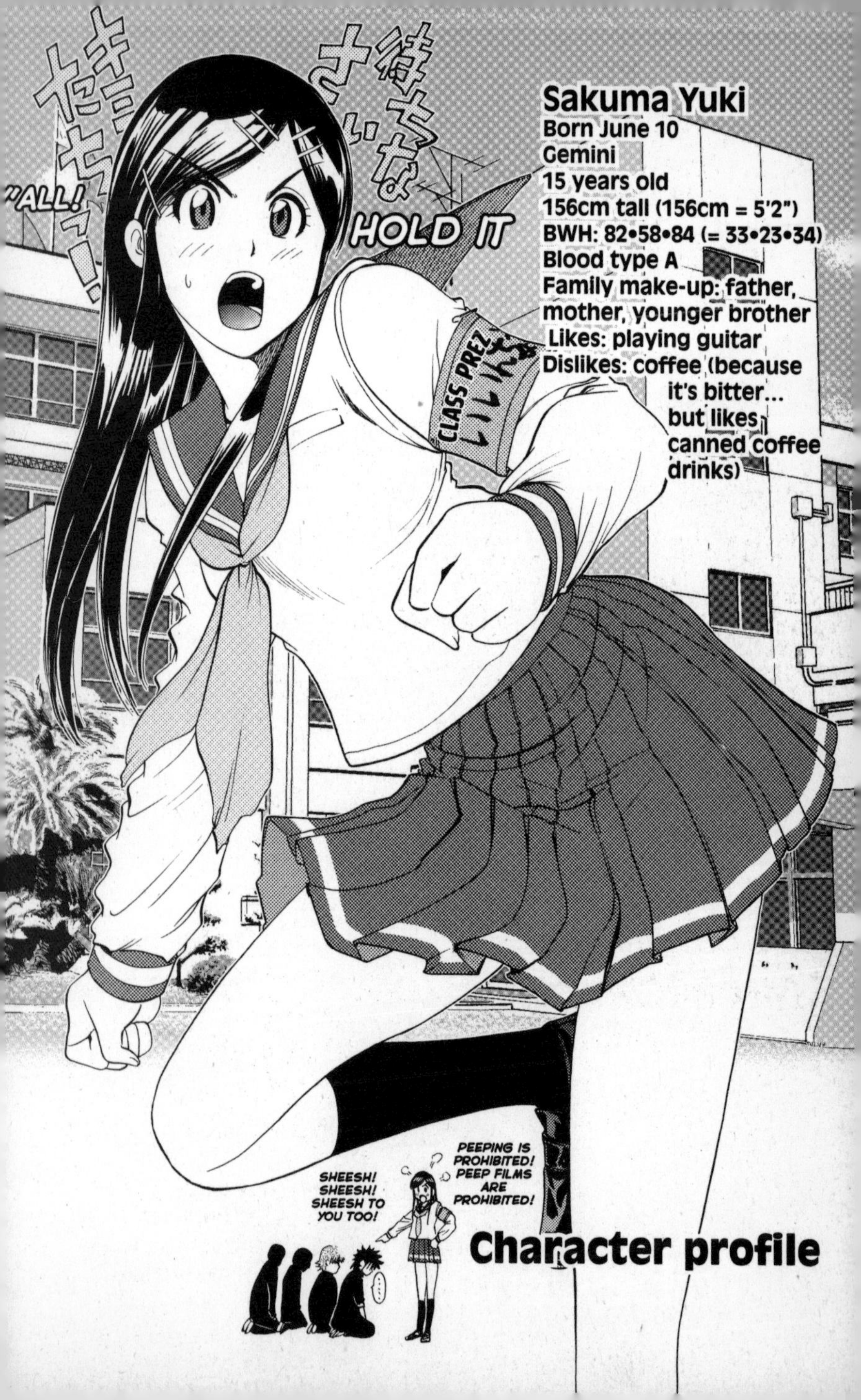
待ちなさい
HOLD IT
"ALL!
Sakuma Yuki
Born June 10
Gemini
15 years old
156cm tall (156cm = 5'2")
BWH: 82•58•84 (= 33•23•34)
Blood type A
Family make-up: father, mother, younger brother
Likes: playing guitar
Dislikes: coffee (because it's bitter... but likes canned coffee drinks)
CLASS PREZ
PEEPING IS PROHIBITED! PEEP FILMS ARE PROHIBITED!
SHEESH! SHEESH! SHEESH TO YOU TOO!
...
Character profile

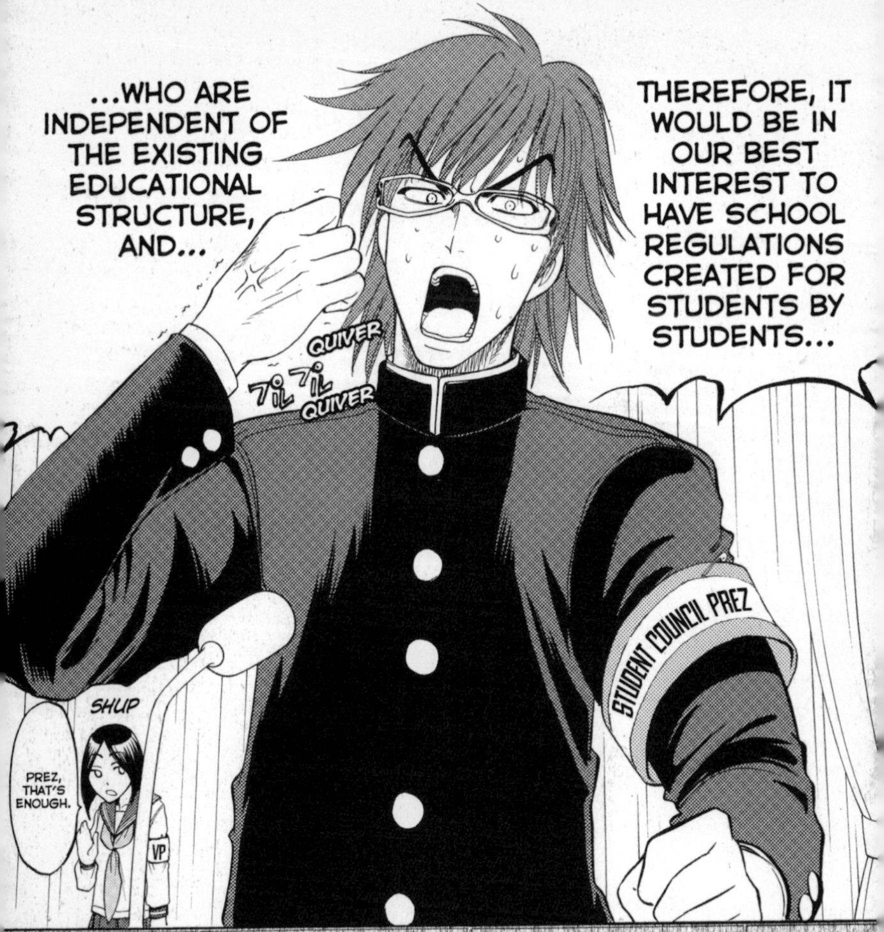
THEREFORE, IT WOULD BE IN OUR BEST INTEREST TO HAVE SCHOOL REGULATIONS CREATED FOR STUDENTS BY STUDENTS...
...WHO ARE INDEPENDENT OF THE EXISTING EDUCATIONAL STRUCTURE, AND...
QUIVER
プルプル
QUIVER
STUDENT COUNCIL PREZ
SHUP
PREZ, THAT'S ENOUGH.
VP

Character profile

Yamaguchi Takashi
Born April 15
Aries
15 years old
175cm tall (175cm = 5'10")
Body weight 60kg (= 132lbs)
Blood type A
Family make-up: father, mothe
older brother
Likes: classical music
Dislikes: rollercoasters

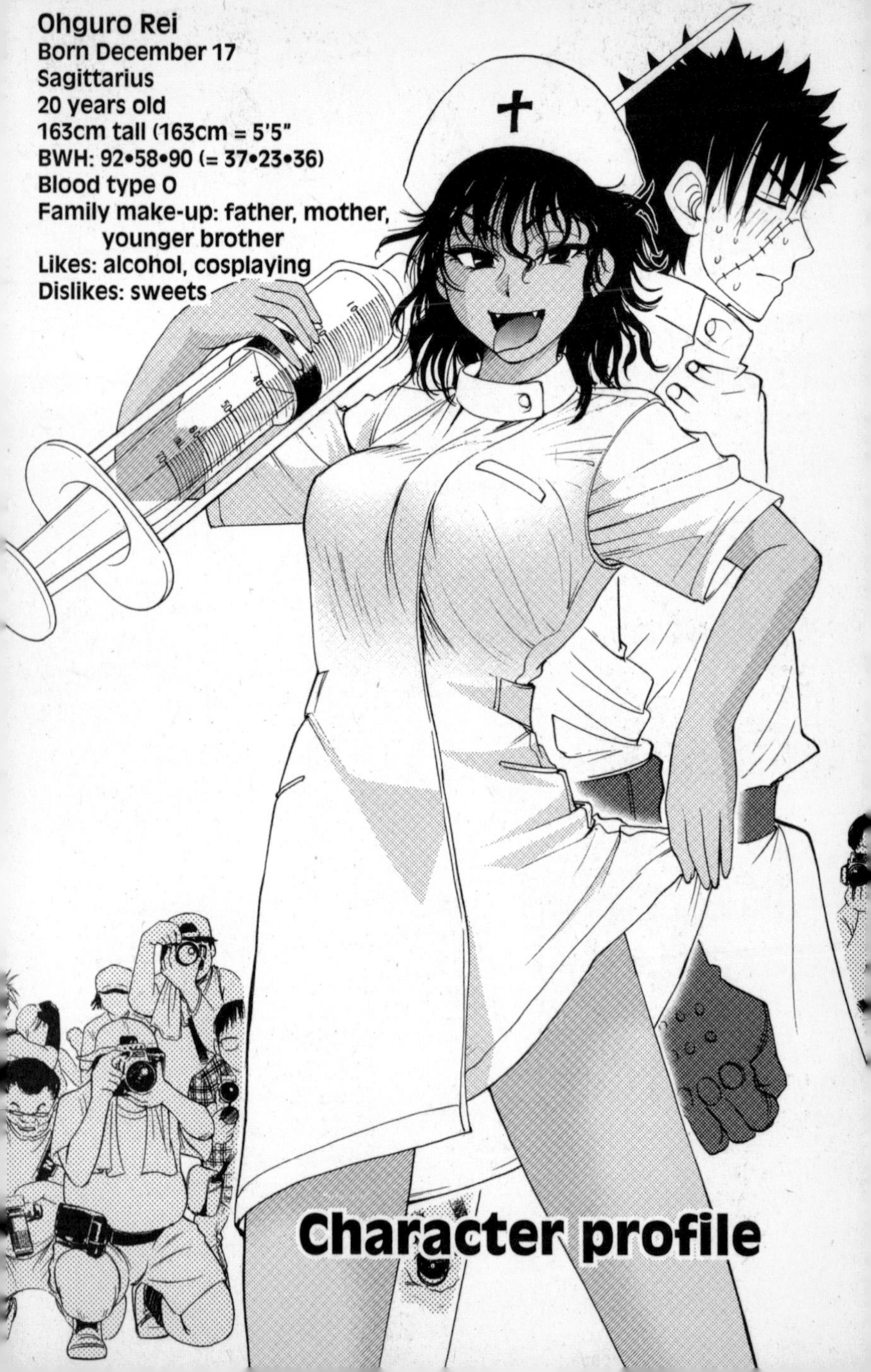
Ohguro Rei
Born December 17
Sagittarius
20 years old
163cm tall (163cm = 5'5"
BWH: 92•58•90 (= 37•23•36)
Blood type O
Family make-up: father, mother, younger brother
Likes: alcohol, cosplaying
Dislikes: sweets
Character profile

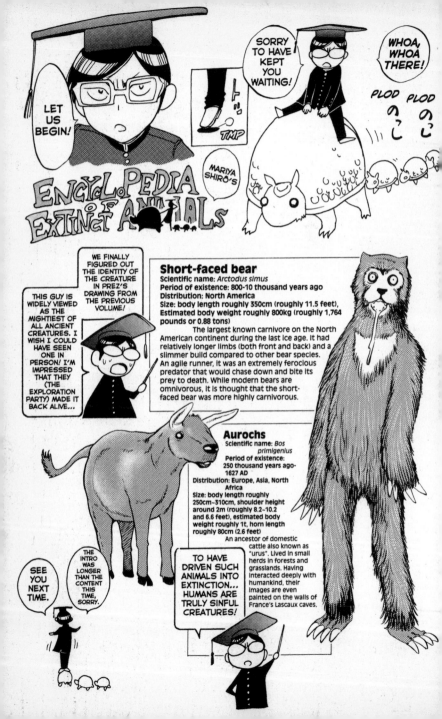

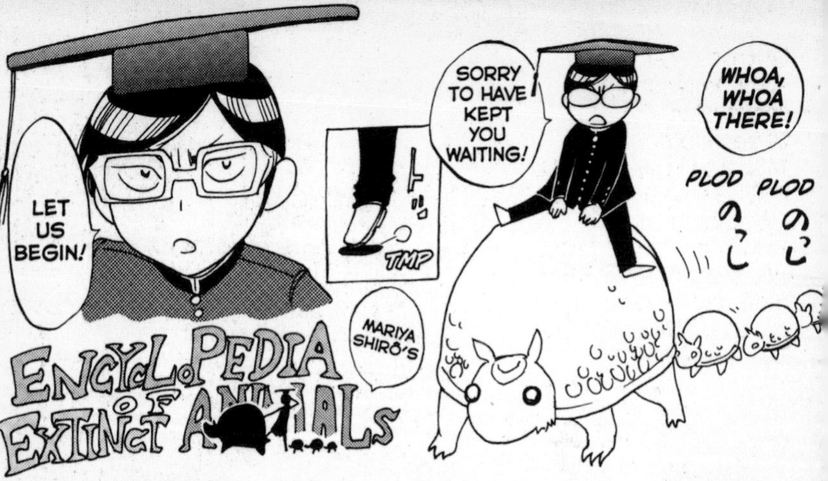
WHOA, WHOA THERE!
PLOD PLOD
のこ のこ
SORRY TO HAVE KEPT YOU WAITING!
TMP
LET US BEGIN!
MARIYA SHIRŌ'S
ENCYCLOPEDIA OF EXTINCT ANIMALS

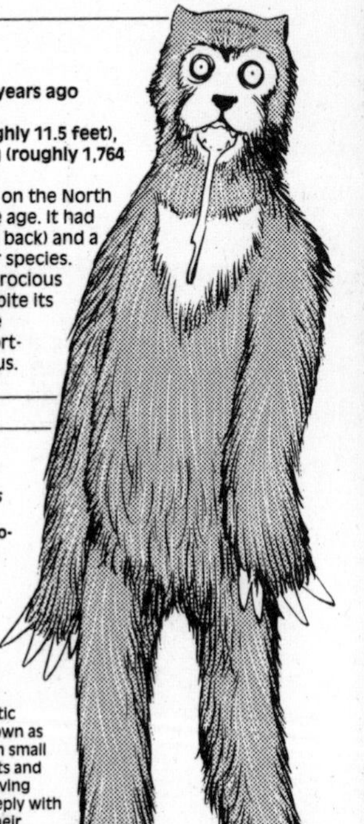

Short-faced bear

Scientific name: *Arctodus simus*
Period of existence: 800-10 thousand years ago
Distribution: North America
Size: body length roughly 350cm (roughly 11.5 feet), Estimated body weight roughly 800kg (roughly 1,764 pounds or 0.88 tons)

The largest known carnivore on the North American continent during the last ice age. It had relatively longer limbs (both front and back) and a slimmer build compared to other bear species. An agile runner, it was an extremely ferocious predator that would chase down and bite its prey to death. While modern bears are omnivorous, it is thought that the short-faced bear was more highly carnivorous.

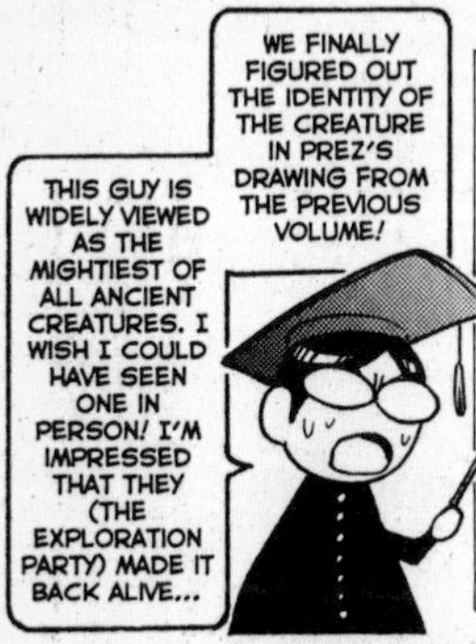
WE FINALLY FIGURED OUT THE IDENTITY OF THE CREATURE IN PREZ'S DRAWING FROM THE PREVIOUS VOLUME!
THIS GUY IS WIDELY VIEWED AS THE MIGHTIEST OF ALL ANCIENT CREATURES. I WISH I COULD HAVE SEEN ONE IN PERSON! I'M IMPRESSED THAT THEY (THE EXPLORATION PARTY) MADE IT BACK ALIVE...

Aurochs

Scientific name: *Bos primigenius*
Period of existence: 250 thousand years ago-1627 AD
Distribution: Europe, Asia, North Africa
Size: body length roughly 250cm~310cm, shoulder height around 2m (roughly 8.2~10.2 and 6.6 feet), estimated body weight roughly 1t, horn length roughly 80cm (2.6 feet)

An ancestor of domestic cattle also known as "urus". Lived in small herds in forests and grasslands. Having interacted deeply with humankind, their images are even painted on the walls of France's Lascaux caves,

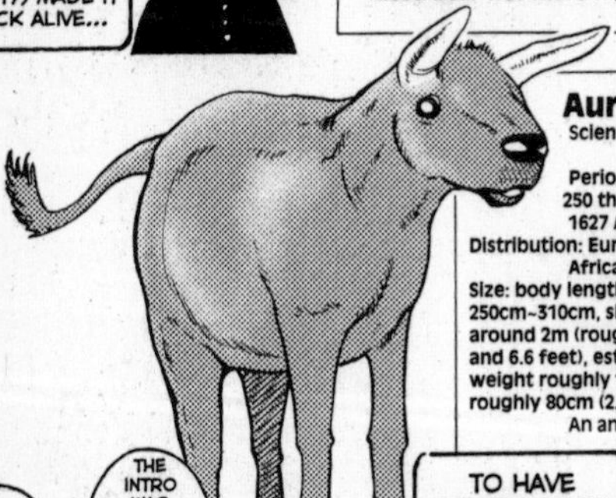

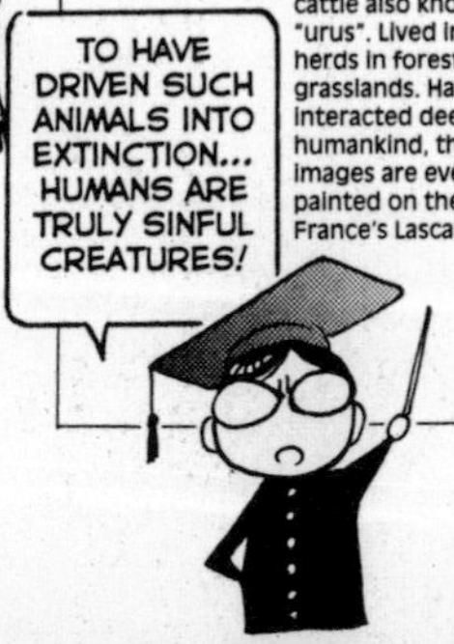
TO HAVE DRIVEN SUCH ANIMALS INTO EXTINCTION... HUMANS ARE TRULY SINFUL CREATURES!

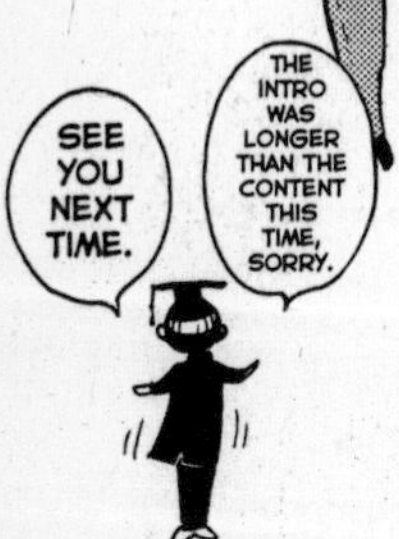
THE INTRO WAS LONGER THAN THE CONTENT THIS TIME, SORRY.
SEE YOU NEXT TIME.

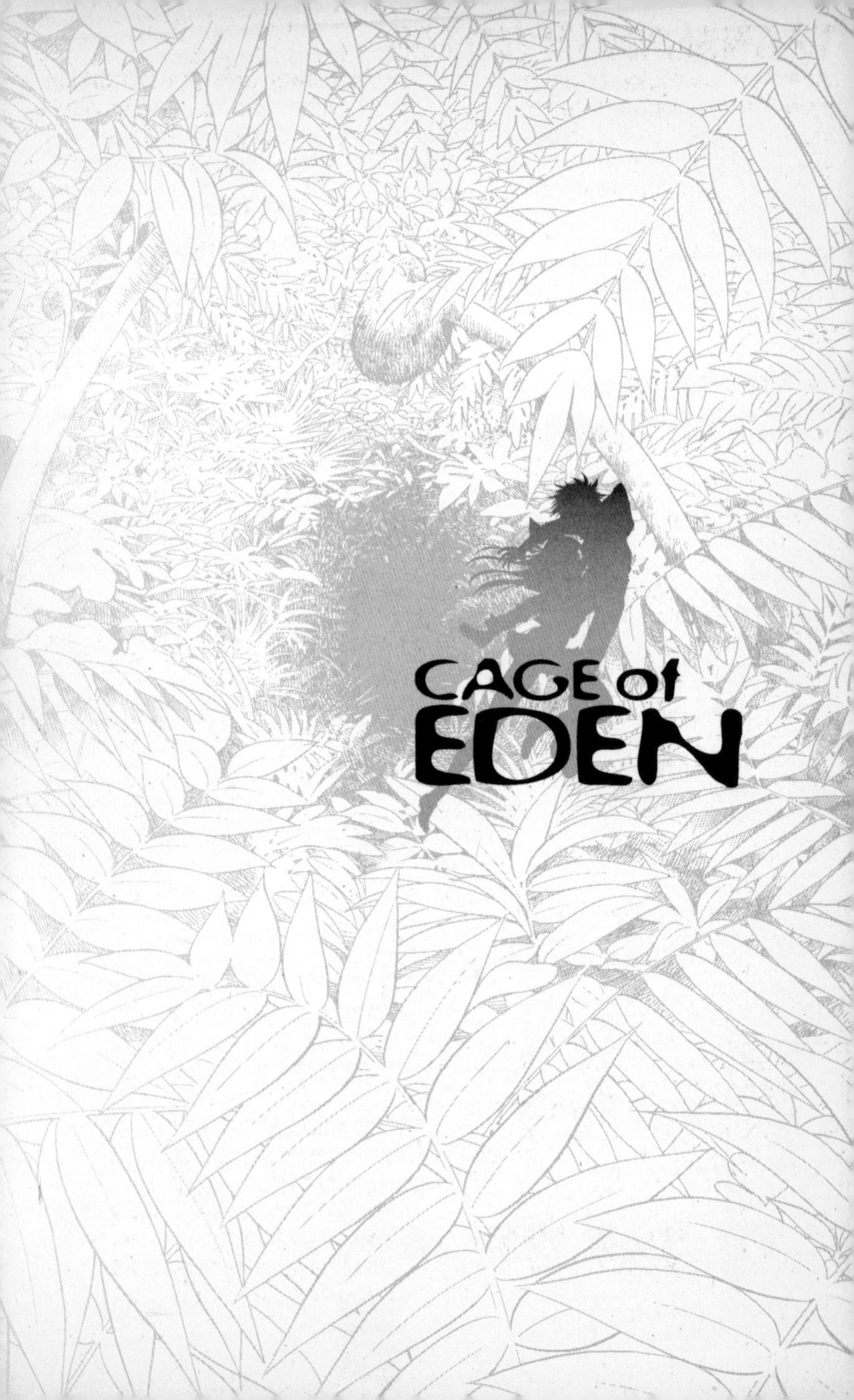
CAGE of
EDEN

TRANSLATION NOTES

Japanese is a tricky language for most Westerners, and translation is often more art than science. For your edification and reading pleasure, here are notes on some of the places where we could have gone in a different direction with our translation of the work, or where a Japanese cultural reference is used.

Zaji, page 16
[016.4]
Zaji is just the nickname this character goes by. His actual name is Saji (family name) Kazuma (given name).

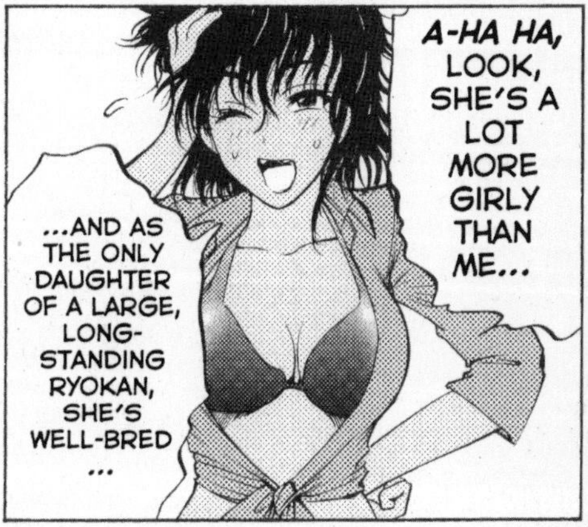
A-HA HA, LOOK, SHE'S A LOT MORE GIRLY THAN ME...
...AND AS THE ONLY DAUGHTER OF A LARGE, LONG-STANDING RYOKAN, SHE'S WELL-BRED ...

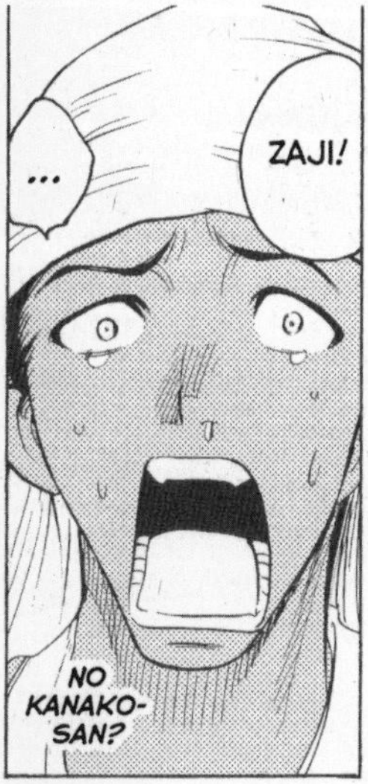
ZAJI!
...
NO KANAKO-SAN?

Ryokan, page 26
[026.5]
Traditional Japanese inns that originally were located along and served travelers of major highways, but are now found more in touristy areas, especially hot spring resorts. Similar to Western bed and breakfasts, one to two meals a day are included in the room rate, and guests may need to share the toilet and/or bathing area.

"When it rains, it pours", page 55
[055.2]
Akira uses the Japanese idiom "fundari kettari dana", which translates more literally to "just kick us when we're down" but because Akira is speaking about the sudden downpour, I felt "when it rains, it pours" to be more apropos.

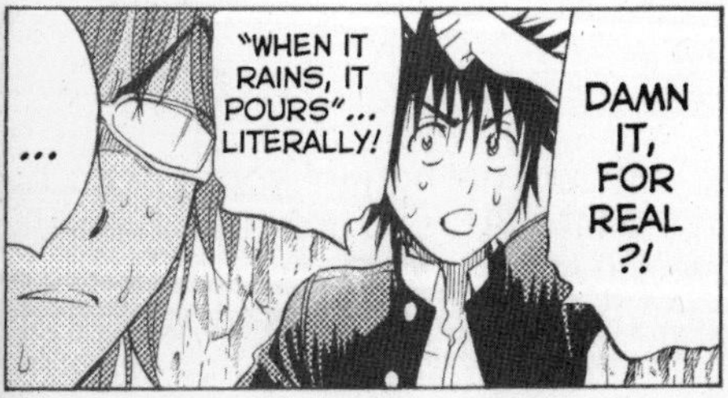
DAMN IT, FOR REAL ?!
"WHEN IT RAINS, IT POURS"... LITERALLY!
...

NHK, page 56
[056.2]
Although Japan's national public broadcasting organization, the Nippon Hôsô Kyôkai, also has an official English name of the Japan Broadcasting Corporation, both domestic and international audiences know it best by its initials NHK. It currently operates both television and radio networks.

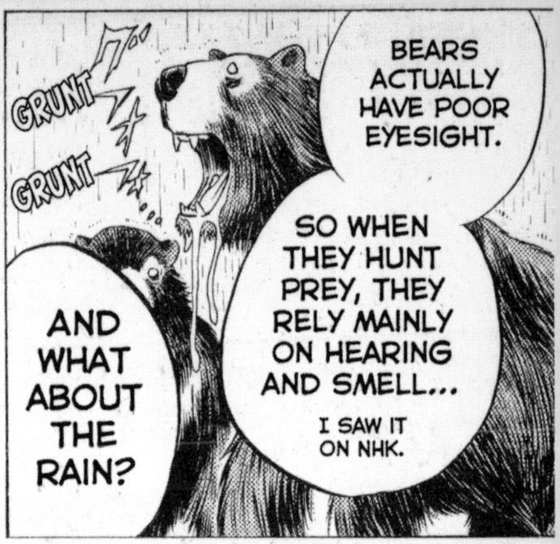
BEARS ACTUALLY HAVE POOR EYESIGHT.
SO WHEN THEY HUNT PREY, THEY RELY MAINLY ON HEARING AND SMELL...
I SAW IT ON NHK.
AND WHAT ABOUT THE RAIN?
GRUNT
GRUNT

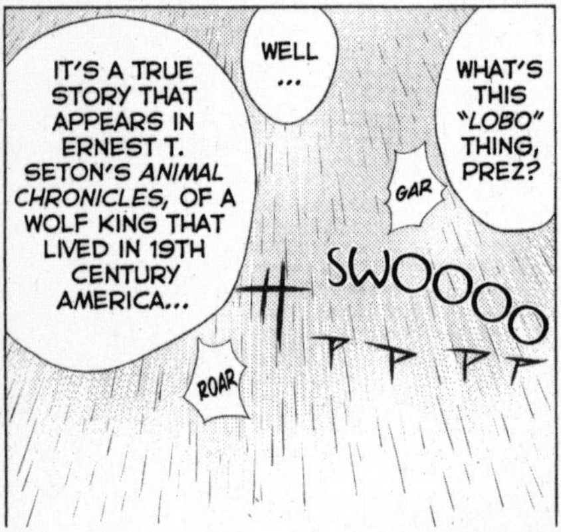
WHAT'S THIS "*LOBO*" THING, PREZ?
WELL...
IT'S A TRUE STORY THAT APPEARS IN ERNEST T. SETON'S *ANIMAL CHRONICLES*, OF A WOLF KING THAT LIVED IN 19TH CENTURY AMERICA...
GAR
SWOOOOP
ROAR

Seton Animal Chronicles, page 74, 108
[074.5, 108.5, 108.6]
Seton Animal Chronicles is the Japanese compilation of author, wildlife artist, and conservationist Ernest Thompson Seton's 55 animal tales that were originally published in many smaller units. For example, "Lobo, the King of Currumpaw" was originally published in Wild Animals I Have Known (1898), and "The Winnipeg Wolf" was originally published in Animal Heroes (1905).

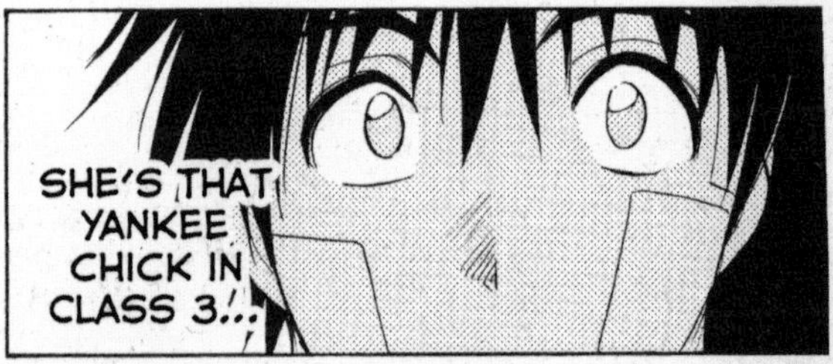
SHE'S THAT YANKEE CHICK IN CLASS 3...!

Yankee, page 148
[148.2]
A Japanese slang term that refers to uncouth delinquent youth of both sexes. It is said to have originated in the late 1970's to describe juvenile delinquents who favored gaudy Hawaiian shirts and baggy pants sold in Osaka's Amerikamura, or "American Village". However, although many yankee boys and girls still sport bleached hair, it does not denote any fascination with America or any attempt to look or be American, and is not meant as a racial slur against Americans despite its use as a derogatory term.

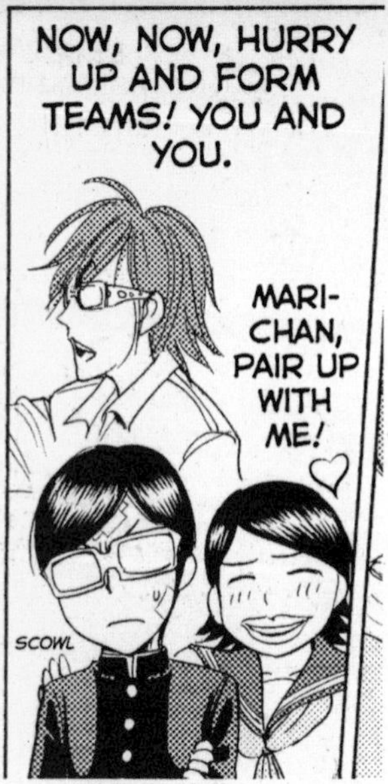
NOW, NOW, HURRY UP AND FORM TEAMS! YOU AND YOU.
MARI-CHAN, PAIR UP WITH ME!
SCOWL

Mari-chan, page 172
[172.7]
The nickname a female classmate affectionately calls Mariya by, although it could also be considered derisive since shortening his family name to "Mari" renders it a female first name. This is further emphasized by the diminutive suffix "-chan" which is used with babies, cute animals, and children (especially girls). One could infer that the appellation originated from brainiac Mariya's small stature and lack of athleticism and other masculine attributes.

BWH (3 Sizes), page 184
[184.1]
An abbreviation for bust, waist, and hip, and denotes each respective circumference measurement. Originally intended for the purpose of aiding seamstresses make or fit clothes, it is currently also used by women in their personal ads or profiles to describe their proportions to the viewer.

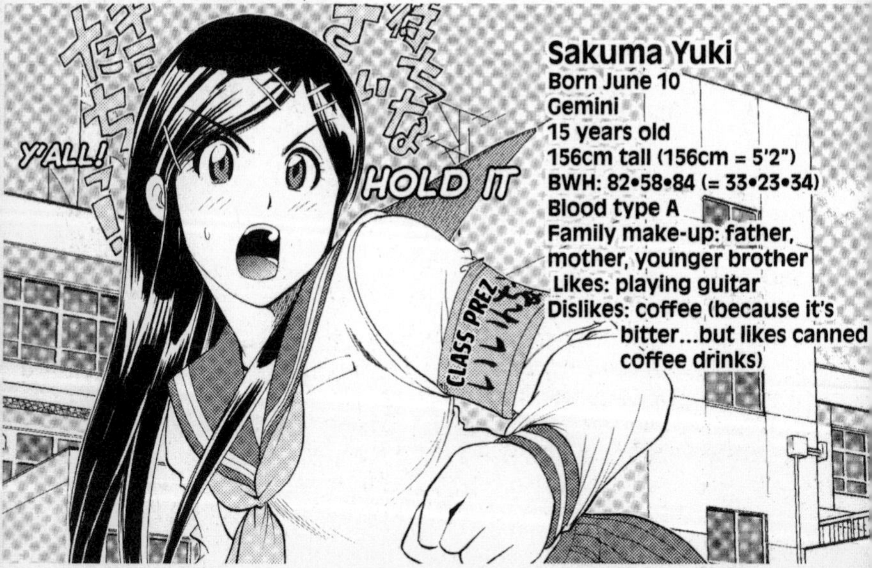
HOLD IT
Y'ALL!
CLASS PREZ
Sakuma Yuki
Born June 10
Gemini
15 years old
156cm tall (156cm = 5'2")
BWH: 82•58•84 (= 33•23•34)
Blood type A
Family make-up: father, mother, younger brother
Likes: playing guitar
Dislikes: coffee (because it's bitter...but likes canned coffee drinks)

Preview of

CAGE of EDEN

We're pleased to present you a preview
from Cage of Eden 7.
Please check our website
(www.kodanshacomics.com) to see when
this volume will be available in English. For
now, you'll have to make do with Japanese!

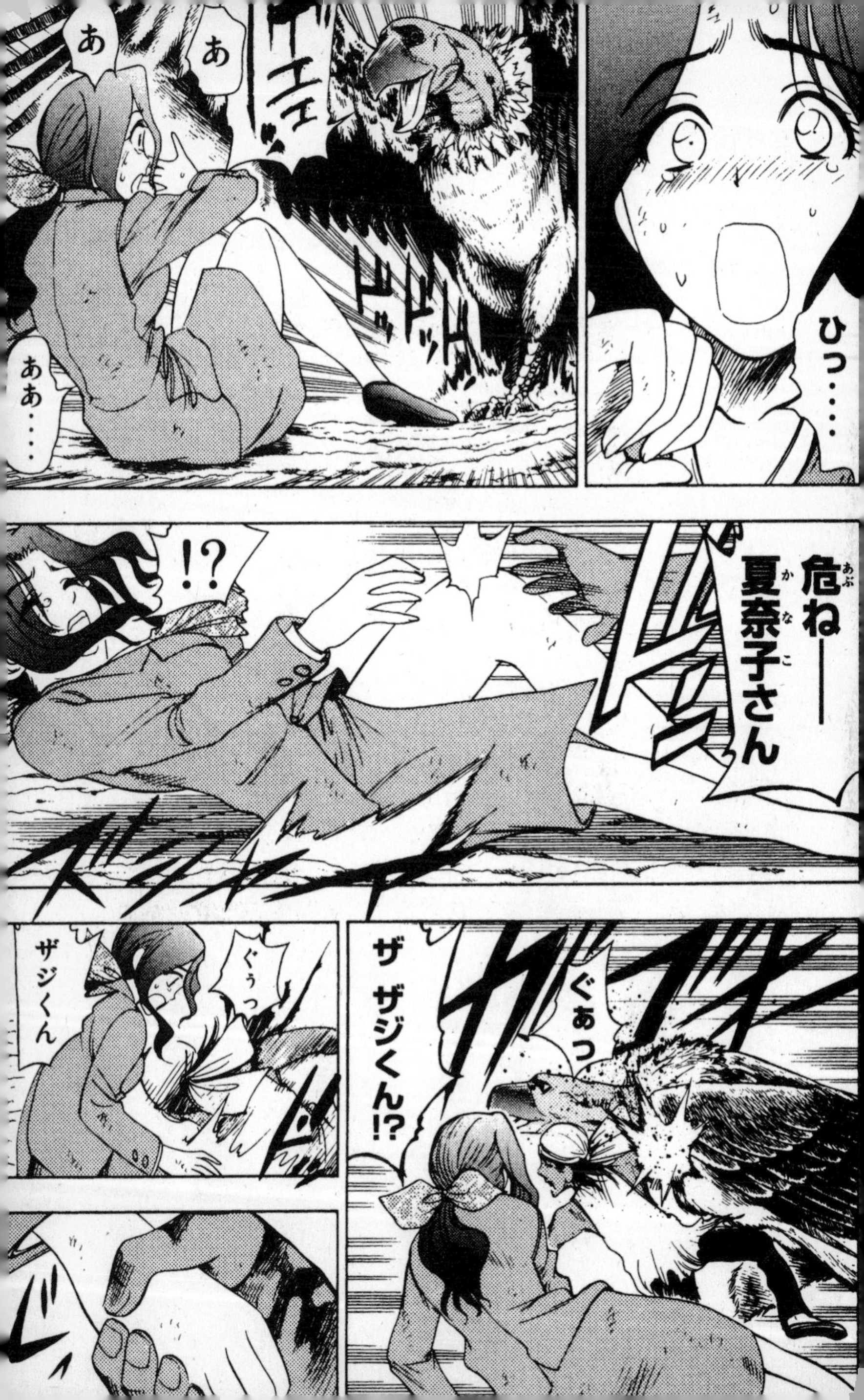
ひっ……
あ
あ
ああ……
危ねー
夏奈子さん
!?
ぐあっ
ザ ザジくん!?
ぐぅっ
ザジくん

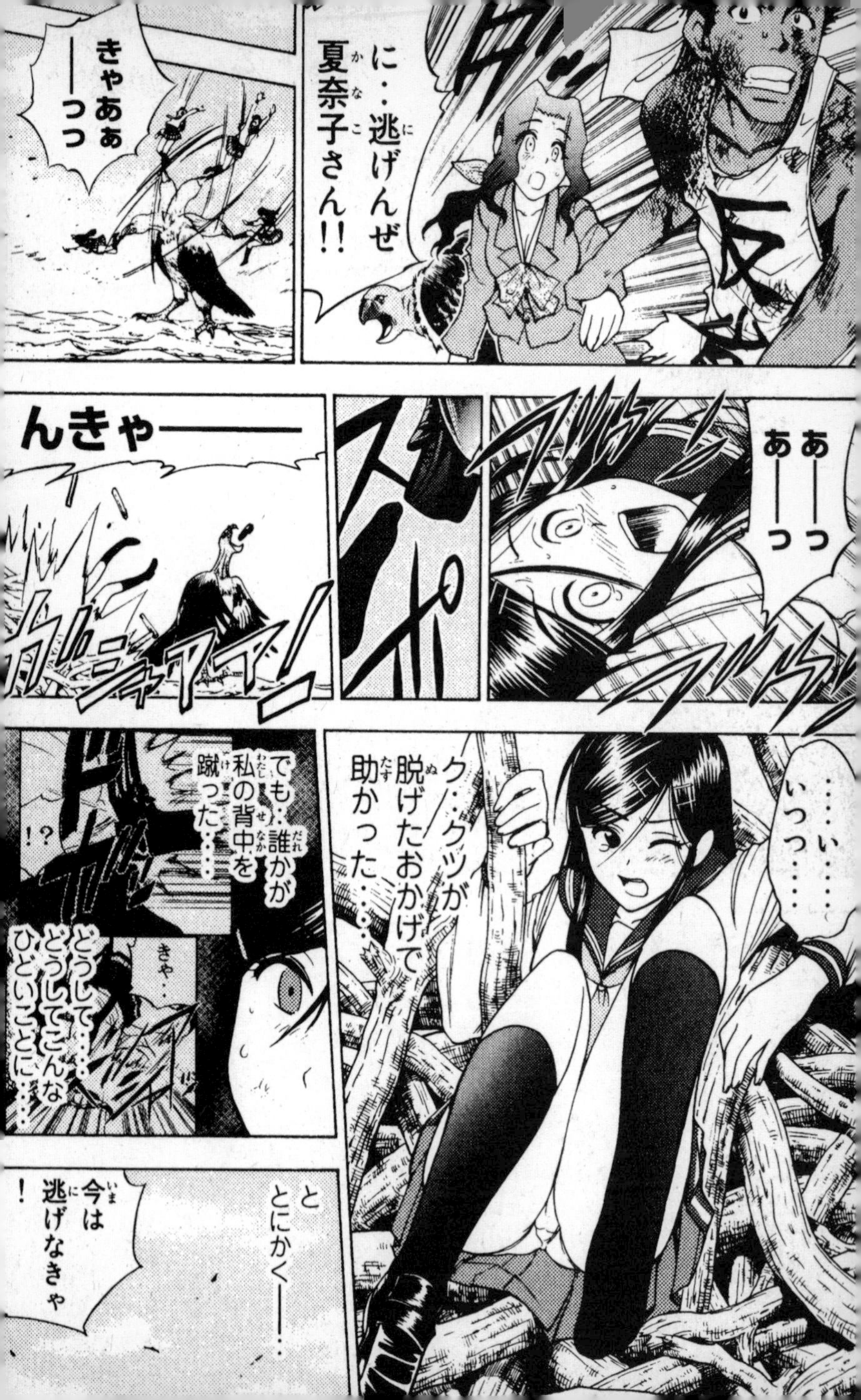
に・・逃げんぜ夏奈子さん!!
きゃあぁ——っっ
あ——っ あ——っ
スポ
んきゃ———
……い……いっっ……
ク・・クツが脱げたおかげで助かった・・・・・
でも・・誰かが私の背中を蹴った・・・・
!?
きゃ・・
どうして・・・どうしてこんなひどいことに・・・
と とにかく——・・
今は逃げなきゃ!

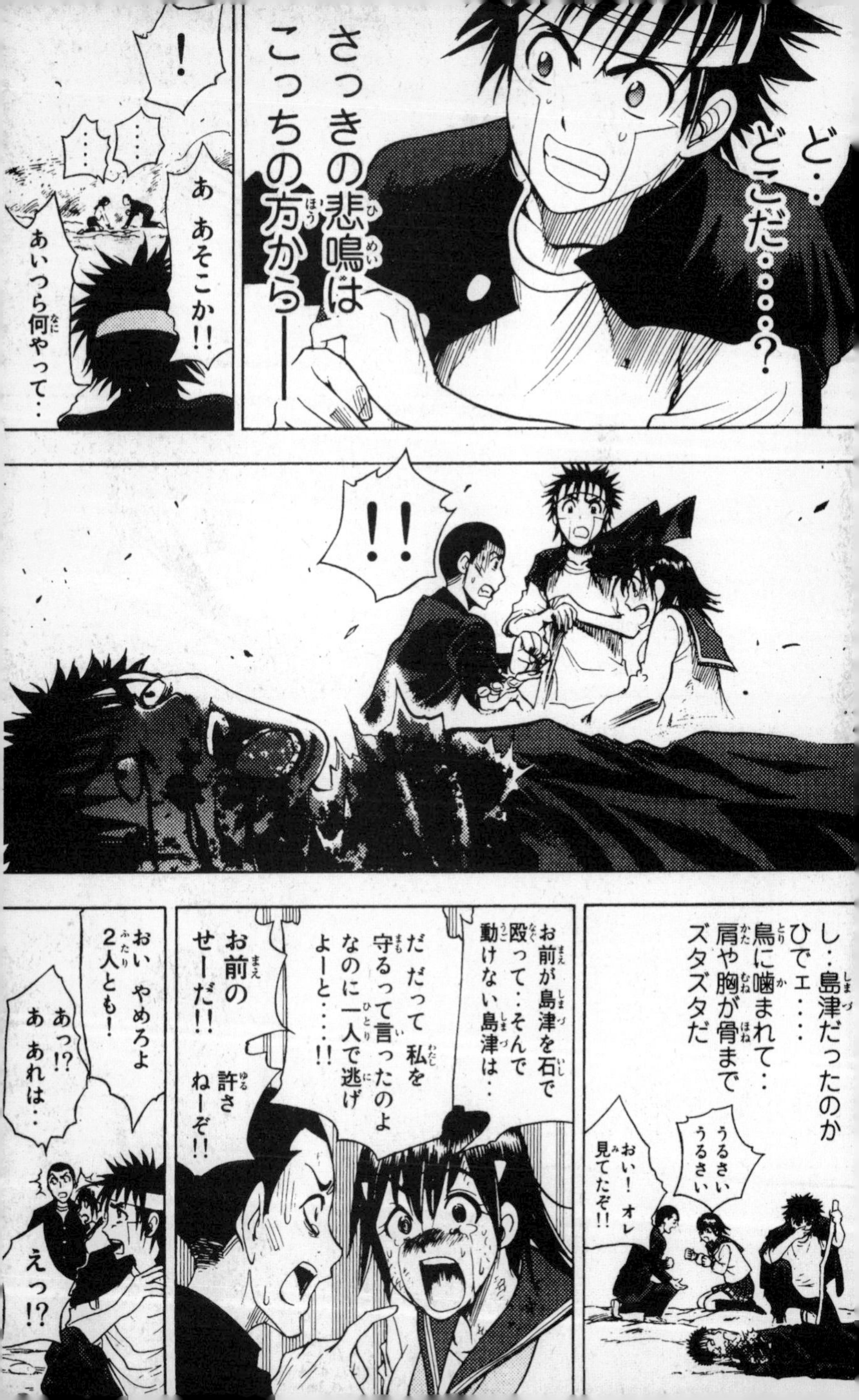
ど・・どこだ・・・？
さっきの悲鳴はこっちの方から——
！
・・・・
・・・・
あ あそこか!!
あいつら何やって・・
!!
し・・島津だったのか ひでエ・・・ 鳥に噛まれて・・ 肩や胸が骨までズタズタだ
うるさい うるさい
おい！ オレ見てたぞ!!
お前が島津を石で殴って・・そんで動けない島津は・・
だだって 私を守るって言ったのよ なのに一人で逃げよーと・・・・!!
お前のせーだ!! 許さねーぞ!!
おい やめろよ 2人とも！
あっ!? あれは・・
えっ!?

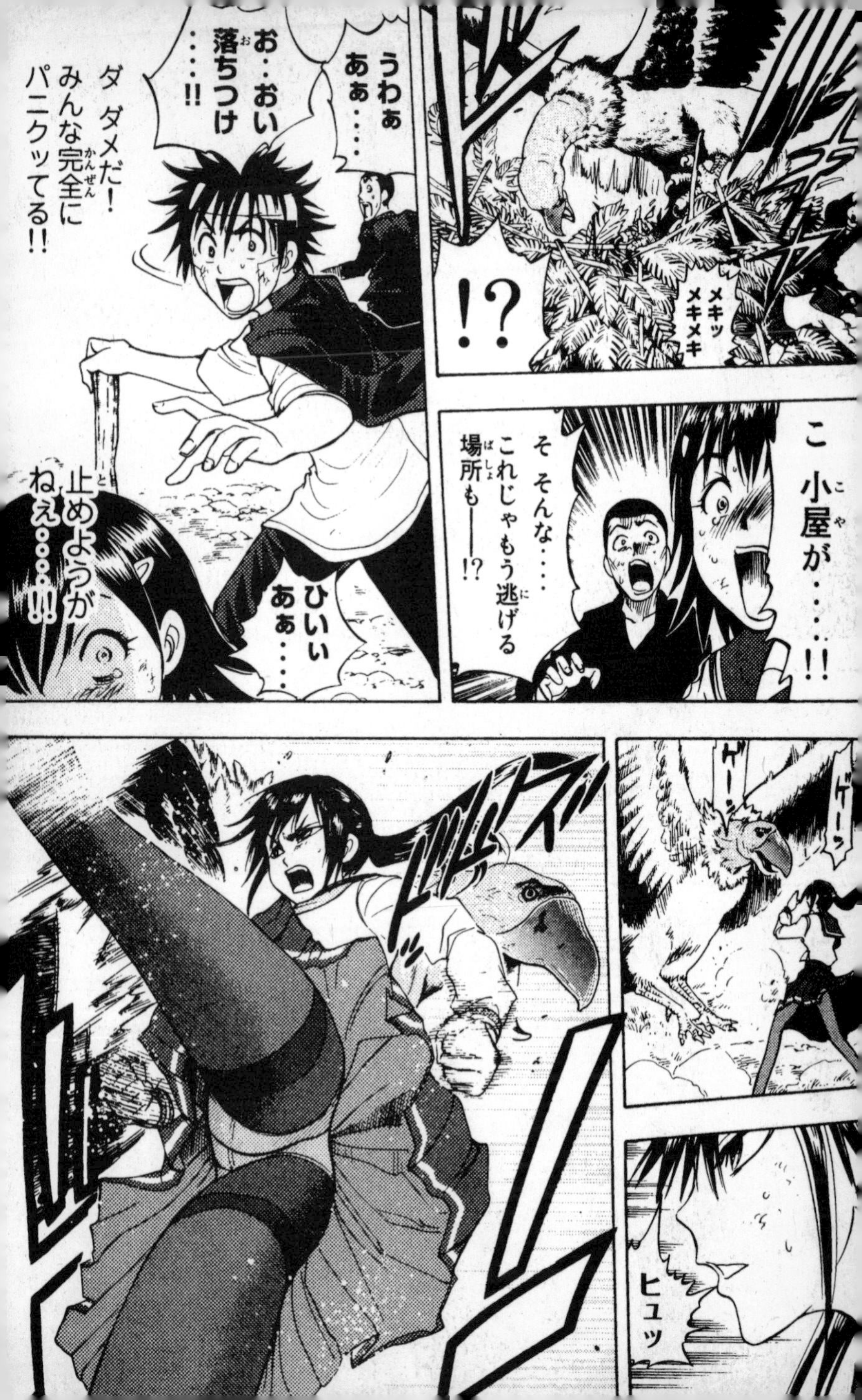
!?
メキッ メキメキ
こ 小屋が・・・・!!
そ そんな・・・・これじゃもう逃げる場所も――!?
うわぁ あぁ・・・・
お・・おい 落ちつけ・・・・!!
ダ ダメだ! みんな完全に パニクッてる!!
ひいい あぁ・・・・
止めようが ねえ・・・・!!
ゲーッ
ゲーッ
ヒュッ

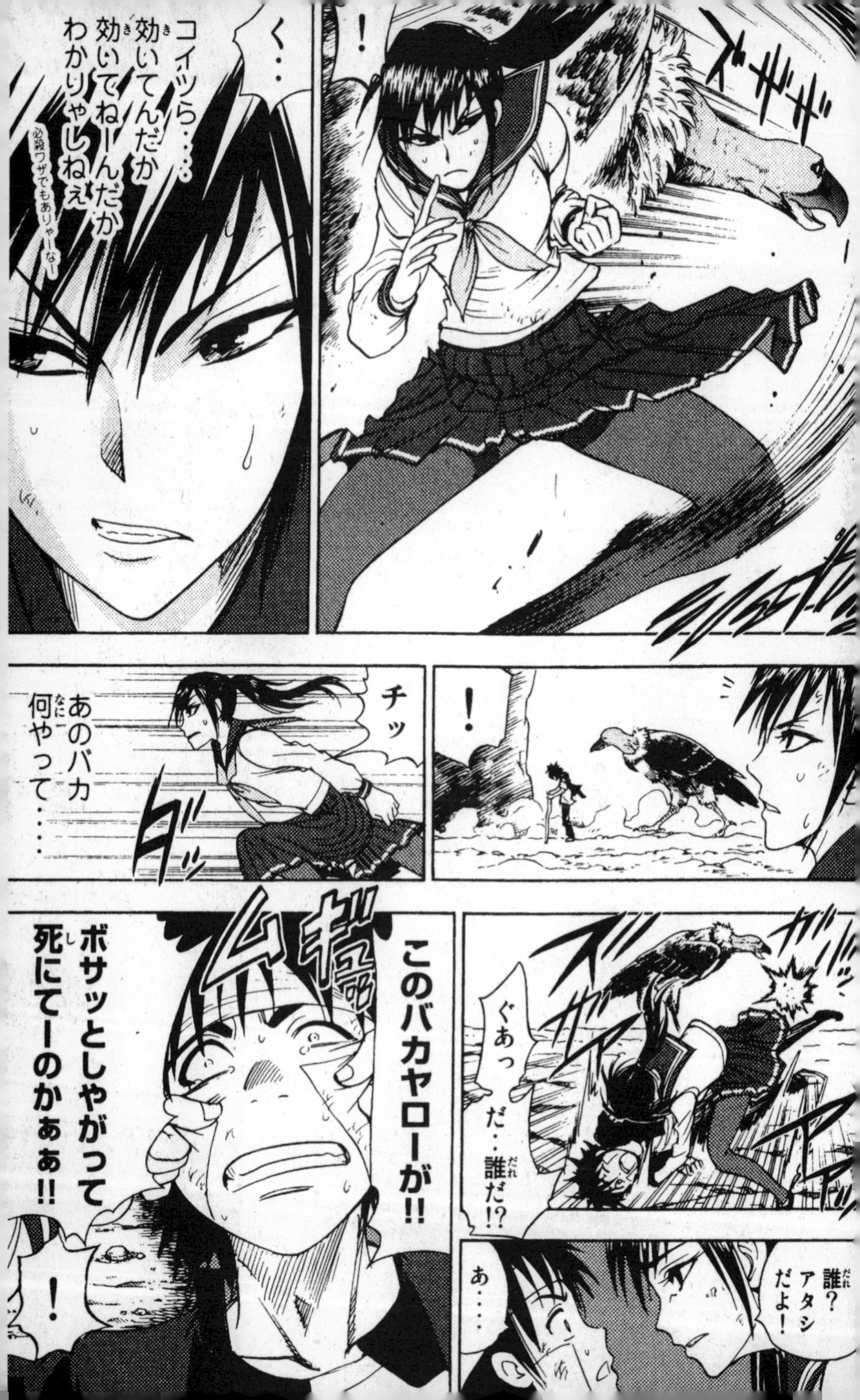
!
く・・・
コイツら・・・・
効いてんだか
効いてねーんだか
わかりゃしねえ
必殺ワザでもありゃーなー
!
チッ
ダッ
あのバカ
何やって・・・・
ぐあっ
だ・・
誰だ!?
誰?
アタシ
だよ!
あ・・・・
このバカヤローが!!
ボサッとしやがって
死にてーのかぁぁ!!
!

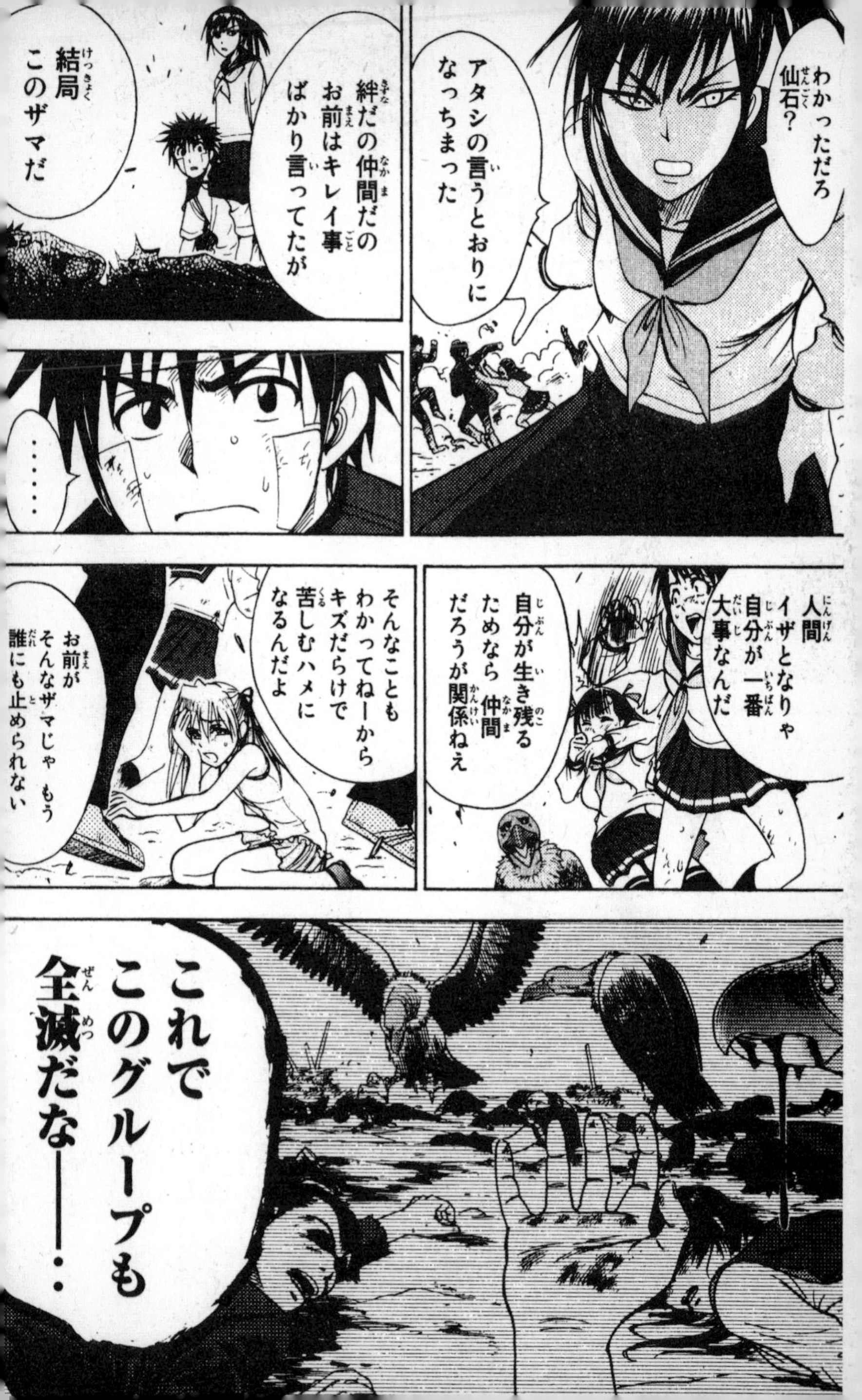

わかっただろ仙石(せんごく)?
アタシの言(い)うとおりになっちまった
絆(きずな)だの仲間(なかま)だのお前(まえ)はキレイ事(ごと)ばかり言(い)ってたが
結局(けっきょく)このザマだ
……
人間(にんげん)イザとなりゃ自分(じぶん)が一番(いちばん)大事(だいじ)なんだ
自分(じぶん)が生(い)き残(のこ)るためなら仲間(なかま)だろうが関係(かんけい)ねえ
そんなこともわかってねーからキズだらけで苦(くる)しむハメになるんだよ
お前(まえ)がそんなザマじゃもう誰(だれ)にも止(と)められない
これでこのグループも全滅(ぜんめつ)だな――・・

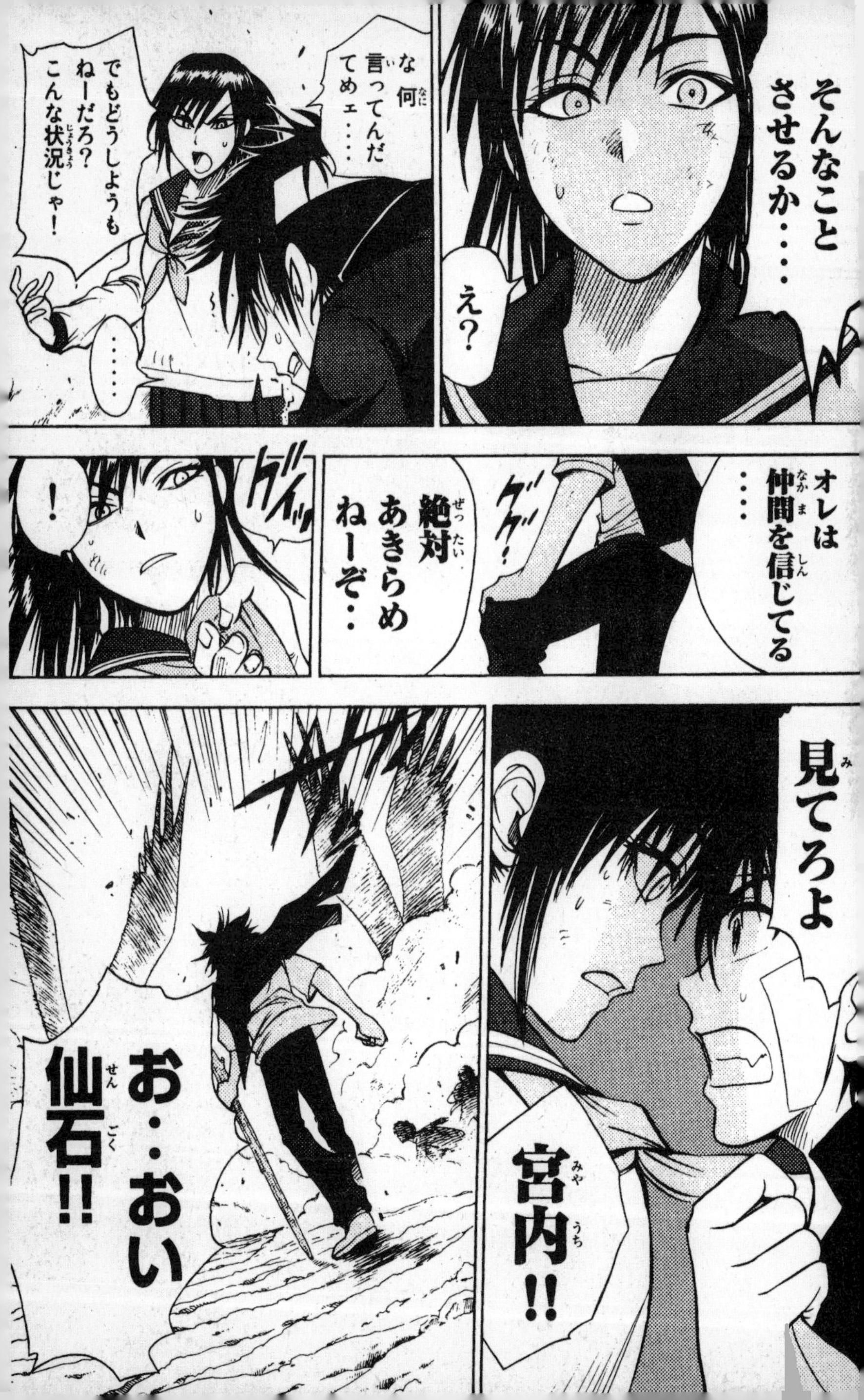

そんなことさせるか・・・・
え？
な何言ってんだてめェ・・・・
でもどうしようもねーだろ？こんな状況じゃ！
・・・・・・
オレは仲間を信じてる・・・・
ググ
絶対あきらめねーぞ・・
グイッ
！
見てろよ
宮内！！
お・・おい仙石！！

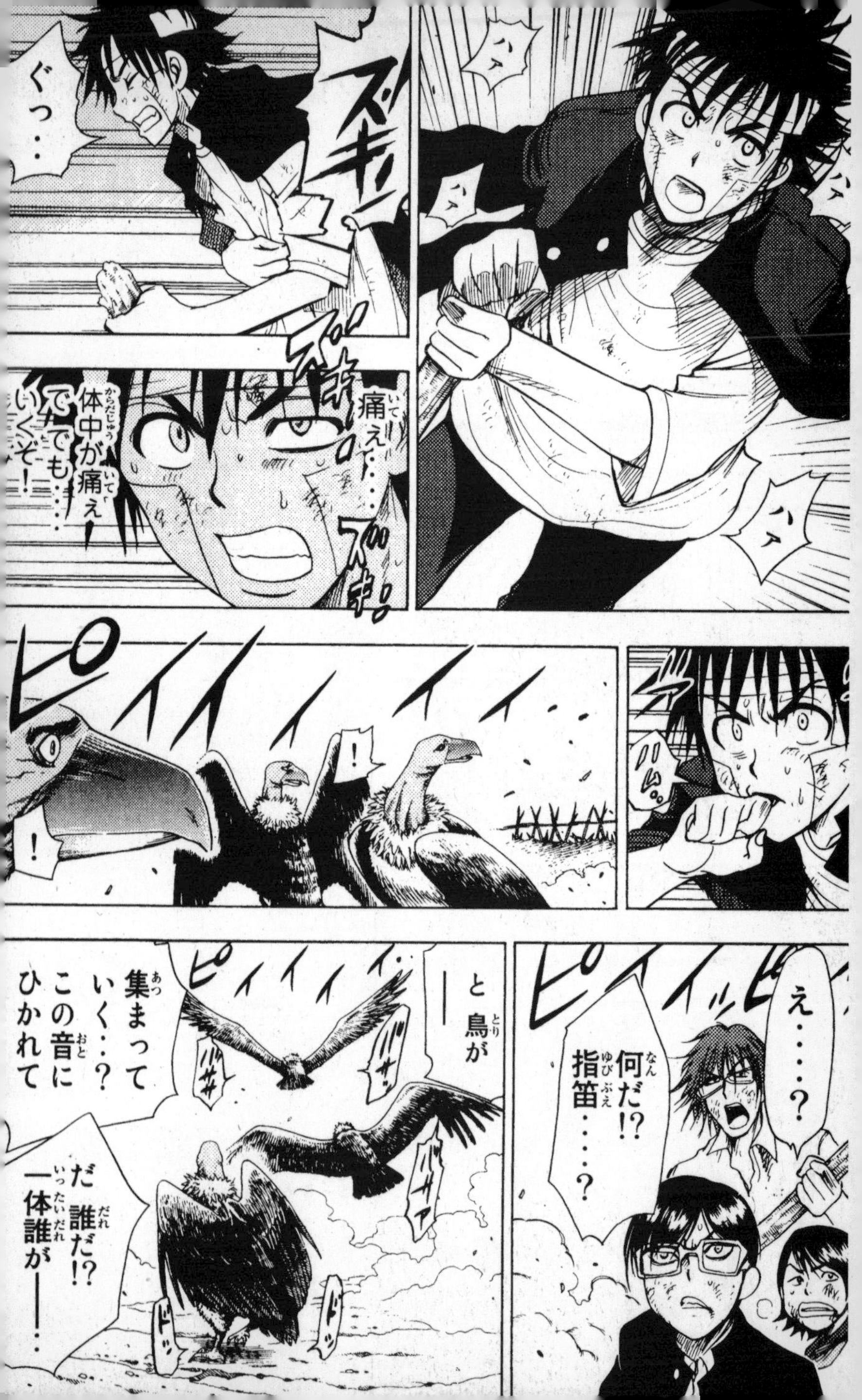
ハァ
ハァ
ハァ
ハァ
ズキン
ぐっ…
痛え…
体中が痛え…
でも……
いくぞ!
ピィイイイイ
!
!
ピィイッピ
え…?
何だ!?
指笛…?
ピィイイイ
と鳥が——
集まっていく…?
この音にひかれて
バサッ
バサァ
ドッ
ドッ
だ誰だ!?
一体誰が——…

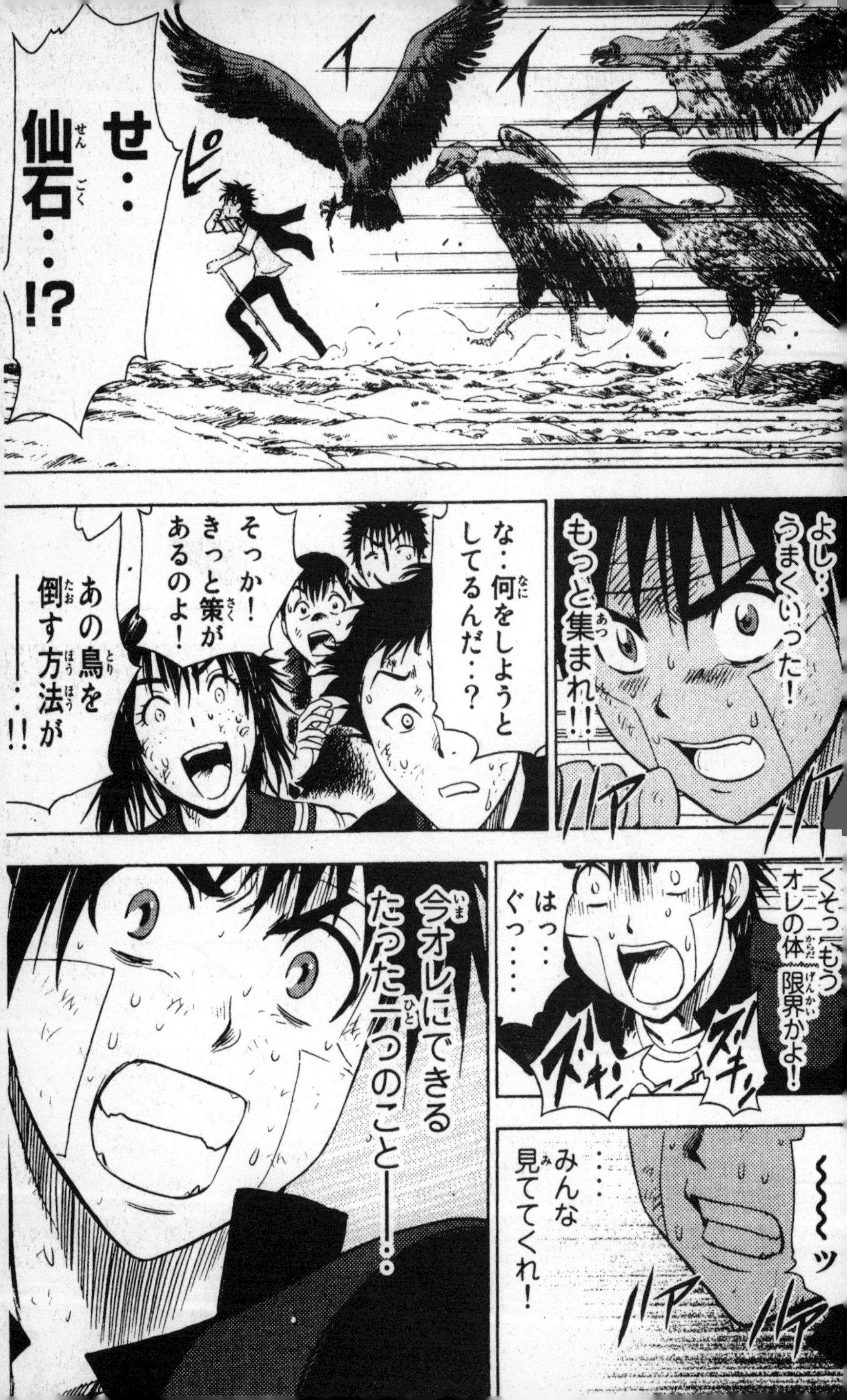
ピ
イイイイ
せ・・仙石・・!?
よし・・うまくいった！
もっと集まれ!!
ハァ ハァ
な・・何をしようとしてるんだ・・？
そっか！きっと策があるのよ！
あの鳥を倒す方法が———・・!!
くそっ・・もうオレの体限界かよ！
はっ・・ぐっ・・・・
ズキン ズキン
〜〜〜ッ
・・・みんな見ててくれ！
ハァ ハァ
今オレにできるたった一つのこと———・・。

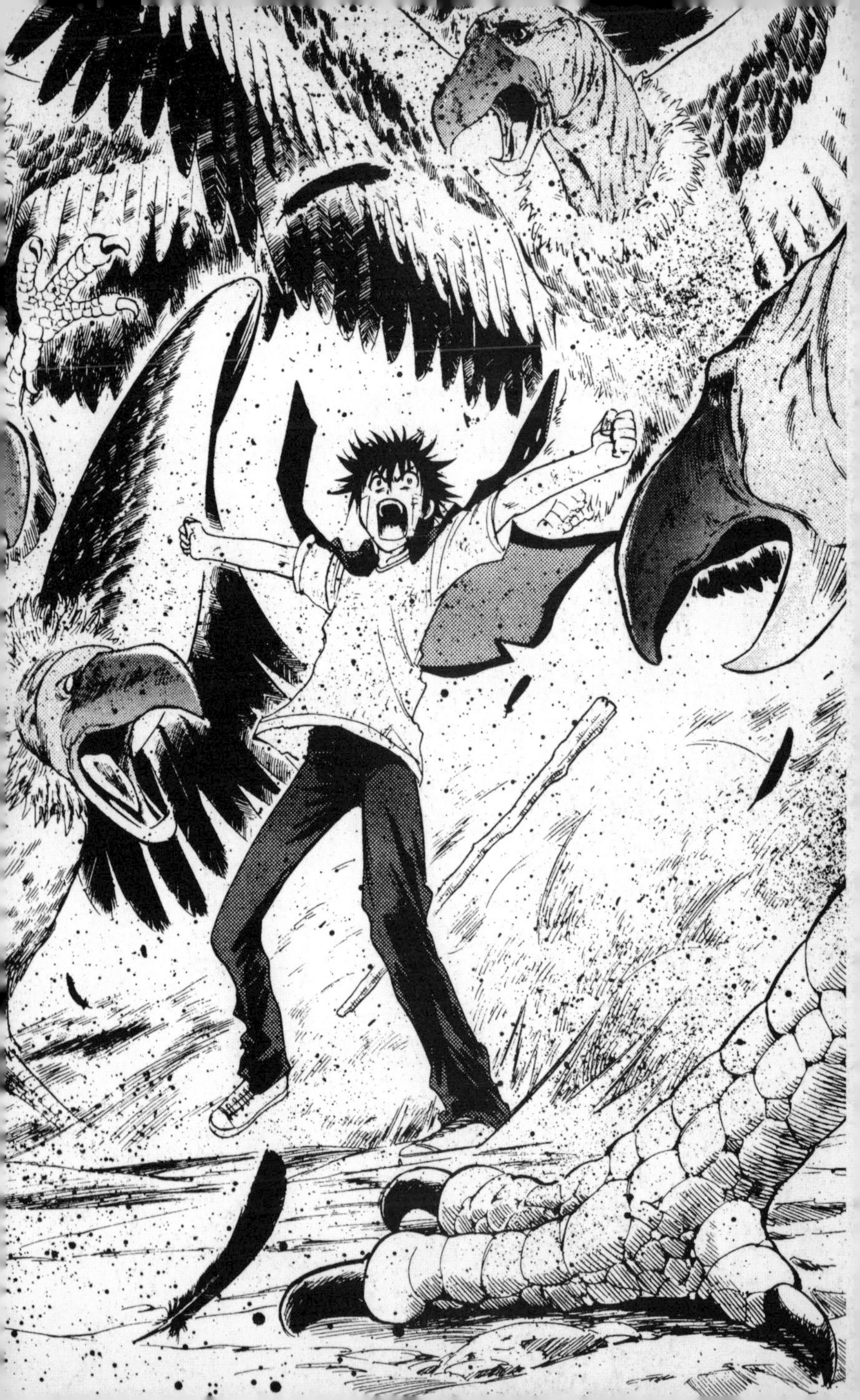

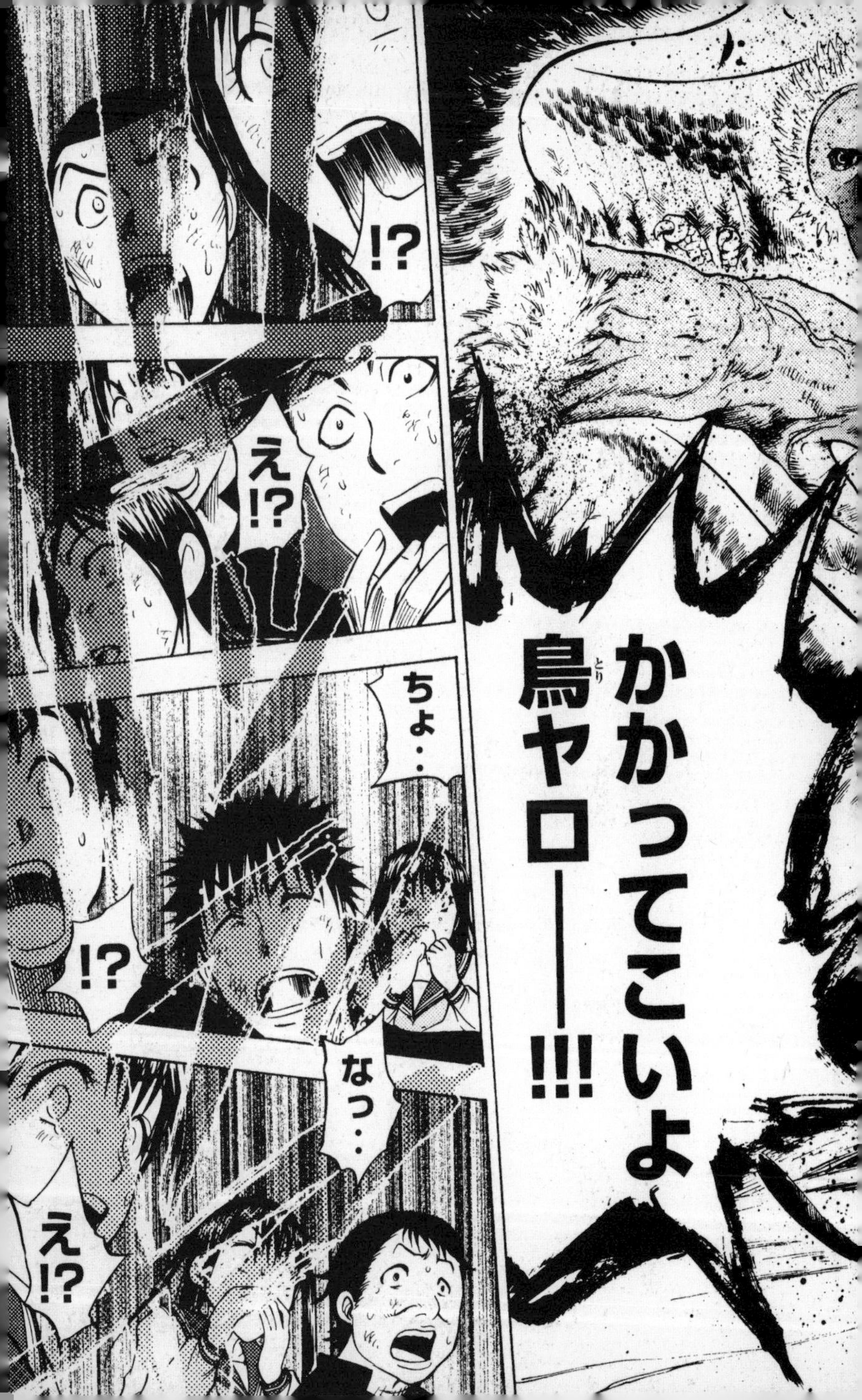
かかってこいよ鳥ヤロ――!!!
!?
え!?
ちょ・・
!?
なっ・・
え!?

FROM HIRO MASHIMA,
CREATOR OF **RAVE MASTER**

Lucy has always dreamed of joining the Fairy Tail, a club for the most powerful sorcerers in the land. But once she becomes a member, the fun really starts!

Special extras in each volume! Read them all!

RATING T AGES 13+

VISIT WWW.KODANSHACOMICS.COM TO:
- View release date calendars for upcoming volumes
- Find out the latest about new Kodansha Comics series

MARDOCK
マルドゥック・スクランブル
SCRAMBLE

**Created by
Tow Ubukata** ✕ **Manga by
Yoshitoki Oima**

"I'd rather be dead."

Rune Balot was a lost girl with
nothing to live for. A man
named Shell took her in and
cared for her...until he tried
to murder her. Standing at
the precipice of death Rune is
saved by Dr. Easter, a private
investigator, who uses an
experimental procedure known
as "Mardock Scramble 09."
The procedure grants Balot
extraordinary abilities. Now,
Rune must decide whether to
use her new powers to help Dr.
Easter bring Shell to justice, or if she even has the will to keep
living a life that's been broken so badly.

Ages: 16+

VISIT KODANSHACOMICS.COM TO:

- View release date calendars for upcoming volumes
- Find out the latest about upcoming Kodansha Comics series

[STOP!]

You are going the wrong way!

Manga is a completely different type of reading experience.

To start at the *beginning*, go to the *end*!

That's right! Authentic manga is read the traditional Japanese way—from right to left, exactly the *opposite* of how American books are read. It's easy to follow: Just go to the other end of the book, and read each page—and each panel—from the right side to the left side, starting at the top right. Now you're experiencing manga as it was meant to be.

ATTACK on TITAN

"A Manga To Look Forward to in 2012" – MTV

FOR THE LAST CENTURY, A GIANT, THREE-WALLED CITY WAS THE ONLY THING STANDING BETWEEN MANKIND AND THE SAVAGE TITANS. BUT WHEN A NEW BREED OF THESE COLOSSAL MONSTERS THREATEN HUMANITY'S HIDDEN FORTRESS, THE REMAINING SURVIVORS MUST BAND TOGETHER...OR FACE TOTAL ANNIHILATION!

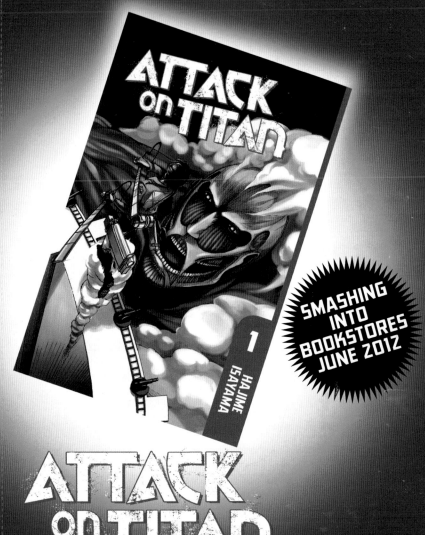

SMASHING INTO BOOKSTORES JUNE 2012

ATTACK on TITAN

BY HAJIME ISAYAMA

KODANSHA COMICS

VISIT KODANSHACOMICS.COM TO:

- View release date calendars for upcoming volumes
- Find out the latest news about new Kodansha Comics series